A TRAILS BOOKS GUIDE

PADDLING IOWA

96 GREAT TRIPS BY CANOE AND KAYAK

NATE HOOGEVEEN

Trails Books
Black Earth, Wisconsin

Library of Congress Control Number: 2003113010
ISBN: 1-931599-33-5

Editor: Stan Stoga
Project Manager: Michael Martin
Assistant Project Manager: Erika Reise
Photos: Nate Hoogeveen
Designer: Colin Harrington
Cover Photo: Nate Hoogeveen

Printed in the United States of America.

09 08 07 06 05 04   6 5 4 3 2 1

Trails Books, a division of Trails Media Group, Inc.
P.O. Box 317 • Black Earth, WI 53515
(800) 236-8088 • e-mail: books@wistrails.com
www.trailsbooks.com

CONTENTS

ACKNOWLEDGMENTS

Many Iowans helped make this book a reality—the efforts of kind people all across the state contributed greatly to this guide, in the form of shuttles, time-saving knowledge of rivers, and knowledge of local history. Countless county conservation board staff members, DNR officers, city parks and recreation personnel, outfitters, and paddlers have been very helpful. I'm especially grateful to Dick Howard, for his good humor, flexibility, and physical suffering that helped make this book a reality; to Peter Komendowski, who understands that rivers have souls; to Greg Beisker, for his on-target advice on locating some of Iowa's most interesting little-paddled waters; to Jeff Holmes, for opening his vault of archives; to Gerry Rowland, for his tireless work on water trails; and to my brother, Kevin, for running some epic shuttles. Paddling leaders like Rick Dietz, Robin Fortney, Jim Searle, Dave Hillman, Steve Weliver, and many, many others have provided much encouragement and information. I'm most deeply grateful to my wife, Vicki, who's been this project's biggest supporter.

LET US HEAR FROM YOU!

We welcome your suggestions and comments about this book. If there are other rivers, creeks, or sections that you would like to see included in the next edition, please let us know. If you find any errors in the text or maps, we would appreciate hearing about them so that we can make the corrections. Send the information, along with your name and address, to:

PADDLING IOWA
Trails Books
P.O. Box 317
1131 Mills Street
Black Earth, WI 52515
e-mail: books@wistrails.com

INTRODUCTION

When people travel across Iowa by highway, they're tempted to generalize that there is little more to the state than cornfields. But, much as John Fogerty never saw the good side of a city till he hitched a ride on a riverboat queen, you haven't seen the good side of Iowa till you've paddled her waters. River corridors offer lengthy, intact wild places where one can truly escape the bustle of modern life. After paddling about 1,800 unique river miles in the state, I'm happy to report that there's a lot more to this place than you might think.

That's probably why many Native American tribes and nations made Iowa their home long before Euro-American settlers arrived. The very name Iowa is thought both to describe a people, the now extinct Iowa nation, and to mean "the beautiful land." In territorial days, the Winnebago were known to deeply love northeast Iowa's waters, even calling one river by the same name they called themselves. The hearts of the Sac and Fox belonged in the Des Moines River Valley, especially near its intersection with White Breast Creek, where a giant sycamore 24 feet wide, since drowned by Lake Red Rock, served as a place of council.

This place called Iowa is flanked by the continent's longest and highest-volume rivers, the Missouri and the Mississippi. Early Iowa pioneers were justifiably enamored with Iowa's waterways and landscape. Over and over, they waxed poetic about the rolling prairies intersected with, as one put it, "magnificent streams of the clearest water, flowing over pebbly and rocky beds." Inside the Washington Monument in Washington, D.C., tourists can view 193 memorial stones inscribed with messages from states, cities, and patriotic organizations across the country. The message Iowans chose for their four-foot-by-two-foot block of Iowa native limestone was: "Iowa. Her Affection, like the Rivers of Her Borders, Flow to an Inseparable Union."

Paddling Iowa today, it's easy to see how waters and landscapes came together to work magic on those early settlers. Land and water, of course, are intricately related. Water flows over and from land and alters it through erosion. Geologists divide Iowa into eight landform regions, but with some exceptions (like the loess hills of western Iowa or the limestone bluffs and hills of northeast Iowa's Paleozoic Plateau), passing across them by car, you may hardly notice a transition. Not so by canoe and kayak.

IOWA'S RIVERS: EARLY BEGINNINGS

In the Des Moines Lobe region (see the accompanying geologic map), between 12,000 and 14,000 years ago the Wisconsin glacier pushed an oven-mitt-shaped mass of ice through north-central Iowa, reaching what's now Des Moines at the southernmost point. Its till created numerous lakes and marshes, many now drained for farmland but some preserved at places like the Trumpeter Trail. Paddlers today can take the route of where all that ice melted and scoured into bedrock in the spectacular Des Moines River Valley, or they can follow along its south-western edge, where the Middle Raccoon flows over and past the numerous glacially smoothed boulders along wooded hills composed of glacial till carried from much farther north. The surprisingly intact prairie landscapes along rivers of the Northwest Iowa Plains show remnants of slightly older advances of the same Wisconsin glacier, with hilly end moraines and glacial rocks at corners here and there on both the Big and Little Sioux Rivers.

The heavily weather-beaten Iowan Surface covers the eastern part of north-central Iowa, and its expanses of wide-open terrain may be best expressed in the big-sky landscapes of the Upper Shell Rock River. The Southern Iowa Drift Plain covering most of the southern third of the state is covered in glacial till from much older glaciers, and rivers like the Grand and the Middle have cut deeply into the land over hundreds of thousands of years, in places exposing limestone bedrock. Much more efficiently draining than northern Iowa's rivers, where the land acts more like a sponge, rivers of entirely southern-Iowa origin usually have to be caught by paddlers shortly after rains.

And no paddler would forget the Paleozoic Plateau, the startlingly different region sometimes referred to as the Driftless Area, which the most recent glaciers largely bypassed. As a result, the area was not scoured and lacks deposits of glacial drift materials. Here, for aeons water has seeped or gushed through cracks in limestone and some sandstone rocks formed in ancient seabeds more than 300 million years ago. The results are the magnificent cliffs, bluffs, and spring-fed waters—and unique pine-and-fir ecosystems growing in microclimates created by the landscapes—that inspire paddlers as they float rivers such as the Upper Iowa or the Volga.

Lollygagging in a shallow stream, such as the Rock at its confluence with the Big Sioux, can be highly pleasurable.

TROUBLED WATERS

For all the magnificence of the state's rivers, in the nineteenth century, Iowans began—in the name of "progress"—to regard both the landscape and the waterways differently. Land was now to be used solely for agricultural production (and 93 percent of it still is, the most in the country), and the rivers were to pump away by-products of the farmers and the cities they fed. Buildings in downtown Des Moines, once constructed to face the Des Moines River as part of the nationwide "Cities Beautiful" movement around the turn of the past century, gradually switched their entrances to the street side, partly to accommodate the rise of the automobile, but also in part so that pedestrians wouldn't have to smell what had become a fouled river. It became obvious, as topsoil depths dwindled from being more than a dozen feet thick to being measured in inches, that such heavy and thoughtless waste of resources was not sustainable.

It took many decades for Iowa's rivers to return to the much-improved state they are in now. Yet, many rivers in Iowa are still listed as "impaired" by the U.S. Environmental Protection Agency. By far the greatest threat to rivers is agribusiness runoff, and headlines seem to pop up every year about fish kills in creeks or rivers. Gradual improvements continue, with riparian buffer strips being added and sensitive lands being purchased along rivers. But much more needs to be done.

In the meantime, paddlers have rediscovered the sense of wonder the earliest Iowans found. Much joy is found along Iowa's waterways, and it's my deep hope that this book can help canoeists and kayakers enjoy stretches of stream they may not have thought to paddle. There is both camaraderie and solitude to be found, often closer to home than you thought possible. Iowa is the beautiful land, and its waterways showcase a disproportionate amount of that beauty.

WHAT'S A "GREAT" PADDLING TRIP?

I believe there is such a thing as a miserable stretch of river. For example, paddling along lines of junked cars nearly a mile long, or next to concrete riprap, or between cornfields or levee walls is not what most paddlers are looking for in a river tour. Iowa certainly has some of those stretches. This book is not a data-dump of maps and accesses. Instead it is a collection of detailed descriptions about waterways on which paddlers will actually want to paddle. Thousands of hours were spent in research, paddling, and bouncing ideas off other paddlers to decide just what to include. And so I hope it lives up to the promise implied in the subtitle on the cover—that it's full of "great trips."

Because rivers are individualistic creatures, most tours are surprisingly different from one another. Paddlers are unique too. Some highly enjoy a sandy-bottomed prairie stream that won't scratch up an expensive canoe's bottom, while others enjoy picking their way through rocky runs. The trips in this book reflect the wide range of paddling opportunities Iowa has to offer and are intended for paddlers of all levels, from novice to expert.

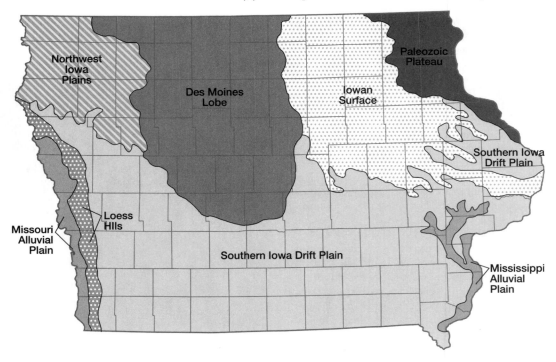

IOWA'S LANDFORM REGIONS

Some general criteria for the rivers that I chose are that they have pleasant scenery, good camping nearby (with riverside camping being a high priority), decent access (in a few cases, just not impossible), adequate water at least semiregularly, and a setting as wild and quiet as possible. Rivers range from tiny, such as the Little Maquoketa or Yellow, to huge, such as the Lower Iowa or Mississippi. Some consideration is given to which riverways are nearby that you may be more likely to paddle. I've included a few of these nearby stretches in inset maps.

There are exceptions to these rules. While a number of Iowa's rivers run nicely throughout the summer, those in south-central Iowa do not because their age-worn valleys drain so efficiently. Some tiny streams are included because they offer a completely unique trip, either in the form of spectacular scenery, a swift challenge, or both. Some parts of the state don't offer good access at all, such as on the Grand River. Most of the trips in the book focus on moving water, but a few exceptional lake and marsh trips are included.

Two vast areas not included are most of the Missouri River (except for a tiny portion on DeSoto Lake) and rivers passing through the Loess Hills. An unfortunate side effect of flood control projects from the 1900s to the 1950s is that rivers passing through the Loess Hills were straightened and channelized with levee walls built around them. The Missouri River along the Iowa-Nebraska border is at least tree-lined, but it has not fared much better, with riprap piled all along, meanders straightened, and wing dams created to keep the channel "self-scouring" for navigation. It's sad that these rivers are all so ditchlike now, but these flood-control efforts have saved Omaha some potentially nasty flooding.

The Mississippi River system, with many wildlife refuges and incredible islands and bluffs all up and down, could easily have taken over this book. Instead, one "gateway" to the great river was included to offer a taste, along with information on how to learn more. The Father of Waters really deserves its own guidebook.

USING THIS BOOK

The basic format that you'll find within these pages was developed by Mike Svob in three useful guides published by Trails Books: *Paddling Northern Wisconsin, Paddling Southern Wisconsin,* and *Paddling Illinois.* I've branched out a bit, including a few new features such as inset maps and appendixes that reflect Iowa's waters and paddling culture, but most of the information is delivered in the same clear, concise design.

This book is intended for paddlers, and as such it contains some paddling language that could initially perplex a first-timer. These are phrases paddlers need to get used to in order to communicate effectively on the water. When directions are given, for instance, you'll notice the phrase "river-left" or "river-right" popping up frequently. This assumes you are facing downstream, as a paddler most often is. This way, if someone warns you to "move right," there is no confusion about whose right he or she means. Other terminology is explained in the "Safe Paddling" section that appears later in the introduction.

Trips are organized into sections (e.g., "Des Moines River 2," "Wapsipinicon River 3"), and each one works out to be roughly a day trip. But there's no reason to be slavish: you can create shorter tours or combine them as you see fit. Information is included to streamline trip planning. The only other resource required is a state highway map to reach the area. If you are planning to paddle sections of river not in this book, two valuable resources are *DeLorme's Iowa Atlas and Gazetteer* and the Sportsman's Atlas Company's *Iowa Sportsman's Atlas.*

The narrative portion of each section begins with a brief overview of the body of water, including the kinds of fish that are present (information taken from DNR publications and personal observation) and why you might or might not enjoy paddling it.

Maps

The description of each river segment section includes a detailed map. In a number of cases, a pair of contiguous sections share a map, arranged that way to include as many stretches as possible. Maps are keyed with symbols, such as a heavy dot for accesses, crosshatches for rapids, different shadings for towns or public areas, etc. To keep the maps easy to read, not all roads are shown—just the ones of some use to paddlers. Riverside roads and roads with bridges across the river are kept because they are good landmarks for paddlers. Roads useful in running shuttles are also shown on the maps.

Each map also has mile markers that run from the put-in for the trip to the takeout, or to the end of the map. Distances are calculated digitally by Mapping Specialists, which has rendered all the maps in this book. You'll notice that distances vary from what you may have seen in Department of Natural Resources publications, and in fact calculating distance on a river is by nature imprecise. That said, these distances have been checked as thoroughly as possible.

Camping

After the narrative portion, nearby options for camping are given, which sometimes also include cushier options such as a riverside cabin or bed and breakfast. But really, rivers offer the best opportunities for a genuine outdoors experience in Iowa, and that experience is enhanced by staying outside. Camping options are described as follows.

If a campground is mentioned but not described, assume it has the basics: pit toilets, campsites with fire rings, and running water. If a campground is described with "full amenities," it has electricity and showers. In Iowa, there are many more publicly operated campgrounds than private ones. Phone numbers are provided for private campgrounds, and most of them take reservations. All state park campgrounds operate on a first-come, first-served basis and do not take reservations. Most county-run campgrounds operate the same way.

The terms "primitive camping," "river camping," or "sandbar camping" mean you'll have no amenities besides fresh air and a level spot to pitch a tent. *When camping along a river, especially a sandbar, be hyperaware of what the river is doing.* Sandbars are deposits of rivers. That means water sometimes rises higher than the sandbar's highest point. Rivers can rise a few feet overnight because of rains near or far from you or water being released from a dam—maybe from one even a hundred miles upstream. Sleep with a light and your personal flotation device (PFD) easily reachable (some even sleep with PFDs on), and make a plan for moving to higher ground should that become necessary. That way, you won't make panic-stricken decisions in the middle of the night as water laps at your tent. See "Property Rights and Paddlers' Rights," later in the introduction, for a discussion of where camping is acceptable.

Shuttle Routes

Next, the most efficient shuttle route for each trip segment is listed. The description assumes you've met other paddlers at the put-in and have more than one vehicle. Shuttling can seem complicated, and I've met intelligent veteran paddlers who always let other paddlers decide on shuttling logistics because they don't like thinking about it. All you need to do is unload the boats at the put-in, have someone stay with the boats, drive more than one vehicle to the takeout, leave at least one vehicle there, and drive one back. Then you have a vehicle waiting for you when you float down to the takeout.

Some prefer to meet at the takeout if there is a vehicle capable of carrying everyone's boat up to the put-in. Using a bicycle for a shuttle is another possibility for experienced cyclists who want an extra workout, especially for solo boaters or when there's only one car. You can simply

A good takeout, like this one at Sutliff on the Cedar, makes a fine end to a fine day.

drop your bike off at the takeout and lock it to something, drive to the put-in, and ride back up after canoeing to get your vehicle. It does take more time, and this is where the shuttle distances listed in each trip can help you decide whether you do have time to get in before dark.

Canoe and Kayak Rentals and Shuttle Services

Rental and shuttle services are listed whenever they are conveniently located, that is, within a reasonable driving distance for you to pick up a boat. If you are picking up a boat, you are usually expected to have a roof rack or some way to carry the boat yourself. Many, but not all, outfitters will shuttle paddlers and/or boats for a fee, even if you don't rent a boat from them.

Water Level

Knowing the water level of every river you plan to paddle is crucial for several reasons. First, it will help you estimate how long your trip will take. Most paddlers want to know exactly how long it will take to navigate a section of river. The true answer is, it depends. Most rivers flow at two miles per hour or more. Paddlers commonly figure they will make two or three miles per hour—assuming they keep paddling—on a normal river outing. But a lot of factors can change your speed. Do you want a lazy float where you let the river do all the work, or do you want to paddle like you're an ancient Aleut chasing down a seal? Do you want an hour-long lunch on a sandbar? Are you on a swift stream or a slowly meandering river? Is the river high, or is it so low you'll be getting out of your boat to drag it over sandbars or shallow riffles? When a river is quite low, plan accordingly, and take a shorter section.

Being aware of the water level is even more important for safety reasons. *All rivers become dangerous and unpredictable at high water levels.* Cold weather amplifies the danger (see "Cold-Season Paddling" later in the introduction). Just because you've driven to a destination doesn't mean you need to perish on a river flowing too high and too fast. Large debris such as tree limbs barreling down a river is one sure sign that no paddler belongs on the water that day.

Each "water levels" section in this book tells you how to go about finding (or at least estimating) current water levels and gives suggestions for a pleasant moderate level. These are suggestions only and are no guarantee you will not hit rocks or dump a canoe. The recommended levels have been determined through both my own observations and suggestions from local paddlers and conservation staff. Where minimum levels are given, be aware these are very subjective—different paddlers will put up with different amounts of bottom-scraping or way-picking, and factors like the amount of gear you have loaded, your own weight or lack thereof, the amount of water your boat displaces, and whether you're paddling tandem or solo all come into play. What is "too high" gets even more subjective depending on skill and the type of boat you're using; paddlers need to use good judgment. The levels suggested here should also give you leeway to paddle at somewhat lower and higher levels. A deeper knowledge of a river can be gleaned by encountering its character at various levels. Most gauges referred to in this book can be found at one of the following Web sites:

U.S. Geological Survey (USGS):
waterdata.usgs.gov/ia/nwis/current/?type=flow
U.S. Army Corps of Engineers:
water.mvr.usace.army.mil/

Most water-level suggestions in this book are given in a volumetric reading of "cubic feet per second," or cfs. A few use the arbitrary gauge heights measured in feet. Besides having the current water level, the Web sites also have a wealth of archival data and information about sedimentation and even pollution levels. Some smaller watersheds, such as the Yellow River and Little Maquoketa River, do not have gauges. In those cases, all you can do from afar is watch for sustained rainfalls over several days or maybe try calling a local (perhaps an outfitter) before driving a long distance and risking disappointment. Better yet, have a backup plan to paddle an alternative river if "plan A" doesn't pan out. **The North Central River Forecast Center** maintains a useful tool for monitoring rainfalls in the eastern two-thirds of Iowa, including color-coded maps of rainfalls with 10 days: www.crh.noaa.gov/cgi-bin-ncrfc/uncgi/igmapx.

For all parts of the state, the **National Weather Service** also publishes statewide rainfall reports: http://iwin.nws.noaa.gov/iwin/ia/climate.html.

Gradient

Also essential for paddling safety is an awareness of the rate of descent, the gradient, of a river. For each river segment in the book, the gradient, calculated by dividing the section's distance by the number of feet in elevation the river surface drops, is given (lakes are not included). A gradient can give clues about a stream's difficulty, although it's just one of many factors. If a gradient is "less than 2 feet per mile," expect a slow river with very few riffles and to make about 3 miles per hour at normal water levels (again, if you paddle the whole way; this does not allow for breaks). Exactly how far below 2 feet per mile is difficult to accurately calculate because of long distances between topographic contour lines, and differences are subtle enough to be meaningless for paddlers.

At gradients between 2 and 5 feet per mile, a river's velocity increases. Expect riffles to be more frequent, and you may make better time with good water levels. At low water, a higher-gradient stream often actually takes *longer* to paddle because you'll get out of your boat more often at rocky riffles. Above 5 feet per mile, you'll encounter swifter water. You may need to get out at a rapids or a sharp turn to scout ahead on foot. Streams exceeding 10 feet per mile demand attention and skill, and you'll likely

encounter rapids. Because only small streams in Iowa drop at rates that high, riverwide snags often compound the danger of swift water.

GEAR CHECKLISTS

This book leaves selecting an appropriate boat and other gear up to you and your local paddle shop. When leaving on a day trip, however, here are some of the items you'll want to make sure you bring:

- Boat, paddle, and an extra paddle (in case you lose the first)
- Personal flotation device (PFD or life vest)
- A first-aid kit
- A sponge for bailing and keeping your boat clean
- A secure place for car keys (many PFDs have key latches)
- Adequate food and plenty of drinking water
- A system for securing gear (carabiners, rope, etc.)
- Sunscreen
- Insect repellant
- Extra clothing in a dry bag (or a watertight bulkhead)
- Weather-appropriate clothing (see "Cold-Season Paddling," later in the introduction)
- Water shoes or old sneakers

In addition, whitewater paddlers should bring the following:

- Flotation bags (lashed in canoes, stuffed in kayaks)
- Rescue rope in a throw-bag
- Helmet
- Spray skirt (for kayakers)
- In cold weather, a wet or dry insulation system (see "Cold-Season Paddling," later in the introduction)

SAFE PADDLING

Like any outdoors experience, paddling has its risks. It's strange that some folks who don't think twice about buckling up in the car won't wear a personal flotation device on moving water. *Always wear your PFD.* In moving-water situations it sometimes barely matters how strong a swimmer you are. If you can afford a boat, you can afford to purchase a PFD comfortable enough to actually wear. Some sections in this book definitely are not appropriate for beginning paddlers, and there is no stretch of river in Iowa that is "perfectly" safe. Rivers are constantly changing, and a free-and-open shallow stretch can transform into a constricted area riddled with dangerous snags after a flood. By getting into a boat, you bear responsibility for knowing something about various features that can spell trouble on the water. The following section is not intended to replace instruction and

Always put in well below killer low-head dams, such as this one at Adel.

practice; rather, it is here to alert you to some hazards and to encourage you to fill in knowledge gaps.

Moving water always has hazards and potentially dangerous features paddlers need to be able to both recognize and avoid. Here are some you should be familiar with.

Low-Head Dams

These are human-created hazards, but very real ones. Dams probably have drowned more paddlers in Iowa in the past two decades than any other feature. The problem is that uniformly falling water below a low-head dam scours a hole where falling water recirculates. Swimmers have little chance of escaping because falling water from both the upstream and downstream directions sucks them down and holds them under water. Unlike in Minnesota and Wisconsin, the effort to remove unnecessary dams here is in its infancy. The trips in this book are very intentionally arranged to avoid having to even portage around dams, and thus eliminate the foolhardy temptation to run them, but on a handful of sections such arrangement didn't make sense. If you care to take a multiday trip in Iowa, most rivers have at least a few dams to portage. Take out as far as feasible upstream, and put in well below the hazardous boil line beneath the dam. Also watch for swift eddies sometimes present below dams that can carry you straight to the dangerous hole.

Snags

Snags—things such as tree limbs or piles of branches—are the most common hazards encountered by paddlers and present on almost every trip you'll take in Iowa. They cause two main problems for paddlers: sweepers and strainers. A sweeper is an overhanging branch or log either just above or below the surface of the water. Structures such as a boat dock in a current, a very low bridge, or a pipe or fence (sometimes electrified) across a river can also be sweepers. They are called sweepers because the boat and occupants can be swept beneath the obstacle. I have

been "swept" only once, but it was a terrifying experience. While tubing as a kid on Wisconsin's Apple River, I figured I'd grab onto a branch at the water's surface. The force of the moderately paced water sucked me under. Fortunately, I popped back up on the other side of the log in short order.

You will not be so lucky if you are flipped at a strainer. In that case, the current under water will pin you in a network of submerged branches, part of a dock, a bridge's structure, underwater fencing, etc. No matter how strong a swimmer you are, it is unlikely you will be able to free yourself. The danger is magnified by the speed of the current. Some streams in this book are likely to have riverwide strainers because they are narrow enough that a bank-side tree will span the entire stream (the North River, South Skunk River, and Grand River are examples). Logjams—strainers caused where logs stack up at high water—can appear in any river, but there are certain corners on certain rivers where they appear time and again over the years.

Pinning

Various stationary obstacles can cause pinning, also called broaching. This hazard is also most dangerous in swift water, best avoided by keeping your boat parallel to the current (i.e., pointed downstream or upstream). That way you tend to graze off obstacles. When you approach them with your boat broadside, a boulder, a bridge pier (probably the most dangerous, and common, pinning hazard), or a post will first stop your boat, and then the current will try to flip it, possibly wrapping your water-filled boat—and perhaps you—around the obstruction. What flips your boat is the current grabbing the upstream side of your boat. You can counter it by aggressively leaning your boat toward the obstacle, exactly the opposite of what a new paddler naturally does. Maintaining the downstream boat tilt, you may then be able to wiggle your boat off the obstacle, often using your hands on the obstacle itself for leverage. If it's a boulder, you might even be able to step out onto it to free your boat. Leaning your boat toward a strainer or sweeper can also help keep you from flipping.

Holes

In some places you'll notice a depression in a river's surface. "Holes" are caused when swift water courses over an irregularity, such as a rock ledge or a boulder, in the river bottom. Whitewater paddlers enjoy "sticky holes," holes that make for good surfing. Naturally occurring large, hazardous holes called "keepers," sticky to the point that they are dangerous or impossible to escape from, are rare in Iowa at normal water levels. However, keeper holes are the norm below low-head dams.

Eddies

Eddies are still (or sometimes reverse-flow) portions of water on a river that occur along the banks behind protrusions into the current or midstream behind obstruc-

At high water, the recirculating holes below low-head dams may look innocuous, when in fact they're at their most powerful.

tions such as rocks. When used properly, they make a good spot to wait for other paddlers or to assess what's ahead. However, when there's a "strong eddy line" where swift water is against quiet water, the differential in current can flip you if you don't tilt your boat while you are entering or leaving the eddy. Essentially, you always want to tilt your boat into the turn you're making. It can take practice to get the hang of this.

Wind

Some of the bigger rivers such as the Lower Iowa, the Cedar, and much of the Des Moines, plus all the lakes, can get extremely large waves in a wind. Anything approaching 30 miles per hour, especially when a current goes directly into the wind, can create waves large enough to crash over the bow of a canoe. Watch for wind advisories and see which direction gusts will blow before heading out on such a body of water. If high waves catch you unawares, you can often move close to the bank where eddies provide more protection. Also realize that even if the waves are not high, a headwind can dramatically slow your progress (this applies doubly to canoes over kayaks). Don't plan a long trip if you know you'll be bucking a headwind.

Cold-Season Paddling

Increasing numbers of gung ho, hardy folks are enjoying paddling in cold weather. It is more dangerous but has its rewards. You'd be surprised how long Iowa's rivers can remain ice-free and how many people enjoy the rivers during late fall and early spring. By late fall, even the biggest and muddiest of Iowa's rivers become crystal clear, and suddenly you can see rocks and a sandy bottom you may not have suspected existed. Dozens—sometimes hundreds—of bald eagles congregate in spots along Iowa's rivers to fish and to gorge on migrating geese or stunned fish.

Late-season paddling in southeast Iowa, where temperatures stay warmer slightly longer and the Skunk, Iowa,

and Des Moines Rivers have relatively dependable flows as waters dwindle elsewhere, can be particularly nice for extending the season. But there are precautions one needs to take before embarking on a cold-season journey. A paddling rule of thumb is that if the water temperature and air temperature don't add up to more than 100 degrees, watch vigilantly for hypothermia. Of course, that varies by individual cold tolerance and the sort of trip you're taking. It's wise to pick warm days, take short trips, and remain nearer to accesses in the cold season. Always paddle with others, and keep talking to check each other for coherence. If you begin hitting even a thin layer of ice, be very cautious—thicker ice that can flip you may lurk just ahead.

Also plan on dumping. You'll need proper clothing layers, in either a wet system or dry system. The wet system uses a wet suit, which, if you dump, allows water next to your skin to warm up to body temperature. A dry suit is (mostly) waterproof with latex gaskets around your ankles, wrists, and neck. "Breathable" dry suits are preferable, allowing your sweat moisture to escape. For each system, some kind of "wicking" layer that keeps sweat moisture off your skin should be next to your skin. Underwear made of a variety of fabrics such as polypropylene or wool does this very well. Next comes the "insulating" layer of either wool or synthetic micro-fleece, both of which continue insulating when wet. In the wet system, a wet suit is the critical part of the insulating layer and should go inside the fleece. The outside layer is a windproof/waterproof layer. A paddling jacket and pants made of a waterproof/breathable fabric such as Gore-Tex works well. Some fabrics are now available in flexing materials that work great for paddling movement. In the dry system, the dry suit itself forms this layer. Kayakers using spray skirts sometimes also use a hybrid of the two systems, with a just a dry top instead of a full dry suit.

Rapids

Rapids are not as common in Iowa as in some states, but there certainly are some. To the uninitiated, rapids can seem scary, while many others don't take them seriously enough. Learning to negotiate them properly is a great joy of paddling, but it's best to learn about moving water first and then work up to easier rapids with formal instruction, learning from a club, or from experienced whitewater paddlers you trust.

Some rapids in Iowa are formed from the rubble of breached or demolished dams. While much safer to run than a low-head dam, concrete rubble is often sharper than natural stone, offering dangers to both boats and paddlers. Also, many dams were built with reinforcing steel rods, which, if a paddler swims (or a kayaker rolls) into them can hook onto paddlers' clothing or gear and pin them under the water, with chances for rescue being low. Some of these are Class II or higher rapids in their own right, so paddlers without whitewater skills and who have not researched hidden hazards have no business in such places.

Fast water comes in a variety of forms. When it courses over a rocky bottom creating choppy water or very small waves, it's called a "riffle." Where water rushes over irregularities in the streambed, such as rocks or bedrock ledges, larger standing waves develop. They also develop at constrictions. Water can actually do a lot of things, such as shoot down sloping rock, cut beneath the bank under rock walls (very dangerous), fall over cascades, and so on. From a paddler's perspective, anything more than a small riffle is a rapids, and to communicate roughly how difficult they'll be for a paddler, a system exists to classify them.

It's important to realize that rapids ratings are imperfect because no two are really alike. Also, when water is high or conditions are cold you should rank them one class higher. This book uses the International Scale of Difficulty ratings to describe the level of rapids you may encounter. Please note that these differ from ratings some Midwesterners use, which consider class I to be flatwater, class II to have riffles, class III to be pretty darned hard, and class IV to be crazy talk.

In fact, most paddlers around the world rank difficulty of rapids from I to VI, with class I rapids being the easiest. Some reserve "class VII" for unrunnable drops that are certain suicide. Class IV to VI rapids or cascades hardly occur in Iowa, and only a tiny fraction of kayakers here are capable of running such drops, so we'll leave them somewhere "utterly beyond imagination" for the purposes of this book. A list of the more difficult rapids in this book appears in Appendix 2. You'll notice some rapids are categorized as class I-II, meaning that they are typically easy rapids that can be more difficult at higher levels. Sometimes it's explained that the rating depends on the route you select. A rating such as I+ or II+ implies that the rapids lie on the more difficult end of the rating. Here's an adaptation of how difficulty is ranked on the International Scale:

Stickle Rapids on Whitebreast Creek. There are few significant rapids in Iowa, but that doesn't mean there aren't any that require skill.

Play-boat design has revolutionized the amount of fun whitewater paddlers can have on Iowa's rivers.

Class I: These are the most common rapids in Iowa. You're in fast water that's a step up from a riffle. You'll see standing waves, but none big enough to top the bow of a canoe. Some maneuvering skills are helpful to avoid rocks, but consequences are usually not dire if you swim. Class I rapids are runnable by novices familiar with moving water.

Class II: The water is fast with larger waves and drops up to three feet. River-reading skills become necessary to navigate around rocks, and turns may need to be made to avoid dumping. These are considered a good start for novices accompanied by more experienced paddlers to learn about somewhat bigger water. Most class IIs in Iowa are very short drops such as rock dams or ledges that are likely to dump a canoeist who hasn't lined up the boat properly. Rescue is not difficult, and swims are usually short.

Class III: The only class III rapids in this book are listed in Appendix 2 and are appropriate only for trained whitewater paddlers. Scouting, if you are not familiar with the rapids, is necessary. Rescue becomes more difficult, and longer swims and injuries while swimming become more likely. Chaotic waves are likely to swamp an open canoe, and large holes may need to be avoided. You may encounter drops of three feet or more and need to use boat control in tight passages.

WHEN YOU DUMP

Blame it on good conversation resulting in poor concentration, but when you paddle with a group, someone almost invariably dumps. If you stick with paddling, it'll happen to you, too. That's why it's important to always keep your gear fastened to the boat. Even kayakers capable of rolling up their boats are sometimes caught off guard and end up swimming.

When you do capsize and find yourself swimming, there's no reason to panic. Try to stay with your boat, recognizing that if you are bound for any of the hazards we've discussed, you should not bother trying to swim your boat away from them—preserve yourself first. If you're in open water, stay on the upstream side of your boat and make your way to shore. Other paddlers can assist.

If you dump your canoe or wet-exit your kayak in swiftly coursing water, a natural impulse is to try to stand up as quickly as possible. Don't do it. Any place where water flows swiftly and is deeper than knee level, be extremely cautious about foot entrapments, a fairly common cause of drowning among paddlers. If your foot becomes wedged between rocks, then the strong pressure of the current can easily bowl you over, and your entrapped foot will keep you stuck beneath the fast water. In that case, the only hope is for a highly skilled rescuer to immediately perform an intricate rescue procedure with ropes or a boat. To avoid foot entrapment, swim with your belly up and your feet pointed downstream, keeping your toes above water. Again, stay with your boat, but try to remain upstream of it (in fast water, if you don't, you can get hit or pinned against an obstruction by your boat). Use your arms to control your direction of downstream travel, and when you near an eddy, swim aggressively toward it.

If you can't stay with your boat, other paddlers can help round it up after you are out of danger. If you are about to go over a drop, don't fight it. Remain floating on your back, tuck your knees into your arms, make the plunge, and when you're flushed through the waves, then you can worry about making the next eddy.

Paddling in groups is a smart way to minimize risks. The most experienced paddlers should take the "lead" and "sweep" positions, or the first and last spots. That way, the first person can watch for hazards out ahead, while the last person is positioned to assist with rescues. All members of the group should agree to follow instructions of trip leaders.

If you paddle solo, be sure you are capable of self-rescue. Paddling alone is not for novices. The same advice as has been given applies, but it's smart to add extra layers of caution when no one is there to help you out of dangerous situations. More attention to water reading and boat handling can help you avoid getting into trouble in the first place.

WATER READING AND BOAT HANDLING

Another aspect of paddling that adds a new dimension of fun to moving water is pairing up good water reading with boat-handling skills. After some practice, you begin to naturally respond to a variety of situations. Water reading includes paddling toward standing waves where the deepest water is found, looking for "friendly Vs" pointing away from you versus "unfriendly Vs" pointing toward you on the water surface to avoid obstructions, seeing a subtle chop in a riffle denoting shallow water, plus recognizing all the hazards already listed. Good boat handling can help ensure you'll avoid such hazards. It's best to practice in nonthreatening situations in preparation for real-world trips out on the water. There are many good books and videos on learning how to maneuver your boat, and numerous instructional opportunities in Iowa and the Midwest are available. See Appendixes 5 and 6 for listings.

PROPERTY RIGHTS AND PADDLERS' RIGHTS

There was a time in Iowa when paddlers had no official legal basis for using many of the state's best paddling streams. In the 1960s, an Iowa attorney general advised a county attorney that canoeists had only the right to paddle publicly owned "meandered streams," called that because of the "meander lines" run by surveyors before and during the decades of Iowa's early statehood. Landowners by the 1960s were advised by the state that they could even construct obstructions across rivers to block boaters. Thanks to 1982 legislation that addressed public access to streams regardless of who owns the riverbeds, the legal framework has shifted favorably for paddlers.

Meandered streams have always been held in a public trust up to the ordinary high-water mark. See the accompanying map to determine these meandered stretches of river where the state owns the riverbed itself as well as the land along it. In practice, permanent vegetation along banks usually defines the ordinary high-water mark on inside bends, and the tops of cut banks define them on outside bends. For paddlers, public banks mean they won't encounter fences across these rivers, and they have the right to camp on sandbars and islands along these streams. Paddlers will usually be on private property if they step into a wooded, cropped, or pastured area along the banks.

There is little rhyme or reason as to which streams were meandered and which weren't, a process that was undertaken rather haphazardly by low-paid surveyors over several decades in the early 19th century. So today, for example, the Little Sioux River, with a drainage area of 3,500 square miles, remains nonmeandered, because in those early days it was considered nonnavigable; whereas the tiny Little Maquoketa, draining about 150 square miles, was meandered to a point a mile or so upstream from its mouth.

Rivers not highlighted on the map are nonmeandered. Streambeds on nonmeandered streams belong to adjacent landowners to the midpoint of the stream. Since 1982, the waters themselves, however, have been considered "navigable," and the definition of what's navigable is fairly liberal. According to the Iowa Code, " 'Navigable waters' means all lakes, rivers, and streams, which can support a vessel capable of carrying one or more persons during a total of six months period in one out of ten years." Paddlecraft firmly fit the bill, and it's pretty easy to make the argument that the fact you're able to pass down a stream—even if you have to wade now and again, considered "incidental use"—proves the navigability of the waterway.

Landowners with property on both sides of the stream are within their rights to put livestock fences across nonmeandered streams. It's worth noting that a 1996 attorney general opinion says such fences should be installed "in a manner that affords boaters safe passage."

As such, there should be a safe way to get over the fence on land or under the fence on water, and landowners would be well advised to mark fences with a piece of fabric tied onto the fence. In practice, this doesn't always happen. The smaller the stream you are paddling, the more vigilant you should be for fences.

Paddlers should also know that criminal trespass is not simply the act of being on someone else's property. The Iowa Code describes it as entering property without permission to use, remove, alter, or damage the land, or to hunt, fish, or trap on the property. Simply crossing someone's property to get around a fence, for example, is not trespassing, an idea supported by case law. However, if a landowner has posted "No Trespassing" or "Keep Out" signs along the riverside, you are violating that landowner's rights if you set foot on his or her property, because you are knowingly going against that person's wishes. If you are stopped at a sandbar along a nonmeandered stream and the property owner notices you, you could be asked to leave. In that case, you should do so immediately and without argument.

Generally, you can avoid problems for all paddlers by treating all riverbanks with the great respect they deserve. Always pack out trash, don't bother any livestock you encounter, leave fences intact, and, wherever camping, be as unobtrusive as possible. Practicing "leave no trace" camping is good for rivers, paddlers, and landowners.

If you intend to camp on the sandbars or riverbank of a nonmeandered stream, secure the landowner's permission first. If you find yourself in a situation where you are unknowingly camping against the wishes of a landowner, you might offer to pay a camping fee. Again, if you are asked to leave, you should move downriver without debate. Keeping landowners on friendly terms is important for all paddlers. Please be considerate of landowners' property—don't litter, don't cut fences, and treat private lands (as well as public lands) as if you want to come back again and again.

On public areas lining rivers, different tracts of land are treated differently. There are only a handful of spots, primarily of archaeological significance, where you are prohibited from stepping out of your boat (the Jefferson Davis Sawmill site at Effigy Mounds National Monument is one). There is a blanket prohibition against camping anywhere on a state park besides designated camping areas, including the river areas. In the many state and county wildlife areas, camping is usually considered an "incidental" use—camping along the river is fine, as long as it doesn't interfere with a primary use of the area, such as hunting. In practice, it is rare that a conflict would occur on public lands because river campers tend to pick secluded spots. At some areas where camping has become a problem—often the problem is underage drinking—it is prohibited.

IOWA'S MEANDERED STREAMS

The river sections in bold are "meandered," meaning their banks are public areas up to the point where permanent vegetation begins.

Accesses

Accessing rivers and creeks where there is an official access with parking is the most cut-and-dried way to get on a river. However, on some very nice stretches of river, there are few official accesses. Because of that, some of the trips in this book suggest using county or state right-of-ways and putting in at bridges. On state and county highways and roads, parking along highways for any nonemergency use is actually a gray area, with the Iowa Department of Transportation officially discouraging the practice. In actuality, however, it is something paddlers often do. DNR canoe publications have even mentioned it as necessary for accessing some portions of stream. Wherever you park, don't block farmers' entrances to fields, and please be considerate of other motorists and farmers with large farm equipment by pulling as far off the roadway as possible.

Registration and Licenses

If you buy a boat, the retailer you purchase it from will alert you to whether you need to register it (unless you purchase out of state). Any boat longer than 12 feet, including paddlecraft, must be registered either here or in another state for you to float on Iowa's waters. Registrations are handled at your county courthouse. You should fish, of course, only if you've purchased an Iowa fishing license, available most places where fishing gear and bait are sold. On border rivers, an Iowa fishing license suffices.

PADDLING ETIQUETTE

Too many paddlers go out looking only for solitude. A great way for beginning paddlers to learn paddling etiquette, to increase safety, and to enjoy the company of other paddlers is to join a local club (see Appendix 6 for a listing). For more advanced paddlers, it's important for the sport that as many skilled people as possible lead trips to keep the cycle of learning going. Newer paddlers can make contributions to clubs in a variety of ways, such as volunteering to handle mailings or cook meals on a trip.

Iowa's rivers are tranquil places where anyone can go to leave the workday world behind for a spell. For the privilege of being able to paddle in such regenerative places, paddlers would do well to be responsible about how they behave on the river. Paddling and alcohol don't mix, for instance; and all cell phones should be kept at home (if you must pack one, keep it switched off and in a dry bag for safety), along with your kids' Game Boy and all other noisy accoutrements of modern life that have no place on a serene and quiet river.

And keep the banks pristine. Don't just refrain from littering; pick up litter when you see it. If you camp along the river, do it in a low-impact way, using a camp stove in favor of a fire if there's no designated fire ring. Plan ahead for packing out all your trash. Treat the rivers well, and they'll continue to be a treat.

Participating in a river cleanup is a great way to deepen your appreciation for Iowa's rivers.

BIG CEDAR CREEK 1 AND 2

Round Prairie Park to Willow Road (8.1 Miles)
Willow Road to Agency Road (11 Miles)

Most rivers are very large when they reach southeast Iowa. Big Cedar Creek offers intimate-scale paddling, languidly winding through two sections of scenic limestone outcroppings and small cliffs. With very few homes near the stream, no paved roads crossing it, and river birch and silver maple and sycamore woods all along, parts of both sections listed have the aura of remoteness.

Draining 530 square miles near its mouth and averaging 60 feet wide, Big Cedar Creek is really a small river with a watershed similar in size to the Upper Iowa River at Decorah. Its flows correspond to agricultural runoff in its headwaters, though, and can be a bit sporadic. Clear-running much of the year, Big Cedar Creek receives an influx of farmers' soil after rains, so water is often muddy brown when paddlers arrive. Extensive pools with just a few short riffles make it passable at fairly low water levels. The river isn't speedy, so you must actually paddle to make good time. Smallmouth bass are common in rocky segments, while catfish are caught in other areas.

For **canoe and kayak rentals** see Des Moines River 9 and Skunk River.

A nice **campground** is available up the hill from the stream at Round Prairie Park, and primitive camping is allowed at Gibson Recreation Area. Also see Skunk River.

The **shuttle route** for the first trip heads south from the put-in on Tamarack Avenue, left at the T intersection, south and east on Timber Road to 120th Street, east to Willow Road, and just north to the bridge over the stream. The second shuttle route heads north on Willow Road and then east on Agency Road to the bridge over Big Cedar Creek.

For **water levels**, see the Cedar Creek near Oakland Mills gauge on the USGS Web site listed in the introduction. Look for at least 120 cfs to pass easily through riffles, although it is possible to carry over the few riffles and paddle long, deep pools at lower water levels.

The total **gradient** for both sections is 2 feet per mile.

Accesses on Big Cedar Creek require fairly steep carries down to the stream, including the **put-in** at the Round Prairie Park canoe access.

Ragged-looking rock outcroppings line the right bank at the base of a 60-foot-high wooded slope. Stands of river birch line the opposite side. Just downstream and still within the park, an easily accessed spot near a gully mouth can make a good streamside camp. Rock outcroppings protrude on the left, and the river diverts south along them. Woods open briefly to a clay slope, followed by more bends along limestone outcroppings and small cliffs.

Numerous limestone outcroppings add to the intimate beauty of Big Cedar Creek.

At a left bend, a fun riffle along moss-covered rocks leads to more bedrock exposures ahead. The stream heads south through deep woods. Flowing generally east along rocky banks, the stream diverts straight north into lowland woods before bending east, where a low mass of limestone appears. The scenery becomes wilder, with deep woods atop limestone walls. More outcroppings are visible after a bend left toward a pleasantly worn-looking steel bridge.

Appealing rock formations continue as the stream curves north along an 80-foot-high wooded ridge on the right. The river doubles back and curves north along another high wooded ridge. Rushing water can be heard, and soon you're at the stream's most significant drop—a 1.5-foot ledge followed by a fun riffle about 20 yards long. Two well-kept cabins are visible as you hook back to the south along flagstone-like rock formations.

Curving left between wooded ridges, a riffle splits around a small island. Past higher outcroppings, you'll see tabletlike limestone formations. After a right bend, prominent limestone outcroppings lead to the Willow Road Bridge. **Take out** downstream of it on the river right. Watch for poison ivy.

Section 2 heads eastward along limestone outcroppings and curves right along a wooded bluff. Bending to the north, the valley widens and woods become sparser. After curving along a wooded bluff on the left, Big Cedar Creek enters a meandering 1.5-mile bottomland river section of cut banks, sandbars, willows, and cottonwoods. Then, at a right bend, the stream turns west along a 300-yard line of limestone outcropping at the base of a heavily wooded bluff. Past a farm, the stream bends south along a higher wooded bluff with limestone outcropping and boulders lining the bank.

The stream drops through a shallow riffle and bends right, followed by some of the river's highest limestone cliffs—only 25 to 35 feet high. Along a left bend are low, tablelike slabs of limestone, perfect for a snack break. Ahead, in two tall sycamore trees is a huge great blue heron rookery with well over 20 nests.

You can take out at the Benton Avenue bridge or continue into lowland woods though a wider valley. Bending north, you reach a dramatic 90-foot oak-topped bluff with a large clay exposure. The next several bends are lined by lowland woods, until curving left along a ridge with limestone rocks and boulders at its base. **Take out** beneath the Agency Road bridge on the river-left.

Other trips. Paddling on Big Cedar Creek is pleasant from the access at Turkey Run in southern Jefferson County to its mouth. The 7.3-mile trip from Turkey Run Wildlife Area to Round Prairie Park passes smaller limestone outcroppings and has an enchanting spring flowing out of a limestone wall just downstream of Peach Avenue. The 5.3-mile section from Agency Road to a boat ramp at Gibson Recreation Area has fewer wooded bluffs and few rock outcroppings, but it does have beautiful sycamore stands.

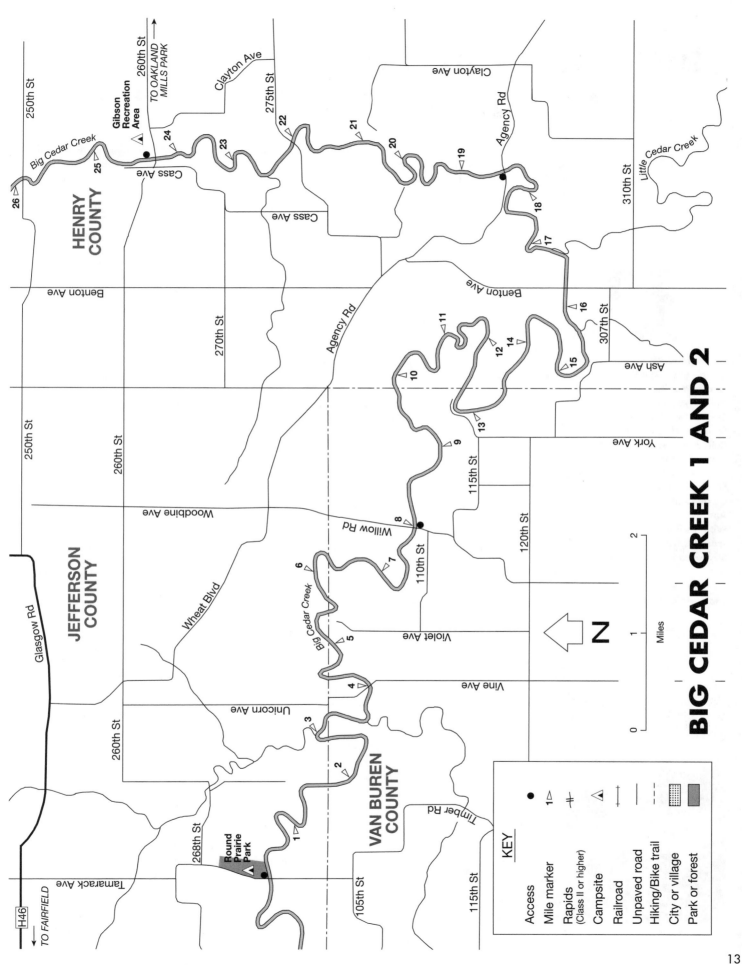

BIG CEDAR CREEK 1 AND 2

KEY

- ● Access
- ⌂ Mile marker
- ╪ Rapids (Class II or higher)
- ⌂ Campsite
- ┼ Railroad
- — Unpaved road
- --- Hiking/Bike trail
- ▦ City or village
- ▓ Park or forest

N

Miles
0   1   2

HENRY COUNTY

JEFFERSON COUNTY

VAN BUREN COUNTY

Big Cedar Creek

Little Cedar Creek

Round Prairie Park

Gibson Recreation Area

TO OAKLAND MILLS PARK →

TO FAIRFIELD

Glasgow Rd

Tamarack Ave

250th St
260th St
250th St
260th St
270th St
260th St
275th St

Cass Ave
Cass Ave
Clayton Ave
Clayton Ave
Agency Rd
Agency Rd
Benton Ave
Benton Ave
Woodbine Ave
Wheat Blvd
Unicorn Ave
Willow Rd
Violet Ave
Vine Ave
York Ave
Ash Ave
Timber Rd
307th St
310th St
105th St
110th St
115th St
115th St
120th St
268th St

BIG SIOUX RIVER 1
Gitchie Manitou State Preserve to Klondike Access (12.8 Miles)

Rising in a rocky region in South Dakota and Minnesota that French fur traders knew as the *Coteau des Prairies*, or Mountains of the Prairies, the Big Sioux cascades dramatically at Sioux Falls, South Dakota, and continues south to form the Iowa–South Dakota border at Gitchie Manitou State Preserve, named for the native Great Spirit. All told, it runs 390 miles before joining the Missouri River near Sioux City.

Upon reaching the Iowa–South Dakota border, the Big Sioux is a mostly lazy, meandering river coursing through pleasant prairie and farmland scenery. The water often appears muddy, thick with silt. It is a midsized river here, ranging from 80 to 150 feet wide, with catfish being the most commonly sought game fish for anglers.

On the Mountains of the Prairie,
On the great Red Pipe-Stone Quarry
Gitchie Manito, the mighty,
He the Master of Life descending,
On the red crags of the quarry
Stood erect, and called the nations
Called the tribes of men together.
From his footprints flowed a river,
Leaped into the light of morning,
O'er the precipice plunging downward
Gleaned like Ishkoodah, the comet.
And the Spirit stooping earthward,
With his finger on the meadow
Traced a winding pathway for it
Saying to it, "Run this way!"

—Henry Wadsworth Longfellow,
The Song of Hiawatha

The preserve is worth exploring before putting in. Native Americans long before the Sioux considered Gitchie Manitou a spiritual place, evidenced by burial mounds more than 1,000 years old dotting the preserve. At the southern reaches of the *Coteau des Prairies*, the reddish quartzite bedrock outcroppings are 1.6 billion years old, Iowa's oldest rock exposures. A quarry last used in 1920 and now filled with water is known as Jasper Pool. Native rock was used to build a Civilian Conservation Corps shelter here in the 1930s, but it has fallen into disrepair. Atypical Iowa plant species, such as prickly pear cactus and a mix of eastern and Great Plains prairie, give the preserve the feel of the West, but with an Iowan tenor.

The **campground** at Lake Pahoja Recreation Area 3 miles east of Klondike Access has full amenities. The Big Sioux along the entire Iowa border is a meandered stream, meaning the state owns the land below the ordinary high-water mark (see the explanation in the introduction), where sandbar camping is acceptable. Similar laws apply on the South Dakota side, with a 50-foot maximum extension of public land from the bank.

Canoe rentals are available in Sioux Falls, South Dakota, from Ace Hardware (605-336-6507) and in Sioux Center at the Rent All Center (712-722-3928).

The **shuttle route** from the put-in (11 miles) goes southeast on County K10, east on County A18, south on County K12, and 1 mile west on County A26, where you turn south onto Ashley Road just before crossing the bridge.

For **water levels**, see the Big Sioux at North Cliff Avenue at Sioux Falls gauge (station 06482020) online at http://waterdata.usgs.gov/sd/nwis/current/?type=flow. Look for more than 250 cfs to avoid occasional scraping on the riffles. The Big Sioux can usually be paddled all season long.

The **gradient** for this section is less than 2 feet per mile.

The **put-in** at Gitchie Manitou requires a 300-yard carry down a trail to a sandbar. Although scenic with grassy pastures and views of distant wooded hills, the trip doesn't kick off in a pristine fashion. A home is soon visible on the left bank, and diesel motors driving irrigation pumps may be heard while you paddle along deep erosion-cut dirt banks. Then the river bends west toward a wooded ridge rising 200 feet above the river with a pretty loess and clay cliff topped by thick oak woods. Ahead, a gravel operation is visible on the left.

Lowland groves of cottonwoods dominate the banks. After Blood Run enters from the left, the view opens to wide grassland vistas reminiscent of the vast prairies that once covered this region. The Big Sioux approaches the bluff on the right once more. As you veer left, crops are visible above a cut bank. After two gentle riffles, past the remains of an old bridge, the river jogs northwest and then hooks back south to the A18 Bridge.

Heading generally southward through several snaggy bends, the Big Sioux approaches a wooded hill and begins heading east. Distant wooded bluffs are ahead. As you draw near them, you'll see beautiful loess cliffs sloping down to the river. As you pass a second cliff, the bottom becomes rocky where pink quartzite rocks poke from a clay cliff. Directly across the river is a private camping retreat. The river bends southeast through a heavily wooded area. Just above a high sandbar on the right in the woods is another private camp. Cottonwood giants grow along the banks just downstream. Hidden Bridge Wildlife Area lines the left bank but is not easily accessible from the river.

For the next several bends, scenery alternates between hilly pastures and woods. You'll pass a silo, barn, and homes on the left bank, and then, curving right along pilings of riprap, you'll view a striking stone home atop a 100-foot-high prairie-covered ridge. As the river bends south, the prairie on the ridge gives way to oak-dominated woods.

The river widens to 200 feet and slows through croplands and then pasture. It curves southeast at a farmyard and then heads south toward the County A26 bridge. Beyond the bridge, a long wooded island splits the river. Either channel works, but novice paddlers should stay left because just below the island is a dangerous dam. **Take out** on the left, 30 yards upstream from the dam.

The best **portage** around the dam at Klondike is on the river-left. Put in again just below the mill foundation and rapids.

**Earthen cliffs and oak-covered bluffs
often line the Big Sioux.**

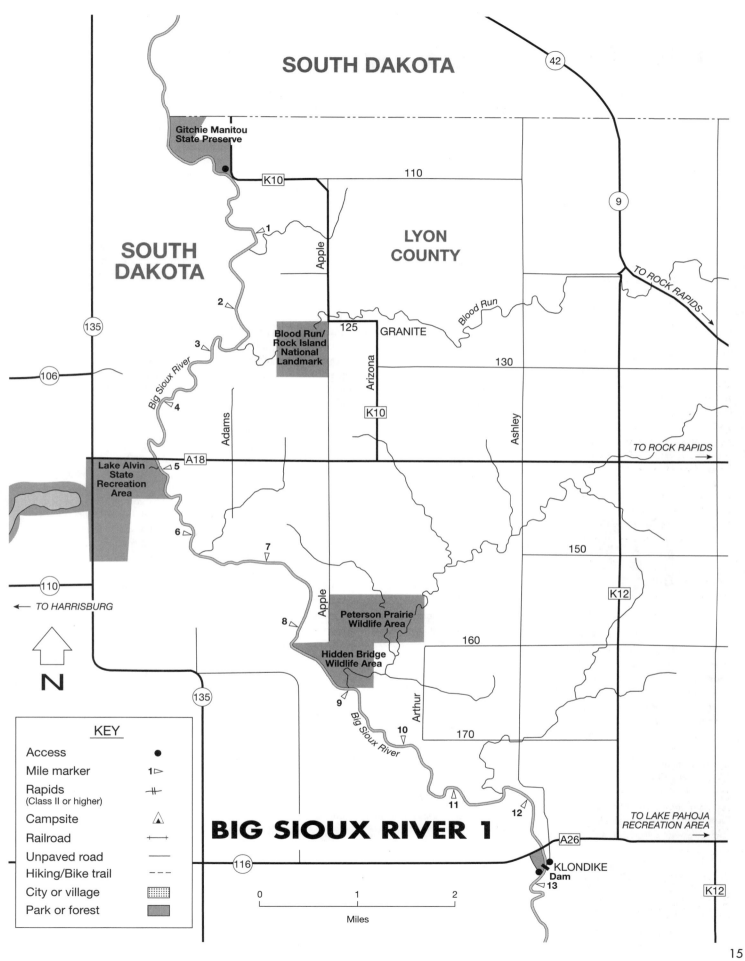

SOUTH DAKOTA

Gitchie Manitou
State Preserve

SOUTH
DAKOTA

LYON
COUNTY

Blood Run/
Rock Island
National
Landmark

GRANITE

Blood Run

Big Sioux River

Lake Alvin
State
Recreation
Area

TO HARRISBURG

Peterson Prairie
Wildlife Area

Hidden Bridge
Wildlife Area

Big Sioux River

TO ROCK RAPIDS

TO ROCK RAPIDS

TO LAKE PAHOJA
RECREATION AREA

KLONDIKE
Dam

BIG SIOUX RIVER 1

KEY

Access	●
Mile marker	1▷
Rapids (Class II or higher)	╫
Campsite	▲
Railroad	┼
Unpaved road	—
Hiking/Bike trail	- - -
City or village	▒
Park or forest	▓

N

0   1   2

Miles

BIG SIOUX RIVER 2
Klondike Access to Canton, South Dakota (12.2 Miles)

This is an entirely pleasant float with some very nice prairie ridge scenery. Perhaps the loess cliffs aren't as dramatic as in the first section, and it doesn't have the riffles and public lands of Big Sioux River 3, but this stretch certainly has long wooded runs and places that feel quite isolated.

It's also a stretch of river with an interesting settlement history. The river at Klondike was once a center of activity for freshwater clamming, an endeavor many began in search of rare pearls. But they soon learned that the shells—shipped to eastern Iowa factories for the button industry—were a more dependable moneymaker. The great snowstorm of 1909 culminated in flooding that changed the river's course in many spots, and to this day it is unclear whether part of the town of Canton—once known as Bijou Island—is really part of Iowa or South Dakota.

Averaging 120 feet wide, the river bends frequently and is fairly shallow. The bottom of the river is most often sandy and occasionally muddy. Catfishing is still the most popular angling opportunity, but walleye can be caught below the dam at Klondike and the rock-dam rapids at Canton.

Canoe rentals are listed in Big Sioux River 1.

The **shuttle route** from the put-in (9.6 miles) runs west on South Dakota Highway 116 and then south on Highway 135 to Canton. Head briefly east on U.S. Highway 18, and then turn south on Lincoln Street. The takeout is behind the Canton public works building.

For **camping**, see the descriptions in Big Sioux River 1 and Big Sioux River 3.

The Big Sioux can usually be paddled all season long. To estimate water levels, see the North Cliff Avenue at Sioux Falls (station 06482020) gauge online at http://waterdata.usgs.gov/sd/nwis/current/?type=flow. Look for more than 250 cfs to avoid running up on sand shoals.

The **gradient** for this section is less than 2 feet per mile.

Put in below the pedestrian bridge on the river-right, on the South Dakota side, a much easier access than the area downstream of the dam on the Iowa side. The foundation of the old Klondike flour mill can be seen across the river, upstream from the bridge. Some rusting gears are still inside it. Camping is prohibited at the Klondike Access on the Iowa side.

Downstream from the pedestrian bridge below the dam the riffle subsides, and the river flows freely over sand shoals and a sandy cut bank on the left. The banks become heavily wooded, and at high-water levels you come to an island. At levels below 400 cfs the left channel becomes the sole channel, which is only about 20 to 30 feet wide and quite swift. Because you cannot see to the end of this narrow chute, get out on the right and scout for dangerous snags before running it.

Past some croplands, woods dominated by silver maple with some elm and basswood surround the river again, and after a left turn the river passes along the base of an oak-topped 160-foot-high ridge on the left with a clay and sand slope reaching down to the waterline. Occasional lines of large glacial-till rocks cover the banks in places.

For the next several miles, the riverbanks are mostly wooded with a few fields of row crops visible. The river joins and leaves the base of the valley ridge on the east side of the river, and distant ridgelines are almost always visible. Just upstream from the rustic-looking trestle bridge on the river-left, a trail leads from 220th Street down to the river for a doable carry-down canoe access.

The stream bends east toward a high, grassy ridge on the left. The river is tree-lined, mostly with cottonwoods and some maples growing in sandy soil. Past a junkyard with old cars stacked on the bank on the right, the river proceeds west and then south. Just downstream from the Highway 18 bridge on the left is a concrete boat ramp.

The next several bends are quite scenic. At the second westward bend, a 220-foot-high prairie-covered ridge slopes down to the river, with loess cliffs flanked by oaks and cedars. A high sandbar on the inside bend here is a good place for primitive camping at moderate water levels. The river proceeds west through a floodplain with wildflowers, native grasses, small cottonwoods, and willow brush. It veers south toward a bluff with a gravelly slope on the left before heading back north into more agricultural lands. Past more lines of glacial-deposit rocks, you head generally west toward Canton. After you pass under a railroad bridge, the concrete ramp **takeout** is on the right, 200 yards upstream from the rock-dam rapids, on the south side of the parking lot for Canton's public works building.

From the concrete ramp near the public works building, you can **portage** your boat down the dirt road approximately 300 yards to the beach below the dam.

Sioux Excursions

Before the days of heavy agricultural runoff, people called the Big Sioux the "Silvery Sioux." At the turn of the past century, the river was clear and narrow, with an average depth of 18 feet. Two 120-foot-long excursion boats, gas-engine paddle wheelers called the *City of Canton* and the *Sioux Queen*, plied the waters between the Iowa towns of Beloit and Klondike in the early 1900s. Beer gardens and picnic spots were set up along the way, where day-trippers stopped for merrymaking. The structure on the west side of the rock dam at Canton, South Dakota, was a landing dock.

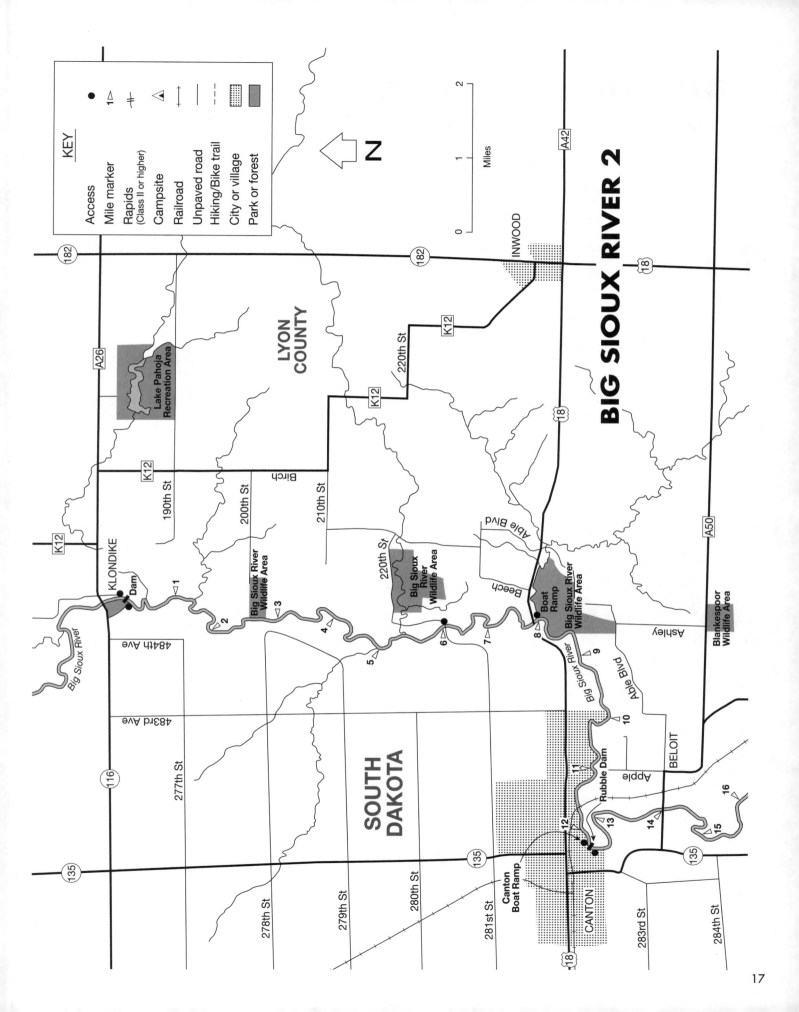

BIG SIOUX RIVER 2

KEY

Access
Mile marker
Rapids (Class II or higher)
Campsite
Railroad
Unpaved road
Hiking/Bike trail
City or village
Park or forest

N

Miles
0   1   2

BIG SIOUX RIVER 3
Canton, South Dakota, to Settler's Access (13.9 Miles)

If you take the time to paddle only one Iowa stretch of the Big Sioux in your lifetime, make it this one. It has the best the Big Sioux has to offer, including heavily wooded bluffs and ridges, a sense of isolation, prairie banks strewn with rocks and boulders, and fun riffles, with the flavor of rural Iowa and South Dakota all the while.

When artist John James Audubon made his way up the Missouri River in 1843, he took a side trip up the Big Sioux and reported an abundance of wildlife and clear waters. Wildlife, from deer and muskrats to waterfowl and turkey vultures, have become abundant once again, but the Big Sioux still runs much muddier these days than in Audubon's time, thanks to agriculture-induced erosion. While some croplands are sometimes visible, there are also sprawling areas of public lands near Newton Hills State Park on the South Dakota side, where high ridgelines lend the river an unspoiled feel.

This section of the Big Sioux also benefits from convenient access. A new boat ramp, the McKee Access was installed in 2002 near Newton Hills. Averaging about 140 feet wide, this stretch, like most of the Big Sioux, is popular for catfishing.

Although it's not directly on the river, the area's best **camping** is at charming Newton Hills State Park in South Dakota, another piece of the *Couteau des Prairies* described in Big Sioux River1. The park has trails winding through forested hills and all modern amenities in the campgrounds, plus heated and air-conditioned cabins available for rental year-round.

Canoe rentals are listed in Big Sioux River 1.

The **shuttle route** (8.4 miles) runs south from Canton on County 135. Turn left at the first paved road, which crosses the river into Iowa and becomes County A50. Head east, south, and east again until reaching County A54B, which curves southeast to the Fairview Bridge just to the south. The takeout is upstream of the bridge on the river-left.

To estimate water levels, see the information in Big Sioux River 2.

The **gradient** is 2.1 feet per mile.

Drive south of the Canton public works compound on Lincoln Street to **put in** below the rock dam, a structure that warrants caution. It was first built in 1917 to pool up the river for ice-skating in the winter, and the area below the dam is now a popular fishing spot. Although there are no dangerous hydraulics, submerged iron rods and foot-entrapment hazards exist, and the dam should not be run.

The river heads south and then east, becoming increasingly wooded. By the time the river bends south again, large rocks jut out midstream and line the left bank with towering cottonwoods on the right. After passing beneath the County A50 bridge near Beloit, Iowa, the river slows above a rocky area before rushing through a brief riffle.

As the river curves northwest and then south, it enters an agricultural plain, with riprap piled on the left bank and crops atop high cut banks. As the river heads southeast, the banks gradually become more wooded. Rocks begin to line the right bank, and then you paddle through calm water past midstream boulders ranging from the size of dogs to the size of cattle.

The view becomes agricultural again, and you pass an old barn. After a southward bend, the stream bottom becomes quite rocky and drops through two riffles past lightly wooded banks. The river flows southeast, past an old barn on an eroding grassy hillside, which transitions to a wooded slope. As you bend south, the pretty slope on the right is dotted with rocks. Prairie grasses and delicate wildflowers grow down to the river. A prominent wooded ridge is visible ahead. The stream bends left, descends a spirited riffle, and bends right again. Just downstream is the McKee Access, a concrete boat ramp that is closest to Newton Hills State Park (2 miles from the park's campground).

For the next several miles, the dramatic oak-covered ridges on the right are almost constantly in view with brief glimpses of crops sometimes visible on the left through the line of trees. Glacially deposited rocks still often line the banks. As you head generally eastward, the topography flattens, with the river flanked by lines of trees.

The river gradually makes it way to the foot of a ridge to the south, where pinkish rocks and boulders are scattered haphazardly near the waterline. As you curve left away from the ridge past young cottonwoods, you can see rolling hills of Iowa cropland, along with a large dairy farm near the river. As you head back toward a high wooded bluff to the south, both banks become increasingly wooded again. Ahead on the left, a high ridge cloaked in savanna with interspersed cedars—the Fairview Wildlife Area—becomes visible. After passing through two short riffles while skirting the wooded ridge along the right, **take out** at the Settler's Access upstream from the Fairview Bridge on the river-left.

Other trips. Another boat ramp added in 2002 allows for a nice 5-mile trip below Settler's Access to the Oak Ridge Access. The river there passes along scenic wooded bluffs and then bends through lowland woods before the takeout on the river-right.

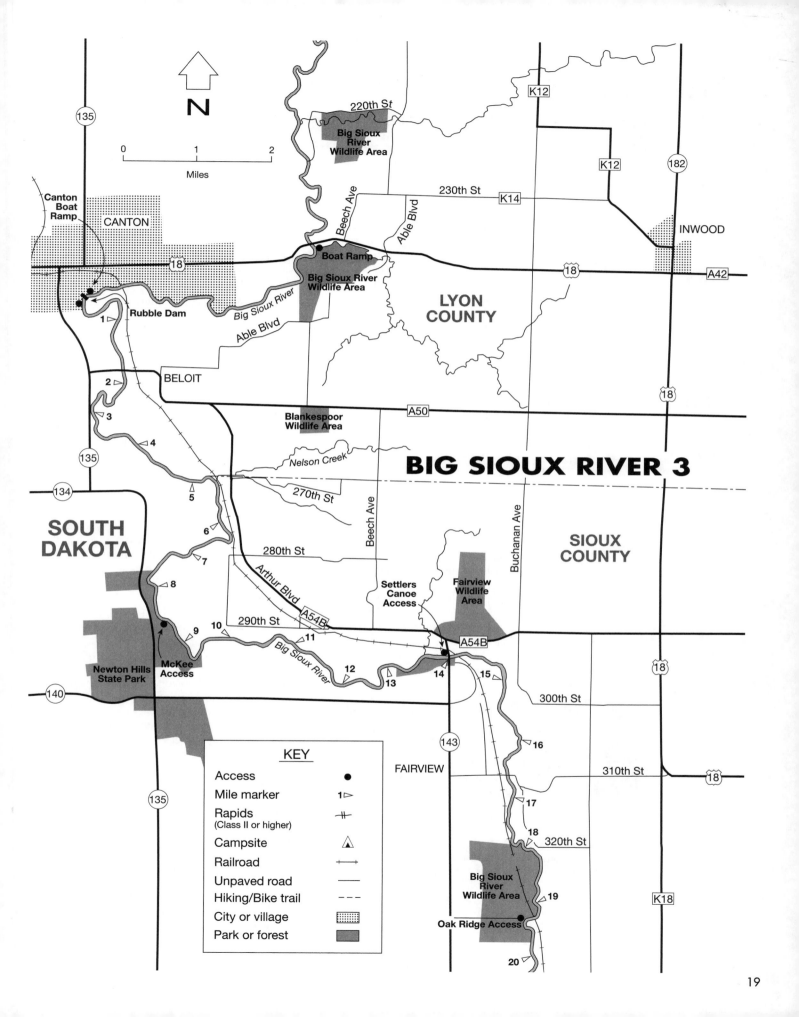

BIG SIOUX RIVER 3

N

0   1   2
Miles

135

Canton Boat Ramp

CANTON

Canton Boat Ramp

18

Rubble Dam

1

Big Sioux River

Able Blvd

2

3

4

135

134

SOUTH DAKOTA

5

6

7

8

Newton Hills State Park

McKee Access

9   10

11

12

13

140

220th St

Big Sioux River Wildlife Area

Beech Ave

Able Blvd

230th St   K14

Boat Ramp

Big Sioux River Wildlife Area

LYON COUNTY

K12

K12

182

INWOOD

18   A42

18

BELOIT

A50

Blankespoor Wildlife Area

Nelson Creek

270th St

280th St

Arthur Blvd

A54B

290th St

Beech Ave

Settlers Canoe Access

Fairview Wildlife Area

A54B

Buchanan Ave

SIOUX COUNTY

18

14   15

300th St

16

143

FAIRVIEW

17

18

320th St

Big Sioux River Wildlife Area

310th St

18

Oak Ridge Access

19

20

K18

140

135

KEY

Access	●
Mile marker	1▷
Rapids (Class II or higher)	╫
Campsite	△
Railroad	┼┼┼
Unpaved road	——
Hiking/Bike trail	- - -
City or village	▦
Park or forest	▬

BOONE RIVER 1 AND 2

Webster City to Albright's Access (8.5 Miles)
Albright's Access to Tunnel Mill (7.6 Miles)

The Boone River is probably the most vaunted of central Iowa's paddling streams. It has all the ingredients a paddler loves: wooded bluffs, a sprinkling of sandstone cliffs, lots of fast riffles, and long tracts of woods; in addition, it tends to run fairly clear at moderate water levels. The Boone was created in much the same way as the deep Des Moines River Valley to which it connects—by a sudden torrent of water caused by glacial meltwater 11,000 years ago. The result here is a narrow valley with a small river coursing down to the Des Moines River.

This section begins in Webster City, a bit above a traditional put-in at Briggs Woods. That inserts the brief hum of traffic noise crossing under U.S. Highway 20, but it also adds a scenic bluff and, at normal water levels, a scenic little waterfall. Catfish are common in the Boone River, but more anglers come to fish the riffles for smallmouth bass.

An excellent riverside campground with full amenities is available at Briggs Woods Park with convenient access to the boat ramp that makes it easy to split the trip into a two-day journey.

For **canoe and kayak rentals**, see Des Moines River 5.

The **shuttle route** (6.5 miles) for the first trip runs south on White Fox Road, west a block on 2nd Street, south on Iowa Highway 17 (Superior Avenue), west on 270th Street, and north on Inkpaduta Avenue to Albright's Canoe Access.

The second shuttle route (5.7 miles) runs south from Albright's on Inkpaduta Avenue, west on 280th Street, and south on County R27 to the Tunnel Mill Access just past the river bridge.

For **water levels**, check the Boone River at Webster City gauge (station 05481000) on the USGS Web site listed in the introduction. A minimum of 200 cfs is required to pass without too much scraping, while 400 cfs makes a great paddling level.

The total **gradient** for both sections is 4 feet per mile.

Swift with rock outcroppings and deep woods, the Boone River is one of central Iowa's best paddling streams.

Put in at the White Fox Road trailhead for the Boone River Nature Trail, either below the rock dam or upstream of it if you care to run one of the three chutes—the far-left chute is most challenging; watch for snags. After passing under the White Fox Road bridge, you enter a wooded area bending south as White Fox Creek enters from the right. The river falls over a drop with a large wave in the center of the stream and then passes beneath a railroad before reaching the Highway 928 bridge. Past a house on the right, Riverside Park lines the right bank until the next street bridge.

Railroad tracks run along the right side of the stream for a half mile, and then the river bends east into a long, swift riffle as the banks grow wild and wooded. A tree-topped ridge with exposed dirt cuts rises on the left before the river jogs right and then curves into a horseshoe loop to the east. At the eastern point of the bend, a 50-foot bluff with loess and stone exposures lines the bank. The woods gradually thin, and you bend left toward the Highway 20 bridges.

A low wooded ridge rises on the right, and rock outcroppings begin to show, as do glacially deposited rocks. Then you pass beneath a railroad bridge. On the nicely wooded ridge to the left, a stream falls six feet over two sandstone ledges that roar spectacularly at high water. You can see more such ledges higher up the creek if you land your boat and hike up. Just downstream on the Boone is a concrete boat ramp near the Briggs Woods Park campground.

A wooded ridge rises just past the Highway 17 bridge, and then you pass some agricultural land before bending east. The river becomes increasingly wooded with all manner of hardwoods, and bluffs begin rising up along the banks with some rock outcroppings. Glacial-erratic boulders protrude from the river above Albright's Bridge. At higher water levels these can look like innocent standing waves from upstream, until they flip your boat when you run into them. The **takeout** for the first section is at Albright's Access, downstream from the bridge on the river-left.

Downstream from Albright's, after a long riffle, the river bends right along a wooded ridge. At the next left bend, the channel splits around a long, heavily wooded island. The left channel passes down an easygoing riffle, while the right channel culminates by dropping over a two-foot ledge rapids with surfable waves. If waves intimidate you, take the left channel. After the channels merge again, the river courses between beautifully wooded ridges, passing a small island on the way to the access upstream of Bever Bridge on the river-left.

The Boone continues along a wooded ridge on the left, heading through a long riffle. Some higher sandstone cliffs briefly line the left bank, then the right. As the river bends right along smaller outcroppings, you pass through a bit of a riffle and see mounds of sand from a gravel quarry ahead.

Rounding a left bend along a ridge wooded with cottonwoods, oaks, elms, and cedars, the river heads east and then begins doubling back swiftly to the west along a dramatic wooded bluff well over a hundred feet high. As the river heads west, the valley begins to constrict after a left bend. The gravel access where you **take out** is ahead 150 yards upstream from Tunnel Mill Bridge.

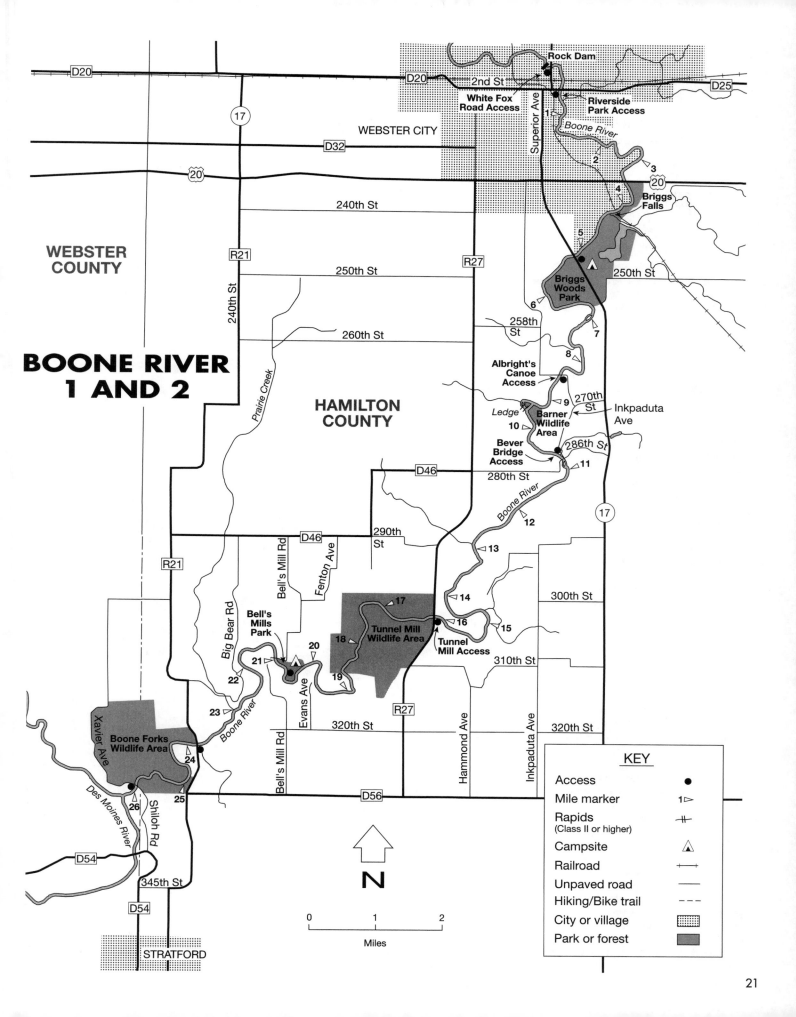

BOONE RIVER
1 AND 2

BOONE RIVER 3

Tunnel Mill to Boone Forks Wildlife Area (9.8 Miles)

Ghost Mills on the Boone River

More than a dozen water-powered grist-mills and sawmills lined the banks of the Boone River in Hamilton County during the nineteenth century. None still stand, but three of them had interesting (and true) stories. The first two could make scary campfire tales with little embellishment.

Did John Ross kill John Ross? Bone's Mill, which stood near today's Bever Bridge, was built in 1854 and purchased by John Ross in 1868. The next year, he was found with a bullet in his back, his body stuffed into the mill wheel's machinery. His nephew, also named John Ross, was accused of murdering his namesake. After being acquitted, he left the county never to return. In 1889, an owner named P. B. Osborne decided to convert Bone's Mill into a steam-powered operation. Ten years later, its boiler exploded, obliterating the mill. The miller's house is still standing east of the bridge.

Even sadder is the story of Bell's Mill, built by a Methodist minister in 1853 and later purchased by the Bell family. The Bells hired Lyman Perry as their miller in 1883. Perry one day noticed the mill had stopped operating. Looking to see why, he was horrified to learn his four-year-old son, Van, had slipped into the mill wheel and drowned. On a rainy spring day in 1888, mill owner Benjamin Bell died, and the same night floodwaters tore out the milldam, rendering the mill useless. It was torn down, and one of its turbines was later placed in Bell's Mill Park. Another turbine was brought to Brewer Creek Park in Webster City. When that turbine was installed, the little boy's shoe fell from the wheel.

Less macabre is the story of Tunnel Mill, whose ingenious builder, Robert Watson, engineered one of the state's most unique mills in the mid-1800s. He carefully surveyed a horseshoe bend about a mile long and found the river dropped 6.5 feet. He knew the distance from his mill to that point through a ridge was only 400 feet. So, he had a tunnel constructed that diverted water directly to the mill, which meant he didn't need to build a precarious dam across the river that, like other dams, would probably be destroyed by flood or ice some spring. But fire did destroy it in 1889. Both ends of the tunnel were later dynamited to keep curious children from being injured inside it.

The Boone River continues its descent to the Des Moines through heavily wooded territory, meandering with easygoing riffles spaced at wider intervals than in the two previous sections of the river. Longer tracts of public lands line the banks of the Boone in this section, offering paddlers good places to beach a craft and explore on foot or to camp along the river.

Anglers will find that catfish gradually become more abundant than smallmouth bass throughout this stretch.

Bell's Mill Park offers a riverside **campground**. You can also canoe camp along public areas shown on the map.

For **canoe and kayak rentals**, see Des Moines River 5.

The **shuttle route** (10.2 miles) runs south on County R27 to County D56, and then west to County R21. Turn south, and where R21 heads west, continue west on a gravel road, 345th Street, to County D54. Head north and then turn right onto Shiloh Road. The takeout is across the bridge on the left side of the road.

For **water levels**, see Boone River 1 and 2.

The **gradient** for this section is 3.8 feet per mile.

Put in upstream from Tunnel Mill Bridge on the river-left. As you head west under the high bridge, the nearly 200-foot-deep river valley rises from both banks of the river; the stretch is narrow and densely covered in deciduous woods. The hills become more gently sloped and grassy until they reach a long curve to the south with a large gravel bar on the left and wooded ridge on the right.

The river heads south toward a wooded bluff and then bends right at its base, where a glacier deposited a moraine of rocks. Then the river curves back north to a bluff that's mostly wooded with a small patch of prairie and back south to some small sandstone cliffs along the left bank. As the river runs back north, the grassy area on the right is Bell's Mill Park. The best access here is 100 yards upstream of Bell's Mill Bridge on the river-right.

Past a hog farm below the bridge, a sloping bank rises on the right where coal deposits run along the river. As the river curves to the left, a pretty bluff with mixed woods, prairie, and earthen exposures rises on the right. A bluff with prairie slopes rises ahead on the left as you curve around to the left. The line of trees along the bank becomes sparser as you head to the next canoe access just upstream of the County R21 bridge on the river-left.

Past the bridge, the Boone Forks Wildlife Area lines the banks until the final takeout. The Boone bends left into a horseshoe bend along a wooded ridge on the right, followed by another on the left. The **takeout** is just downstream from the Shiloh Road bridge, sometimes called Vegor Bridge after the Indian burial grounds and pioneer cemetery perched atop the hill north of the river.

The deep, wooded valley of the Boone continues to its mouth at the Des Moines River.

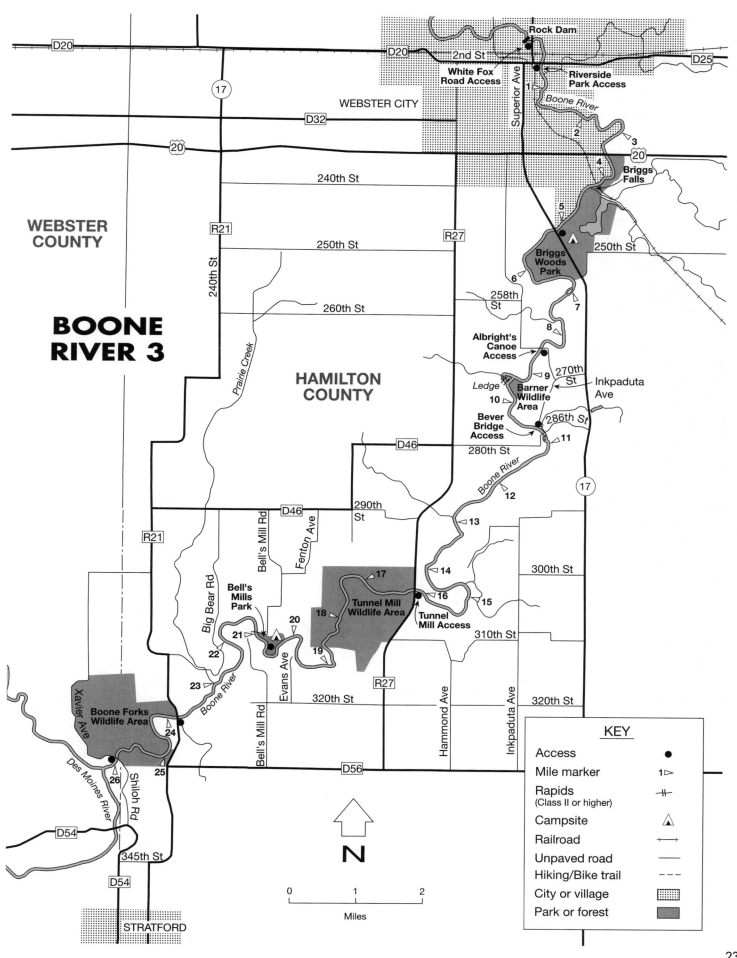

BOONE RIVER 3

WEBSTER COUNTY

HAMILTON COUNTY

Rock Dam

White Fox Road Access

Riverside Park Access

WEBSTER CITY

Boone River

Briggs Falls

Briggs Woods Park

Albright's Canoe Access

Ledge

Barner Wildlife Area

Bever Bridge Access

Inkpaduta Ave

Bell's Mills Park

Tunnel Mill Wildlife Area

Tunnel Mill Access

Boone River

Boone Forks Wildlife Area

Xavier Ave

Des Moines River

STRATFORD

Prairie Creek

Big Bear Rd

Bell's Mill Rd

Fenton Ave

Evans Ave

Bell's Mill Rd

Hammond Ave

Inkpaduta Ave

Shiloh Rd

KEY

Access ●

Mile marker 1▷

Rapids ─╫─
(Class II or higher)

Campsite △

Railroad ─┼─

Unpaved road ──

Hiking/Bike trail ----

City or village ▦

Park or forest ▨

N

0   1   2
Miles

23

CEDAR RIVER 1 AND 2
Mitchell to County T38 (8.6 Miles)
County T38 to Rotary Park (15.7 Miles)

Left to its own devices, the upper Cedar River from the Minnesota border to Charles City was once quite a swift-flowing stream. Now impounded by four dams in 13 river miles from Otranto to Mitchell, the Cedar River finally cuts loose below the Interstate Power Dam, and for more than 20 miles modern-day paddlers can paddle this joyously uninhibited stream.

Perhaps in part because of all the dams, the waters of the Cedar tend to run fairly clear. It courses along numerous wooded bluffs with limestone cliffs and outcroppings that are quite attractive but perhaps not as dramatic as those along other Iowa rivers. But don't mind that, because this is a fun river in a mostly natural setting. Smallmouth and rock bass offer the best angling opportunities.

Interstate Park at the put-in has a riverside **campground** with full amenities. There are also riverside campgrounds at Osage Spring Park and Idlewild Wildlife Area.

The nearest **canoe rentals** available are from the River Ranch Campground (641-435-2108) near Nashua, about 20 miles southeast of Floyd.

The **shuttle route** for the first trip heads south from the town of Mitchell on Hickory Avenue to Iowa Highway 9, east through Osage to County T38, and south to the takeout on the Cedar River.

For the second trip, head north of the put-in on County T38 to 340th Street, east to County T42, south to County B17 at Orchard, east to U.S. Highway 218, south to County B33, east to Redwood Avenue, south to 165th Street, and west to Rotary Park.

For **water levels**, see the Cedar River at Charles City gauge (station 05457700) on the USGS Web site listed in the introduction. Releases from the dam at Charles City don't perfectly match the releases upstream, but look for a bare minimum of 200 cfs to avoid scraping up the bottom of your boat at the riffles. A nice level is 400 to 600 cfs.

The **gradient** for the first section is 5.6 feet per mile, and it is 2.8 feet per mile for the second section.

Put in downstream of the dam at Interstate Park on the river-left. You pass under a bridge and run through a fast section of tight channels braiding between islands. After a low bluff and a long, wooded island, the channels rejoin and the river widens to 140 feet.

The banks are heavily wooded, and the bottom is uneven and rocky. The river passes over wide riffles and along a road on the left. A wooded bluff begins to rise on the right with a few limestone outcroppings, and you pass the Bennett Access on the left. The channel continues along wooded bluffs and after a right bend splits around a long, tree-covered island. Stay left in the main left channel.

At the Falk Wildlife Area on the right, a scenic bluff rises, wooded with limestone cliffs. At a shallow riffle, the river bends right near a bluff with pretty limestone clefts and stands of birch trees. To Highway 9, the river remains riffly. As the river bends right, more small cliffs rise up, and a wooded island splits swift riffles. As the river bends left, limestone outcroppings appear. Ahead on the left is access at Osage Spring Park, just upstream from a spirited riffle over concrete riprap.

The river continues east, curving right along a small wooded bluff and through riffles to the County T34 bridge. Bending 90 degrees left along some very scenic limestone cliffs, the river turns right and heads into the Sunny Brae Golf Club, where you'll portage the low-clearance pontoon bridge—a sweeper hazard. Just past here at a left bend, a high cliff rises. Past the next bridge, at County T38, the takeout for section 1 is on the river-right.

For the second segment, past the County T38 access, the river passes along lowland trees and through more riffles. After you pass a few homes and a field, the right bank becomes rocky. Limestone outcroppings begin rising with a wooded ridge. Past a series of islands, Rock Creek, clear and beautiful, tumbles into the Cedar.

The river heads east toward the River Road bridge, slowing through a lightly wooded area. As the river hooks southwest, a small cliff topped with birch and cedars appears. More limestone cliffs emerge downstream. Beyond a home and several islands that you pass as you head generally south, the river bends east and past three small wooded islands, the second of which, inside the Idlewild Wildlife Area, is high and sandy enough for river camping at moderate water levels.

On the right, past a park building, the boat ramp is at the Idlewild campground. The valley becomes narrow, the river riffly. After it passes a clearing with three homes, the river becomes heavily wooded, winding gently back and forth between wooded bluffs and rock outcroppings. Past another home is a gap through the bluff, cut for a quarry. After bending left at a wooded ridge on the right, the Cedar passes beneath the Highway 218 bridge. The banks become sparsely wooded. Beyond several islands after a right bend, a shelter house is visible through trees on the left ridge. The dirt **takeout** at Rotary Park is ahead on the river-left.

Ioway, or Red Cedar?

Native Americans called this the Mosk-Wah-Wak-Wah, or Red Cedar River, which irritated explorer Albert Lea. The Cedar River is much bigger than the Iowa River at their forks, where the streams combined have always taken the name "Iowa" to the Mississippi. Lea figured people should ditch the name "Cedar" altogether, calling the smaller branch the "Buffalo River." That way, what's now still the Cedar River above the forks could be called the "Ioway." Obviously, his scheme never caught on.

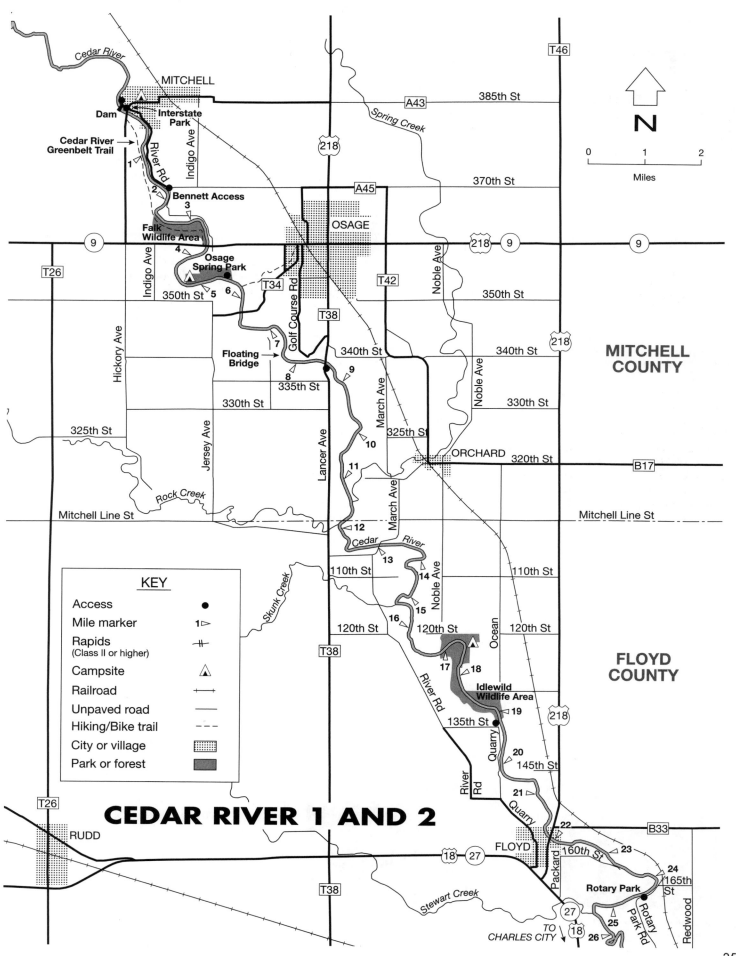

CEDAR RIVER 1 AND 2

CEDAR RIVER 3
Palisades-Kepler State Park to Sutliff (9.8 Miles)

Above Cedar Falls, the Shell Rock, West Fork Cedar, and Cedar Rivers merge, creating a wide river that tends to be shallow with occasional deep holes over a sandy or rocky bottom. Arguably the most scenic area anywhere on the Cedar is in the striking limestone gorge well over 100 feet deep at Palisades-Kepler State Park. Perhaps the state's best takeout spot is Sutliff, where you can enjoy a beverage and greasy food from a pub built in 1899, either inside or on a huge pedestrian trestle bridge across the river.

This trip does include a difficult portage around the rapids at the dam-breach at the park; you can put in at the boat ramp below, but you'll miss some of the best of the rugged riverside cliffs if you do. See the upcoming note on water levels. Smallmouth bass, walleye, and striped bass are commonly caught below the dam breach, as well as in other areas, and catfishing can be good near snags all along.

Excellent **campgrounds** are up the bluff from the river at Palisades-Kepler State Park (full amenities) and riverside at South Cedar Natural Area.

The **shuttle route** (17 miles) from the put-in runs southwest on Palisades Access Road, east on Ivanhoe Road, south on Iowa Highway 1, and east on County F14. After crossing the river, turn right onto White Oak Avenue, which leads to the takeout at Sutliff.

For **water levels**, see the Cedar River at Cedar Rapids gauge (station 05464500) on the USGS Web site listed in the introduction. The upcoming portage instructions are appropriate at moderate levels to approximately 6,500 cfs. Above 6,500 cfs, water also courses over a second breach, but experienced paddlers can still portage across what becomes the island. Don't put in at the Upper Palisades access at levels above 9,500 cfs, at which a very dangerous breach in the center of the dam begins running. The sandy-bottomed Cedar is rarely too low to paddle.

The **gradient** is less than 2 feet per mile.

Check water levels before you **put in** at the Upper Palisades boat ramp. Downstream of the access are three homes on the left, and ahead you see the first of the limestone cliffs. Here, in the middle of Palisades-Kepler State Park, the river bends right, with bluffs visible on both sides as the gorge bottom narrows to just 150 yards. Cedars cling to rocky clefts, and wooded hollows leave gaps in the valley walls. Vines hang from sheer rock walls that rise from the river. One cliff on the left has jagged-looking rocks with a multileveled cave.

As the river bends right, the cliffs are close by on the right, and small caves and fossilized sea creatures can be seen in the limestone strata near a set of stairs that head up the bluff. Branches hang out over the river.

Ahead you'll see a breached dam. RUNNING THE RAPIDS THROUGH THE BREECH IS NOT RECOMMENDED. Although to experienced paddlers they look like runnable, solid class II rapids with some potentially sticky holes, pieces of steel that once reinforced the concrete dam below the surface can pierce a boat's hull and/or entrap a swimming paddler. Numerous people have perished while wading. Pull out on the sandbar on the river left and **portage** across rocks and the dry portion of the dam, putting in at the sandbar below the rapids.

Past the boat ramp on the left, the river leaves the cliffs and bluff along the right, and more scenic bluffs join the left bank. Then it flows past the base of one more high, heavily vegetated bluff on the right with limestone exposures. Passing some rock shelves covered with wildflowers on the right, the river at high levels will fork around an island as the valley widens and bluffs become less prominent.

After floating under Highway 1, you'll spot a collection of houses on the left, and the banks are otherwise wooded. Downstream, another pretty bluff briefly joins the river on the right. Past one more home, there is a boat ramp on the right at South Cedar Natural Area. The bank on the right becomes rocky, and the river heads northeast. After bending right at a small wooded ridge, the big lazy river extends, flanked by thick swaths of woods on either bank. Depending on water levels, you may pass two wooded islands or just see desertlike channels of sand where the river flows at higher levels.

A ridge rises on the right, and you can just barely see small limestone walls through the base of trees. Just ahead, you'll paddle under the County F14 bridge, which has a canoe access on the right. Another quarter mile downriver, the **takeout**, the boat ramp at Sutliff, is just upstream from the high trestle bridge.

Other trips. Most of the free-flowing 75 miles of the Cedar River between the Mitchell Access in Waterloo and the Seminole Access in Cedar Rapids is of interest to paddlers. Two segments in Benton County deserve particular attention. The 11.3 miles from the Minne Estema Area (has camping) on 24th Avenue north of Vinton to the boat ramp at the 1,600-acre Dudgeon Lake Wildlife Area is flanked by long tracts of public land through mostly lowland woods. You can camp at the put-in. From the Milroy Canoe Access on County E18 north of Vinton to Wildcat Bluff (has camping), 9.9 miles, expect to see numerous homes in some areas, as well as spectacular wooded bluffs up to 150 feet tall. Accesses between (with distance from the put-in) are Hooefle-Dulin (2.6 miles, has camping) and Benton City-Fry (6.3 miles, has camping).

The idyllic access at Sutliff may be Iowa's best place to end a trip—with food and cold beverages from a tavern built in 1899 that you can enjoy outside on a pedestrian bridge.

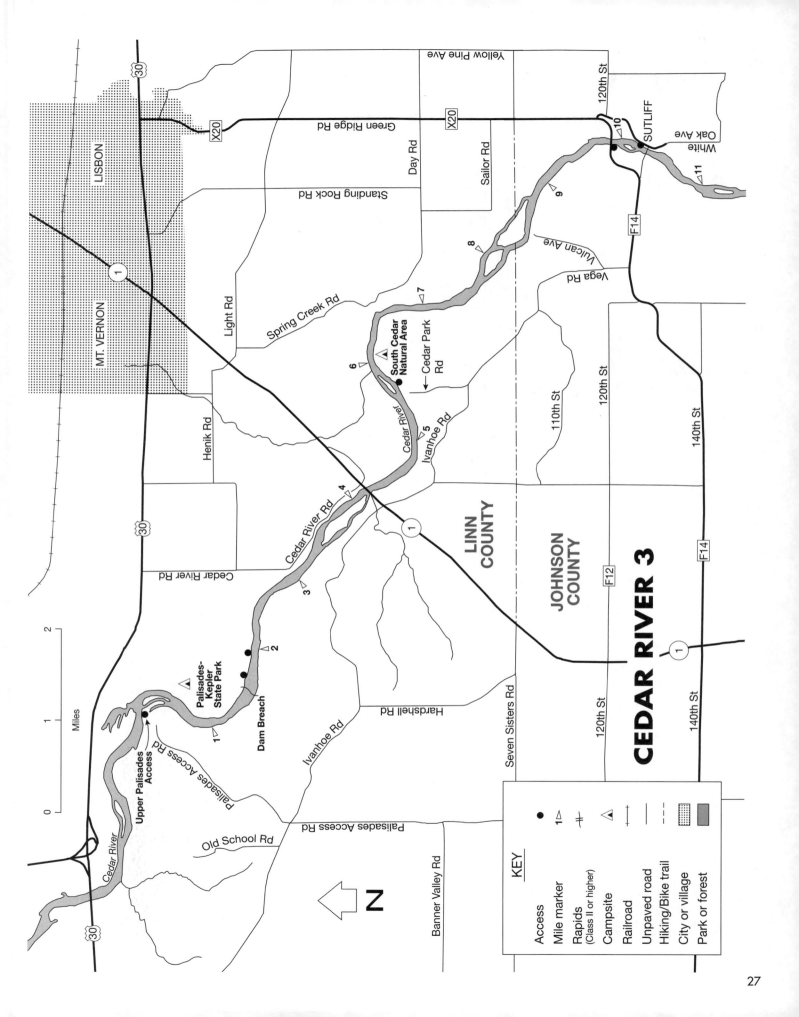

CEDAR RIVER 3

KEY

●	Access
△1	Mile marker
⚱	Rapids (Class II or higher)
⛺	Campsite
✝	Railroad
――	Unpaved road
―·―	Hiking/Bike trail
▦	City or village
▨	Park or forest

N

CEDAR RIVER 4
Cedar Bluff to Rochester (12.5 Miles)

Rock outcroppings along the Cedar in Cedar County are occasionally spectacular.

A stretch of lazy, sandy river flowing past occasional wooded bluffs, limestone cliffs, and scenic islands, this is an excellent section to get the feel for the lower Cedar River. The Cedar in these parts averages 600 feet wide and is usually neither crystal clear nor muddy, appearing a glassy green from reflecting the billowy lines of maples, elms, cottonwoods, and ash trees that almost continuously line the banks.

Sandbar camping can be a pleasurable experience here. In fact, the river runs freely through undeveloped areas from Palisades-Kepler State Park into the Iowa River at Columbus Junction, and then all the way to the mouth of that river (see Iowa River 4 and 5), with good places to camp on sandbars scattered all along. Make sure to select as high a spot as possible without crossing the "ordinary high-water mark" (see the introduction), and sleep with your PFD nearby or even on, because heavy rains up north can cause the river level to rise a few feet very quickly. You'll pass a home now and again, but the lower Cedar passes mainly through very rural areas with only tiny settlements along its banks.

Anglers will find catfish—this section is celebrated for yielding some of the Iowa River's largest flatheads.

A riverside **campground** is at Cedar Valley Park near the boat ramp.

The **shuttle route** (17 miles) from the put-in runs east on County F28, south on County X40, east on County F44, and south on Atalissa Road to Rochester Park.

For **water levels**, see the Cedar River at Cedar Rapids gauge (station 05464500) on the USGS Web site listed in the introduction. The sandy-bottomed Cedar is rarely too low to paddle.

The **gradient** is less than 2 feet per mile.

Put in at the boat ramp on the river-right 300 yards upstream from the bridge at Cedar Bluff. Downstream from the bridge on the right, a row of cracked-looking limestone outcroppings lines the bank before the river passes by homes on both banks. The river is forced left at a wooded bluff with 20- to 30-foot limestone cliffs at its base.

Through a sparse line of trees on the right, you can see a cornfield and meadow-covered hills with a farm and a wooded ridge in the background. The valley widens, and wooded ridges can be seen in the distance. Ahead, after a small island covered in willow shrubs, you'll pass a private boat ramp on the right. As woods become thicker along the banks, the river flows by four old stone-and-concrete bridge supports.

Ahead, ridgelines closing together are visible, and you paddle into a narrow valley first along a wooded bluff on the right; then the river bends slightly left to a rocky bank with limestone exposures. Behind an elephant-sized boulder at a striking cliff with overhanging protrusions, a cave near the river level is tucked into the base of the cliff, making a fine place to stop.

As you continue southeast, a bridge adds perspective to the valley, and beyond it are limestone block supports—all that remain of a previous bridge. Riverside cabins appear on the left, and just beyond them the concrete boat ramp at Cedar Valley Park is on the right. Ahead on the right, a bluff rises with a prominent cliff and is followed by lower exposures covered with moss and lichens beneath moist, cool woods. This bluff continues along the right bank for nearly two miles with intermittent limestone outcroppings.

Long, forested islands—connected to shore by sandbars at low levels—begin appearing to the river-left. The bluff across the river rises behind them, affording the valley a hemmed-in feeling. As the river bends right slightly, a wooded island rises a bit higher from the river where crystal-clear Rock Run Creek enters from the left. An imposing home tops the bluff to the left. The downstream side of the island has a long sandbar.

Ahead, riverside cabins and mobile homes appear above a rip-rapped bank. Wooded ridges become less prominent from the river, and homes become more common along the banks as you approach the little town of Rochester. The next long, wooded island is a state preserve, and soon you pass under the next bridge. **Take out** at the boat ramp about a quarter mile downstream on the right.

Other trips. The verdant Cedar River continues to offer good paddling below Rochester into Muscatine County, passing along thousands of publicly held acres of fens, sloughs, and woodlands. Approximate distances include Rochester to Moscow (9.3 miles), Moscow to Saulsbury Bridge Recreation Area (9.7 miles), and Saulsbury Bridge to McKeown Bridge (11.6 miles). Shuttles and canoe rentals are available from the Muscatine County Conservation Board at (563) 264-5922.

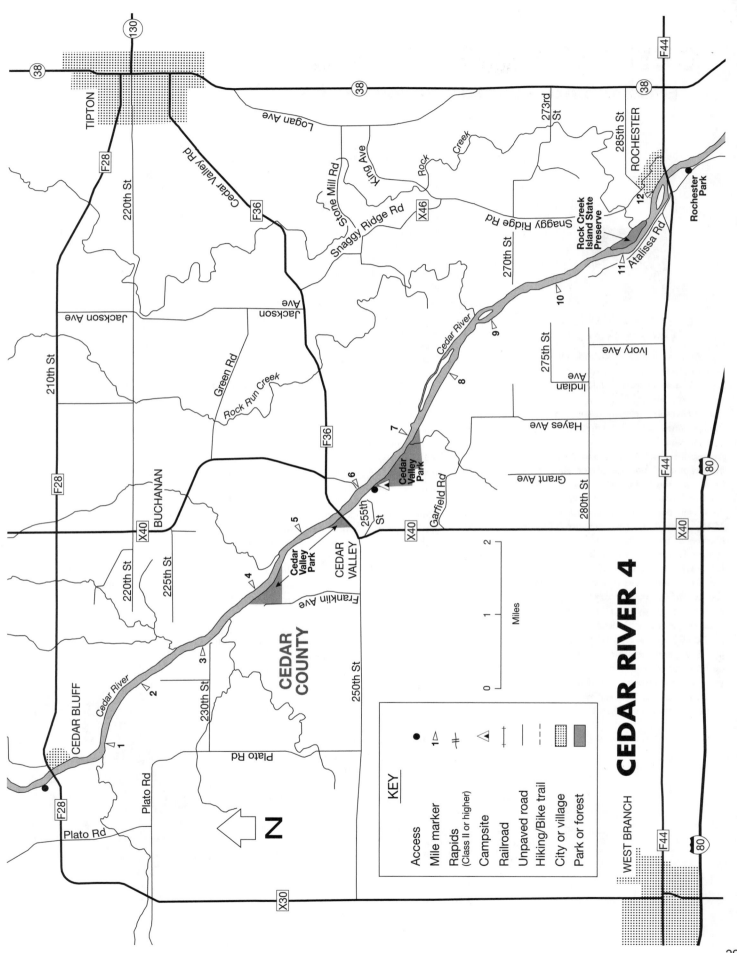

CEDAR RIVER 4

KEY

Access	●
Mile marker	1△
Rapids (Class II or higher)	≠
Campsite	◁
Railroad	
Unpaved road	
Hiking/Bike trail	
City or village	
Park or forest	

N

Miles

0   1   2

CEDAR COUNTY

DES MOINES RIVER 1
Erickson's Access to Fort Dodge (14.1 Miles)

When a lobe of the Wisconsin glacier covering central Iowa melted more than 11,000 years ago, it went in a hurry. A raging torrent rapidly incised what are otherwise central Iowa's pancake-flat plains into the narrow Des Moines River Valley, one of the state's most unique topographical features.

This trip from just below the confluence of the east and west forks of the river makes a great entrance into the valley, traveling along rock walls and light woods, over bedrock ledges, and finally along impressive bluffs north of Fort Dodge. Occasional boulders left by the glacier protrude from the riverbed along the way, and waters of several clear little creeks tumble into the Des Moines here. The water is that of a typical Iowa river—mud-tinted in the summer, clearing by late fall. Smallmouth bass prowl the riffles and several tributary streams, and catfish can be caught throughout this section. The entire Des Moines River is a "meandered stream" (see the introduction), so sandbar camping is acceptable.

Two public **campgrounds** are near the river here, including one at Kennedy Memorial Park three miles north of Fort Dodge and another at Frank A. Gotch Park, just north of the put-in.

For **canoe and kayak rentals**, see Des Moines River 5.

The **shuttle route** (14.2 miles) from the put-in goes west a mile on 270th Street and west one more mile on County C49. Turn south onto U.S. Highway 169, head south to the four-way stop sign at Iowa Highway 7, and turn left. Proceed to 2nd Street and turn left, heading north to 6th Avenue, and turn right toward the takeout, just upstream from Hydroelectric Park.

Water levels are found at the Des Moines River at Fort Dodge gauge (station 05480500) on the USGS Web site listed in the introduction. Look for 500 cfs to avoid scraping in riffles.

The **gradient** for this section is 3 feet per mile.

The **put-in** is at a private fishing access where you are encouraged to leave a donation. If the access is locked, ask for permission to enter from the farmer living north of 270th Street on County C49, on the east side of the road. Soon after the put-in, the river makes a small hook to the west, flowing slowly around boulders and rocks that jut from the water at lower levels. Small lime-stone outcroppings join the left bank, and the river heads straight south along lightly tree-lined banks.

Ahead, the river passes through a small riffle and past two cottages. A low bluff rises with limestone walls at its base where the river curves southwest. Swift riffles, rocks that poke above the waterline, and limestone outcroppings continue until you bend left and head toward the 120th Street bridge, above which a large in-stream boulder displays a devotional message.

The river follows along a limestone wall and then courses over a sheet of bedrock. Just upstream from the mouth of rocky little Deer Creek is a canoe launch. You head toward the base of a scenic wooded bluff on the left, and then a long riffle flows to a higher bluff with rugged 30- to 40-foot rock cliffs multihued with reds, grays of the rock, and bluish-green lichens.

A small cottage is visible atop a limestone wall set into the woods. After the river bends right, a small limestone cliff joins the left bank. Where it ends, Badger Creek delicately pours in from the left. Several riffles lead to a light line of trees along a pasture before a wooded ridge rises on the right. Ahead is an orchard, followed by a long line of riverside homes. At a left bend past the homes, midstream boulders announce the entrance to Breen's Rapids, which is an easy set of class I ledges at levels up to 1,500 cfs. But at higher levels, a sticky solid class II wave hole forms across most of the river-left—fun for whitewater boaters but intimidating for others. The river-right is still easily passable.

A much less intense rapids begins just upstream of the County D14 bridge. A quarter mile ahead is a canoe access at the Becker Wildlife Area. Heading east, the river begins slowing and widening. You'll pass several riverside homes on the right, and then a wooded bluff rises. Bending south along another wooded bluff on the left, the river splits around a wooded island and passes the nicely wooded bluff of Fort Dodge's Loomis Park on the left. **Take out** at the boat ramp, ahead on the river-right.

Can You Believe These Guys?

After a farmer in Cardiff, New York, dug up a petrified, naked, anatomically correct, 10-foot-tall man in 1869, popular science went abuzz. The world wanted to know: had some ancient race of super-sized humans once roamed North America?

A similarly breathtaking discovery centered around Father Louis Hennepin, a 17th-century French explorer thought to have been the first European to lay eyes on the Des Moines River. Debate on that topic was considered to be settled when, in 1912, picnickers at what's now Dolliver Memorial State Park southeast of Fort Dodge found a lead tablet inscribed by Hennepin himself, in Latin!

Both discoveries proved to be hoaxes. The Cardiff Giant was carved from a block of Fort Dodge gypsum in the likeness of cigar manufacturer George Hull, who pulled in $30,000 by charging admission to see his petrified giant. Eventually, the game was up. The giant returned, spending several years in Iowa. Now it's on display in Cooperstown, New York. A replica is on display at the Fort Museum in Fort Dodge.

This section of the Des Moines is swifter than others and has excellent scenery, as well.

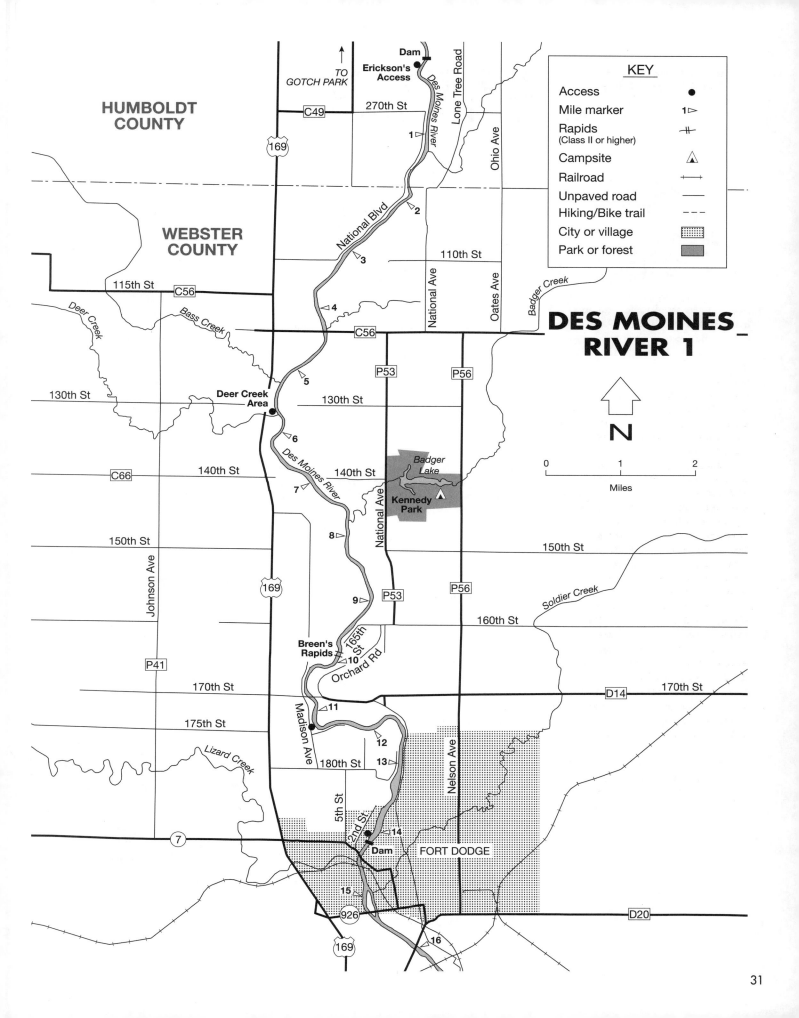

DES MOINES RIVER 1

DES MOINES RIVER 2
Kalo to Dolliver Memorial State Park (8.8 Miles)

Three Hollows

Although they go unnoticed from the river due to the forested canopy, paddlers pass very near three remarkable hollows during the run to Dolliver Memorial State Park. Woodman Hollow is inaccessible from the river because of steep banks and poison ivy. A little spring-fed brook trickles through sandstone-walled canyon here, topography that allows for a great diversity of woodland plants that thrive in the cool, moist environment.

Boneyard Hollow, inside the park, is a narrow gorge with sandstone ledges 40 to 70 feet high. Pioneer settlers found troves of buffalo bones here. Some theorize that Native Americans once drove buffalo, deer, and elk over the cliff walls to their deaths here. Others speculate that they drove the beasts from below, finding the narrow canyon convenient for slaughtering.

The third hollow surrounds Prairie Creek, the beautiful brook that flows over a ford in the park. A trail leads to a 150-foot-high sandstone cliff, with the creek gurgling along its base. Numerous multicolored minerals such as calcite and sulfur seeped into the sandstone as the bedrock formed 150 million years ago, forming what are known today as the "copperas beds." Petrified logs and sticks can be seen in the bluff, and natives and settlers alike were reputed to use the copperas powder for anything from war paint to dye for clothing.

For 50 miles, the Des Moines River from Fort Dodge down to Ledges State Park remains confined to a narrow, V-shaped valley up to 200 feet deep by the time the river nears Boone County. This section is one of the most beautifully sculpted of all in the heavily wooded valley, with sandstone outcroppings and low rocky walls along the river, as well as some pristine pieces of public lands.

The Des Moines River during the beginning of this section gradually loses the swift character it has above Fort Dodge, becoming a slowly meandering river averaging 200 feet wide. Agricultural lands can briefly be seen through lines of trees, but most of this trip is quite wild in character. Expect the muddy waters of a typical prairie stream in the summer. Abundant wildlife and surprisingly rugged scenery, along with excellent camping nearby make this river an attractive destination for leaving life's daily rigors behind.

For anglers, catfishing is good on this stretch, especially near snags. Walleye can be found in the stretches closer to Kalo.

Dolliver Memorial State Park has a **campground** with full amenities in a wooded setting.

For **canoe and kayak rentals**, see Des Moines River 5.

The **shuttle route** (5.5 miles) runs southeast on Riverside Trail to County P59, south to County D33, and southeast to the boat ramp at Dolliver Memorial State Park.

For **water levels**, check the Des Moines River at Fort Dodge gauge (station 05480500) on the USGS Web site listed in the introduction. This section is almost always paddleable.

The **gradient** for this section is less than 2 feet per mile.

Downstream from the dirt **put-in**, a cottonwood- and elm-dominated bluff rises on the right, with occasional rock faces visible high on the bluff. The bluff becomes lower as the river curves east past riverside homes in tiny Kalo and through a riffle that runs beneath Kalo Bridge.

The valley becomes deeply wooded with oaks and maples on the uplands. A steep wooded slope joins the bank on the right, with a forested bluff visible across the stream ahead. The river continues around midstream boulders through a riffle, and after power lines cross the river, a planting of evergreens is seen on the left bank at a Girl Scout camp. Just downstream an impressive sandstone cliff appears on the right, striated with reddish and greenish layers.

You may briefly see crops on the left before the river bends southward as a bluff on the left nears the bank. As you continue the bend to the right, low cliffs join the left bank while the woods thin briefly on the right with agricultural views. Brick and concrete riprap briefly lines the left bank, followed by a sheer cliff up to 30 feet high extending a half mile downstream, overgrown with vines, moss, and ferns. As you pass around a rocky island, the cliff fades away, and after you go by a shanty in the woods, the cliff briefly rejoins the bank before the river flows west to even more impressive sandstone cliffs up to 50 feet high along the river-right.

As the river bends left, smaller rock outcroppings continue until it approaches a scenic island and curves gently left. A lush understory of woodland plants is visible through dark woods on the right. Little hollows can be discerned as depressions in the leafy canopy carpeting the slopes. Angular rock outcroppings jut from the banks, and then, as the river bends south, low sandstone walls join the left bank for a few hundred yards. Ahead, the undulating wooded bluffs of Dolliver Memorial State Park become visible. A couple of higher cliffs rise from the waterline on the left. Past a home in the woods, **take out** at a boat ramp in the state park on the river-right.

Other trips. Thanks to a new boat ramp in Fort Dodge, just south of Business Highway 169 on the southwest side of the Des Moines River, you can extend the beginning of this journey by approximately 3 miles. The paddling is quite scenic, with more wooded bluffs before the river bends under the Highway 20 Bridge to the Kalo access.

Sandstone cliffs at Dolliver State Park and Woodman Hollow State Preserve are especially impressive.

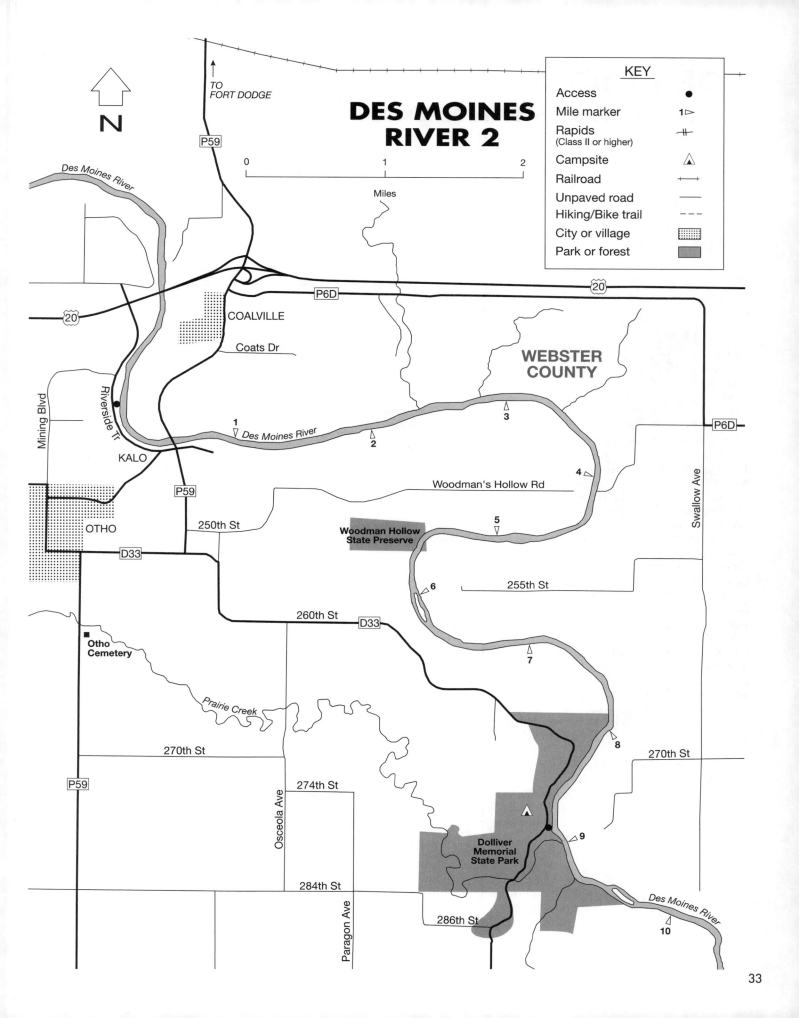

DES MOINES RIVER 2

N

TO FORT DODGE

P59

Des Moines River

KEY

Access ●
Mile marker 1▷
Rapids (Class II or higher) ╫
Campsite ⏏
Railroad ┼┼┼
Unpaved road ──────
Hiking/Bike trail ─ ─ ─
City or village ▦
Park or forest ▓

0   1   2
Miles

20

P6D

COALVILLE

Coats Dr

20

Mining Blvd

Riverside Tr

KALO

P59

OTHO

250th St

D33

Otho Cemetery

Prairie Creek

270th St

P59

260th St

D33

274th St

Osceola Ave

270th St

284th St

286th St

Paragon Ave

WEBSTER COUNTY

1▷ Des Moines River

2▷

3▷

4▷

Woodman's Hollow Rd

Woodman Hollow State Preserve

5▷

6▷

255th St

7▷

Swallow Ave

P6D

8▷

9●

Dolliver Memorial State Park

⏏

10▷ Des Moines River

DES MOINES RIVER 3
Dolliver Memorial State Park to Skillet Creek Access (20.7 Miles)

With all the accesses along this stretch, you can choose to either paddle one long day-trip or select your own portions from an array of configurations, each with something worthwhile along the way. The scenery continues to be excellent, with forested bluffs, rock outcroppings and cliffs, and long strips of public areas along the river. The river also flows through Lehigh, a historic coal mining and brick- and tile-producing town as well as the consummate river village of the upper Des Moines. Brick architecture displays Lehigh's heritage.

Catfishing is good throughout this section, and walleye are often sought at the Lehigh rock dam; mouths of tributary streams are popular places to fish for smallmouth bass and walleye, as well.

The **campground** at Dolliver Memorial State Park has full amenities in a wooded setting. Brushy Creek State Recreation Area has two modern campgrounds, neither near the river (see map).

For **canoe and kayak rentals**, see Des Moines River 5.

The **shuttle route** (approximately 14 miles) from the put-in at the Dolliver boat ramp heads south of the park and then east on Iowa Highway 50 into Lehigh. Turn south onto County P73, and follow it to the north edge of Dayton. Turn south onto Iowa Highway 175, and follow it as the highway curves east toward the Des Moines River. Right before the bridge, take River Road north to the Skillet Creek boat ramp.

For **water levels**, see Des Moines River 2 and also the Des Moines River near Stratford gauge (station 05481300) on the USGS Web site listed in the introduction. Water levels are usually adequate.

The **gradient** for this section is less than 2 feet per mile.

Put in at the boat ramp in Dolliver Memorial State Park. A wooded bluff rises on the right and then recedes as you head southeast. The upstream side of a long wooded island has a high sandbar good for a break or camping. Beyond the island, old concrete bridge pylons project from the river.

After you pass a home, bluffs become distant as you bend right toward Lehigh next to a long gravel bar. The concrete boat ramp in town is on the left, well above the rock-dam rapids at Lehigh. The rapids are a short class II run over a rock dam. If you aren't sure about running them, **portage** to the canoe access below the bridge. At higher levels, waves on the river-right can swamp a canoe. Smaller waves on the river-left are more easily run.

The river continues south along a road. Then the setting becomes serene, with a shale outcropping at the base of a wooded slope. As you bend right past glacial moraine rocks, crops are visible for a bit. At a pretty wooded bluff with sandstone walls rising from the river, you bend south into a 3.5-mile horseshoe bend. Past an island, more crops are briefly visible, followed by another reddish sandstone outcropping. Between outcroppings are thin-soiled prairie glades. From here, Brushy Creek State Recreation Area lines the left bank for 7 miles. The bluff tapers off into a lowland planting of young cottonwoods.

Ahead on the right is the Deception Hollow boat ramp. The river widens and heads east and then southeast, with a high wooded bluff ahead. Riprap fishing jetties stick out into the river from the right, and the river arcs back north between cottonwoods and a wooded bluff.

At the horseshoe's end, bluffs of the Brushy Creek area are visible ahead. The river curves generally east, joining a crumbly sandstone wall. Past a wooded island, a line of maples on the right gives way to a willow shrub thicket and sandy gravel bar. Brushy Creek joins from the left. If the water level is high enough to paddle up it, a trail can be found that accesses the park's trail network.

Downstream, another tree-topped bluff rises, with bedrock exposures, grasses, and wildflowers sloping down to the water, followed by an area of lightly wooded cut banks. Forested bluffs on both sides, set back from the bank, define the valley. The river meanders between valley walls for several bends, with sandbars lining inside bends. As you approach the Boone River, the valley widens as the smaller river enters from its own deep valley on the left.

Past the County D54 bridge, the river flows through a riffle and past a home and joins a wooded bluff that rises on the left. Heading west, the river leaves and rejoins the bluff. Sandbars and willows are common until the river curves south along a wooded bluff on the right. The valley tightens again, and you can see wooded bluffs ahead on both sides of the river, which meanders between them. Beyond mixed woods and prairie sloping down to the river on the left, the **takeout** at the Skillet Creek boat ramp is just ahead on the right.

515 Tons, and What Do You Get?

The little Des Moines River town of Lehigh was once an important mining center, shipping 515 tons of coal a day. Webster City entrepreneur Walter C. Willson founded the Crooked Creek Railroad and Coal Company in 1875. He had narrow-gauge tracks built out of the valley, along with a 370-foot wooden span across the Des Moines River to the mines. Immigrant laborers mined coal from deep shafts with rooms supported by timbers. The dangers of cave-ins, explosions, and deadly gases always lurked. Willson was known for working alongside the miners. Perhaps that was a mistake. In 1900, as he helped unload slag, a railcar toppled, crushing him. Miners paid tribute at Willson's funeral—to date Webster City's largest ever—traveling to town on the Crooked Creek line.

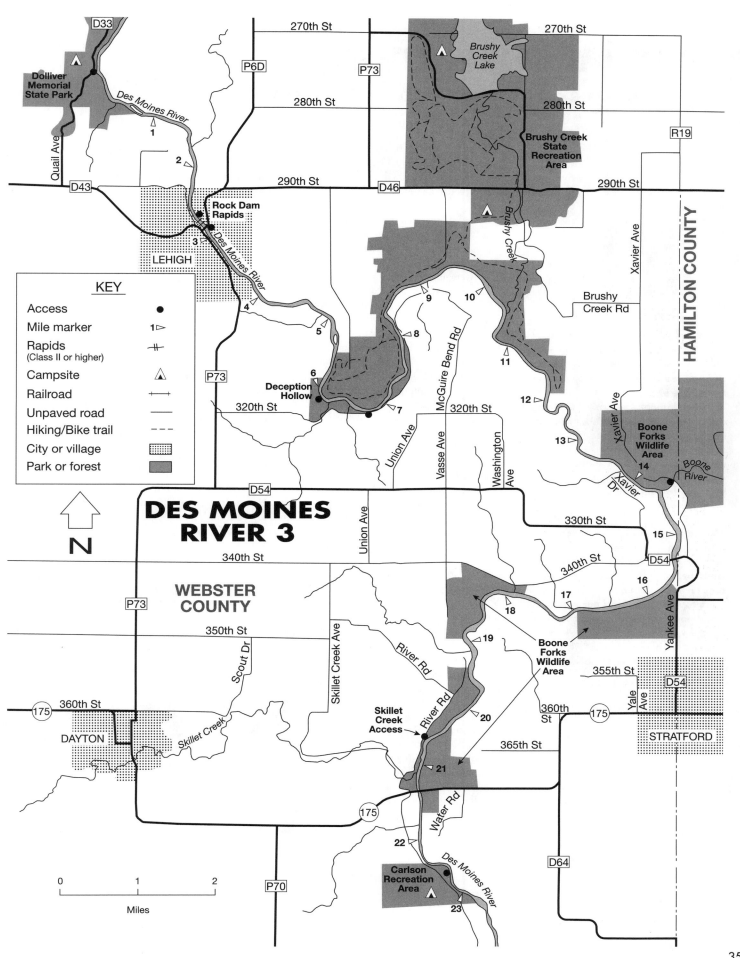

KEY

Access	●
Mile marker	1▷
Rapids (Class II or higher)	⊢⊦
Campsite	⚐
Railroad	┼─┼
Unpaved road	───
Hiking/Bike trail	---
City or village	▦
Park or forest	▨

N

DES MOINES RIVER 3

WEBSTER COUNTY

Dolliver Memorial State Park

Des Moines River

Brushy Creek Lake

Brushy Creek State Recreation Area

HAMILTON COUNTY

Rock Dam Rapids

LEHIGH

Brushy Creek

Deception Hollow

Brushy Creek Rd

Boone Forks Wildlife Area

Boone River

McGuire Bend Rd

Union Ave

Vasse Ave

Washington Ave

Xavier Ave

Xavier Ave

Xavier Dr

Boone Forks Wildlife Area

River Rd

Scout Dr

Skillet Creek Ave

Skillet Creek Access

River Rd

DAYTON

Skillet Creek

Yale Ave

Yankee Ave

STRATFORD

Carlson Recreation Area

Des Moines River

Water Rd

270th St
280th St
290th St
320th St
330th St
340th St
350th St
360th St
355th St
360th St
365th St

Quail Ave

D33
P6D
P73
R19
D43
D46
P73
D54
P73
P70
175
D54
D54
D64
175

0   1   2
Miles

DES MOINES RIVER 4

Skillet Creek Access to North Fraser Access (12.4 Miles)

The Dragoons

Running a shuttle pretty much anywhere in the Des Moines River Valley, you can't help but notice the "Dragoon Trail" signs posted all over the place. Who were these people?

The Dragoons were sort of the special forces of the early 1800s, mounted on horseback and using breech-loading percussion weapons while everyone else was still using muzzle loaders. Brazen and rather flamboyant, they wore their hair long, accompanied by earrings and colorful scarves around their necks.

In 1835, the U.S. government sent a 150-man expedition of dragoons along with native guides to explore the wild prairies, sticky marshes, and lush woodlands between the Missouri and Mississippi Rivers. Lt. Albert M. Lea was the mission's topographer. Lea later popularized many now-familiar place names, including the word Iowa, in his book that described "the beautiful land." The state of Iowa established the Dragoon auto tour trail in 1933.

Perhaps the scenery is grander on the sections upstream and downstream of this one. Occasionally, the river here skirts glacier-deposited rocks, but unlike other sections between Fort Dodge and Madrid, bedrock outcroppings are not seen along this stretch. Still, most of the way passes trees, and ridges often line the banks in a narrow valley. Plus, wildlife viewing is superb. Like the rest of the Des Moines River between Fort Dodge and Saylorville, the river is slow and easygoing.

Averaging about 280 feet wide, due to the infusion of waters from the Boone River (see Des Moines River 3), the river is becoming a larger waterway as it flows south. Fishing is best for catfish on this stretch, although walleye and some bass can sometimes be caught at lower water levels upstream from Fraser Dam.

There is **camping** near the river at Carlson Recreation Area, although it may soon close. Don Williams Park south of Pilot Mound has camping with all amenities, and the privately run Duncan Campground is across Juniper Road from the river a half mile north of the Fraser access.

For **canoe and kayak rentals**, see Des Moines River 5.

The **shuttle route** (17 miles) from the put-in runs south of the Skillet Creek access on River Road, west on Iowa Highway 175, south on County P70, east on County E26, and north toward Fraser on Kale Road. Before the Des Moines River bridge, turn left onto Juniper Road and proceed to the second boat ramp, upstream from the dam.

For **water levels**, check the Des Moines River near Stratford gauge (station 05481300) on the USGS Web site listed in the introduction. The Des Moines River is usually paddleable.

The **gradient** for this section is less than 2 feet per mile.

Put in at the Skillet Creek Access boat ramp, and just ahead you'll paddle past two limestone towers—one of them midstream—supports for an old bridge. Past the Highway 175 bridge, the river flows due south. Where the river bends left, the wooded Carlson Recreation Area lines the right bank. There is a carry-down access that can be used for a hike to campsites, although the area has had some law-and-order problems, and the county has considered closing it.

The river heads through lowland woods and then past a wooded island. A couple farms on the right can be seen through a clearing in the trees, and wooded ridgelines can be seen ahead. The valley seems to tighten as the river runs along a ridge on the left and then bends slightly away from the bluff. The maple-dominated woods thin, and a grassy hill with shrubs and trees joins the left bank where the river begins to curve west into a horseshoe bend at Rohades Acres, a public hunting and fishing area.

Just south of here, the river has recently cut off an old oxbow. The main channel runs along a dunelike sandbar 300 yards long and curves east and then south, where a small lake connects with the river on the right. The lake can be a good place to view aquatic birds such as herons and egrets.

The river bends east and approaches a ridge wooded with sycamores and other hardwoods. After you pass a home tucked in the woods, a more dramatic wooded ridge on the right slopes with glacial rocks, grasses, and wildflowers down to the waterline. Ahead, a large, wooded island rises from the river. Bending right, the river follows a wooded bluff to the E18 bridge, with a few homes downstream of it.

As the river heads south, the valley gradually narrows. Homes are occasionally visible, and a mix of woods and hilly pastures lines the banks. **Take out** at the boat ramp on the right, well upstream of the dam.

Portage: If you are through-paddling the Des Moines, paddle a bit farther down to a dirt access on the right. Carry your boat down the road along the river and then the trail to the dam. Put in below the dam. The portage is approximately a fifth of a mile.

Undulating ridgelines become a familiar sight as you paddle down the Des Moines River above Fraser.

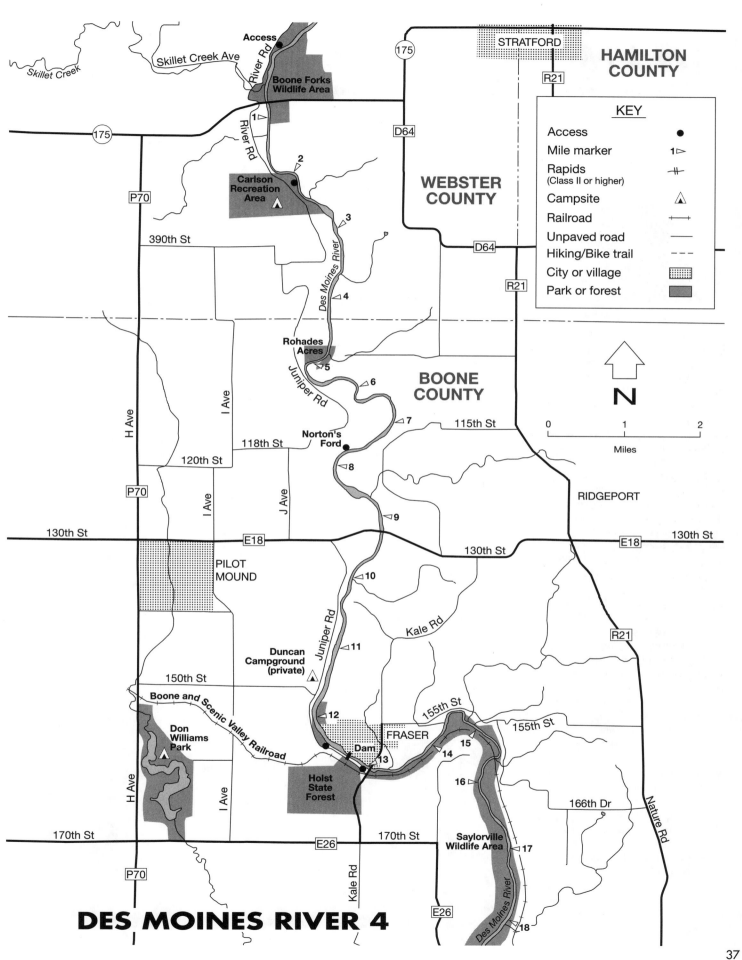

DES MOINES RIVER 4

DES MOINES RIVER 5
South Fraser Access to Highway 30 (12.4 Miles)

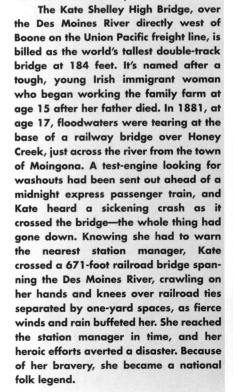

Paddling Beneath the Rails

The low-head dam at Fraser is the last relic of a hydroelectric facility that created power for the interurban line running between Des Moines and Fort Dodge from 1907 to 1955. From Boone on a Boone and Scenic Valley Railroad steam train from Memorial Day to October 31, you can experience a small piece of the trip thousands of passengers made on the interurban. The scenery offers an occasionally vertigo-inducing perspective on the valley. The deciduous hardwoods in the Des Moines River Valley put on a spectacular show of colors in October. (It's smart to call ahead for tickets in the fall at 515-432-4249.)

The Kate Shelley High Bridge, over the Des Moines River directly west of Boone on the Union Pacific freight line, is billed as the world's tallest double-track bridge at 184 feet. It's named after a tough, young Irish immigrant woman who began working the family farm at age 15 after her father died. In 1881, at age 17, floodwaters were tearing at the base of a railway bridge over Honey Creek, just across the river from the town of Moingona. A test-engine looking for washouts had been sent out ahead of a midnight express passenger train, and Kate heard a sickening crash as it crossed the bridge—the whole thing had gone down. Knowing she had to warn the nearest station manager, Kate crossed a 671-foot railroad bridge spanning the Des Moines River, crawling on her hands and knees over railroad ties separated by one-yard spaces, as fierce winds and rain buffeted her. She reached the station manager in time, and her heroic efforts averted a disaster. Because of her bravery, she became a national folk legend.

This popular stretch of the Des Moines is a lazy river meandering through a heavily wooded segment of deep, narrow valley. The mix of dozens of types of hardwoods here is particularly pleasing, and nearly all the land along the banks below Fraser is public, all the way to Saylorville Dam just north of Des Moines.

It also has something you'll rarely find in this book—a portage around a low-head dam at the Boone Waterworks. If you're not confident in your ability to keep from going over the dam, please divide the trip so you take out above the E26 bridge at the concrete access well above the dam, and then drive to the access downstream of the dam to put in again. Fishing is primarily for catfish, although walleye are sometimes caught below the dams.

For **camping**, see Des Moines River 4 and Des Moines River 6 and 7.

Seven Oaks Recreation Area (515-432-9457) near Boone offers **canoe and kayak rentals**, as well as shuttles. Ames Outdoor Gear (515-292-2276) also rents out canoes and kayaks.

From the put-in, the **shuttle route** (14.9 miles) runs south on Kale Road, west on E26, and then south on P70 to U.S. Highway 30. Just before the bridge over the Des Moines River, head east to the access on the left side of this four-lane highway,

For **water levels**, see Des Moines River 4.

The **gradient** for this section is less than 2 feet per mile.

Put in at the boat ramp downstream of Fraser Dam. The river heads through light woods, with riprap on the bank as you bend right. As you curve south, you see a forested ridge ahead and soon pass the YMCA camp on the right, just before crossing under a bridge where the Boone and Scenic Valley Railroad (see sidebar) crosses at a right bend. Past it is a wooded island with a long gravel bar, a nice spot to stretch your legs.

As it moves southward, the river is enclosed in a narrow valley with heavily wooded bluffs on both sides of the river. After you go by a clearing on the left and pass two old concrete bridge pylons, look left, where a Boone and Scenic Valley Railroad bridge spans the hollow. The river continues generally south past steep, wooded ridges. A boat ramp is upstream from the bridge on the river-left. Past the bridge is a dam that has killed paddlers in the past. There is a concrete access below it on the river-left. But the easiest **portage** doesn't use the official accesses—take out 30 yards upstream from the dam on the river-right, and carry around it, putting in well below it.

The river bends right at a rocky glacial moraine at the base of some tall cottonwood trees and then southwest along wooded slopes. After a left bend, two bridges are visible to the south. The first is a rusted steel trestle bridge. The second is the massive Kate Shelley High Bridge (see sidebar). Built more than a century ago, it spans the edges of the valley 184 feet above the river and puts the valley's grand scale in perspective. On the busy Union Pacific line, 50 trains traverse the bridge daily, so it's likely you'll see one cross.

Downstream on the right is a rare grassy hillside, but woods soon cover the serene valley slopes again. Colorful, sloping rock and coal outcroppings begin appearing on the right bank. As the river rounds a southeast bend to the right, higher yellowish rock outcroppings appear, with coal visible closer to the river level. If there have been recent rains, a small waterfall can be visible on the left. Just ahead on the right, upstream from the Highway 30 bridge, **take out** at the boat ramp on the right.

The Kate Shelley High Bridge is a familiar landmark for paddlers on the Des Moines below Boone.

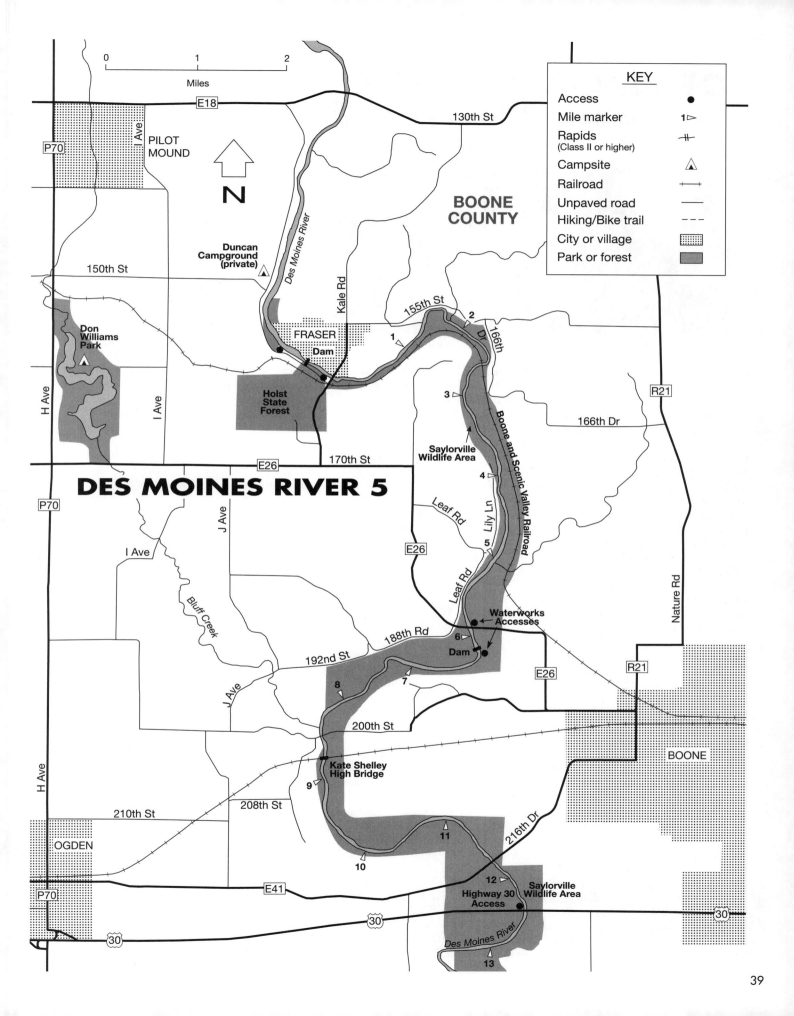

KEY

Access	●
Mile marker	1▷
Rapids (Class II or higher)	‡
Campsite	▲
Railroad	┼
Unpaved road	——
Hiking/Bike trail	- - -
City or village	▦
Park or forest	▓

DES MOINES RIVER 5

BOONE COUNTY

PILOT MOUND

P70

E18

I Ave

Des Moines River

130th St

Duncan Campground (private)

150th St

Don Williams Park

H Ave

I Ave

Kale Rd

FRASER

Dam

Holst State Forest

155th St

1▷

2▷

166th Dr

R21

3▷

Saylorville Wildlife Area

Boone and Scenic Valley Railroad

170th St

E26

4▷

Leaf Rd

Lily Ln

5▷

J Ave

I Ave

Bluff Creek

E26

Leaf Rd

Waterworks Accesses

6▷

Dam

188th Rd

192nd St

E26

R21

7▷

8▷

J Ave

200th St

BOONE

Kate Shelley High Bridge

9▷

210th St

208th St

216th Dr

11▲

OGDEN

H Ave

10▷

E41

P70

12▷

Highway 30 Access

Saylorville Wildlife Area

30

30

Des Moines River

13

Nature Rd

39

DES MOINES RIVER 6 AND 7

Highway 30 to Sugar Valley Access (11.6 Miles)
Sugar Valley Access to Laurie Boat Ramp (5.7 Miles)

Ledges State Park has magnificent views—both from the river and above it.

On these two sections, the Des Moines River flows through a narrow valley and past scenic bluffs at Ledges State Park and beyond. The river is still slow, and the valley bottom sporadically widens into a plain that sometimes spreads a mile wide. During flood periods, Saylorville Lake can back up this far, helping create the marshland vegetation and sparse woods you'll see in parts of both trips. With the Saylorville Wildlife Area surrounding the river all along, these are fine areas to see all kinds of aquatic birds, from shorebirds to waterfowl. The river also keeps winding back and forth between the wooded valley walls with rugged sandstone outcroppings, adding a periodic scenic spark to an otherwise lackadaisical journey. Snags are a usual hazard, but high winds can be more surprising—high waves can develop on the river, which becomes well over 300 feet wide. Anglers will have best luck with catfish.

Good **campgrounds** with all amenities are atop the bluffs—not at the river level—at both Ledges State Park near Boone and Swede Point Park near Madrid.

For **canoe and kayak rentals** and shuttles see Des Moines River 5.

For the first trip, the **shuttle route** runs east on Highway 30, south on County R27, then west on County E57 to Peach Avenue; continue, going south on Peach, west on 280th Street, and southwest on Opal Lane to Sugar Valley Access.

For the second trip, head northeast on Opal Lane from Sugar Valley Access, east on 280th Street, north on Peach Avenue, west on County E57, south on County R26, east and south on County E62, and east on Iowa Highway 210. Cross the river and turn left to the Laurie Boat Ramp.

If you care to combine these trips for one long daytrip, go west from the put-in on Highway 30 to County R18, south to County E62, then east on Iowa Highway 210; cross the river and turn left to the Laurie Boat Ramp (17.3 miles for the combined route).

For **water levels**, see Des Moines River 4.

The **gradient** for this section is less than 2 feet per mile.

Put in and float beneath the bridges of Highway 30 and past a grassy hill on the left. Sandy slopes appear as the river continues bending to the right. Sandstone outcroppings are seen on the left as the river heads west into a long horseshoe bend, and low outcroppings pick up on the right bank as you begin the curve back around to the east toward an imposing bluff ahead with loess faces, sand slopes, and sandstone exposures.

As you head south, the bluff ends and the river enters a grassy lowlands with thickets of willow shrubs and trees sparsely spaced along the banks. Bluffs are visible ahead in the distance, and the river gradually nears them flowing southeast. This time the river doesn't get right up to the base of the bluffs, and you head generally south until reaching a creek's mouth on the left.

When water levels are high, you can paddle up to a small bridge where you can take out to explore the sandstone cliffs of Ledges State Park. Downstream on the Des Moines, a slight left bend brings you to the most spectacular sandstone cliffs anywhere along the Des Moines River, with sheer faces 50 feet or so high and wooded bluffs rising behind them. The river curves right and then southeast toward more bluffs. Downstream, the bridge for County E57 becomes visible. Although there is officially an access here, it is usually silted in and inconvenient to use.

Past a wooded ridge on the right, a bluff rises on the left with low slopes and coal outcroppings near the river. The river flows due west toward 200-foot-high Buffalo Ridge. Heading south and then west, you come upon a pretty bluff with loess and sandstone exposures split in the middle by a wooded ravine. As the river heads southeast, a plain to the left is studded by the skeletons of dead trees. The **takeout**, Sugar Valley Access, is ahead on the left.

The Des Moines River 7 segment begins as you head southeast from the Sugar Valley Access and approach a forested hill near the right bank. At a right bend, low sandstone outcroppings line the left bank at the base of a sloping, heavily wooded ridge. The valley bottom tightens to just a quarter mile wide as the river flows slowly southward. The river hooks briefly to the east, and tiny Richardson Creek enters via a deep hollow it has cut through the bluff on the left side of the river.

The valley bottom gradually widens again, and reeds, grasses, and young willows are common along the banks. When the river does approach the valley edges, slopes are more gradual, until one last curve to the east brings you to a battered-looking sandstone outcropping. After a left bend, you'll see the Highway 210 bridge ahead. **Take out** at the boat ramp upstream of it on the river-left.

Other trips. The 12-mile trip to the boat ramp at Jester Park on Saylorville Lake is also quite scenic. Stay on the right fork where the river splits around an island 5 miles into the trip for adequate water. Below the lake's normal pool, 836 feet (check Saylorville Lake on the Corps of Engineers Web site listed in the introduction), you will reach a silted-in section where water slows going into the lake—this may involve getting out of your boat and pulling it. For information on the section below Saylorville Dam in Des Moines, see Appendix 1.

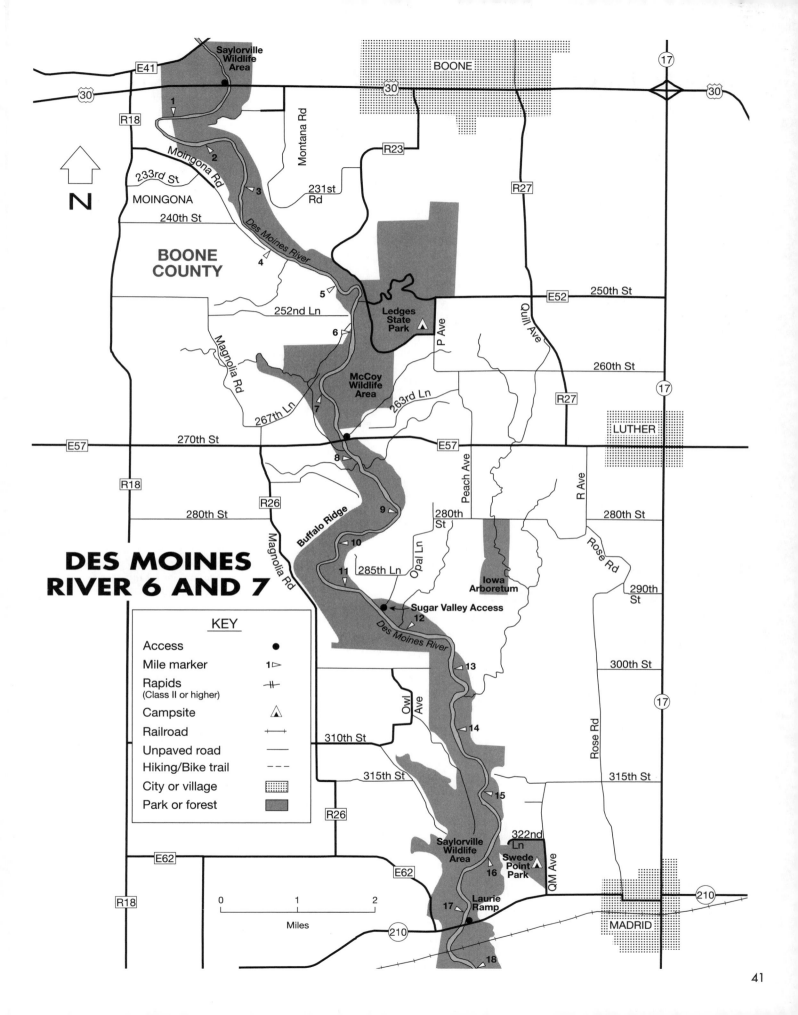

DES MOINES RIVER 6 AND 7

BOONE COUNTY

MOINGONA

Roads and labels:
E41, US 30, R18, 233rd St, 240th St, 252nd Ln, 267th Ln, 270th St, E57, 280th St, R26, Magnolia Rd, 285th Ln, Opal Ln, Owl Ave, 310th St, 315th St, E62, R18, Moingona Rd, Montana Rd, 231st Rd, R23, R27, P Ave, Quill Ave, E52, 250th St, 260th St, 263rd Ln, Peach Ave, R Ave, Rose Rd, 280th St, 290th St, 300th St, 315th St, 322nd Ln, QM Ave, 17, 210, 30

Saylorville Wildlife Area

Ledges State Park

McCoy Wildlife Area

BOONE

LUTHER

Iowa Arboretum

Sugar Valley Access

Buffalo Ridge

Des Moines River

Saylorville Wildlife Area

Swede Point Park

Laurie Ramp

MADRID

KEY

Access	●
Mile marker	1▷
Rapids (Class II or higher)	⌗
Campsite	⚠
Railroad	┼
Unpaved road	——
Hiking/Bike trail	– – –
City or village	▦
Park or forest	▨

0   1   2
Miles

N

41

DES MOINES RIVER 8
Yellow Banks Park to Bennington Township (18.7 Miles)

Beginning along high loess bluffs and continuing into a sprawling, 28,000-acre wildlife area, this unique trip often feels quite remote, and yet it is easily accessible for central Iowa urbanites. The Red Rock Wildlife Area, managed by the state, is a birdwatchers' paradise in the summer months, but during the fall waterfowl season expect to encounter hunters with blinds set up. Motorboats that you'll encounter the rest of the season are, for the most part, just anglers—the Jet Ski set prefers nearby Lake Red Rock.

As with sections above Saylorville Lake, there are not many riffles, and the water is usually muddy in the spring and early summer. Because the river is quite wide, averaging more than 350 feet, and usually unprotected by bluffs, strong winds can cause large waves that will spell trouble for inexperienced paddlers, so check for wind advisories before you leave.

A public **campground** with full amenities is located at Yellow Banks Park. Privately run Webb's Campground is located near the Runnells Access in Warren County on Carpenter Place.

Canoe and kayak rentals are available at Canoesport Outfitters (515-961-6117) in Indianola.

The **shuttle route** (13.9 miles) from the entrance of Yellow Banks Park runs east on SE 32nd Avenue for a very short distance, southeast on County E70, briefly south on Iowa Highway 316, and east on County F70 to West 117th Street S in Jasper County. Head south, and, after crossing into Marion County, the gravel road's name changes to 40th Avenue. Just after the road curves to the west, the Bennington Township boat ramp is on the left.

Near the entrance of the Middle River into the Des Moines, wooded bluffs begin rising again.

For water levels, see Des Moines River below Raccoon River gauge (station 05485500) on the USGS Web site listed in the introduction. Paddlers will usually find this stretch passable.

The **gradient** for this section is less than 2 feet per mile.

Just beyond the **put-in** at the Yellow Banks Park boat ramp, you'll paddle briefly along the 140-foot-high bluff on the left, with two tiers of loess cliffs. Beyond here the banks are deeply erosion cut and lined with trees. From here on, the U.S. Army Corps of Engineers

owns lands all along the banks, defined between bluffs in a valley ranging between one and three miles wide. Motorized vehicles are prohibited, and the trip becomes wild and serene. Views of the distant wooded bluffs lining the valley arise now and then, and after the North River enters from the right, you'll run through a brief riffle and enter the first of four long horseshoe bends.

You'll pass a familiar pattern of sandbars on inside bends along with willow shrubs, with tree-lined erosion-cut banks on the outsides of the bends. After the third horseshoe and a bend left from a run to the southwest, the river nears the pretty wooded bluff along the south side of the river. The Middle River joins from the right as the river heads east, and the Hartford boat ramp is just downstream on the right. The river curves north into one last shorter horseshoe, and as it heads back south, the wooded bluff joins the right bank. A few rock outcroppings are visible.

The river begins heading due east through a straightened stretch, and its pace quickens. One-half mile ahead on the right is the Runnells boat ramp, and then the South River pours into the Des Moines just upstream from the Highway 316 bridge. Past the bridge, the river begins meandering again northeast, where the channel diverges in opposite directions around a huge wooded island. The south channel remains in a lowland area of cottonwoods and willows, while the branch heading north skirts bluffs before the two channels' water swirls back together at a high sandbar.

A wooded ridge again joins on the right for a bit, and then reeds and grasses of marshlands line the banks, affording views of distant bluffs along the edges of the valley; aquatic bird sightings become common. Heading generally east, the river then bends left toward a wooded bluff, and approaching it, sandstone outcroppings appear on the left bank. After the river bends sharply to the right, the **takeout** in Bennington Township is just ahead on the river-left.

Other trips. For information on areas downstream of this section, see Lake Red Rock, and for information on areas upstream from here, see Appendix 1. Also, the 20-mile section of the Des Moines from the boat ramp at the northeast side of the tailrace of the Red Rock Dam to the Eveland Access has its nice points, flowing past a scenic limestone cliff, over one invigorating ledge drop, and through some wooded territory, although numerous shoddy-looking cabins and crops planted close to the bank detract somewhat from the experience. Both accesses have excellent campgrounds. There is one access between them at a small settlement just south of Highway 92.

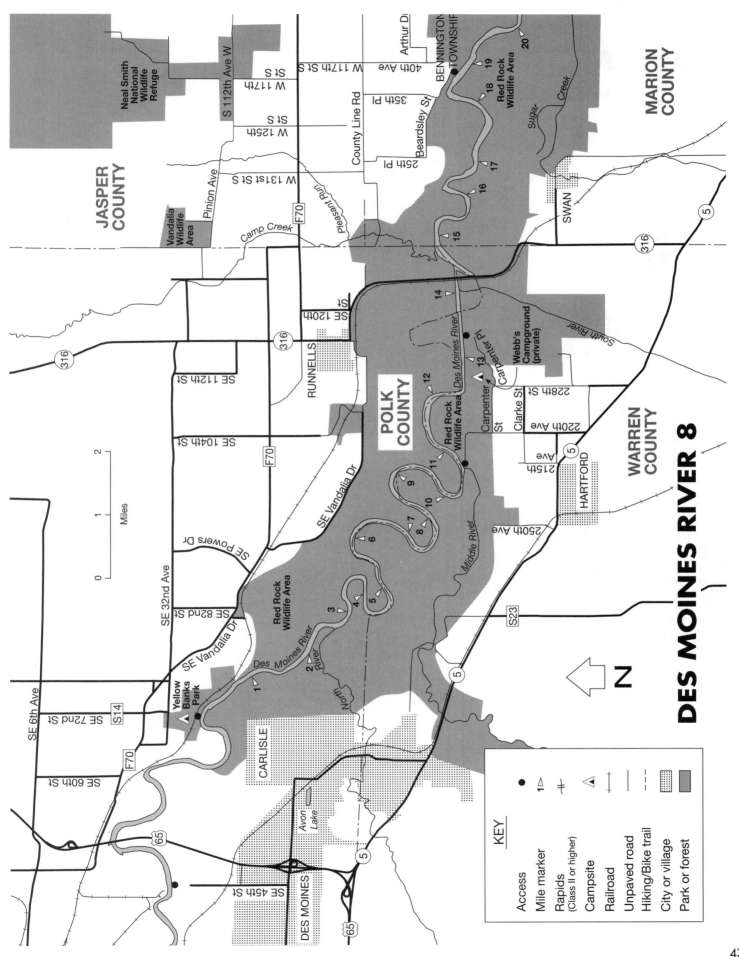

DES MOINES RIVER 8

KEY

●	Access
△ 1	Mile marker
╫	Rapids (Class II or higher)
◁	Campsite
┼	Railroad
│	Unpaved road
┆	Hiking/Bike trail
▨	City or village
▩	Park or forest

N

DES MOINES RIVER 9
Douds to Keosauqua (16.2 Miles)

Paddling in Van Buren County is a thoroughly unique experience. The scenery of forested bluffs and limestone cliffs is superb, but what really sets this and the Des Moines River 10 section apart are the historic little river villages spaced all along the river. Combining the two trips makes a pleasant weekend. Camping options are excellent—you can choose anything from an island or sandbar to a state park with showers—or you can spend your nights in a reasonably priced historic hotel, bed and breakfast, or cabin, none far from a river landing. Plus, locals have embraced the river here by designating it as the first official segment of the Des Moines River Water Trail.

The Des Moines here is a big muddy river, belying its steamboat days. The river averages 500 feet wide, and a windy day can create large waves, especially on the long unprotected stretch near Austin Park. The river at normal flows will do much of the work for you here in a part of Iowa where life seems to slow down. Because bends last for two miles or more, even the river seemingly meanders in slow motion. Incidentally, Van Buren County boasts an utter lack of fast-food chains or traffic lights. Due to this region's sparse population and the river's rocky and sandy shoals, powerboat traffic tends not to be troublesome. You'll likely encounter some anglers in motorboats, mainly after catfish and smallmouth bass.

Riverside **camping** is available at Austin Park north of Keosauqua. A campground with full amenities and cabins is well up the bluff from the river at Lacey-Keosauqua State Park. Riverside lodging is also available in Keosauqua at the Hotel Manning (800-728-2718), Iowa's oldest continuously running hotel, which also rents riverfront cabins.

Canoe and kayak rentals are available from Hawkeye Canoe Rental (800-484-9733) in Keosauqua, and Riverview Retreat (319-878-3715) in Farmington.

The **shuttle route** (17.2 miles) from the put-in runs south of Leando on County V64 and east on County J40 to Iowa Highway 1 in Keosauqua. Take a right and follow Highway 1 to near the river in town. The boat ramp is just downstream of the bridge and the Hotel Manning on the left.

For **water levels**, see Des Moines River 10. Because this stretch has few shoals, it can be paddled at somewhat lower water levels.

The **gradient** for this section is less than 2 feet per mile.

Put in at the Douds boat ramp (slated for completion in the summer of 2004; until then a dirt bank suffices) upstream of the bridge on the river-left. The banks are tree-lined, with pastures and croplands sometimes visible behind the woodlands. A wooded area rises along the left bank. Some limestone outcroppings and boulders appear, and ahead a high trestle bridge spans the river at the ghost village of Kilbourn.

As you go past a farm and round a long curve to the right, a nicely wooded bluff rises on the left, and a scenic island—a good spot for river camping—rises from the left side of the channel. Downriver, the river moves away from the bluff. The concrete boat ramp at Austin Park is just ahead on the right.

The river continues southeast along low, tree-lined banks. Past the County J40 bridge are some small riverside homes along the left. The right bank then becomes rocky, and soon you are paddling along limestone cliffs 20 to 30 feet high, topped with dark woods. At one point, a Civilian Conservation Corps–era shelter house in Lacey-Keosauqua State Park is visible. Attractive rock overhangs and boulders in the stream—plus the fact that the bluff provides shade by the time you arrive—make this a prime area for dillydallying. At "Name Rocks" you can look for the oldest names and dates carved in stone. Across the river, the bank is very lightly lined with maples.

For a quarter mile or so, the bluff continues without the rock outcroppings until you reach the Keosauqua Bridge. The **takeout** at the boat ramp is just downstream, on the river-left. As the signs will tell you, don't try to approach the dock from upstream—this is a classic (and dangerous) sweeper that can flip your boat as efficiently as any log could.

Other trips. If you care to extend your trip by 5 miles, put in near Selma at the Shidepoke Access, upstream from Douds. This adds flatwater paddling between lightly tree-lined banks with no high ridges close to the river. There is a long tradition of local performers showing up to jam on the porch of Selma's R and L Country Store the third Sunday afternoon of each month; usually they are playing bluegrass, gospel, or country.

The Villages of Van Buren County

Van Buren County is a land of undulating hills covered with forest, pasture, and crops. Many of its little towns were dying slow deaths by the 1960s, bypassed not only by major highways but also by most of the industrial revolution. Recognizing the beauty in its towns—especially those along the river in the first part of Iowa's interior settled in the 1830s—locals began lovingly restoring the brick architecture of homes and buildings. Nowadays, especially in Bentonsport and Bonaparte, there's plenty to do in addition to paddling, such as shopping for antiques, sampling fudge, learning to blacksmith or create pottery, or eating in an elegant riverside restaurant in an old mill. Sports activities other than paddling are also popular; little-traveled, hilly county roads make for scenic workouts on bikes, and the Shimek State Forest near both Keosauqua and Farmington has some of the state's longest hiking and equestrian trails. For more info, see www.800-tourvbc.com.

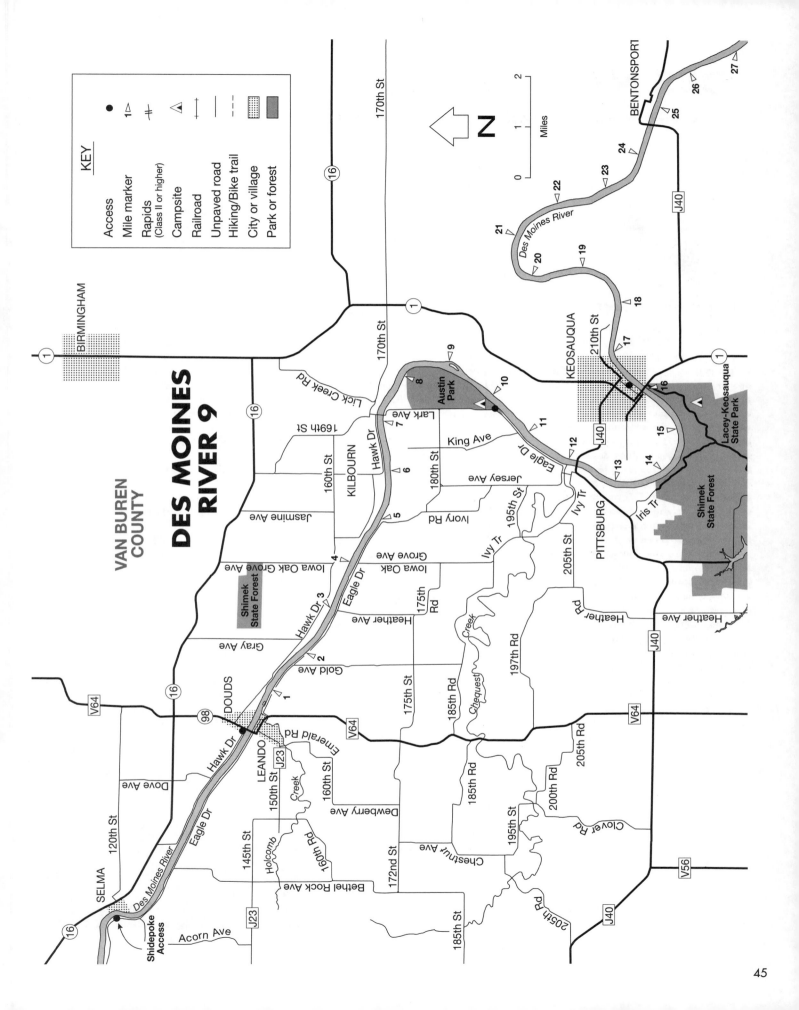

DES MOINES RIVER 10
Keosauqua to Farmington (17.9 Miles)

A charming continuation of the previous segment of the Des Moines, this trip connects the most interesting of the little river towns in Van Buren County. In places, the rocky streambed adds occasional riffles to make the trip more exciting. The wooded bluffs are high and breathtaking. It's easy to take a breather in either Bentonsport or Bonaparte, where you can browse locally created art, find homemade fudge and other victuals, or just laze around in pleasant parks.

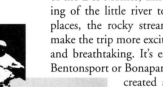

Mormon Influences

Several towns in southeast Iowa owe much to the Mormons who fled Nauvoo, Illinois, in 1846 after a series of violent acts against them. Skilled craftspeople and hard workers, they passed through and camped in this part of the state. Locals employed many of them, especially to build new homes and other buildings. As a 1967 booklet, *History of Bonaparte*, suggests, "They drove resistless bargains with the Iowa farmers . . . as a result, the spring of 1846 in the Des Moines valley above Farmington saw more frontier shanties replaced by two-story dwellings than has occurred in any like time and area in any western state." Iowa was one of the few places where Mormons were not harassed on their westward journey to Utah. Incidentally, the Des Moines River's water quality was in a different state in those days. As Brigham Young's party crossed the river at Bonaparte, one woman reported dipping her tin cup into the Des Moines River and drinking the "refreshing" water.

Headwinds on long straight sections can cause large waves. You can easily modify the length of this trip with a choice of five accesses, and options abound for camping or cushier lodging.

Riverside **camping** is available at Bentonsport Riverside Park and at Riverview Retreat near Farmington. More campgrounds are in the Shimek State Forest east of Farmington and at Indian Lake Park in Farmington, which also has cabins. The Mason House Bed and Breakfast (319-592-3133) and Alexander's Bed and Breakfast (319-592-3152) in Bentonsport are both a very short walk from the river. The Cottage (319-592-3620) in Bonaparte is another option. Also see Des Moines River 9.

For **canoe and kayak rentals**, see Des Moines River 9.

The **shuttle route** (16 miles) heads south across the river bridge on Iowa Highway 1 to Iowa Highway 2, and then it heads east all the way to Farmington. Turn right onto the first street past the river, and the boat ramp is just past the city park to your right.

Water levels can fluctuate dramatically, depending on releases from Lake Red Rock, and this section has rocky shoals. See the Des Moines River at Keosauqua gauge (station 05490500) on the USGS Web site listed in the introduction. Look for at least 1,200 cfs for easy paddling. You'll be all right down to 800 cfs if you read water well, but below that, pick a sandy stretch upstream or downstream of here.

The **gradient** for this section is 2.6 feet per mile.

Put in at the boat ramp in Keosauqua. Just downstream you pass down a long riffle and past several homes. On the right is a bluff with vertical limestone outcroppings, and both banks are wooded with rock outcroppings as you bend north toward a scenic wooded bluff with the prominent white trunks of large sycamores mixed with other hardwoods. Crops are perilously close to the river on the inside bend.

As the river curves south, the bluff gradually tapers off, and woods continue to the left after a private camping area. The woods grow increasingly dense, and ahead two bridges become visible. Beyond the first, a boat ramp is on the left. The next is a pedestrian trestle bridge connecting the artisan village of Bentonsport to its sleepy suburb, Vernon.

The river constricts, and beginning just above the bridge is a long, fun riffle. The river again joins a high bluff, this one wooded with expansive cedar thickets and hardwoods, and bends right along it. At Bonaparte you begin to hear the roar of a rapids, and a boat ramp is on the left well above it at the city park. If you are not confident with boat control, stay along the river-left through the rapids, really just an energetic riffle there. The wide rapids (class II) in the center of the river have more impressive waves, one or two of them big enough to splash over the bow of a canoe. The rapids are caused by the remains of a lock and dam once used by steamboats. Two mills that used a Des Moines River millrace still stand on the banks, one housing a restaurant, the other an antique shop.

The river heads east and bends right along a wooded bluff with a house visible midway up it. Both banks are tree-lined, and river shacks start appearing on the lower right bank. Ahead on the right is a boat ramp. A lower wooded ridge begins to rise on the right bank. As you pass a silo on the left, a bridge is visible in the distance. The **takeout** at the Farmington boat ramp is downstream approximately one-sixth of a mile.

Other trips. The 18.5 miles of the Des Moines between Farmington and Saint Francisville, Missouri, which defines a small portion of the Iowa-Missouri border, offers more paddling along forested bluffs. Similar laws regarding sandbar camping apply on the Missouri side. A sandy bottom makes for a pleasant journey when the river is fairly low (down to 500 cfs), and you'll pass Croton, where the northernmost battle of the Civil War was fought. Access distances from the put-in at Farmington are Croton Civil War Memorial Park, 5 miles; Turkey Run Access, 10 miles; and Saint Francisville Access, 18.5 miles.

At Keosauqua, paddlers can enjoy the architecture that hails from the days when lower Des Moines River villages were in their riverboat heyday.

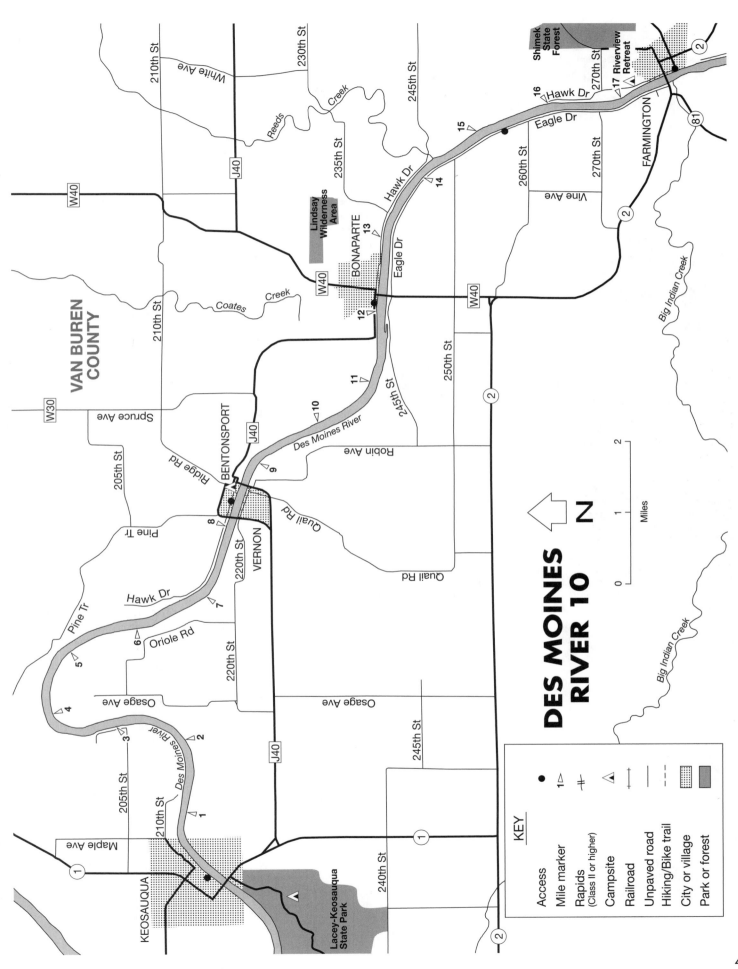

DES MOINES RIVER 10

KEY

- ● Access
- △1 Mile marker
- ✳ Rapids (Class II or higher)
- ◮ Campsite
- ╫ Railroad
- Unpaved road
- Hiking/Bike trail
- City or village
- Park or forest

N

Miles
0 1 2

VAN BUREN COUNTY

Lindsay Wilderness Area

Shimek State Forest

Riverview Retreat

Lacey-Keosauqua State Park

KEOSAUQUA

BENTONSPORT

VERNON

BONAPARTE

FARMINGTON

Des Moines River

Big Indian Creek

Coates Creek

Reeds Creek

DESOTO LAKE
South Gate Access to Mile Marker 642 (9.9 Miles)

There are few spots along the Iowa-Nebraska border where you'd want to head up the Missouri River, as Lewis and Clark's expedition did in 1804. That's essentially what this route does, following a sliced-off bend of the Missouri that was intact when the Corps of Discovery members passed. Now landlocked by a different Corps—the U.S. Army Corps of Engineers—old DeSoto Bend is now considered a lake. The going will be easier for you, too, because the lake has no current. Then, the swift DeSoto Cutoff (dug between the two ends of the old bend) of the Missouri River shuttles you back close to the put-in.

This unique loop route, north of Council Bluffs and Omaha, is a fine way to explore the DeSoto National Wildlife Refuge, which teems with wildlife. Hundreds of thousands of aquatic birds, from pelicans to snow geese, use the refuge as a stopping point on northern and southern flyways in the fall and spring. A number of them raise young in the marshes lining the lake.

Because the Missouri—also known as the Big Muddy—presented navigation challenges (see the sidebar) and caused flooding, the U.S. Army Corps of Engineers was keen on engineering the river to better match human requirements. The Corps hatched a plan to cut off DeSoto Bend, running the river through a two-mile channel between each end. The idea met much opposition until it was decided the bend could become a wildlife refuge. Now, with the adjacent Wilson Island State Recreation Area, the area is attractive for outdoor recreation.

The scenery along the lake is pristine in many spots, with either woods or marsh reeds lining the shores, but there are also some erosion-control pilings now and again. A 5-mile-per-hour speed limit is enforced, so primarily it's anglers who show up with powerboats, usually seeking crappie, bluegill, bass, or northern pike.

So as not to disturb the migrations (yes, even paddlers' mere presence would do so), the lake is closed from October 15 to April 14. There is a modest fee for entering the National Wildlife Refuge. Also, some areas in the refuge are off-limits, and such boundaries change, so please pick up a map at an entrance to the refuge and check so that you know where you can step out of your boat. The portage areas are open to foot traffic.

Adjacent Wilson Island State Recreation Area has **campgrounds** with full amenities.

Canoe and kayak rentals are available from Canoesport Outfitters (402-296-0522) in Plattsmouth, Nebraska, south of Omaha.

Although no **shuttle** is needed for the suggested route, if you'd like to save yourself a portage, an alternative is to take out at the boat ramp at Wilson Island State Recreation Area and run a 1.2-mile shuttle to the South Gate boat ramp on park roads.

For **water levels**, see the Cedar Rapids gauge on the USGS Web site listed in the introduction. The sandy-bottomed Cedar is rarely too low to paddle.

The **gradient** on the Missouri River portion of this section is less than 2 feet per mile.

Put in at the boat ramp in the South Gate Area of the refuge. As you paddle northeast and put distance between you and the boat ramp, the banks become more natural for the next two miles, with woods along the right and marsh grasses on the left until a road joins the left shore.

Past a boat ramp, the scenery again becomes wilder until traffic on Highway 30 is briefly visible above a dirt cut bank to the north. Follow the lake's bend to the left, and soon you'll pass wildlife observation blinds at a beach on the left, a good place to observe shorebirds. Ahead on the right is the glass-and-concrete visitor center. Past here, the scenery is quite nice, with a wooded ridge joining the left bank, where colonies of cliff swallows make their homes in the banks. One arm of the lake diverts from the right into a marshy area paddlers can explore.

As you near the end of the lake, a small inlet shoots off to the left; paddle into it. It ends in a grassy area. Portage 50 yards across the park road to the river, putting in on the riprap. Because the Missouri River is tightly constricted, bound by riprap, it can flow quite fast, sometimes with swirly currents. Stay near the left bank, and paddle down the tree-lined river. Each mile is marked for navigation on the river. When you reach the sign for mile 642, take out on the left by the culvert and portage 60 yards across the park road and then put in again on the lake. Paddle about a half mile to the **takeout** on the right, the same spot where you put in.

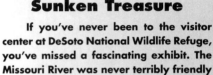

Sunken Treasure

If you've never been to the visitor center at DeSoto National Wildlife Refuge, you've missed a fascinating exhibit. The Missouri River was never terribly friendly toward navigation, and it swallowed up more than 800 steamboats by the early 1900s. The steamboat Bertrand hit a snag and sank as it rounded DeSoto Bend in 1865. A century passed, and in 1968 the boat was rediscovered and excavated. Now the Civil War–era cargo—anything from mercury to clothing and tools originally bound for gold mines and logging camps in the Montana Territory—is displayed at the visitor center, along with wildlife displays and films. In the fall, massive migrations of snow geese can be viewed from an observation area.

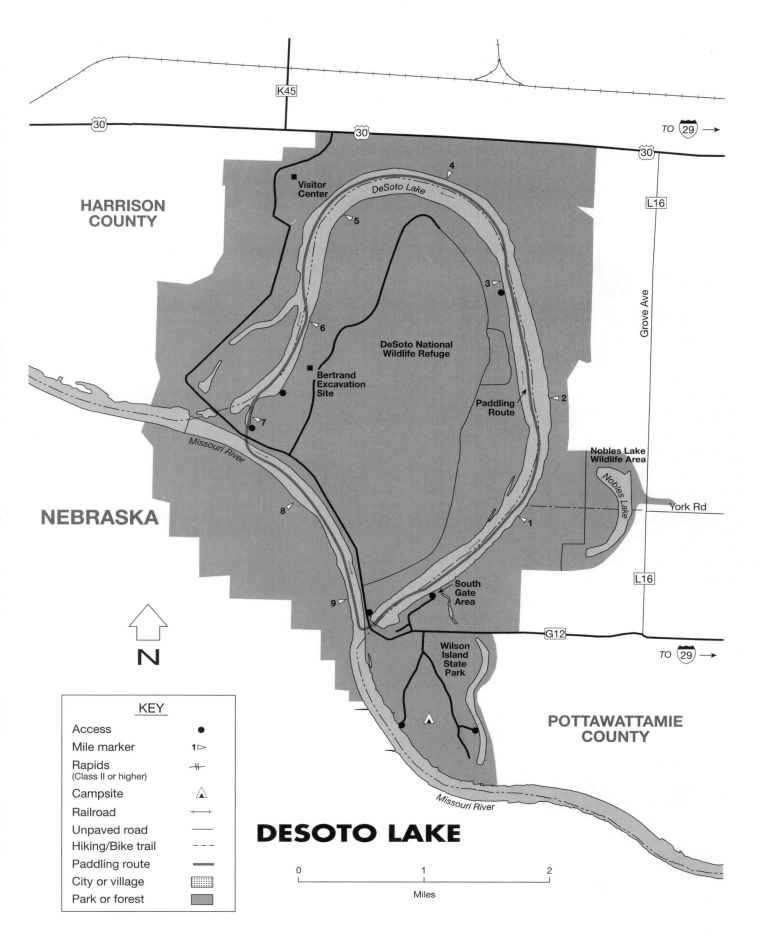

DESOTO LAKE

HARRISON COUNTY

Visitor Center

DeSoto Lake

DeSoto National Wildlife Refuge

Bertrand Excavation Site

Paddling Route

NEBRASKA

Missouri River

Nobles Lake Wildlife Area

Nobles Lake

York Rd

South Gate Area

Wilson Island State Park

POTTAWATTAMIE COUNTY

Missouri River

Grove Ave

TO 29 →

TO 29 →

KEY

Access	●
Mile marker	1▷
Rapids (Class II or higher)	─╫─
Campsite	⛺
Railroad	┼─┼
Unpaved road	──
Hiking/Bike trail	─ ─
Paddling route	━━
City or village	▦
Park or forest	▨

0   1   2
Miles

N

EAST NISHNABOTNA RIVER
Lewis to Griswold (8.1 Miles)

In a part of the state largely bereft of exceptional river paddling due to past channel straightening and farming up to the edges of banks, this beautiful section of river really shines. In places, rock outcroppings and scenic ridges line the river's edge, and at one nifty river-wide rock outcropping called the Nishnabotna Rock Cut, you could believe you're paddling Nebraska's storied Niobrara River rather than anything in southwest Iowa. The short, easy rapids at it are exhilarating.

That said, the river usually runs with a heavy silt load, and you'll encounter cut banks, sometimes with crops on them. More often the banks are lined with trees. The put-in west of Lewis is historically interesting—the Mormon Trail out to Utah crossed the East Nishnabotna River here, and just east of the bridge a shanty for the people who operated the ferry still stands. Another historic footnote: the town of Lewis claims to be where Kool-Aid was invented.

Channel catfish are the main prey species for anglers on this river, which averages 100 feet wide.

Cold Springs State Park has a **campground** well up the ridge from the river.

Canoe and kayak rentals are available from Botna Bend Park (712-741-5465) and Canoesport Outfitters (402-296-0522) in Plattsmouth, Nebraska, south of Omaha.

The **shuttle route** (approximately 9 miles) from the put-in runs briefly east into Lewis on Nishna Valley Road, south and then west on Lewis Road, south on Iowa Highway 48 to Griswold, and west on Iowa Highway 92 to the bridge crossing the river.

For **water levels**, see the East Nishnabotna River at Atlantic gauge on the USGS Web site listed in the introduction. Look for a minimum of 150 cfs, although you may occasionally scrape bottom in the riffles at that level. The **gradient** is 2.9 feet per mile.

The **put-in** and takeout for this trip are not official accesses. There are adequate carry-downs through grassy areas at bridges, but watch out for nettles. Just down-stream from the Nishna Valley Road bridge, limestone outcroppings appear at the base of a high wooded ridge on the right. The line of trees thins a bit as the bluff tapers off, and a pastured hill appears.

Bending left again, you'll see the beginning of the Nishnabotna Rock Cut, a picturesque little ravine with blocky-looking limestone walls 8 to 10 feet high on both sides of the river. At low water levels, most of the water courses to the right side of the channel into a fast chute that can have fun, small waves. Above approximately 300 cfs, some water pours over a 3-foot ledge on the left but is rarely runnable. Scout first if it is, because sticky holes are likely to develop. A large sandbar below the ledge is a nice place to enjoy the scenery.

Downstream, the river splits around a long, sandy island and bends right at a high cut bank with a clearing. Heading west through modestly wooded lowlands, the river becomes a more typical prairie stream with stands of lofty cottonwoods. Spring Creek enters from the right, and the river flows over a light riffle. A long clearing overtakes the right bank along a sandbar on the left. Beyond a high, sloping ridge with an unfortunately placed steel building atop that joins the left bank briefly, Indian Creek runs in from the right.

The river bends left and offers an expansive view of crop fields before a distant wooded ridge. Then, a pretty bluff wooded with elms, oaks, basswood, and maples rises on the left bank with limestone outcroppings. A long, gentle riffle leads to the Highway 48 bridge, and the limestone outcroppings continue along the left bank. Heading southeast, the river falls through shorter riffles, and as the bluff tapers off, the right bank grows wooded. Past the Quimby Road bridge, both banks are lined with maples and willow trees.

The next several bends reveal a mix of grass-covered and cut banks with occasional clearings that give glimpses of distant fields and farms. Sandbars are numerous. Heading southwest, the river comes to the base of a heavily wooded ridge and turns left. At the base of a clay slope, solid, undulating limestone outcroppings appear near the waterline. The river bends left away from the ridge briefly and then rejoins a smaller slope on the right, grassy with cedars and willows. The easiest **takeout** is ahead to the south, just downstream of the bridge on the left.

Other trips. Southwest of Griswold, the 12-mile section of the East Nishnabotna from the boat ramp on Highway 48 west of Elliot to the boat ramp at the Coolbaugh Avenue Bridge in Red Oak is generally tree-lined, with frequent glimpses of nearby crop fields. The bridges between don't make great accesses. Wildlife sightings are frequent. Be cautious as you approach Red Oak—past the Highway 48 bridge, a half-mile-long section has midstream steel pilings installed as part of a Superfund cleanup site, where, sadly, hazardous industrial waste was dumped near the river in the 1970s. Keep well clear of the pilings, which could flip and pin both boat and paddler.

The Underground Rails

The Hitchcock House, built by the Rev. George Hitchcock, stands on the ridge just west of the put-in for this section. He ran his home as a "station" in the Underground Railroad, which helped free escaped slaves, mostly refugees from the Kansas Territory. The house is made of cocoa-colored sandstone from a quarry across the river (just north of Cold Springs State Park, you'll pass the quarry on the shuttle route). Rocks had to be hauled to the river by oxcart, floated across, and then hauled two miles up the slope.

The Nishnabotna Rock Cut is an uncommon type of limestone formation to find in southwestern Iowa.

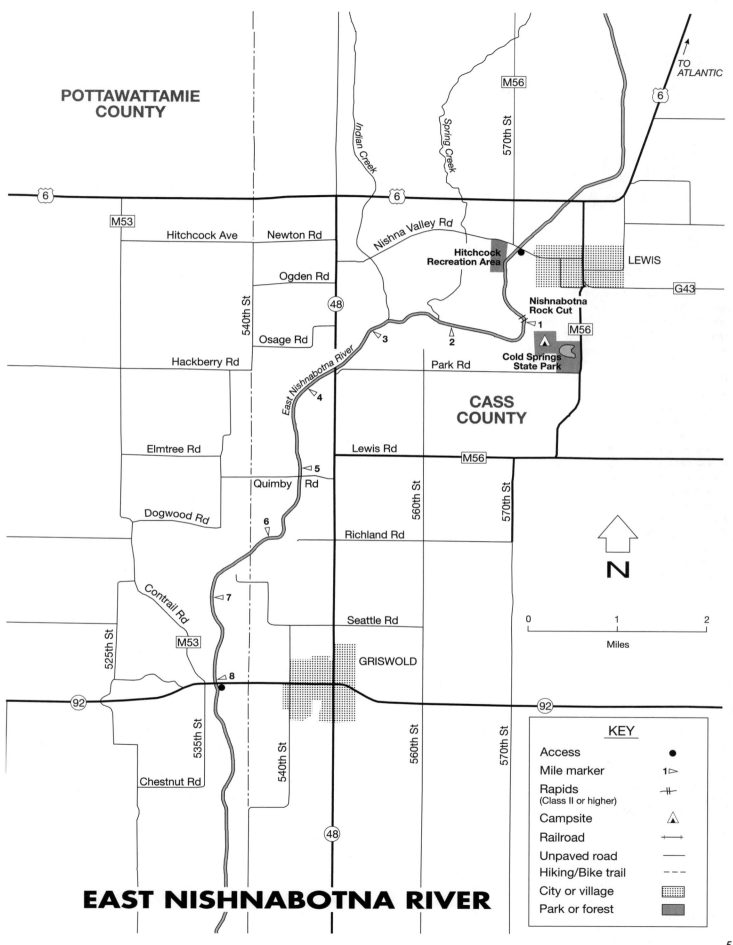

POTTAWATTAMIE COUNTY

M56

570th St

Spring Creek

TO ATLANTIC

Indian Creek

6

6

M53

Hitchcock Ave

Newton Rd

Nishna Valley Rd

Hitchcock Recreation Area

LEWIS

G43

Ogden Rd

540th St

48

Osage Rd

East Nishnabotna River

◁ 3

Nishnabotna Rock Cut

▷ 1

M56

△ Camp

Cold Springs State Park

Hackberry Rd

△ 2

Park Rd

CASS COUNTY

◁ 4

Elmtree Rd

Lewis Rd

M56

◁ 5

Quimby Rd

560th St

570th St

Dogwood Rd

Richland Rd

6 ▽

N

525th St

Contrail Rd

◁ 7

M53

Seattle Rd

0   1   2
Miles

535th St

540th St

560th St

570th St

92

◁ 8

GRISWOLD

92

48

Chestnut Rd

KEY	
Access	●
Mile marker	1▷
Rapids (Class II or higher)	╫
Campsite	△
Railroad	┼┼
Unpaved road	—
Hiking/Bike trail	- - -
City or village	▦
Park or forest	▨

EAST NISHNABOTNA RIVER

GRAND RIVER 1
County P64 to County R15 (14.8 Miles)

The Four Corners

The area where Ringgold, Union, Clark, and Decatur Counties join is known as the Four Corners—and was before Colorado, Utah, Arizona, and New Mexico joined the Union. An ancient buffalo migration route crossed the Grand River in extreme southeastern Union County, and an Indian trail followed. Eventually, the Dragoons (see Des Moines River 4) began using the trail as a route between Fort Des Moines and Fort Leavenworth in the Kansas Territory, and it became known as the Dragoon Trace. In 1855, a notorious farmer named, of all things, Silas Rude, was accused of murdering a neighbor after they disagreed about who owned some cattle and the boundaries of their land. Rude fled, but a posse hunted him down. He was brought to the Four Corners intersection, a man from each county formed part of a firing squad, and Rude was shot. From then, the event was known as the Four Corners Execution.

By the time it reaches the Missouri River, the Grand River is the Muddy Mo's largest tributary in Missouri, impressive enough that early explorers simply called it the Grand. In this stretch, where the river is only 35 feet wide, you'll notice that like many enormous things, the Grand River has humble beginnings.

It is an unassuming, pleasant paddling river, winding through its age-worn valley among the lightly glaciated wooded hills of sparsely populated southern Iowa. Rarely swift, it's not so slow, either. Never bold or dramatic, this river has a low-key beauty about it, passing along stretches with small limestone outcroppings, under wooded canopies, past pastures, and sometimes by fields of crops. At paddleable levels, it runs muddy. One definite drawback of paddling the Grand is that in Iowa there is only one official canoe access on the length of it (at Davis City)—most put-ins and takeouts involve steep-incline carries at bridge crossings.

Technically known as the "Thompson Fork of the Grand River," this is called Thompson River in Missouri, where it eventually joins the main branch of the Grand River. But don't fret over what Missourians say—it's the Grand here, and that's that. Catfish are the primary game fish species.

Thayer Pond Park, southwest of Thayer on Thayer Lake Road, has a **campground**, as does Talmage Hill Park west on U.S. Highway 34.

The **shuttle route** (12.6 miles) from the put-in runs south on County P64, east on 230th Street, which becomes Freedom Street in Clarke County, and south on County R15 to the takeout.

Water levels tend to fluctuate more than on other rivers. They can be approximated by checking the Thompson River at Davis City gauge (station 06898000) on the USGS Web site listed in the introduction. This stretch is well above the gauge, but a reading of more than 250 cfs usually will yield adequate levels for this section.

The **gradient** is 2.6 feet per mile.

Put in down the grassy incline on the river-right, downstream of the County P64 bridge. As the river heads east, maple limbs hang over the water, forming a wooded canopy. Bending south, the river splits around a small island—the left channel is a 10-foot-wide riffly chute with deeper water. At a left bend, small limestone outcroppings line the bank and an iron trestle bridge is ahead.

As you pass thick tangles of tree roots, the cathedral of trees continues. Past a clearing, the river curves right, and some limestone shelves join the left bank heading southwest. As it bends left, and then right at a small wooded ridge in a tiny horseshoe bend to the north, limestone shelves again join the bank. Beyond a riffle, you bend left and pass beneath County P64 again, which has decent access on the river-right. Bending left at a rock outcropping, you head south along heavily wooded banks and then bend right at a small ridge toward a grassy hill. As you bend south at the pasture clearing past a farm, the banks are lightly wooded with clearings and cut banks for several bends until you curve right at 15-foot-high rock protrusions.

The river heads generally south through a mix of lowland woods, pastures, and croplands, until it bends left and reaches the Willow Avenue Bridge, with more mixed woods and clearings to the 275th Street iron trestle bridge, which has decent access on the downstream river-left side.

Past here, the banks grow densely wooded, and heading generally southeast into the somewhat remote "Four Corners" area, the river passes through three counties in a quarter mile. A wooded ridge joins and rejoins the right bank several times, with a pretty combination of deciduous trees and ferns. The line of trees thins for a bit, and then the river joins another beautiful wooded ridge with 30-foot sloping clay exposures contrasting with the deep woods of the Sand Creek Wildlife Area.

As you bend eastward away from the ridges, you pass a home set back in the woods. After a sharp left, the river begins a long right curve through lowland woods, culminating in a little northwest jog. Hooking back south at a wooded ridge, you wind through more lowland woods until, heading west, you bend left at a scenic clay bluff. As you head east past tall cottonwoods and sycamores, limestone outcroppings jut from the bank like large gravestones. The **takeout** is downstream of the County R15 bridge on the river-right.

Several ridges line the pretty little Grand at Sand Creek Wildlife Area.

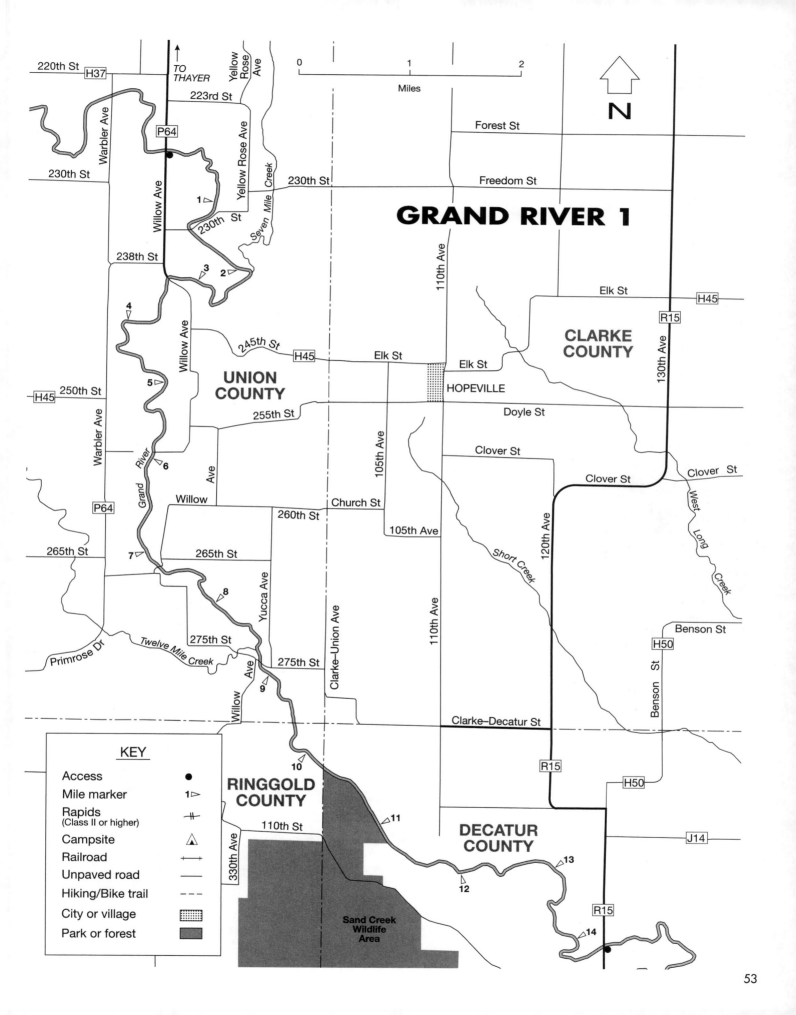

GRAND RIVER 1

GRAND RIVER 2
County R15 to County R26 (12.2 Miles)

The Grand continues its meandering route in this section with somewhat more frequent and prominent limestone outcroppings. The river remains quite intimate, averaging 50 feet wide, usually surrounded by lines of trees.

You may notice the lack of road names on the map. They aren't missing—they don't exist, because some of Iowa's southern tier of counties haven't gotten around to labeling roads with street names for 911 emergency systems.

Catfish are the primary game fish species.

Shewmaker Park on the river has a **campground** but no river access. Also see Grand River 3.

The **shuttle route** (6.7 miles) from the put-in runs south on County R15 and east on County J20. Watch carefully, because the turnoff is unmarked: Past the river bridge, take the second right turn onto a gravel road (County R26 on the map) heading southeast to the next river bridge, your takeout.

For **water levels** see Grand River 1.

The **gradient** is 2.6 feet per mile.

Put in downstream from the County R15 bridge on the river-right. The river flows slowly east past woods, cut banks, and fields in a series of bends so that by the time you near R15 again you'll have paddled in all directions. As the river bends east into a clearing with a sloping grass bank, woods gradually take over and small limestone outcroppings appear.

Bending right near a quarry, you run a riffle past more prominent limestone outcroppings and head southwest along a lightly wooded pasture. As you bend left into an interesting area near where the town of Westerville once stood, large limestone slabs appear on the banks with the sketchy remains of an old mill built in the 1850s and limestone-block pillars near the twisted wreckage of an iron bridge they once supported.

The banks become more densely wooded as you follow along rock outcroppings, and large Sand Creek joins from the right. The river heads east, and slablike boulders and shelves line the right bank to the next bridge. Heading south through placid water along a lightly wooded area with an occasional clearing, the river to the County J20 bridge passes occasional short clearings and small rock outcroppings.

The river heads straight south beyond the bridge, and at Shewmaker Park, where there is no good access, a solid limestone outcropping about 6 feet tall and 100 yards long stretches along the right bank as you turn eastward. Past smaller limestone formations the river drops over a small ledge into a short riffle.

Curving right and then looping left through lowland woods, the river turns southeast at a small limestone outcropping. Logjams sometimes accumulate at this corner, so a portage may be necessary. At the next left bend, the scenery becomes quite pretty, with crumbling rock forming the base of a nicely wooded 100-foot-high slope for three-quarters of a mile. Through lowland woods, the river doubles back to the south, and at the second bend in the S-turn ahead is another spot where logjams can accumulate. The **takeout** at the County R26 bridge is on the river-left, with a steep carry.

Other trips. The 6.5-mile section between the Grand River 2 and Grand River 3 segments can be paddled, but be warned that logjams more frequently accumulate in this section and that scenic rewards are not all that great. Agricultural clearings are much more common until a mile upstream from State Highway 2, where the river becomes wilder and more wooded past a farm at a bend to the west. The gravel road bridge upstream from Highway 2 could be used as a very steep put-in, adding 2 miles to Grand River 3, but it is less than ideal.

Sightings of wildlife, such as this Canada goose trying to lure a predator from its goslings, are common all along the nicely wooded Grand River.

A Safer Route

Fur traders bound for the Dakotas enjoyed paddling up the Grand River before Iowa was settled. The Sac and Fox tribes inhabiting this area were much friendlier than warlike tribes in western Missouri and eastern Kansas along the Missouri River. After the Sac and Fox were removed to Council Bluffs in 1845, they returned for several years to the Grand River Valley to collect maple syrup.

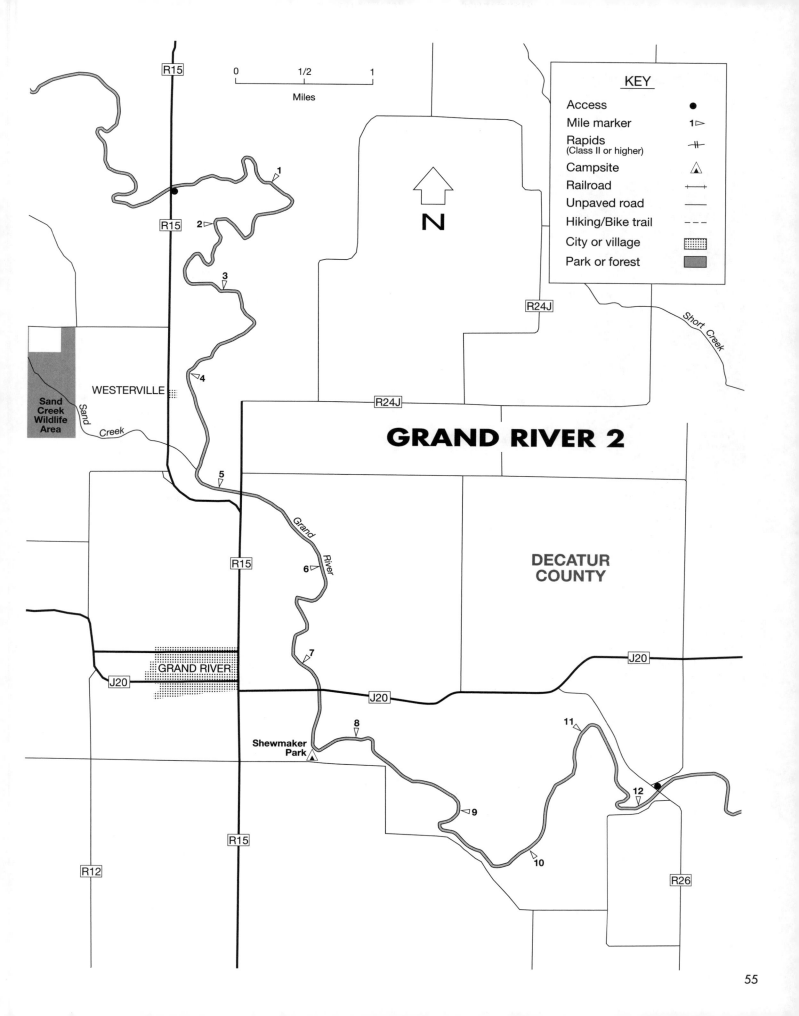

KEY

Access ●

Mile marker 1▷

Rapids ━╫━
(Class II or higher)

Campsite ▲

Railroad ━┼┼━

Unpaved road ━━━

Hiking/Bike trail ----

City or village

Park or forest

N

R15

0   1/2   1

Miles

R24J

Short Creek

1

2▷

3

4

Sand
Creek
Wildlife
Area

WESTERVILLE

Sand   Creek

R24J

GRAND RIVER 2

5

Grand

River

6

R15

DECATUR
COUNTY

J20

GRAND RIVER

J20

J20

J20

8

11

Shewmaker
Park ▲

7

R15

9

12

10

R12

R26

GRAND RIVER 3
Highway 2 to Davis City (18.2 Miles)

A scenic creek makes an entrance to the Grand.

This long day-trip is by far the most varied trip on the Grand in Iowa. Here, it has grown into a midsized river about 70 feet wide with a 700-square-mile drainage basin. Scenery includes enclosed woods, the river's most impressive limestone outcroppings, wide-open scenery lined with the river's highest wooded bluffs, and finally an unfortunate 3-mile channelized stretch at the end through dirt canyons of cut banks.

This section could be divided into two shorter tours, the first 9.9 miles and the second and 6.4 miles, by using the R30 bridge as a put-in, although access there is steep and fairly inconvenient. Catfish are the primary game fish species.

Davis City Park has a riverside **campground**. Slip Bluff Park has a campground up the bluff from the river (no canoe access). Nine Eagles Park, 6 miles southeast of Davis City, has a campground with all amenities.

The **shuttle route** (16.5 miles) from the put-in runs east on Highway 2, south on Interstate 35, and east and northeast on U.S. Highway 69 to Davis City. The take-out is at Davis City Park on the river-left.

Despite the basin's larger size, like many southern Iowa rivers, **water levels** tend to fluctuate widely. Check the Thompson River at Davis City gauge (station 06898000) on the USGS Web site listed in the introduction. Look for more than approximately 200 cfs to avoid scraping in riffles, although the stretch can be paddled at lower levels.

The **gradient** is 2.2 feet per mile.

Heading south from the put-in at U.S. Highway 2, the river bends slightly right at a wooded slope and runs past towering cottonwoods. Bending left, at a pretty wooded ridge, the river heads east past recently logged woods.

After a right bend followed by a left along lightly wooded low banks, you curve to the right past small limestone outcroppings at the base of a pasture hill. Heading south through deeper woods, the river bends left and then makes a 120-degree bend along limestone rocks near a quarry into a 50-yard riffle. Limestone forms 15-foot rock walls on the left, leading to a high, scenic steel bridge. Just past it on the left, a little creek leads in along a pretty limestone wall just above a riffle.

Bending right, you briefly pass crop fields before approaching a wooded ridge. Bending left at its base, you head south into a wild area with mature cottonwoods and maples. Then you head southeast, and sporadic bedrock exposures are visible. At a long curve to the right, a 140-foot wooded bluff rises, and you head northwest past little limestone outcroppings to a clearing with a high, sloping clay bank. Young willows and cottonwoods line the banks, followed by taller trees at a left bend where a wooded ridge joins the bank.

In a long, tree-lined stretch, the river heads southeast, bending right past a high sandbar into a sparsely wooded area where Elk Creek joins and the Grand River flows southeast into riffles past sandbars. Past higher trees in this lowland area, you begin winding past high cut banks with some piles of riprap, until you bend east along a wooded ridge with limestone outcroppings at its base.

The ridge tapers away, and you approach a concrete bridge, with steep access on the river-left. Past a riffle where you can see the sketchy remains of an old mill dam at what remains of the town of Terre Haute, you bend south at a timbered bluff, and limestone/shale cliffs up to 25 feet high line the left bank. After a rain, you may see a small waterfall. Smaller limestone outcroppings continue for a third of a mile, and gradually you hear traffic noise where the river passes close to Interstate 35. Bend right along a high cut bank where cliff swallows make their home, and then head west and then south to a striking reddish cliff, inhabited by more swallows that have hollowed out homes into soft rock and clay.

Bend left at a pretty wooded ridge, and take the deeper left channel around the island, where the river snakes through a fun riffle 200 yards long. Soon, you pass under the I-35 bridges. Passing through another riffle and along cut banks, the river bends right toward the base of Slip Bluff, a 150-foot forested ridge. The river bends left, and the ridge tapers off, the woods thin, and soon you are weaving between deeply erosion-cut banks. They continue until you bend south, and the banks become more wooded approaching Davis City. The **takeout** is at a dirt carry-down, just past the mouth of a gully about 300 yards upstream of the U.S. Highway 69 bridge on the river-left.

Other trips. See Appendix 2, "Whitewater Playspots and Runs," for information on the ledges just downstream of this segment of the Grand River.

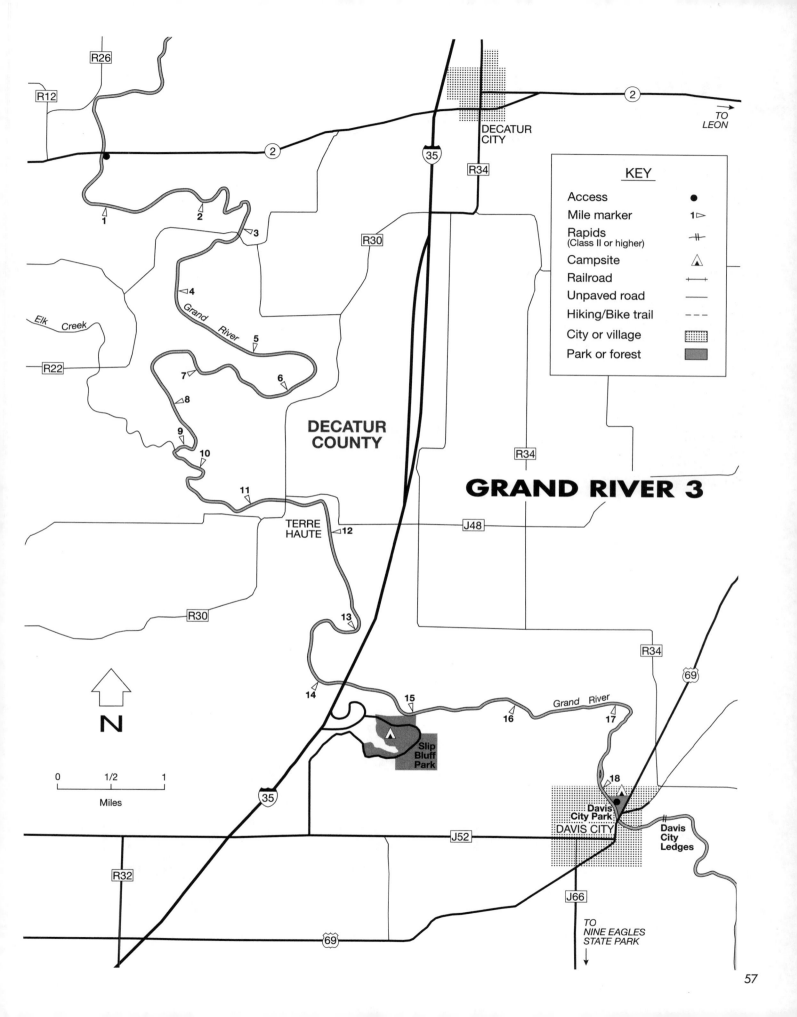

IOWA RIVER 1
Alden to Iowa Falls (6.7 Miles)

As the name suggests, the Iowa River is an entirely Iowa creation. Its headwaters are in the north-central part of the state, where lakes, marshes, and drainage tiles feed it to a paddleable size in Wright County. Near Interstate 35, the Iowa runs through marshes and backwaters, emerging as a clear-running stream in Hardin County, where local government has worked to protect thousands of acres along its scenic banks from development.

Connecting two pleasant, Rockwell-esque towns, this short section actually has quite a bit of development, passing by numerous riverside homes and under several bridges. But that can be forgiven, for it is a delight to paddle, falling swiftly through numerous riffles and thick woods and past pretty rock formations. Slowing near the Weaver's Cove access and becoming a lake behind the tall dam in Iowa Falls, the river passes a high cliff before entering a scenic little gorge running to downtown Iowa Falls. Although the views are enjoyable in the lake section, Jet Skis and powerboats tear through the narrow strip of lake, and their drivers often aren't considerate of paddlers, so hug the shore if you continue to Dougan's Landing.

Riverside **camping** is available at Bessman-Kemp Park northwest of Alden, upstream of the dam.

For **canoe and kayak rentals**, see Iowa River 3.

The **shuttle route** (5.4 miles) from the put-in runs east on County D15, east on State Highway 941, and south two blocks on River Street in Iowa Falls to Dougan's Landing.

To approximate water levels, take the average of readings from the Iowa River near Rowan (station 5449500) and the Iowa River at Marshalltown (station 5451500) gauges on the USGS Web site listed in the introduction. Look for an average above 250 cfs.

The **gradient** in the free-running portion of river to Weaver's Cove is 7.3 feet per mile.

Put in below the dam on the river-left at the canoe access in Alden. The river is immediately swift, running through fast riffles along a limestone bank through town. Past a second canoe access, the river flows past more rock outcroppings and a quarry to two islands, where the channel braids briefly.

Channels rejoined, the river bends right, and you pass under the Highway 941 bridge. Through a riffle, you pass homes and other buildings as you approach an attractive limestone wall with trees and ferns growing from it. Bending left, you head east between wooded banks. Bending left at a bluff, you pass more homes in a densely wooded setting. As you curve right along another bluff, rocks and boulders are midstream in the riffles. The trees thin on the left heading east where rounded rocks have been stacked along the bank at a home on the left with a large grassy yard. Here, a long spirited riffle begins, leading along a charming bluff with limestone outcroppings on the right.

You pass beneath the railroad bridge and under Highway 941 again, heading north. Beyond riverside homes on the right, a nicely wooded island splits energetic riffles. As the river bends right at the base of a wooded bluff, the water slows substantially entering Iowa Falls. A sheer 50-foot-high limestone cliff rises on the right, undercut at its base and topped with homes. Homes with parklike lawns are on the left, and just ahead on the river-left is the boat ramp at Weaver's Cove. You may want to **take out** here.

Proceed eastward into the lake (again, watch out for powerboaters and personal watercraft), where there is usually a small natural limestone wall on one bank or the other at the waterline, and sometimes along both banks where the little gorge narrows. After you pass a small lighthouse and two parks, you'll see a number of homes set above the river. After paddling beneath two bridges in quick succession (one for Highway 941—yet again—and the second for River Street), on the left is Dougan's Landing, the final **takeout** before the dam. If you're still not quite ready to end your trip, you can also paddle just a bit farther down, where, as you round the cliff on the left side, you'll see a peculiar thing: a glass elevator running up the bluff. There is a landing at its base where you can tie your boat and then take the elevator three stories up to Camp David, a bar and grill with a nice view of the river. Don't paddle closer to the dangerous dam.

The Iowa River below Alden is an invigorating swift run at decent water levels.

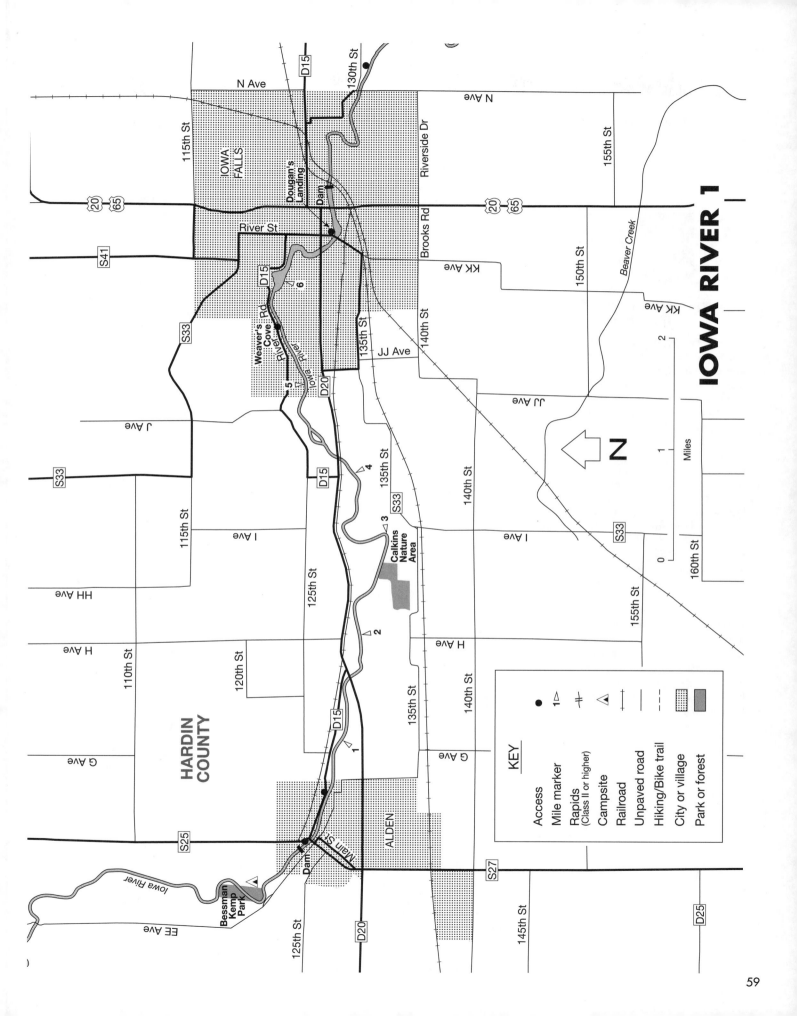

IOWA RIVER 1

KEY

●	Access
1△	Mile marker
≠	Rapids (Class II or higher)
◁	Campsite
†	Railroad
—	Unpaved road
- - -	Hiking/Bike trail
▦	City or village
▨	Park or forest

N

Miles
0   1   2

HARDIN COUNTY

IOWA FALLS

Dougan's Landing

Dam

Weaver's Cove Rd.

Iowa River

Calkins Nature Area

Bessman Kemp Park

ALDEN

Dam

Main St

Beaver Creek

IOWA RIVER 2
Iowa Falls to Hardin City (15.5 Miles)

The Highway 20 Bridge

Hardin County loves its Iowa River Greenbelt. So, when locals caught wind that a newer, straighter, four-lane Highway 20 would slice through the middle of it, some were angry. They didn't spend years protecting old-growth forest and rare species just so the Iowa Department of Transportation could have a swath bulldozed and paved right through sensitive lands. Eventually, a compromise was reached. Instead of bringing heavy equipment to the valley bottom, a special bridge was constructed using an expensive technique called "launching," commonly used in Europe but never before done on a large project in the United States. No part of the bridge touches the water, and to minimize disturbance for the midsupport piers, preformed piers were carried across the valley and inserted in holes drilled down to bedrock, rather than being poured on-site as they typically would. The $20 million bridge is 137 feet above the water, spanning 1,510 feet between the valley edges. Runoff from the bridge goes to silt basins rather than directly into the river, and the bridge was designed to have as little visual and noise impact as possible.

This section runs through the heart of Hardin County's splendid Iowa River Greenbelt. It's a midsized river averaging 70 feet wide. The first 5 miles to Cross's Ford are swift, falling about 5.5 feet per mile and coursing along scenic, low limestone cliffs and outcroppings. The next 9 miles wind along high ridges covered in old-growth woods and unique landforms.

The Iowa River Greenbelt includes eight riverside tracts of wildlife areas, wilderness preserves, and county parks. These areas help conserve remarkable stands of woodlands, lowland marshes, and sand bluffs. Wildlife, from several raptor species to mammals like woodchucks and raccoons, is abundant and commonly seen. Woods of walnut, maple, and elm can be quite dense and give a feeling of remoteness in stretches between pastures. Where there are agricultural settings, they are of the hilly, bucolic variety rather than row-crop monocultures. The excellent canoe accesses at Cross's Ford and Eagle City can be used to add variety to the length of this trip. The riffles provide excellent smallmouth bass fishing.

The Eagle City access has a riverside **campground**. Primitive camping is allowed at the Cross's Ford Access. Also see Iowa River 3.

For **canoe and kayak rentals**, see Iowa River 3.

The **shuttle route** (13.8 miles) from the put-in runs west on 130th Street to N Avenue, south across the bridge, and right onto Riverside Drive to U.S. Highway 65. Go south on 65, then east on County D35; continue east on 185th Street, north on SS Avenue, and briefly east on 170th Street to the access on the right before the bridge.

For **water levels**, see Iowa River 1. The overall **gradient** is 2.9 feet per mile.

At the **put-in**, on the east edge of Iowa Falls, the ride begins fairly swiftly, falling about 9 feet in the first mile. After the first bend to the right, the river divides around a large island in Welden Woods. A logjam typically blocks off the smaller left chute. The swift right channel requires some maneuvering around snags and smaller islands before it rejoins the other channel at a small sandy island. The river turns abruptly left, and it's wise to cut this corner short to avoid running into a potential fast-current sweeper on the river's south bank.

After a series of riffles, a 15-foot limestone wall topped with red cedars rises on the left. A taller limestone formation pockmarked with tiny caves appears downstream, followed by a wavier riffle. The river widens and then passes around a wooded island; the left channel has deeper water and a view of an undercut limestone cliff capped with a grassy glade. Around a long, gradual bend to the right, the wall recedes. A home is visible straight ahead on the south bank atop a 40-foot bluff. A rock here hangs out several feet over the left-turning channel. The high banks drop away, and half a mile downriver, sandy Cross's Ford Access appears on the left.

The river slows and widens, entering a wooded area. A high sand bluff appears on the left. Past an island, 100-foot wooded bluffs are seen to the right all along a horseshoe bend. Small limestone walls are visible on the right, and on the left is the grassy lowland Parlina Pierce Wildlife Area. A riffle ensues, followed by the 160th Street bridge and Eagle City Park access on the left. Two fun riffles ahead sweep past appliance-sized boulders and tree-studded savanna lowlands. Past the RR Avenue bridge, the current slows, and a steep bank heavily wooded with walnut trees is visible on the left. At the second bend southward, just after an island, is the Mann Wilderness State Preserve, a biologically rich area with steep ravines carved in limestone; it's worth exploring for those with time and inclination to bushwhack up the bluff.

The river quickens pace again as pastoral hills capped with woods can be seen in the distance beyond cow pastures. At a right bend, a 60-foot-high sandy bluff capped with towering cottonwoods appears on the left. If rainfall has been normal, a tiny spring will trickle from the bluff. The bottom turns to gravel, and the current slows through a snaggy area. After the river bends back to the south, a long riffle weaving through dozens of rounded boulders leads to the Hardin City Bridge, where the **takeout** is on the right, downstream from the bridge.

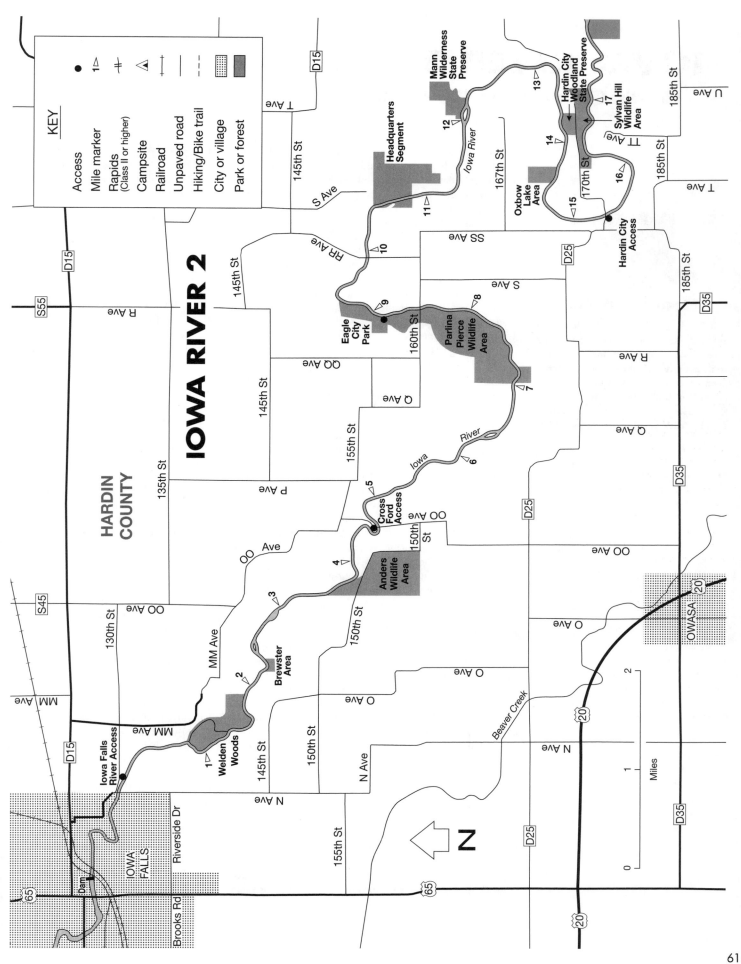

IOWA RIVER 2

HARDIN COUNTY

KEY

- Access
- Mile marker
- Rapids (Class II or higher)
- Campsite
- Railroad
- Unpaved road
- Hiking/Bike trail
- City or village
- Park or forest

Mann Wilderness State Preserve

Headquarters Segment

Hardin City Woodland State Preserve

Sylvan Hill Wildlife Area

Oxbow Lake Area

Hardin City Access

Iowa River

Eagle City Park

Partina Pierce Wildlife Area

Cross Ford Access

Anders Wildlife Area

Brewster Area

Welden Woods

Iowa Falls River Access

IOWA FALLS

Dam

Riverside Dr

Brooks Rd

Beaver Creek

OWASA

Miles

N

IOWA RIVER 3
Hardin City to Eldora (13.6 Miles)

One of central Iowa's most scenic river trips, this section links two distinct halves often paddled in the same day, split by a portage around a dangerous low-head dam. You can avoid the portage by basing your trip at Pine Ridge Park and shuttling your boat to the Steamboat Rock access downstream of the bridge.

The first 6.3 miles wind lazily through more of the Iowa River Greenbelt, along ridges with old-growth stands of walnuts and oaks, and under what may be the United States' most environmentally correct bridge (see sidebar in Iowa River 2). At Steamboat Rock, the stream adopts the character of a northeast Iowa bluff country river, running fairly clear through swift riffles along beautiful sandstone bluffs adorned with hardwoods, pines, and birch. The entire stretch passes through numerous state preserves and wildlife areas. Fishing is best for smallmouth bass.

Pine Ridge Park has a riverside **campground** with all amenities. Primitive river camping is allowed in a portion of Tower Rock Park, where there is also a campground. Pine Lake State Park has a lakeside campground with full amenities up the bluff from the river, as well as riverside cabin rentals (641-858-3626).

Kayak rentals and shuttles are available from Rock 'n Row River Adventures (641-858-5516) in Eldora. **Canoe rentals** and shuttles are available at Twin Lakes Bait Shop (641-858-3626) at Pine Lake State Park.

The **shuttle route** (10 miles) from the put-in at Hardin City runs briefly west on 170th Street, south on SS Avenue, west on 185th Street, south on County D35, south on County S55, south on County D41, and east on State Highway 175 into Eldora. Turn right onto Washington Street and left onto 14th Avenue, heading east and southeast. The takeout, on the left, is a boat ramp near Eldora's Wastewater Treatment Plant.

To approximate **water levels**, take the average readings of the Iowa River near Rowan (station 5449500) and the Iowa River at Marshalltown (station 5451500) gauges on the USGS Web site listed in the introduction. To avoid dragging bottom in wide riffles below Steamboat Rock, look for more than 300 cfs.

The overall **gradient** is 3 feet per mile. The swifter stretch below Steamboat Rock falls at 5.2 feet per mile.

The **put-in** at Hardin City (formerly a town) is just downstream of the bridge. The river curves left along a 120-foot wooded bluff, entering a series of small bends through lines of lowland silver maples and briefly skirting wooded ridges on either side of the narrow valley. The river bends right, and a high clay slope appears ahead, where little iron-rich springs trickle down the ridge.

Past a timbered island, you curve south through lowland woods. At a left bend, the new U.S. Highway 20 bridge appears. The river bends right, sandy-bottomed and slow, and a view opens up to grassy hills in the distance. Through more lowland woods, winding back and forth between occasional wooded ridges, you come upon Pine Ridge Park on the river-right.

A county brochure suggests a **portage** from the Pine Ridge Park boat ramp (about one-fifth mile). More paddlers head closer to the dam, where on the river-left next to an amorphous chunk of concrete, a steep dirt portage trail goes around it. DO NOT ATTEMPT THIS PORTAGE AT HIGH WATER.

After a small rapids below the dam and the County D35 bridge, just ahead on the left is Steamboat Rock's canoe access. Past it, you curve along the Steamboat Rock formation. As the river bends left at Tower Rock Park, a striking namesake sandstone monolith does tower, clad in birch and oaks. Through light woods, the river drops through riffles and past boulders along Fallen Rock State Preserve. Another beautiful bluff rises on the left, with hardwoods and paper birch. Ahead are swift riffles past boulders, and at a left bend past a home, a high, wooded bluff appears, with a few native white pines jutting above birch and hardwoods. Along the next riffle, the woods hold moss-and-fern-covered rock faces.

A bluff joins the right bank, diverting the river left toward the 215th Street trestle bridge. The river bends east at the base of a rugged, wooded bluff 100 feet high. Bending northeast and hooking back to the south, the river bends along steep, rocky banks past the Wildcat Cave area.

The river runs south into a narrow valley along pretty pine-topped bluffs and steep, rocky banks. Several riffles follow. The valley is very defined, with occasional rock outcroppings visible through deep woods. Pines top bluffs all along. Beyond riverfront cabins on the left is the Pine Lake State Park canoe access. The scenic bluffs continue past the high bridge at Eldora, after which the river drops through a quick rapids (the remains of a demolished dam) on the way to the **takeout**, a boat ramp on the river-right, just above the bridge at 14th Avenue.

Other trips. Immediately below the Eldora access, paddling is nice enough at first, as the river passes small rock outcroppings, pastures, and woodlands for part of the 8 miles to the Bates Memorial Park. Near its juncture with the South Iowa River, the Iowa assumes its smaller branch's heavily agricultural ambiance. A better trip begins at Marshalltown's Riverview Park, where you'll run the remains of a dam and slowly meander along timbered ridges and lowland woods to the Furrow Access (4.2 miles), Three Bridges Park (8.2 miles, riverside camping), or Tama County's McCoy Landing (12.2 miles).

Steamboat Rock

In old photographs, the long sandstone "Steamboat Rock" outcropping looked more rugged. It has since eroded to its present smoothed-out appearance. Locals thought it looked like several anchored steamboats, so they changed their town's name from Lithopolis (in Greek, "rock city") to Steamboat Rock.

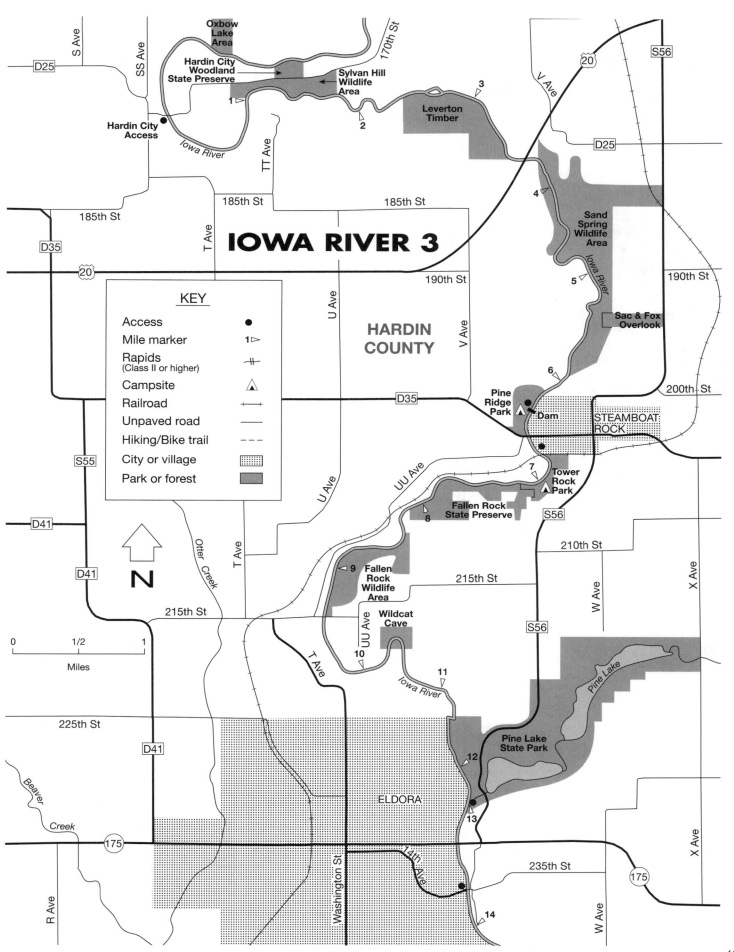

IOWA RIVER 3

KEY

Access	●
Mile marker	1 ▷
Rapids (Class II or higher)	⫣
Campsite	▲
Railroad	┼┼┼
Unpaved road	—
Hiking/Bike trail	- - -
City or village	▦
Park or forest	▨

HARDIN COUNTY

Oxbow Lake Area

Hardin City Woodland State Preserve

Sylvan Hill Wildlife Area

Hardin City Access

Iowa River

Leverton Timber

Sand Spring Wildlife Area

Sac & Fox Overlook

Pine Ridge Park

Dam

STEAMBOAT ROCK

Tower Rock Park

Fallen Rock State Preserve

Fallen Rock Wildlife Area

Wildcat Cave

Pine Lake

Pine Lake State Park

ELDORA

Beaver Creek

Otter Creek

N

0   1/2   1
Miles

IOWA RIVER 4 AND 5

Fredonia to Wapello (13.3 Miles)
Wapello to the Mississippi River (16 Miles)

Beginning and ending at the confluences of three great rivers, these two trips offer excellent big-river paddling. Where the Iowa and Cedar Rivers join at Columbus Junction, you can see why explorer Albert Lea suggested that the Cedar, the larger branch, should have the same name above and below the forks (see sidebar for Cedar River 1 and 2). After the confluence, the Iowa takes on the personality of the Cedar: wide and sandy—only there's a lot more of it. The river averages 800 feet wide, but the water often runs only a few feet deep, although drop-offs along sandbars can plunge much deeper.

With a foot or so of visibility, the big Iowa River in these parts is rarely muddy, passing beautiful islands and long tracts of public lands, with some wooded bluffs but more often floodplains lining the banks of the river set 10 or 20 feet down in its broad channel. Entirely a "meandered" stream, the Iowa offers sandbar camping, which is more popular here than in most other places in Iowa. With the sprawling, tall sandbars lining the insides of many bends and forming tails on islands, it's an ideal stretch of river for sandbar activities (but please do see the introduction for precautions).

There is a riverside **campground** at Ferry Landing Park on the Mississippi, and camping is allowed at the River Fork access in Fredonia and at the Schwob access in Wapello. See the introduction for information on sandbar camping. There is also a campground at the Snively access on Lake Odessa.

Canoe and kayak rentals and shuttles are available from River Basin (800-748-3712) near Burlington, about 30 miles south.

The **shuttle route** (14.8 miles) for the first segment heads south to State Highway 92, east on 92, south on U.S. Highway 61, and east on County Highway 99. In Wapello turn south onto 2nd Avenue, then left onto Vernon Street to the access.

For the second segment, go back through Wapello to Highway 99, heading east over the river bridge and then southeast to Oakville. Turn north onto Oakville's Russell Street and then east on River Road, which becomes County X71; follow it northeast to Ferry Landing Park.

For **water levels**, check the Iowa River at Wapello gauge (station 5465500) on the USGS Web site listed in the introduction.

The **gradient** is less than 2 feet per mile.

Put in at the River Fork boat ramp in Fredonia, just downriver of the merger of the Iowa and Cedar Rivers. Flowing under the Highway 92 bridge, the river passes a few homes and shacks atop riprapped banks. You will come to a wooded island, and a scenic bluff covered in a mix of hardwoods is just beyond it. Beyond a few more

houses heading east, the river bends southeast approaching another wooded island. The banks become heavily treelined as the river splits around several wooded islands, one two-thirds of a mile long, where a large wetlands, Indian Slough Wildlife Area, begins lining the banks.

At a left bend, a high sandbar lines the inside bank for half a mile. Just past the Highway 61 bridge, a canoe access is downstream on the river-left. A ridge joins the left bank where a farmstead overlooks the river. Past a few more homes, the ridge tapers off, and lowland woods, sandbars, and islands are visible as the river curves left toward the businesses and homes of Wapello. Past the next bridge, a few hundred yards downstream is the Schwob access, the **takeout** for this segment.

For the next leg, after a right bend, the river leaves town heading south along a small ridge, becoming quite scenic past a series of long, wooded islands. As the river bends right and then left, trees become sparser where the vistas include mobile homes, riprap, and junked cars.

Where 410th Street leaves the right bank, the scenery becomes pristine again, running between woods along the Port Louisa National Wildlife Refuge, where river sightings of waterfowl such as cormorants and geese are common in the spring and fall. Bending left, you come to Highway 99 again, reaching a boat ramp on the right.

As you pass it heading north, dense woods of tall trees line the banks. Beyond two large islands, a 100-foot wooded bluff briefly joins the left bank where the channel divides for 1.5 miles around Cuba Island. Aquatic bird sightings of pelicans, cormorants, and other waterfowl are likely here. When the channels rejoin, stay to the right of the next two islands—the **takeout** at Ferry Landing is on the right, where the Iowa joins the Mississippi River.

Other trips. Lake Odessa and its series of interconnected smaller ponds and lakes is a remarkable area to paddle. On part of the main lake, some bluff-top homes overlook the waters. The rest of the setting is quite secluded, running through clear backwaters surrounded by dense woods separated from the Mississippi River by a levee. Partly managed as a national wildlife refuge, some areas are closed in the fall for waterfowl migrations; call (319) 523-6982 for details and a refuge map.

Sandbars at the tails of the Iowa's numerous islands in southeast Iowa make fine places to take breaks.

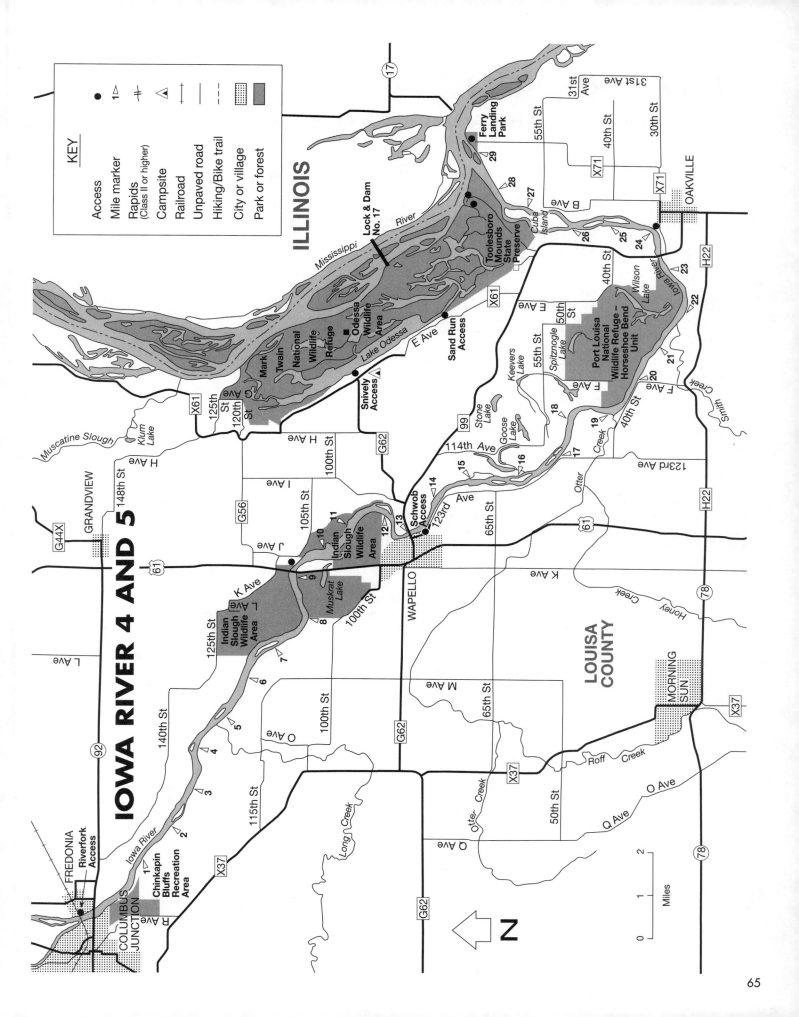

IOWA RIVER 4 AND 5

LAKE RED ROCK
Bennington Township Access to Elk Rock State Park (14.8 Miles)

With spectacular sandstone cliffs (see photo, page 183), excellent beaches, and somewhat less buzzing from powerboats than lakes closer to urban areas like Saylorville and Coralville, Lake Red Rock is a great destination for touring kayakers. There are surprising features you may not expect, like a paddle-through sandstone cave.

As the Des Moines River widens and braids nearing the lake, it spills through the huge Red Rock Wildlife Area, spanning about 28,000 acres of marshy areas that are flooded periodically. Thousands of shorebirds, pelicans, herons, egrets, ducks, and geese make the sprawling wetlands their summertime home. Hunters take over in the fall waterfowl season. The trip described here links this area with the main lake's best cliffs.

Except for short out-and-back trips, a touring kayak (or "sea kayak") is highly recommended. About 12 miles long and averaging a mile wide, with cliffs that can block access to shore, Lake Red Rock is no place to be caught by high winds in an undecked or recreational boat. Waves can top five feet, immensely dangerous for anyone not prepared with the right equipment and skills.

In early spring, the lake's excellent clarity and un-crowdedness are attractive, but another level of skills and gear—wet suits or dry suits, a touring kayak with bulkheads, self-rescue gear, etc.—are required. Hypothermia is a potentially lethal risk early in the season.

Campground options are abundant. The U.S. Army Corps of Engineers has five lakeside campgrounds with all amenities, including Howell Station, Ivan's, North Overlook Camp, Wallashuck, and Whitebreast. ReserveUSA (toll-free at 877-444-6777) handles reservations. Elk Rock State Park also has campgrounds (one lakeside) with full amenities and mountain biking trails. Robert's Creek Park has a campground with full amenities on a separate lake. Cordova Park has lakeside rental cabins (641-627-5935). The U.S. Army Corps of Engineers allows camping only in designated areas.

Canoesport Outfitters in Indianola (515-961-6117) **rents touring kayaks**, periodically offering instruction and guided trips.

The **shuttle route** from the put-in at the Bennington Township access runs north on 40th Avenue, continuing north on 117th Street in Jasper County to County F70, and then east into Monroe, and south on State Highway 14. After you pass over Mile-Long Bridge and the entrance to Elk Rock State Park, turn east on Hayes Drive, and follow the signs to the ranger station and boat ramp.

For **water levels**, check the Lake Red Rock Pool gauge (station PELI4) on the Corps of Engineers Web site listed in the introduction. Below "normal pool" at 744 feet, shoals entering the lake lengthen. In the fall, the pool level is raised for migrating waterfowl. Shore scenery changes at various levels (the description here is at normal pool).

Gradient is negligible on the river portion.

Put in on the Des Moines River. Paddling generally southeast, you cross a wide, remote floodplain bound by bluffs. Head south into a horseshoe bend, where small channels join and can be explored for wildlife viewing. Near the south bluff, a more significant channel siphons a quarter of the river's flow off to the right, running swiftly toward the bluff. Take it. (Alternatively, heading through the main channel to the Boxcars Access adds 1.5 miles to the trip.) At the bluff, you can hike up a shale slope for a view over the expanse of wetlands you've paddled across.

Head east along the bluff, past an island, and into Lake Red Rock. For a short bit you may need to scoot over sandy shoals. Don't curse them: they're the reason powerboats and Jet Skis avoid the shallow west end of the lake. Hug the south shore and continue east past a pastured hillside. You'll paddle through a skeleton forest of trees flooded when the dam was built in 1969. Lines of bluffs with sandstone outcroppings become visible on shore, all part of the Red Rock Wildlife Area.

Past coves and bluffs, you pass a point with a higher wooded bluff, approaching a marvelous beach with sandstone cliffs immediately behind it. It's a great spot to climb around on scenic rocks. As you paddle northeast of the beach, some of the lake's most incredible cliffs rise up to 100 feet above the water, with cedars clinging to promontories hanging out over the lake. Little caves appear above and at the waterline. The largest, barely big enough to fit one kayak, is mossy with rounded columns.

Impressive cliffs divided by coves continue to Mile-Long Bridge. On the right, the bay past the next point harbors one of Elk Rock State Park's two boat ramps. Crossing the bay, past several coves, you reach another long line of dramatic cliffs. For the next half mile, there is no break in the vertical walls. Watch the cliff line for one fascinating spot where a piece of the cliff has fissured. There is a slot in the rock where you can paddle into a narrow, 30-foot cave and out a separate opening.

Past more cliffs and coves, just past a turn to the south is the second Elk Rock State Park Boat Ramp, the **takeout**.

Other trips. The map shows mostly the western two-thirds of the lake, typically less traffic congested and with prime areas of interest to kayakers. Along the north side of the lake beginning at the Boxcars Access, kayakers can follow a line of dead trees to a high, sandy island, and then along wooded bluffs with sandstone outcroppings on the way to the Painted Rock cliffs. More beautiful cliffs line Cordova Park. Paddlers can select any route using the map, or they can go farther east, where there are also scenic cliffs. For a map including boat ramps on the east side of the lake, call the Army Corps of Engineers (800-362-2001).

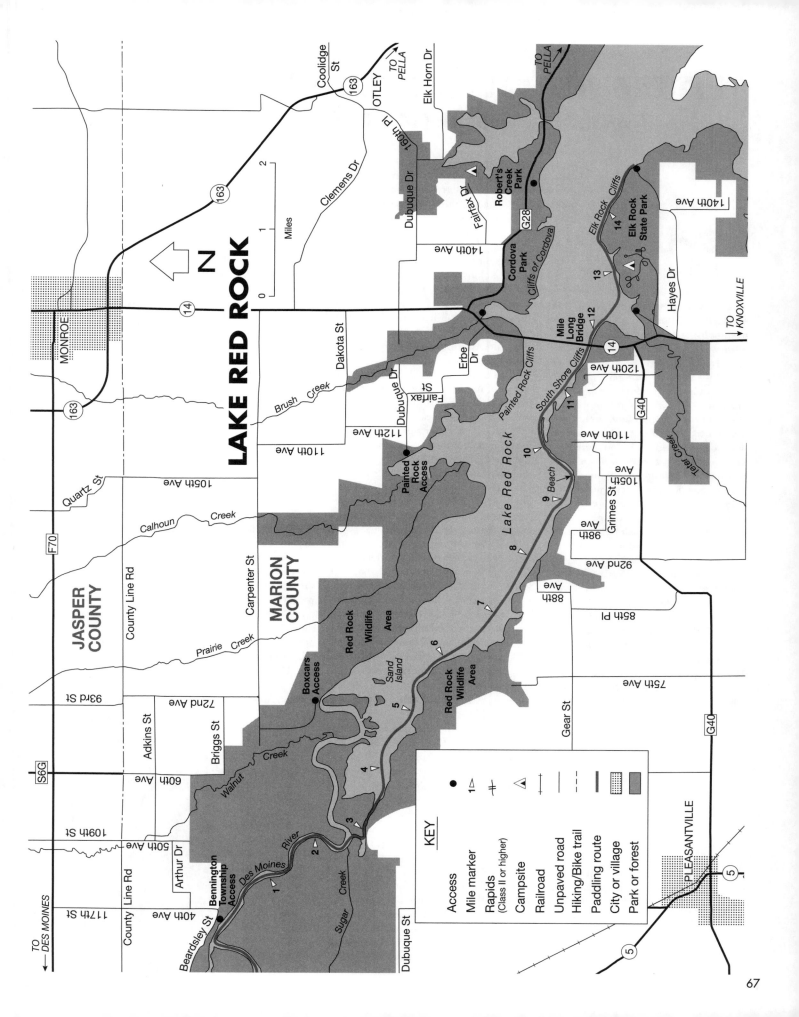

LAKE RED ROCK

N

Miles
0   1   2

KEY

Access ●
Mile marker 1△
Rapids (Class II or higher) ⊨
Campsite ◁
Railroad ⊥
Unpaved road |
Hiking/Bike trail ⌇
Paddling route
City or village
Park or forest

TO DES MOINES

JASPER COUNTY

MARION COUNTY

Bennington Township Access

Des Moines River

Sugar Creek

Walnut Creek

Boxcars Access

Red Rock Wildlife Area

Sand Island

Red Rock Wildlife Area

Painted Rock Access

Lake Red Rock

Prairie Creek

Calhoun Creek

Brush Creek

Cliffs of Cordova

Cordova Park

Robert's Creek Park

Painted Rock Cliffs

South Shore Cliffs

Mile Long Bridge

Elk Rock Cliffs

Elk Rock State Park

TO PELLA

OTLEY

MONROE

PLEASANTVILLE

TO KNOXVILLE

LITTLE MAQUOKETA RIVER
Durango to Mud Lake Park (10.1 Miles)

Julien Dubuque

Lead was in high demand for musket and cannonballs in the late eighteenth century, and mines were eventually established all through this area where three states meet. Iowa's first European settler, a diminutive, swarthy French Canadian named Julien Dubuque paddled into these parts in 1788 with designs on mining. The local Mesquakie band, with a village on the banks of Catfish Creek at the southern edge of modern-day Dubuque, had promised the British to ban mining. Dubuque responded with both goodwill and subterfuge, apparently wooing and eventually marrying Potosa, Chief Peosta's daughter, but also setting Catfish Creek ablaze (using an oil slick a comrade poured) to demonstrate his great power. He threatened to torch the Mississippi next if he didn't get his way. Integrated into the tribe, he was called "Little Night," and the coveted mining rights were granted. His mines, later sanctioned by the territory's Spanish governor, were successful. By the time Dubuque died in 1810, he was buried with tribal honors on the bluff overlooking Catfish Creek, where a monument now stands at the Mines of Spain State Recreation Area.

This trip is one of this book's most diverse, passing from a tiny stream to the country's largest river. Within two miles of tiny Durango, three branches of the tiny Little Maquoketa River converge forming a small, swift river just 45 feet wide. From there, it's six miles to the Father of Waters, coursing through one of Iowa's deepest valleys, with wooded bluffs rising 200 feet from the valley floor. Then it meanders slowly in a wooded floodplain, finally opening into an expansive, bluff-lined pool of the Mississippi River (check for wind advisories that can create high waves before running your shuttle).

Running along the Little Maquoketa is one of Iowa's most scenic cycling trails, the 26-mile Heritage Trail, which connects Dyersville to near the north edge of Dubuque. Fishing for smallmouth bass is good in the upstream portions, and catfishing is better downstream of State Highway 3/U.S. Highway 52.

A riverside **campground** with full amenities is at Mud Lake Park, the takeout. Another good campground is at Swiss Valley Park southwest of Dubuque.

Canoe and kayak rentals are available from Fever River Outfitters (815-776-9425) in Galena, Illinois, about 15 miles southeast of Dubuque.

The **shuttle route** (7.2 miles) from the put-in at Durango heads east on Highway 3/52, briefly north on County C9Y, and northeast on Mud Lake Road to Mud Lake Park.

For good **water levels**, normal rainfalls are required, and by July the river is often not runnable. DANGEROUS AT HIGH LEVELS, THIS RIVER CAN FLOOD QUICKLY. After heavy rains, the National Weather Service (563-386-3976) can tell you if the river has reached flood stage (15 feet) from manual readings at a gauge near Clay Hill Road.

The **gradient** for the Little Maquoketa part of this section is 3.1 feet per mile.

Put in at the trailhead for the Heritage Trail in Durango, just upstream of the river bridge on the river-right. Past the bridge you'll curve left into the first riffle and then bend right into another. The valley bottom is just a quarter mile wide. As you head east, you see a high, cedar-topped wooded bluff on the left. Turn right, and at another wooded bluff the river rounds a left bend and descends a long riffle along a bluff with jagged boulders in the stream.

Briefly coursing straight north, the Little Maquoketa makes a hard right along another pretty wooded bluff, curves along it to a bridge, and slows. A riffle leads along limestone boulders at the base of a nicely wooded bluff. The stream runs fast for the next half mile, and turning left along a scenic bluff you pass three car-sized boulders and an island with a fun chute on the left channel. Crops are occasionally seen through a line of trees. After a hook to the left, you pass beneath the Heritage Trail bridge and wind swiftly through more lowlands with crops visible atop cut banks. Then, a charming cedar-topped bluff appears on the left as the river slows.

Curve left along another wooded bluff, and just ahead a home sits atop a crumbly, undercut limestone wall leading to the Highway 3/52 bridge at Sageville. Past the bridge, another limestone wall appears on the left, and the stream passes through one last riffle, nearing a bluff to the north. Lowland woods line low dirt banks. Around a right bend, the Herber Road bridge is usable as a takeout, but it entails a steep carry up unstable riprap.

Past the bridge, the river is quite sluggish. Nearing a bluff and quarry, it bends sharply to the right through more lowland woods. After a railroad bridge across the river, the channel splits. Either channel can work, but the right route adds about 1.5 miles to your trip. Through the left channel, the woods thin, and the sloughlike river takes on marshy qualities with grassy banks. A bluff is visible on the left, and as you enter the Mississippi, the view opens dramatically across the lakelike pool of the Mississippi to spectacular limestone bluffs across the river. Paddle north along the lily beds to your left, hugging the shoreline. On a windy day, large waves that can easily capsize a canoe develop here, but it's also a great place to view waterfowl during spring and fall migrations.

Paddle toward the tip of a peninsula jutting from the shoreline near the navigation channel markers. Round the point, and paddle northwest toward the marina; just left of it is the **takeout** at Mud Lake Park.

Other trips. See Appendix 2 for information on the Little Maquoketa above Durango and the Dubuque entry in Appendix 1 for information on Catfish Creek.

Scenic woods and boulders line the banks of this little river north of Dubuque.

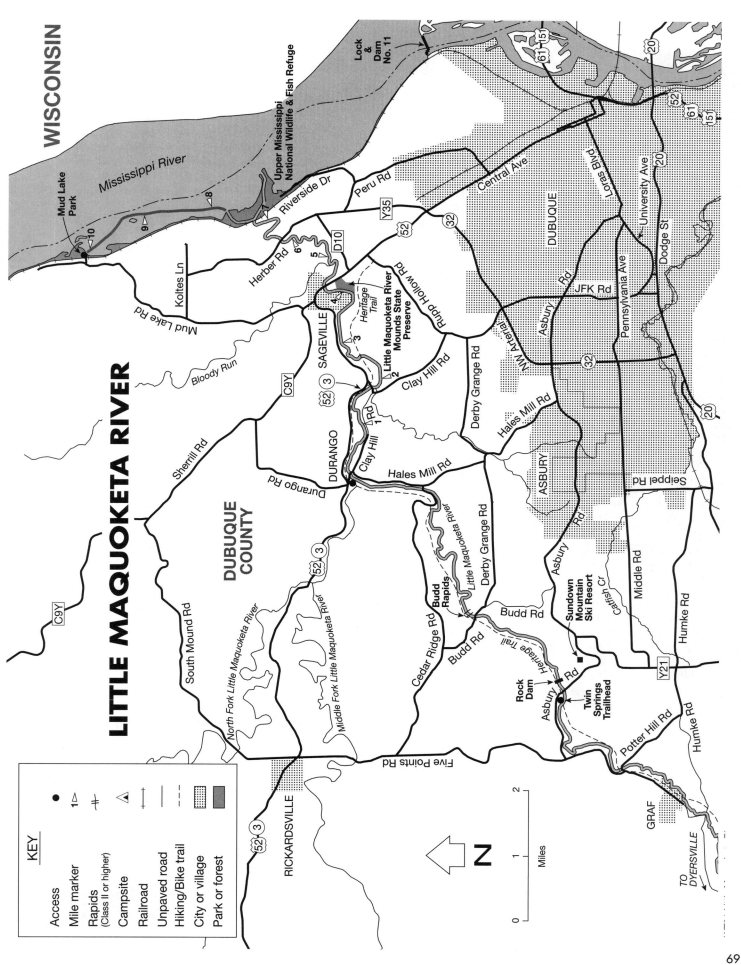

LITTLE MAQUOKETA RIVER

WISCONSIN

Mississippi River

Upper Mississippi National Wildlife & Fish Refuge

Lock & Dam No. 11

Mud Lake Park

Riverside Dr

Peru Rd

Central Ave

DUBUQUE

Koltes Ln

Mud Lake Rd

Herber Rd

Y35

52

32

Loras Blvd

University Ave

Dodge St

JFK Rd

Pennsylvania Ave

Asbury Rd

Bloody Run

SAGEVILLE

Heritage Trail

Little Maquoketa River Mounds State Preserve

Rupp Hollow Rd

Clay Hill Rd

Derby Grange Rd

NW Arterial

Hales Mill Rd

C9Y

52

3

52

DURANGO

Clay Hill Rd

Hales Mill Rd

ASBURY

Sherrill Rd

Durango Rd

Little Maquoketa River

Derby Grange Rd

Seippel Rd

DUBUQUE COUNTY

North Fork Little Maquoketa River

Middle Fork Little Maquoketa River

52

3

South Mound Rd

Cedar Ridge Rd

Budd Rapids

Little Maquoketa River

Budd Rd

Budd Rd

Sundown Mountain Ski Resort

Catfish Cr

Middle Rd

Asbury Rd

Humke Rd

C9Y

RICKARDSVILLE

52

3

Five Points Rd

Heritage Trail

Rock Dam

Twin Springs Trailhead

Asbury Rd

Potter Hill Rd

Humke Rd

Y21

GRAF

TO DYERSVILLE

KEY

- ● Access
- 1△ Mile marker
- ⊬ Rapids (Class II or higher)
- △ Campsite
- ┼┼ Railroad
- ─── Unpaved road
- ---- Hiking/Bike trail
- ▦ City or village
- ▓ Park or forest

N

Miles
0   1   2

LITTLE SIOUX RIVER 1
Spencer to Little Sioux Wildlife Area (15 Miles)

The Little Sioux River is the quintessential Iowa prairie stream. Fed by the numerous lakes and drainage districts in the Iowa Great Lakes environs, the river is sometimes paddleable in Dickinson and northern Clay Counties, but joined by the Ocheydan River in Spencer, its flows become more consistent. Not really "little," in its most-paddled portions it is a midsized river. At its mouth, the Little Sioux is Iowa's largest interior tributary to the Missouri River.

Running muddy most of the paddling season, the river is usually very slow. Scenically intact, it enjoys Iowa Protected Water Area status from Spencer to Linn Grove, making it eligible for public land acquisitions. This section, in particular, has long, very secluded areas of woodlands and prairie with few modern intrusions. Unbridled in a fairly wide plain, it constantly and lazily meanders, forming new channels at high water. Fishing is quite productive in the Little Sioux for walleye, catfish, and, in the upper stretches like this one, northern pike.

There is a **campground** at Oneota Park, not near the river access. Also see Trumpeter Trail and Little Sioux River 2.

Canoe rentals are available from Linn Grove Landing (712-296-3635) in Linn Grove, about 5 miles west of Sioux Rapids. For **kayak rentals**, see the Expedition Co. (712-332-9001) in Arnold's Park on Lake Okoboji, about 15 miles north of Spencer.

The **shuttle route** (10.2 miles) runs south on U.S. Highway 71, east on U.S. Highway 18, south on County M50, and east on 420th Street. Turn left into the wildlife area to reach the access.

For **water levels**, see the Little Sioux at Linn Grove gauge (station 06605850) on the USGS Web site listed in the introduction. With few riffles, it can be paddled at fairly low levels, down to 200 cfs. The **gradient** is less than 2 feet per mile.

The **put-in** is at West Leach Park at Spencer, just upstream from the Highway 71 bridge. Beyond it, the river has been channelized and concrete riprap lines the banks through town. A pedestrian bridge crosses the river, and as it bends right, the banks become more wooded. As you head southeast along riprap, watch out for the remains of a dam, where dangerous steel rods jut from the riverbed.

A ridge rises on the right bank, and past an apartment complex, both sides become increasingly wooded as you pass a home. The river bends away from the ridge heading generally northeast through little bends, the banks become grassy curving right, and you pass through the southeastern corner of Oneota Park and paddle under the M50 bridge, which can be used as an access on the river-left.

Past the bridge, the river passes through lightly wooded areas with cut banks. At a right bend, an imposing home stands atop a high loess bluff, and the river diverts left at its base into a long section of low, wooded banks. The river bends right toward a more pristine bluff, and prairie and light woods line the next several bends in the Stouffer Wildlife Area. Past the Highway 18 bridge, you'll see the last small ridge for several miles as the valley becomes broad, with no signs of civilization.

The river meanders almost constantly through light woods and prairie in the Hawk Valley Wildlife Area. You find Lost Outlet entering from the left, and after a right bend you'll notice a 15-foot-wide channel that shoots off to the right. It can be choked off in snags, or it can be an interesting diversion, cutting off several bends of the snaggy, meandering main channel.

Beyond the 390th Street Bridge, the river constricts to 35 feet wide in a recent cut off an old meander between newly cut banks topped with grass and stands of young cottonwoods. At a right bend, the still backwater of the old channel joins from the river-left, and the woods are suddenly mature.

With a sparser line of trees giving glimpses of fields, the river turns sharply right and circles around to the left where you see a pastured hill and a private camp. There are more pastured hills in the distance, and with occasional riprap, the river continues meandering, often approaching the ridges lining the valley. Past some views of crops near the river above riprapped banks, the woods grow denser. Heading west to the base of a pasture hillside, the river bends left and the ridge grows heavily wooded. The concrete boat ramp at Little Sioux Wildlife Area, the **takeout**, is ahead on the river-right.

Other trips. See the Spencer entry in Appendix 1.

A few scenic bluffs near Spencer appear before the river enters a long stretch of lowland woods.

The Inkpaduta Canoe Trail

West Leach Park is the starting point for the Inkpaduta Canoe Trail, Iowa's longest and most complete canoe trail. (See Little Sioux River 6 sidebar for the story of the Dakota warrior the trail was named after.) A paddler can spend a full leisurely week on the Inkpaduta, with only one dam to portage (a long one at Linn Grove) in 134 miles between Spencer and Smithland to the southwest. There are many places to camp in between. Generally, accesses are well marked with wooden signs visible from the river, giving the distance to the next access. Except for a small section at the end, Little Sioux maps in this book include the entire trail (with some sections in smaller inset maps). A foldout trail map (somewhat dated—certain accesses listed on it have been washed out) is available from the Clay County Conservation Board at (712) 262-2187.

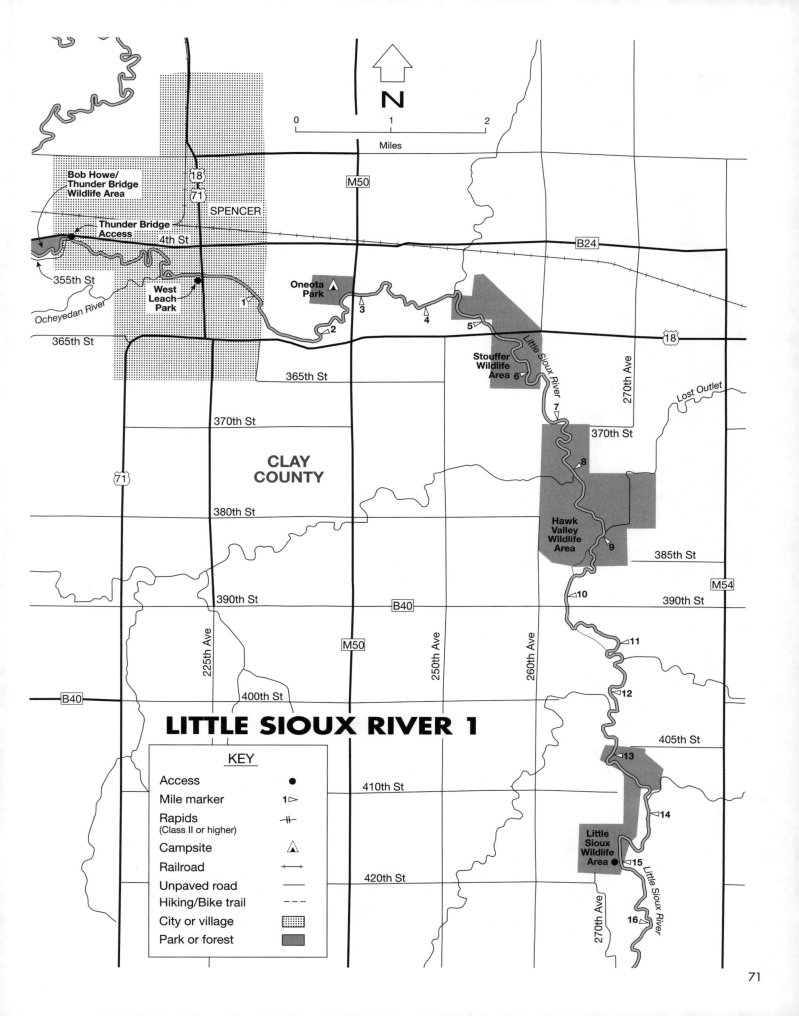

LITTLE SIOUX RIVER 1

Bob Howe/
Thunder Bridge
Wildlife Area

SPENCER

Thunder Bridge
Access

4th St

355th St

West
Leach
Park

Ocheyedan River

365th St

Oneota Park

365th St

CLAY
COUNTY

370th St

380th St

390th St

225th Ave

400th St

B40

Stouffer
Wildlife
Area

Little Sioux River

370th St

Lost Outlet

270th Ave

385th St

M54

Hawk
Valley
Wildlife
Area

B40

M50

250th Ave

260th Ave

390th St

405th St

Little
Sioux
Wildlife
Area

Little Sioux River

270th Ave

18
71

M50

B24

18

KEY

Access	●
Mile marker	1▷
Rapids (Class II or higher)	─╫─
Campsite	△
Railroad	─┼─
Unpaved road	———
Hiking/Bike trail	– – –
City or village	▓▓▓
Park or forest	■

410th St

420th St

LITLE SIOUX RIVER 2
Little Sioux Wildlife Area to Burr Oak Bridge (14.3 Miles)

Woven Rock

The Sioux-speaking Indians who lived in these parts actually referred to themselves as the Dakota (now called the Santee Sioux), and they didn't call the Little Sioux River by that name. They preferred *Eaneah Waupedan*, meaning either Stone River or Woven Rock River, after the numerous glacial erratic rocks deposited in its valley. Even though it's by no means a small river, French fur traders first assigned the current name when they began calling it the *Petite Rivere de Cuouex*, comparing it to the Big Sioux.

Seldom is the Little Sioux's scenery called dramatic, but this section certainly passes along impressive wooded ridges and bluffs. In the first part of the trip, the valley is narrower than is typical of this stream. Throughout, the river runs along timbered stretches or pastures. Riffles are still rare. Wildlife, from river otters to waterfowl, is abundant.

The terrain here has a somewhat different texture than along most of the state's rivers, with some obvious relics of the most recent glaciers to cover Iowa. The hills and ridges undulate along, and piles of rocks laid bare by the river appear in outside bends. Averaging 75 feet wide, the river has carved scenic wooded bluffs into the glacial till in places. Fishing is good for catfish, walleye, and northern pike.

Kindlespire Little Sioux access has a **campground** near the river that makes a good base for a weekend trip. Gabrielson Park, just south of Sioux Rapids, also has a campground.

Canoe rentals are available from Linn Grove Landing (712-296-3635) in Linn Grove, about 5 miles west of Sioux Rapids.

The **shuttle route** (15.8 miles) runs west on 420th Street, south on 260th Avenue, west on County B53, south on U.S. Highway 71, east on 485th Street, southeast and east on 490th Street, southwest on 245th Avenue, and briefly east to Burr Oak Bridge on 495th Street.

For **water levels**, see the Little Sioux at Linn Grove gauge (station 06605850) on the USGS Web site listed in the introduction. With few riffles, it can be paddled at fairly low levels, down to 200 cfs.

The **gradient** is less than 2 feet per mile.

From the **put-in**, the river veers southeast where, at the edge of the Little Sioux Wildlife Area, a prairie hillside abruptly turns to pastured hillside. The valley has narrowed, imparting an enclosed feeling between ridges as the river winds between them. Bending right along some riprap, you approach the base of the wooded west ridge and then bend away from it. As you approach it again, it appears as an impressive 100-foot timbered bluff with clay cliffs sloping down to the river.

After a little hook to the north, you reach the Gillett Grove Bridge. Beyond it, you pass along a wooded ridge on the right and run south through a 100-yard-long riffle to join a small glacial moraine ridge on the left with rounded rocks at its base. Heading west, you'll see some crops and pasture on the left. Gradually the terrain becomes wilder again, with prairie and light woods through several bends until you see telephone poles and approach the 260th Avenue bridge.

With woods on the right and pasture on the left, you continue west to a wooded bluff. The next few bends run past light woods and pastured hillsides. After a long, straight stretch to the southwest, the river begins curving left and heads toward a high bluff to the west, entering the High Bridge Wildlife Area. Bending south at the bluff's base, you pass beneath an abandoned railroad bridge about 40 feet above the river. Along a nice prairie ridge on the left with glacially worn rocks at its base, you head generally southwest until reaching the 240th Avenue bridge, which could be used as an access on the river-right.

Past lightly wooded banks, you reach the County B63 bridge, where an impressive wooded ridge rises in the background. Here the river becomes snaggy, but also quite scenic, joining 100-foot wooded ridges with loess or clay cliffs exposed. At a right bend, you'll see the Kindlespire Little Sioux boat ramp, a possible takeout with riverside camping. It's also a great place to get out and stretch your legs on the area's excellent hiking trails traversing the bluffs you're about to paddle along.

The bluffs on the south side of the river are earthen and heavily wooded, delicately beautiful with some mossy slopes. The river leaves and rejoins them several times heading generally east. The ridge tapers off, and heading right, you bend south and meander past low, lightly wooded banks. Bending northwest toward a hillside farm, the river turns right toward the Burr Oak Bridge. The **takeout** is downstream of the bridge on the river-right.

Other trips. The next 5.3 miles from the Burr Oak Bridge to the Sioux Rapids access actually has some very nicely wooded terrain lining it, as well as a scenic high ridge that the river curves along nearing Sioux Rapids. Unfortunately, even though this is still part of the so-called Iowa Protected Water Area, there is also a large hog confinement on an east bank that can literally make it difficult to breathe for several minutes if the wind is coming from the east.

An abandoned railroad bridge spans the river at the High Bridge Wildlife Area.

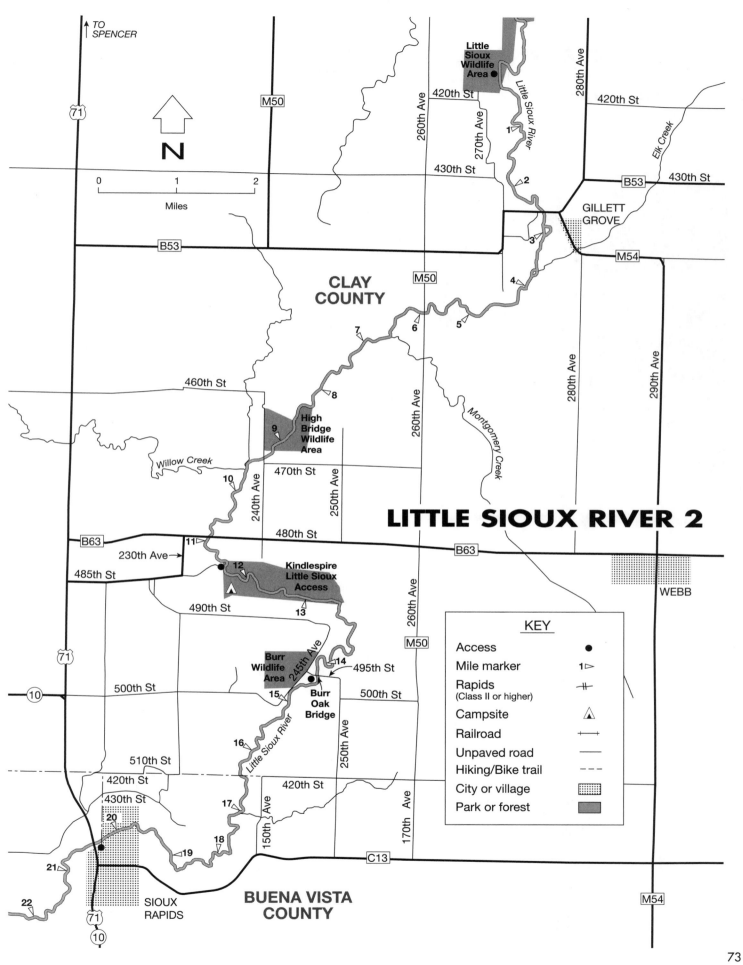

TO
SPENCER

N

0   1   2
Miles

71

M50

280th Ave

**Little
Sioux
Wildlife
Area**

Little Sioux River

420th St

420th St

260th Ave

270th Ave

430th St

B53

430th St

Elk Creek

GILLETT
GROVE

B53

M54

**CLAY
COUNTY**

M50

290th Ave

280th Ave

260th Ave

Montgomery Creek

460th St

**High
Bridge
Wildlife
Area**

Willow Creek

470th St

250th Ave

240th Ave

480th St

LITTLE SIOUX RIVER 2

B63

B63

230th Ave

485th St

260th Ave

M50

**Kindlespire
Little Sioux
Access**

WEBB

490th St

**Burr
Wildlife
Area**

245th Ave

495th St

**Burr
Oak
Bridge**

500th St

500th St

250th Ave

KEY

Access ●

Mile marker 1▷

Rapids
(Class II or higher)

Campsite ⚠

Railroad ┼┼┼

Unpaved road ──

Hiking/Bike trail - - -

City or village

Park or forest

10

Little Sioux River

510th St

420th St

420th St

150th Ave

170th Ave

430th St

71

SIOUX
RAPIDS

C13

M54

**BUENA VISTA
COUNTY**

71

10

1
2
3
4
5
6
7
8
9
10
11
12
13
14
15
16
17
18
19
20
21
22

LITTLE SIOUX RIVER 3
Sioux Rapids to Linn Grove (8.2 Miles)

Slow and glassy, the Little Sioux passes along remarkably pristine scenery on the way to Linn Grove.

Another showpiece section, the Little Sioux here winds through some quite isolated territory, along more pretty, wooded ridges. Running through a very rural area, this section also offers expansive vistas of distant ridges at clearings. The river is at its lowest gradient here, and backing up behind the dam, the current is very slow for about the last third of the trip, so expect to paddle, but the trip is short. That also makes this a favorable stretch when the river is too low to paddle elsewhere. Cut banks are rare, while low, grassy banks are the norm. Fishing is still good for catfish. One of the state's hot spots for walleye and northern is in the swift waters below the dam at Linn Grove, especially productive in spring spawning runs. (The dam is dangerous—under no circumstances should you paddle near it.)

There is a riverside **campground** at the Linn Grove access. Gabrielson Park, just south of Sioux Rapids, also has a campground.

Canoe rentals and shuttles are available from Linn Grove Landing (712-296-3635) in Linn Grove.

The **shuttle route** (8.9 miles) from the Sioux Rapids put-in runs north on U.S. Highway 71, west on State Highway 10, south on County M36, east on 430th Street, and south on the access road to the takeout.

For **water levels**, see the Little Sioux at Linn Grove gauge (station 06605850) on the USGS Web site listed in the introduction. With few riffles and deeper water near the dam, this stretch can almost always be paddled.

The **gradient** is less than 2 feet per mile.

Beyond the Highway 71 bridge from the **put-in** on the river-left, the Little Sioux heads southwest near a mix of woods and prairie, bending left at a wooded ridge with grain silos visible ahead. Ahead, the river begins working its delicate magic, with a small prairie hill studded with cedars on the left. The banks are covered in a pleasant mix of grasses and woods, with views of distant ridgelines carpeted in trees ahead.

After a long, straight stretch, the river bends right at a small ridge heading generally northwest. Through a clearing on the right you see pastured hills and a radio tower off in the distance. Wooded again, the river joins an otherwise pretty wooded slope that has a talus of junked appliances and cars.

Through more lowland woods, occasional clearings give vistas of distant high ridges with grassy hillsides topped with trees. Now and again you catch glimpses of farmyards at the base of a ridge.

At a left bend, the current begins to turn sluggish. Bending right, part of the channel has cut through the bank creating a shortcut and a small island. Past trees and prairie grasses with distant ridges still visible now and again, the channel splits around a large island. If water levels are adequate to get past snags, take the more serene, narrower left channel, which passes along a pretty, wooded ridge rather than by a farm.

Where the right channel rejoins, you bend right at two small islands. Passing a lightly wooded ridge and a home, you paddle southwest between grassy banks quite low to the water. After you head east and then bend 90 degrees to the right, if the water level is high enough, a small channel connects the river to a little lake on the right. Bending left, the Little Sioux reaches the boat ramp on the river-right, your **takeout**. If you are continuing on, there is a one-third-mile **portage** down the access road around the very dangerous Linn Grove Dam.

Other trips. The 10.9-mile section from Linn Grove to Peterson is perhaps not quite as impressive as some others on the Little Sioux, but it's still worth paddling. You'll pass along some pretty ridges wooded with hardwoods and cedars and longer stretches through row crop areas. Where the river enters a third-mile swift stretch between high cut banks, use caution because the area is prone to potentially dangerous logjams. At the trip's end, very pretty wooded ridges along Wanata State Park (with nice hiking but no river access) line the banks to the takeout.

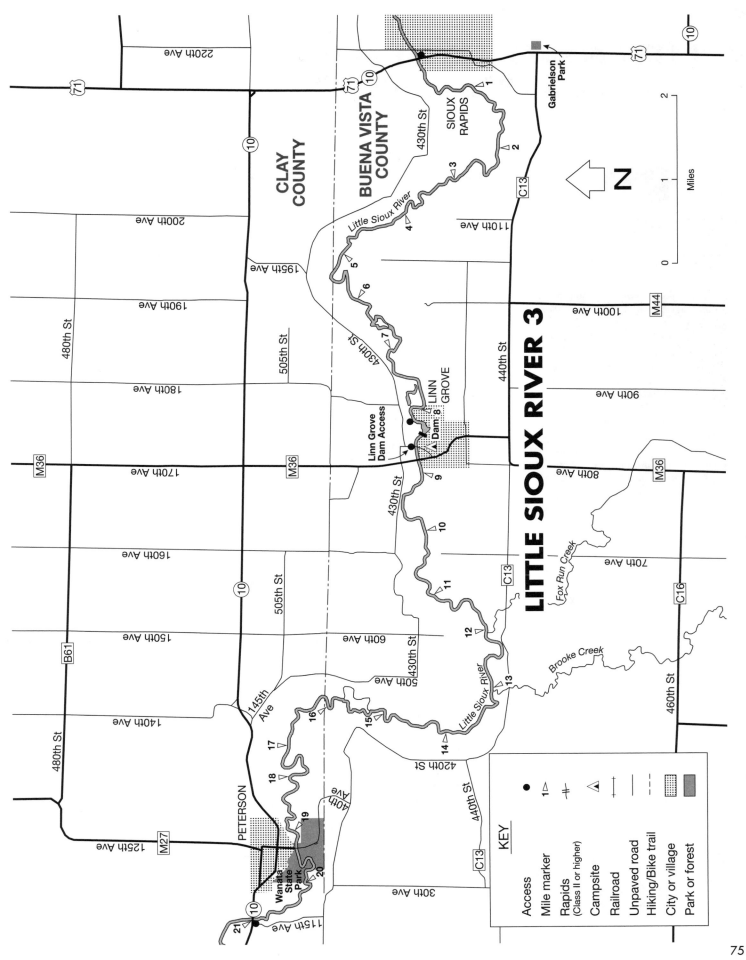

LITTLE SIOUX RIVER 3

KEY

●	Access
1△	Mile marker
≠	Rapids (Class II or higher)
◁	Campsite
╪	Railroad
—	Unpaved road
– –	Hiking/Bike trail
▦	City or village
▬	Park or forest

CLAY COUNTY

BUENA VISTA COUNTY

SIOUX RAPIDS

Gabrielson Park

LINN GROVE

Linn Grove Dam Access

Dam

PETERSON

Wanata State Park

Little Sioux River

Fox Run Creek

Brooke Creek

N

Miles

0   1   2

LITTLE SIOUX RIVER 4
Peterson to Martin Access (15.6 Miles)

Mill Creek Culture

Along the banks of this segment of the Little Sioux, along the one in Little Sioux River 5, and along several nearby tributary creeks, the Mill Creek Culture of Native Americans reached its zenith about 1,000 years ago. Numerous archaeological sites located throughout the valleys are shedding light on this highly organized people. One site, at Wittrock Indian Village State Preserve on Waterman Creek, was a village that lasted 300 years. Surrounded by a stockade of wooden posts to protect the people from marauding tribes, the village had 20 earthen lodges, each 20 by 30 feet with it's own central fireplace. Villagers grew corn, beans, and squash and hunted bison.

You'd figure this trip for a dud at the very beginning, passing by deep-cut banks, sandbars, and row crops. Everything changes entering O'Brien County, where the river becomes uniquely scenic, meandering through excellent tracts of public land.

There's intimate beauty winding close to remnant prairie and wooded ridges both small and tall. Past Highway 10, the river becomes more open to views of sprawling tallgrass ridges with interspersed cedars, a scene that may spur you into whistling the theme song to Little House on the Prairie. The river also passes long stretches of valley-bottom farmland, and ridges dominated by oak groves become more common toward the end of the trip, but this is one of the finest stretches in the state to get a feel for what extensive prairie ridges once looked like. With the river width averaging about 80 feet here, riffles become slightly more common than in the stretches upstream, sometimes with glacial-deposit rocks and boulders.

Three canoe accesses—Nelson, Soo, and Old Dutch Fred—that appear on county government Inkpaduta Canoe Trail maps are no longer convenient for boaters due to bank erosion. The trip can still be shortened considerably by taking out at the Burned Bridge access. Catfish and walleye are common catches for anglers.

Dog Creek Park on County M12 has a **campground** as does the Martin Access Area. River camping is allowed at Burned Bridge and other tracts of public land along the river.

Canoe rentals are available from Linn Grove Landing (712-296-3635) in Linn Grove.

The **shuttle route** (8.2 miles) from the put-in near Peterson runs west on State Highway 10, south on County M27, west on County C16, and south on Martin Access Road to the Martin Access Area.

For **water levels**, see the Little Sioux at Linn Grove gauge (station 06605850) on the USGS Web site listed in the introduction. Paddling conditions are pleasant in the few rocky areas with at least 250 cfs.

The **gradient** is 2.1 feet per mile.

Put in at the Riverside access just west of Peterson, upriver-left from the Highway 10 bridge. After passing the bridge, you bend gradually left past a shack and toward a crop-covered hill to the southwest. Curving northwest and then southwest, you pass high cut banks with more views of crops, and as you head west, the banks become more wooded heading generally west-northwest. A grassy ridge and crops are seen on the left, and you approach the base of a glacial moraine ridge and bend right. After a left turn at a 25-foot cut bank, the setting becomes quite beautiful. A scenic prairie hill with cedars becomes visible next to the river. Bending left, you approach a 150-foot wooded ridge, loop to the right away from it, and then approach it again at piles of glacial rocks.

Through several bends, the banks are deeply wooded, with occasional glimpses of mixed prairie and wooded slopes. Waterman Creek enters from the right, and after a left bend, a small riffle leads to some old steel pillars at the Burned Bridge access, where there's a boat ramp on the river-right.

Bending north toward a distant grassy ridge studded with cedars, the river diverts south into a sparsely wooded area with crops visible. Then the channel becomes riffly and splits around midstream boulders—run right at lower water levels.

After passing under another Highway 10 bridge, the river enters another long, bridgeless tract past mature stands of cottonwoods and silver maples. Passing along cornfields and pastures and bending to the right, you get the next of many views of the impressive grassy ridges dotted with cedars lining the valley.

Gravel bars line inside bends. The river heads straight east past cut banks and cornfields toward a farmstead atop a small, wooded ridge with glacial rocks at its base; then it bends southwest toward another grassy ridge view, this time with shrubs defining gullies running down the slopes. Bending right, you enter the Waterman Wildlife Area, snaking toward and away from a 150-foot prairie ridge. At the third bend toward it, you approach its scenic base sloping down to the bank.

Entering Cherokee County, you bend away from and approach the prairie slope one last time. Heading generally southward, you see high, wooded ridges on the east flank of the valley in the distance as the scene near the river becomes sparsely tree-lined and more agricultural. You'll see a tidy, red barn from several angles at different bends, and the river enters a long stretch between cornfields straight to the west, with another view of the now-distant west grassy ridge.

As you head southwest, a gravel road cuts straight up the savanna ridge to the west, and as you bend south, the ridge becomes increasingly wooded, crowned with cedars. Through a series of bends with views of alternating grassy or wooded slopes, you bend right along a line of concrete riprap and turn left under the C16 bridge. Passing a quarry, you bend left toward a wooded ridge, where the dirt **takeout**, the Martin Access, is on the river-left at the river's bend to the right.

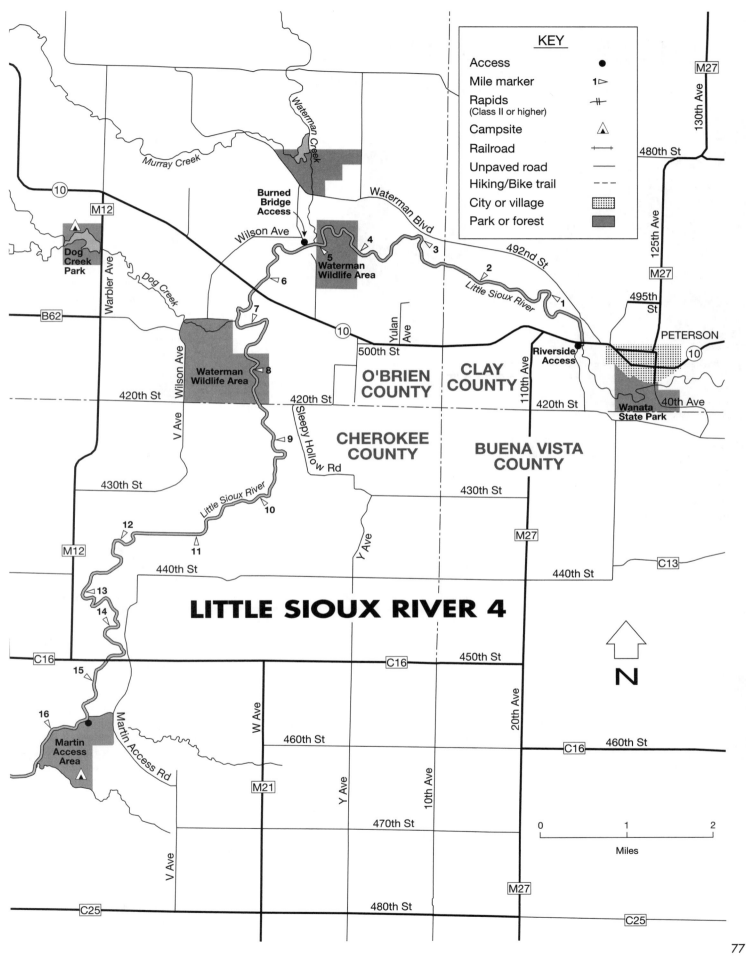

KEY

Access ●
Mile marker 1▷
Rapids +⊢+
(Class II or higher)
Campsite ▲
Railroad +┼+
Unpaved road ────
Hiking/Bike trail ─ ─ ─
City or village
Park or forest

LITTLE SIOUX RIVER 4

Murray Creek

Waterman Creek

Dog Creek Park

Burned Bridge Access

Wilson Ave

Waterman Blvd

Waterman Wildlife Area

Little Sioux River

492nd St

PETERSON

Riverside Access

Wanata State Park

O'BRIEN COUNTY

CLAY COUNTY

CHEROKEE COUNTY

BUENA VISTA COUNTY

Dog Creek

Warbler Ave

Wilson Ave

Waterman Wildlife Area

Sleepy Hollow Rd

Yulan Ave

500th St

420th St

430th St

440th St

450th St

460th St

470th St

480th St

Little Sioux River

Martin Access Area

Martin Access Rd

N

0 1 2
Miles

LITTLE SIOUX RIVER 5
Martin Access to Cherokee (12.8 Miles)

Rockier than most other parts of the Little Sioux, this section also is more heavily wooded with a few pretty bluffs.

On this especially delightful stretch of the Little Sioux, the banks tend to be more wooded and the stream bottom rockier. Although the overall gradient is low, from the Martin Access to the Barnes Access, the stream uncharacteristically drops over several back-to-back riffles and even passes a little spring, a rarity in this part of the state.

Averaging 90 feet wide, the river is slower the rest of the way to Cherokee, bending through woods and past some farmland and one dramatic bluff. Catfish and walleye are common catches for anglers.

The Martin Access has a **campground** well up the ridge from the river. The campground at Spring Lake Park, across U.S. Highway 59 from the access at Westcott Park on the south edge of Cherokee, is riverside. River camping is also allowed at the Martin, Barnes, and Jordahl accesses.

Summer's Canoe Rental (712-372-4774) in Correctionville, about 25 miles southwest of Cherokee, **rents kayaks and canoes** and runs shuttles. Canoe rentals are also available from Linn Grove Landing (712-296-3635) in Linn Grove.

The **shuttle route** (7.7 miles) from the put-in runs north on Martin Access Road, west on County C16, and south on U.S. Highway 59 to Westcott Park in Cherokee.

To approximate **water levels**, average the Little Sioux at Linn Grove gauge (station 06605850) with the Little Sioux at Correctionville gauge (station 06606600) on the USGS Web site listed in the introduction. Look for a minimum average of 300 cfs.

The **gradient** is less than 2 feet per mile.

The dirt **put-in** at the Martin Access can be muddy. Heading southwest and then west along rocky banks, the river drops down a brief riffle, widening and passing a livestock corral with a view of a distant grassy hill to the west. Bending left, the river passes along more rocks and gentle riffles. Hooking around to the right, the channel tightens and drops swiftly over a rocky riffle and heads west toward a hill. After the river takes a right bend followed quickly by a left, the right bank is rocky with glacial moraine and cedar trees, and at lower water levels a little coldwater spring tumbles a foot or two into the river.

Past a small island to the south, cottonwoods and willows line the banks to a left bend toward a wooded hill. Hooking back to the west, the river falls through a rocky chute. The Barnes Access is ahead on the right, just before the bend to the left.

Through wood-lined banks, you pass a private recreation area and some nice sandbars. The left bank rises higher where a quaint cabin is tucked into the woods on the river-left. At a right bend, the river courses swiftly through a garden of microwave-sized rocks. Wooded ridges are visible to the west. As the river turns south, the banks are grassy and tree-lined, and beyond the 480th Street bridge, the river bends right and heads for a pretty, grassy hill. You head generally southwest, and trees become sparse as you pass along crops, with cottonwoods lining the left bank.

Use caution in a snaggy area with moderately fast current. The next several bends through a lightly wooded area also can have numerous snags along with sandbars in insides of bends. Occasionally, there's a view of distant wooded hills and, approaching them, piles of glacial rocks often line the base.

Past power lines, the river enters a lowland plain and flows past cornfields in gentle bends, and ridge-top homes are sometimes visible. A larger tributary, Mill Creek, enters from the right. A little bit south, after a left bend, the Jordahl access is on the river-right—a good access at very low water, but not ideal at higher levels.

The river rounds a bend to the right, and a striking 150-foot bluff looms on the left, with loess cliffs, grass, oaks, and sumac growing up its slopes. As you head south, you see that the bluff has been desecrated with junked cars and trucks. Bending right, you briefly see a warehouse on the north edge of Cherokee and then bend left through deep woods toward the Highway 3 bridge. Past a rocky island heading into the outskirts of Cherokee, you reach the Highway 977 bridge. A small ridge rises on the left as you bend right past more woods. The **takeout** at Westcott Park is ahead on the river-left, 200 yards upstream from the Highway 59 bridge.

Other trips. Swift and rocky with numerous short class I rapids and long riffles, Mill Creek is a largish creek with a radically different character than most northwest Iowa rivers. Unfortunately, you need to wait for rainy spells to enjoyably run it, and there are no gauges on the stream. Multicolored glacial boulders as large as bison periodically jut from the streambed and banks. Prairie ridges, slopes with red cedar groves, and pastures line the banks. With a few tricky turns, numerous fences to negotiate, and dropping at an average gradient of 5 feet per mile in the 13.8 miles from Middle Road to the takeout on Riverview Drive, Mill Creek is not everyone's cup of tea; it's best left to experienced paddlers. For those who enjoy a fast run and paddling in quite secluded areas, though, it's well worth the trouble.

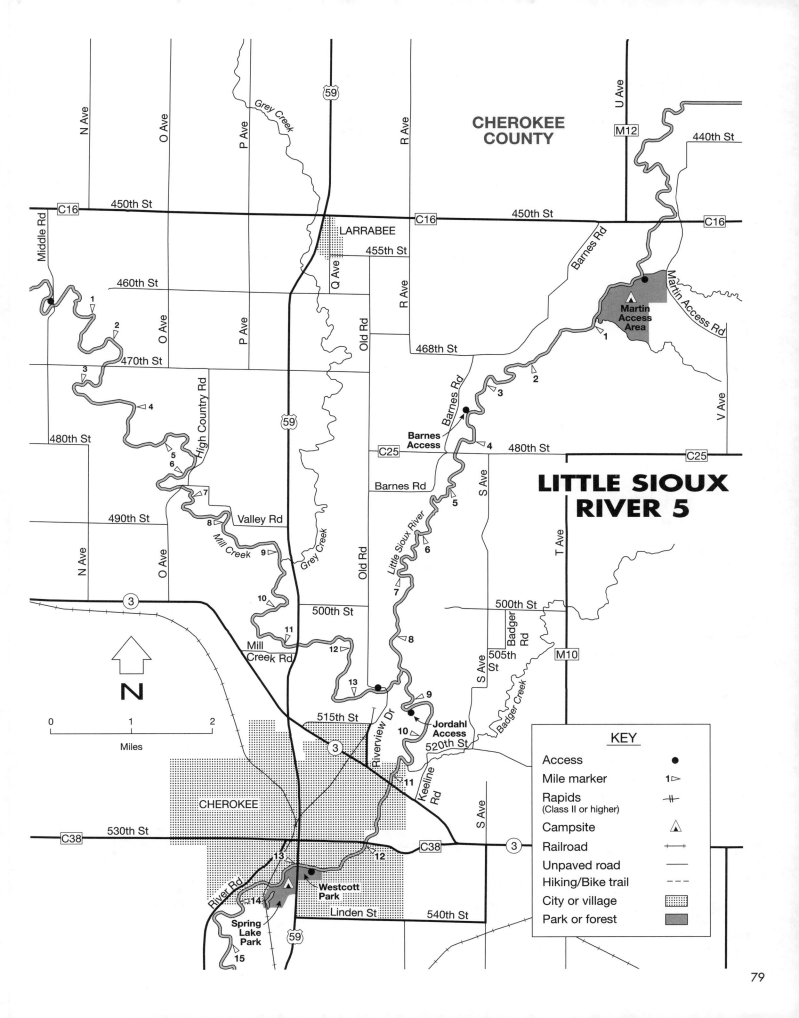

LITTLE SIOUX RIVER 5

CHEROKEE COUNTY

LARRABEE

CHEROKEE

Martin Access Area

Barnes Access

Jordahl Access

Westcott Park

Spring Lake Park

KEY

Access	●
Mile marker	1▷
Rapids (Class II or higher)	⫚
Campsite	⛺
Railroad	┼┼┼
Unpaved road	—
Hiking/Bike trail	- - -
City or village	▦
Park or forest	▨

N

0 1 2
Miles

LITTLE SIOUX RIVER 6
Cherokee to Pearse Access (14.1 Miles)

Perhaps not quite as endearing as some other parts of the Little Sioux, this segment does have its nice points, including some very scenic wooded ridges and excellent camping areas. Not at all swift, and averaging 100 feet wide, the river passes some nicely wooded areas as well as farm ground. As in all sections of the Little Sioux, expect muddy waters except when the river is low or during the fall. Catfish and walleye are common catches for anglers.

There is a riverside **campground** at Spring Lake Park, across U.S. Highway 59 from the access at Westcott Park on the south edge of Cherokee. The wooded campground at the Silver Sioux Recreation Area is not far from the river.

Summer's Canoe Rental (712-372-4774) in Correctionville, about 25 miles southwest of Cherokee, rents **kayaks and canoes** and runs shuttles. Canoe rentals are also available from Linn Grove Landing (712-296-3635) in Linn Grove.

The **shuttle route** (13.5 miles) from the put-in runs south on U.S. Highway 59, west on County C44, and southwest on County L56 to the Pearse access.

For **water levels**, average the Little Sioux at Linn Grove gauge (station 06605850) with the Little Sioux at Correctionville gauge (station 06606600) on the USGS Web site listed in the introduction. Look for a minimum average of 250 cfs.

The **gradient** is less than 2 feet per mile.

Put in at Westcott Park in Cherokee, then float beneath the Highway 59 bridge and past Spring Lake Park on the left. The way out of town isn't particularly pleasant, bending past a quarry, junked cars on a bank, the wastewater treatment plant, a packing plant, and a humming power substation.

The river heads generally south, and the banks are lightly timbered. You pass through a wide, lowland plain with occasional views of high grassy ridges. For several miles, you pass some pastures, but more often you go by stands of cottonwoods and willows. Past a decrepit old railroad bridge, a few locust trees line the left bank near some glacial erratic rocks. Redtail Ridge begins to rise on the left at a left bend toward the C44 bridge. The access just past the bridge on the river-left is somewhat steep, making a much better put-in than takeout. This is the Redtail Habitat Area, which has hiking trails beginning just up the hill from the river access.

As you head south, the bank at the base of the wooded ridge is rocky. The river curves right and then bends left back toward the ridge lined with glacial rocks and boulders. You head southeast, crops line the right bank, and there is a pretty view of undulating forested hills to the south. As you approach them, they remain set back a few hundred yards from the wooded banks for the next mile, where the river bends straight north and then west. At a left bend, you'll notice a private recreation area on the right heading southeast toward a beautiful 70-foot wooded ridge.

Bending right at the mouth of a creek, you'll notice an Inkpaduta Canoe Trail sign up a dirt bank. Proceed 50 yards downstream where you'll find a boat ramp on the river-left.

Bending to the right around a high sandbar, you head northeast along 30-foot-high sandy banks past the private recreation area's shelter house. Along a small grassy ridge with stands of cedars, locusts, walnuts, and cottonwoods, you pass a small cabin and the remains of a high railroad bridge ahead. Past a bend to the right and under the bridge, you come to the **takeout** at the Pearse access, which is on the river-right along the rocks, very close to County L56.

Other trips. For a couple of miles beyond the Pearse access area, the paddling is reasonably good to the bridge in Quimby, which serves as a passable access. Past Quimby, the 9.1 miles to Ranney Knob Park includes occasional views of distant ridges, but the wide valley bottom is heavily used for agriculture, so for very long distances you'll paddle between dirt cut-bank canyons topped with corn or beans. There are some pleasant qualities, such as long sandbars, willow thickets, and some tree-lined ridges. The Steineke Access has a good campground with drinking water, but it is at an unmarked sandbar, tricky to locate from the river.

Inkpaduta

The Inkpaduta Canoe Trail was named for the chief of a Dakota band best remembered for a diabolical act: the Spirit Lake Massacre. For years, Inkpaduta—never captured—was sort of a boogeyman thought to be lurking in some Iowa grove, thinking murderous thoughts toward whites he baselessly hated. His band, in fact, had suffered years of persecution by whites. When uneasy settlers near Smithland took their guns as they hunted elk to feed themselves in a bitter winter, Inkpaduta seems to have snapped. Following the Little Sioux River northward, Inkpaduta's men helped themselves to settlers' food, guns, and ammunition and raped women. Word of the rampage spread, but some remote lake-area settlements never got the news. Settlers there were caught unawares. The situation quickly escalated. In two days, 38 settlers were dead and several women were abducted, depopulating Dickinson County. Inkpaduta was never captured, and he died a natural death in Canada.

Views of distant wooded ridges become common downstream of the Redtail Habitat Area.

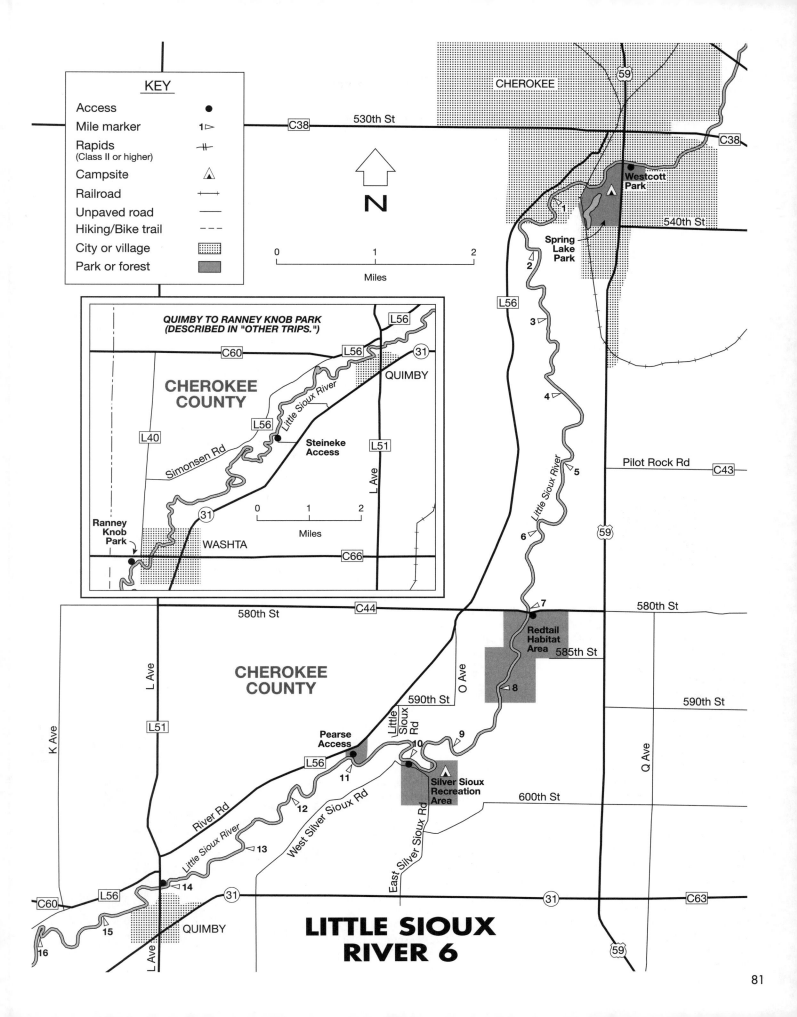

LITTLE SIOUX RIVER 7
Washta to Correctionville (12.8 Miles)

Near Washta, the Little Sioux River regains its exceedingly scenic character. For a brief stretch past the Washta Access, it speeds up through a succession of entertaining riffles as well. Nearing Iowa's loess hills (unfortunately all river routes through the loess hills have been channelized with levees built around their banks), the terrain becomes quite hilly with ridges up to 200 feet high, and the woods are dense with occasional views of prairie, pasture, or farmland. The section is a pleasant, quiet stream to paddle, where fishing is best for catfish.

There are excellent riverside **campgrounds** at both ends of this trip: at Ranney Knob Park and Little Sioux Park. The latter has all amenities.

Summer's Canoe Rental (712-372-4774) in Correctionville **rents kayaks and canoes** and runs shuttles.

The **shuttle route** (12.5 miles) from the put-in runs north on the park road, east on County C66, southwest on State Highway 31 through Correctionville, south on O'Brien Avenue, east through the Little Sioux Park entrance, and north to the takeout near the RV camping area.

For **water levels**, check the Little Sioux at Correctionville gauge (station 06606600) on the USGS Web site listed in the introduction. About 450 cfs is pleasant.

The **gradient** is less than 2 feet per mile.

Put in at the campground at Ranney Knob Park, just southwest of Washta. The river heads south along a pretty bluff with loess cliffs sloping down to the water. The scenic ridge tapers off, and as the river bends east from the park, banks become sparsely wooded. Bending right, the river has cut off a long oxbow still connected to the river. Bending right again, you pass agricultural and prairie lands until you reach a rocky bank at a low grassy ridge.

Winding into Ida County, you begin seeing graceful prairie hills on either side of the river on the outsides of bends. As the river curves right past the Washta Access, a quite spirited riffle splits around a small rock island, where snags can make for tricky turns. Two more riffles ensue, and the river widens flowing west past trees toward a distant ridge.

Bending south near the base of a pretty pasture savanna ridge, the river enters a swift, constricted area where dodging fallen trees can be a challenge. Heading southeast, you see a scenic ridge in the distance and paddle past a rock-lined bank and then a crop field.

You bend southwest, occasionally past crops, and serene savanna hills are visible on the right. Coming to a left bend, you pass beneath an abandoned railroad bridge toward a grassy hill. The next several bends tend to be quite snaggy, running past cottonwood, silver maple, and willow woods. As you reach a point near Highway 31, a scenic prairie ridge rises with red cedar thickets. Bending southwest, the river zigzags through more snags between lowland woods until straightening a bit, heading south past lightly wooded banks.

At a farmyard, the river heads westward, making small bends along the way and passing the Walling Access on the left. Beyond an abandoned railroad trestle bridge, you see a densely forested hill in the distance and bend left toward the County L36 bridge. A few hundred yards ahead, the river passes two small rocky islands and then narrows under the Highway 20 bridge. After a right bend, the river curves left near a 200-foot-high ridge heavily wooded with mature hardwoods.

Passing along Copeland Park, you come to the next river access underneath the Highway 31 bridge on the river-left. Leaving the ridges, the river passes through lowland woods heading generally south. After it takes a tiny horseshoe bend to the east, the river heads southwest. A quarter mile ahead, the **takeout**, at Little Sioux Park just south of Correctionville, is at a gravel access on the river-right.

Other trips. The Little Sioux continues to offer interesting paddling as far south as the County Bridge Access (see inset map). In the 8.4 miles from Little Sioux Park to Anthon's Stahl Park (which has a campground), the river very lazily meanders between some of the Little Sioux Valley's highest ridges, passing both heavy woods and long stretches of farmland. The 3.4-mile stretch from Stahl Park to County Bridge Access is perhaps a bit less scenic, but the river itself becomes the most challenging, dropping over a rocky substrate through a half mile of riffles and small rapids, with a tricky wave that may dump novice paddlers. Only those wishing to run the entire Inkpaduta Canoe Trail to its official end at Smithland would care to paddle the rest of the channelized river between corn and bean fields from County Bridge Access to Smithland.

Woods and sky over the Little Sioux.

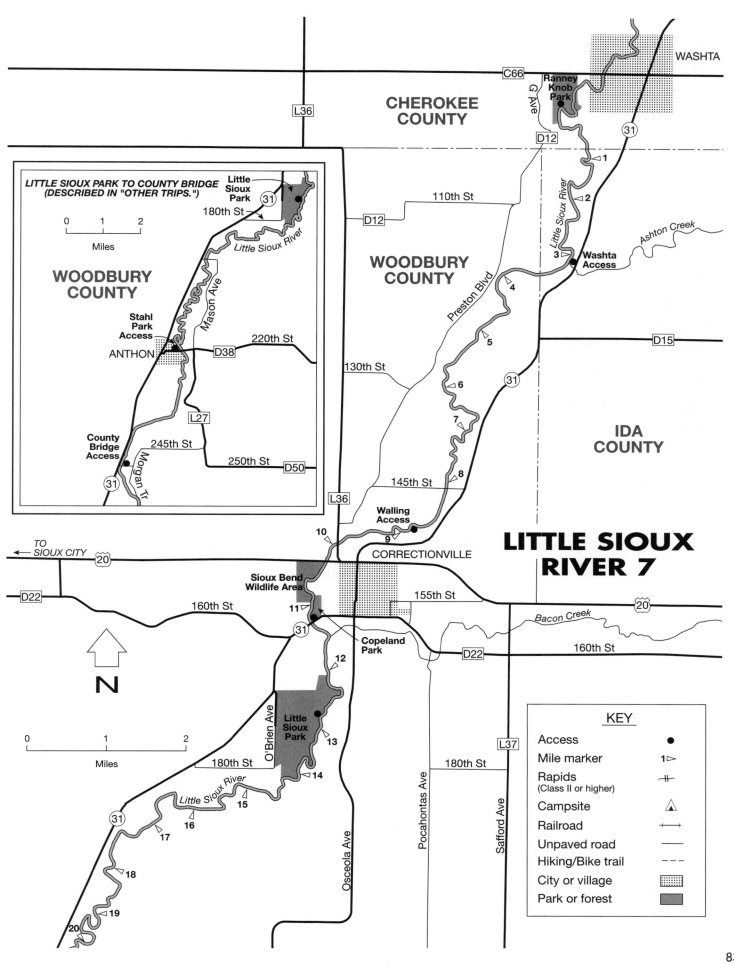

WASHTA

C66

CHEROKEE COUNTY

L36

G Ave

Ranney Knob Park

D12

31

1

2

110th St

D12

Little Sioux River

Ashton Creek

WOODBURY COUNTY

3

Washta Access

LITTLE SIOUX PARK TO COUNTY BRIDGE
(DESCRIBED IN "OTHER TRIPS.")

0   1   2
Miles

Little Sioux Park

31

180th St

Little Sioux River

WOODBURY COUNTY

Mason Ave

Stahl Park Access

ANTHON

D38

220th St

Preston Blvd

4

5

D15

130th St

6

IDA COUNTY

L27

7

County Bridge Access

245th St

250th St

D50

Morgan Tr

31

8

145th St

L36

Walling Access

10

9

CORRECTIONVILLE

LITTLE SIOUX RIVER 7

TO SIOUX CITY

20

D22

160th St

Sioux Bend Wildlife Area

11

31

155th St

Copeland Park

D22

Bacon Creek

20

160th St

N

0   1   2
Miles

O'Brien Ave

12

Little Sioux Park

13

Osceola Ave

Pocahontas Ave

180th St

L37

Safford Ave

180th St

14

Little Sioux River

15

16

31

17

18

19

20

KEY

Access   ●

Mile marker   1▷

Rapids
(Class II or higher)

Campsite   △

Railroad   +—+—+

Unpaved road   ————

Hiking/Bike trail   - - - -

City or village

Park or forest

83

LITTLE TURKEY RIVER

U Avenue to Neon Road (11 Miles)

This section begins not on the Little Turkey River but on Crane Creek. Starting on Crane (which averages 60 feet wide) adds an enchanting, swift 4.4 miles past impressive wooded bluffs with fragrant undergrowth of coniferous yew, numerous scenic rock formations, and a few sheer cliffs. The Little Turkey itself has somewhat fewer rock outcroppings, but it passes through delightfully serene landscapes past large boulders and birch-fringed bluffs. Taking out at Neon Road allows you to focus on the best scenery (see "Other trips"). Both streams run clear over a rock or sand bottom.

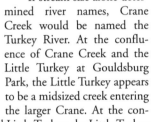

Crane Creek makes a delightful primer to a trip on the Little Turkey River.

If stream size alone determined river names, Crane Creek would be named the Turkey River. At the confluence of Crane Creek and the Little Turkey at Gouldsburg Park, the Little Turkey appears to be a midsized creek entering the larger Crane. At the confluence of the Turkey and Little Turkey, the Little Turkey is the larger river.

This is a somewhat adventurous trip, likely requiring portages around two (or more) fences and using bridge crossings for put-ins and takeouts. Some paddlers may prefer putting in below the fence at Gouldsburg Park and taking out at Eldorado (see "Other trips"). Fishing is best for smallmouth bass.

There are riverside **campgrounds** at Waucoma Park and Gouldsburg Park, and there is another campground overlooking the river valley at Goeken Park.

The **shuttle route** (9.7 miles) from the put-in runs south on U Avenue, east on 250th, north on County W14, and east and south on County B44; on Neon Road, the takeout is just past the bridge, on the right.

Estimate **water levels** by checking the Turkey River near Eldorado on the USGS Web site listed in the introduction. A combined level of 250 to 300 cfs is usually enough to run this section without much scraping, but if the Turkey River level is higher than normal, it can skew the reading.

The **gradient** is 5.7 feet per mile.

The **put-in**, about 4 miles southeast of Waucoma on Crane Creek, is upstream, river-right of the U Avenue bridge. The stream heads into woods, bending right at a small ridge through a riffle. As it curves north along a ridge, prominent limestone outcroppings appear. The river falls through a long riffle and bends south at a pretty limestone wall 200 yards long, perched with cedars.

At a 1-foot drop with an electrified wire across it, **portage** at the pasture on the right. The river then flows past a home; as it bends left along a wooded ridge, a long riffle leads north past refrigerator-sized boulders and midstream bedrock outcroppings. Bending right, the stream turns rapidly left into a riffle along a small undercut cliff.

At a sharp right turn, the stream continues through riffles into mixed woods and pasture. As you slow into a right bend, you see a beautiful and sheer limestone cliff up to 30 feet high topped with cedars and yew. You head south and then bend left along a high wooded bluff with thick yew undergrowth and mossy rocks; limestone outcroppings appear here and there. Bending east along pretty little rock walls, you reach the Spruce Road bridge, usable as an access on the river-left.

Past a cornfield, you run through riffles in a leftward loop. The stream bends right at a rising bank near a home. As it bends right through more riffles, woods and prairie line the banks. As you head northeast, Crane Creek is joined on the left by the Little Turkey.

You run through a long riffle, and numerous spots on grass banks work for taking out at Gouldsburg Park. At the park bridge in warm seasons, a barbed-wire fence crosses the river at the entrance to a riffle. You may want to **portage**.

Through a pasture, the Little Turkey parallels County W14 for a while. The banks become more wooded. A couple dozen junked cars line the left bank before the river passes under a bridge for the road. As the river bends right, the scenery changes for the better. A long riffle leads to the base of a wooded bluff with an elephant-sized limestone boulder at its base. Slowing and following along the bluff, the river bends left, picking up pace eastward toward a higher bluff on the left with pretty birch trees among hardwoods high above the valley. Heading southeast, the river bends left at a creek mouth into a 300-yard-long riffle, with mixed woods and prairie on ridges in the narrow valley.

A wooded ridge joins the left bank, and a small island divides a riffle. Curving right, the river drops over an 18-inch ledge. Bending left, you reach the Otter Road bridge. Heading east, you reach the base of a clay-banked bluff. At a left bend, you enter a long, spirited riffle to the base of a higher bluff on the right with a van-sized, slanting boulder at its base.

The setting is quite serene, as you bend through riffles heading generally north past more high ridges. At a right bend to the southeast along a lightly wooded ridge, you pass through a long riffle. After another right bend, two bridges appear, one abandoned and one new. **Take out** at the first bridge on the river-right, and carry up the grassy slope.

Other trips. The 5.7-mile trip from Neon Road to the Eldorado canoe access is pleasant with frequent riffles. In a widening valley, pastures become common as the river passes several riverside farms and few bluffs. The 6.3-mile stretch of the Little Turkey from Waucoma Park to Gouldsburg Park can also be paddled when water is plentiful. It's a swift run winding through low woodlands, pasture (watch for fences across the stream), and some cropland, with a gradient of 9.7 feet per mile. In the last mile approaching Crane Creek, scenic bluffs rise and surround the stream.

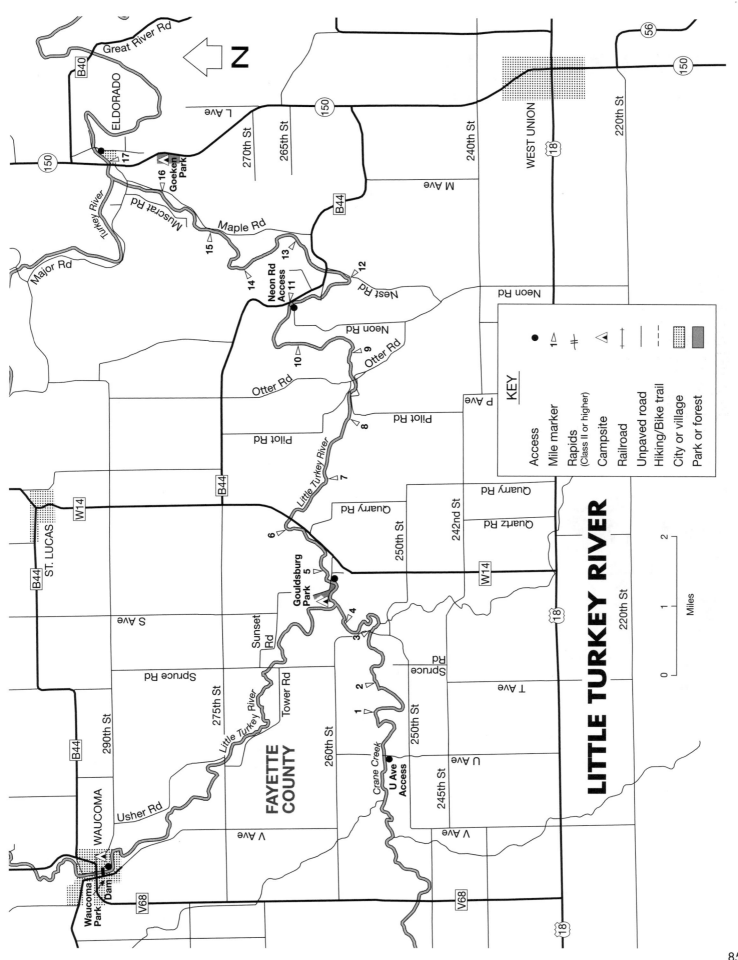

LITTLE TURKEY RIVER

LIZARD CREEK
County P29 to Fort Dodge (13.6 Miles)

Early settlers translated the native name of these swift and scenic waters as "River of the Lizards." The original name may actually have referred to salamanders, common here in the past. With a watershed comparable in size to northeast Iowa's Yellow River, you must likewise wait for rains to run it.

Born in Rush Lake and fed by marshes and drainage tiles in the plains between Pocahontas and Emmetsburg, the Lizard begins a meandering descent in Webster County to the Des Moines River over bedrock. Averaging 50 feet wide, the stream offers intimate paddling though an enchanting valley of woods and prairie, numerous riffles and small rapids, bedrock outcroppings, and scenic loess or clay cliffs. At the end moraine of the Clare Advance of the Wisconsin Glacier, abundant rocks and boulders jut from the streambed. Moderate flows usually translate into clarity of a mountain stream.

Close to a city, the banks remain largely undeveloped (a colossal exception being the gypsum mine near Fort Dodge). The last mile is a fun ride through a series of rock-garden rapids, mostly class I–II, not for novices because boat-handling skills are required to avoid the hazards described here. You may encounter fences across the stream

A boulder-strewn stream in a nicely wooded valley, Lizard Creek is simply a delight to paddle.

where it passes along private land. Smallmouth bass fishing can be good, and walleye are taken in the lower parts.

For **campgrounds**, see Des Moines River 1 and Des Moines River 2.

The **shuttle route** (11 miles) from the put-in runs south on County P29, about 2 miles south of the town of Clare, and east on State Highway 7 into Fort Dodge, where it turns into Hawkeye Avenue curving southeast. Just before the Des Moines River Bridge, turn right onto Second Street and head south over Lizard Creek. The takeout is on the Des Moines River under the railroad tracks at the entrance to Phinney Park.

For **water levels**, see the Lizard Creek gauge (station FLZI4) on the Army Corps of Engineers Web site listed in the introduction. Five feet is the minimum for decent paddling. Readings can be skewed by flows from the South Branch below the gauge. Usually, rapids are most enjoyable between 5.5 and 6 feet. AT 7 FEET, THE WAVES BECOME UNORGANIZED, PUSHY, AND UNPREDICTABLE.

The **gradient** is 7.2 feet per mile.

After the **put-in** downstream-left of the southernmost County P29 bridge, Lizard Creek bends right along a rock wall and homes, with several riffles leading southward over a rocky streambed. Soon, a high bluff with red-tinted sand forces the river left. Some rock outcroppings appear following the bluff northeast. Briefly slowing, the stream then drops over two small ledges and a 2-foot ledge. The rest of the way to the Hayes Avenue bridge is swift, with hardwoods lining both banks.

Beyond the bridge, you veer sharply north past a pretty loess bluff and boulders. Bending right, the stream courses east into a long stretch of pasture (watch for fences) where the stream is boulder-strewn in near-continuous riffles for more than a quarter mile. Just upstream from a railroad bridge, watch for a potentially dangerous fence in fast water.

Eastward, banks grow lightly wooded. Slowing into a northwest bend toward a loess bluff, the creek then quickens while circling southeast and then south through woods with large glacial-erratic boulders midstream. At an elephant-sized boulder, the stream heads toward a sandy prairie slope.

The woods thin, the current slows, and the valley widens. Bending south toward a high, loess bluff, the stream picks up speed. At a right bend it heads toward another loess bluff. Past concrete chunks on a bluff and rows of crops, the stream drops through chutes around a small island. Hooking left, you arrive at the P41 bridge, the last convenient **takeout** before committing to the final, more challenging section.

Heading generally east and then south, the stream meanders between high clay and loess bluffs, dropping over a ford. Rocks and boulders continue protruding from the streambed. Homes are sometimes visible atop the bluffs. A sharp westward bend brings you to the base of a bluff with bedrock exposures.

As you pass beneath Highway 7, the current slows. Railroad tracks are seen ahead, and South Branch Lizard Creek enters. A long riffle begins past mounds of crushed gypsum at a mine, and you pass beneath the mine's bridge. As the river bends slightly right, riffles begin. The stream curves left and constricts into short Gypsum Mine Rapids (class I–II), best run straight through the center. Stay right at the island, and keep right to avoid pinning on the Highway 169 bridge pylon on the river-left. Beyond the bridge, pretty limestone walls line the creek.

Approaching railroad tracks, the stream bends left into a 200-yard-long set of class I–II boulder garden rapids. At the right bend just downstream of the rapids, stay right of the sometimes-dangerous hydraulics at the remains of a low-head dam on the left half of the channel. A short class I rapids follows, and the river slows past more low limestone cliffs to its mouth. **Take out** 125 yards downstream on the Des Moines River beneath the railroad bridge, on the river-right.

Other trips. You can also put in farther north on County P29, but homes are more frequent. There's a 2.5-foot ledge upstream of the last County P29 bridge. South Branch Lizard Creek is also scenic, with numerous riffles, although several fences across the creek and more agricultural views detract somewhat from the experience. Put in either at Hayes Avenue south of County D22 or at the D22 bridge just west of Fort Dodge for the quickest access to the mile of rapids described here.

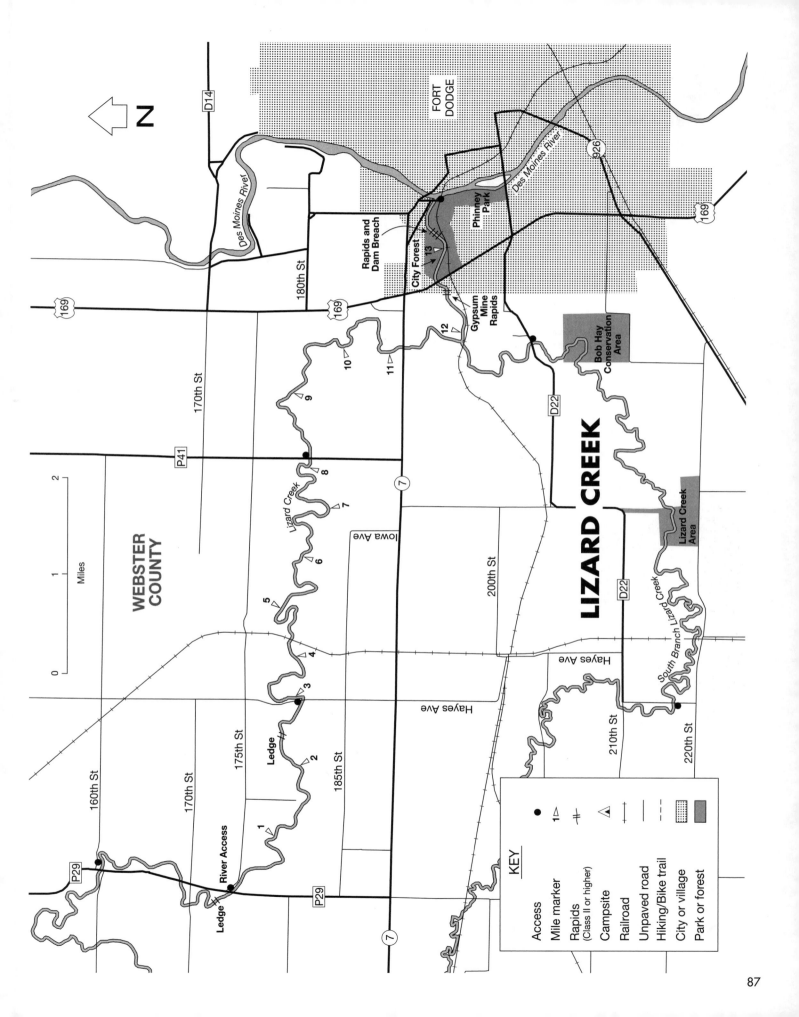

MAQUOKETA RIVER 1 AND 2

Delhi to Hopkinton (9.3 Miles)
Hopkinton to Monticello (11.1 Miles)

The Maquoketa River is a great paddling river. At moderate levels it runs clear over an undulating, scalloped, sand bottom with gentle waters just deep enough to cruise a canoe or kayak. The river also passes numerous scenic bluffs, the most impressive of which you'll find along the Maquoketa River 3 and 4 segments. The two sections described here are the river less paddled, each beginning with very isolated, narrow, deeply wooded and rocky valleys and ending with long stretches of low, wooded banks.

Delaware County recently altered the dams on both river channels at the County D47 bridges at Hopkinton, under construction at press time. The smaller left channel now has rock-dam riffle, expected normally to have too little water to run. On the main right channel, at the Dunlap Park access, the original low-head dam was lowered in the center, and boulders were added downstream of it. The danger of running it is unknown; assume it's unsafe. A portage trail was added, which paddlers are advised to take.

Heavy rains usually muddy the waters for a few days. For 4.5 miles below Lake Delhi Dam, the river is a catch-and-release smallmouth bass fishery. Bass and catfish are common throughout the river.

The Retz Wildlife Area access has excellent **campsites** for primitive river camping. Privately run, riverside Walnut Acres Campground (319-465-4665), north of Monticello on Highway 38 has full amenities and cabin rentals. Backbone State Park has a campground with full amenities, as well as cabin rentals, on Backbone Lake (563-933-4225).

The **shuttle route** (9.1 miles) for section 1 from the put-in at Lake Delhi Dam runs south on County X31 and east on County D47 to the Dunlap Park access at Hopkinton.

For section 2, from the put-in, head northeast on County D47, east and south on Highway 38, and southeast on River Road, continuing across U.S. Highway 151 to the takeout above Mon-Maq Dam (10.5 miles).

Water levels can be approximated by checking the Maquoketa River at Manchester gauge (station 05416900) on the USGS Web site listed in the introduction. There is usually only occasional scraping in riffles at levels as low as 100 cfs.

The overall **gradient** for both sections is 3.2 feet per mile.

At the **put-in**, downstream-left of the Lake Delhi Dam, the river runs in a small canyon at the bottom of a 200-foot valley. Heading east, you turn south at a high, wooded bluff along a boulder-lined bank. Continuing southward, you reach another wooded bluff and bend east, running through several riffles in the secluded valley. As you bend right, the woods thin to meadow on the right. The river approaches another wooded bluff, curving left. Bend-

ing right again, where a line of riprap ends on the river-left, you'll find the Retz campsites above the dirt access.

You bend right along one wooded bluff toward another and turn south. Scenic limestone faces are exposed in vertical shafts jutting from the trees. The valley is quite narrow again, and straight ahead a 200-foot bluff looms, diverting the river left. As you course northeast, another timbered bluff rises on the left. As you head east through riffles, the ridges recede, and you curve south toward the bridge at Pioneer Road and the Pioneer Road access, a possible takeout.

The landscape changes considerably as the valley widens as you head south to the next bridge. The riverbed changes to a mix of sand and gravel. You join and rejoin a small ridge on the wooded left, and on the right bank you'll see a mix of pastures, farms, crops, wildflowers, and distant ridges. Past the 295th Street bridge, the stream enters a deeply wooded lowland area. After several bends, the river splits into two channels that don't rejoin for nearly a mile. Take the right channel—if you don't you will miss the **takeout** for section 1 at the Dunlap Park access.

For the next segment, from Hopkinton head southwest past a home; the river then bends left at a wooded bluff with limestone outcroppings and rock-lined banks. Bluffs on either side draw near the banks. Bending right, you reach a high, sloping, wooded ridge with mossy boulders on the right bank at Hardscrabble Park. Heading south, the river remains hemmed in by wooded and pastured ridgelines over glassy water.

You bend left at a rocky 150-foot ridge, and the deep woods and narrow valley continue. At a right bend along another high ridge, the bluffs taper off and the river enters a section of maple-dominated woods. As you enter Jones County, clearings reveal farmland between lines of trees, and then you reach a rocky ridge that diverts the river left. Heading south, the river bends along lines of riprap ending at an A-frame house. Bending left, you reach a limestone outcropping with a few mobile homes atop it; bend right, and continue southeast along tree-lined banks.

Silver Creek enters from the right. In a lowland plain, the river is lined by woods and willow shrubs near sandbars through several bends. Bending east to the Highway 38 bridge, the river continues into woods near Monticello, becoming sluggish behind the Mon-Maq Dam. The channel divides around a large island, rejoins, and passes beneath the Highway 151 bridge. **Take out** 50 yards upstream of the dam on the river-left. If you are continuing on, **portage** 100 yards on the left.

Other trips. Upriver, the short, 2-mile trip from the dam at Backbone State Park to the Dundee Access (on 3rd Street in town) is very sweet, past scenic little bluffs with numerous limestone outcroppings and riffles over a rocky streambed. Look for a bare minimum of 75 cfs on the Manchester gauge.

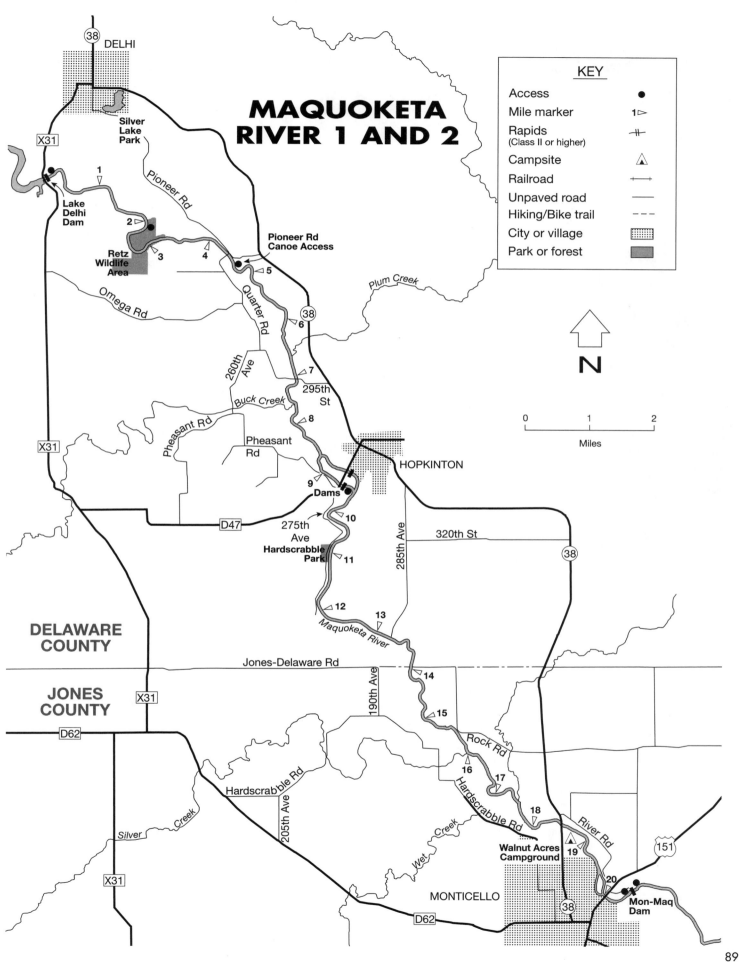

MAQUOKETA RIVER 1 AND 2

KEY

Access   •

Mile marker   1▷

Rapids   ╫
(Class II or higher)

Campsite   ⛺

Railroad   +—+—+

Unpaved road   ———

Hiking/Bike trail   - - -

City or village

Park or forest

N

0   1   2

Miles

DELHI

Silver Lake Park

Lake Delhi Dam

Pioneer Rd

Retz Wildlife Area

Omega Rd

Pioneer Rd Canoe Access

Quarter Rd

Plum Creek

260th Ave

Buck Creek

295th St

Pheasant Rd

Pheasant Rd

Dams

HOPKINTON

275th Ave

Hardscrabble Park

285th Ave

320th St

DELAWARE COUNTY

JONES COUNTY

Maquoketa River

Jones-Delaware Rd

190th Ave

Rock Rd

Hardscrabble Rd

205th Ave

Silver Creek

Wet Creek

River Rd

Walnut Acres Campground

MONTICELLO

Mon-Maq Dam

89

MAQUOKETA RIVER 3
Monticello to Highway 136 (20.3 Miles)

This section and Maquoketa River 4 are high on the list of Iowa's finest trips. Why? The scenery is superb, with long stretches of narrow valley between thickly wooded bluffs and numerous rock exposures. In fact, all the trees cloister the valley's rugged reality. Its jagged rock outcroppings often are not visible, obscured by a dense canopy of leaves. Rock climbers know better, regularly scaling rigid limestone walls of the Pictured Rocks and Indian Bluffs wildlife areas. The river also passes some rather dull agricultural areas, worth paddling through to reach the good stuff.

This trip is paddled more often than the next section, probably due to its proximity to Dubuque and Cedar Rapids. With 2,000 acres of public lands snaking along the banks, in many places, you can land to explore beneath the woods. This long section can be split up into a weekend excursion with an easy day of paddling (7 miles), an overnight stay at the Pictured Rocks campground, and then a second day continuing on to Highway 136 (11 miles). There are a few rocky riffles, but more often the river is a languid stream. Fishing is best for smallmouth bass and walleye.

There is a primitive, wooded, riverside **campground** at the Pictured Rocks Access, with no drinking water, as well as riverside campsites at the Indian Bluffs Wildlife Area. (Also see Maquoketa River 1 and 2.)

Appleby Canoe Rentals (319-465-3697) near the put-in **rents canoes** and runs shuttles, as does Bickford Canoe Rental (563-652-5855) in Canton.

The **shuttle route** (13.5 miles) from the put-in at Monticello runs west on River Road, southwest on U.S. Highway 151, southeast on Highway 38, east on County E17, and north on Highway 136 to the takeout across the river bridge on the west side of the road.

Water levels can be approximated by checking the Maquoketa River at Manchester gauge (station 05416900) on the USGS Web site listed in the introduction. About 150 cfs is usually pleasant.

The **gradient** is 2.3 feet per mile.

Put in on a sandbar downstream-left from the Mon-Maq Dam. After a right bend, you pass beneath the new Highway 151 bridge—in the first phase of construction at press time—and past it on the right is a limestone outcropping. As the river bends right again, a pretty cliff with a cave at its base comes into view. As you head southeast, wooded ridges line the valley and then taper off. The river bends left into a long section heading generally east, and the banks are low with numerous clearings, with views of hillside cornfields and farmhouses for almost two miles.

You bend south along a timbered ridge with rocks and boulders beside the bank, and the view changes, gradually becoming wilder. A home on the left is just visible, set back in the woods. The valley narrows. Limestone cliffs poke through woods, and you bend left 90 degrees. Scenic, heavily timbered bluffs exchange sides with each bend for the next 6 miles. Curve northeast along a wooded bluff, and at the bend right, you see how this area, called Picture Rocks, got its name: dramatic 150-foot bluffs with high, sheer limestone faces appear ahead. Curving right along the bluffs, you bend left and the river widens, flowing swiftly around a sandy island with a backdrop of bluffs.

As you head south, bluffs on both sides draw into a wooded gorge, with rugged rock outcroppings sporadically poking out through the trees. At the Pictured Rocks Access and campground on the river-right, the bluffs are a bit lower, but still quite rugged. Passing through a riffle and then a private camp on the right, the river joins a high bluff on the right and bends left along it, circling north through a wide riffle.

The setting remains isolated, with bluffs near both banks; you curve right until you're heading south. At the point you begin heading north, a 20-foot mossy limestone cliff at the base of a forested ridge joins the right bank. Passing cottage-sized boulders, you curve north. At the next right bend are tortured-looking rock outcroppings near the riverbank. The bluff recedes from the river as you head generally east along sandy banks. On the left bank near a gully is the Indian Bluffs canoe access. A few hundred yards downstream near old bridge pylons (once Dales Ford) are primitive riverside campsites on the river-left.

At the next southward bend, a small, rocky ridge joins the left bank. Bending left, to the east, you paddle along another rocky slope. Follow it south, and the bluff recedes, heading into lowland woods. Curving west and then gradually bending right to a ridge, you see abandoned Eby's Mill Bridge near a luxurious log home. At a second bridge, the river bends south toward a rocky ridge before heading straight east where it widens. Limestone outcroppings become smaller and less common. The river flows southeast through lowland woods into a long horseshoe bend. As you head back north, wooded hills appear in the distance above croplands and cut banks.

Bending east, you see one last high bluff with an impressive limestone face rising on the river-left. After looping north and circling in a rightward bend, you bend left to the **takeout** in the sandy area on the river-left, just upstream of the Highway 136 bridge.

Three Bears

Before pioneer settlers extirpated them in the late 1800s, the heavily forested and cave-riddled Maquoketa Valley was prime black bear habitat. Native American hunters sometimes captured hibernating bears, and they were abundant enough here that they gave the river their name for black bear, Maquoketa ("muh-KO-ket-uh"). Bear sightings began increasing in northeast Iowa in the 1990s. Likely, they've been wandering down from Minnesota just for visits—not to stay permanently.

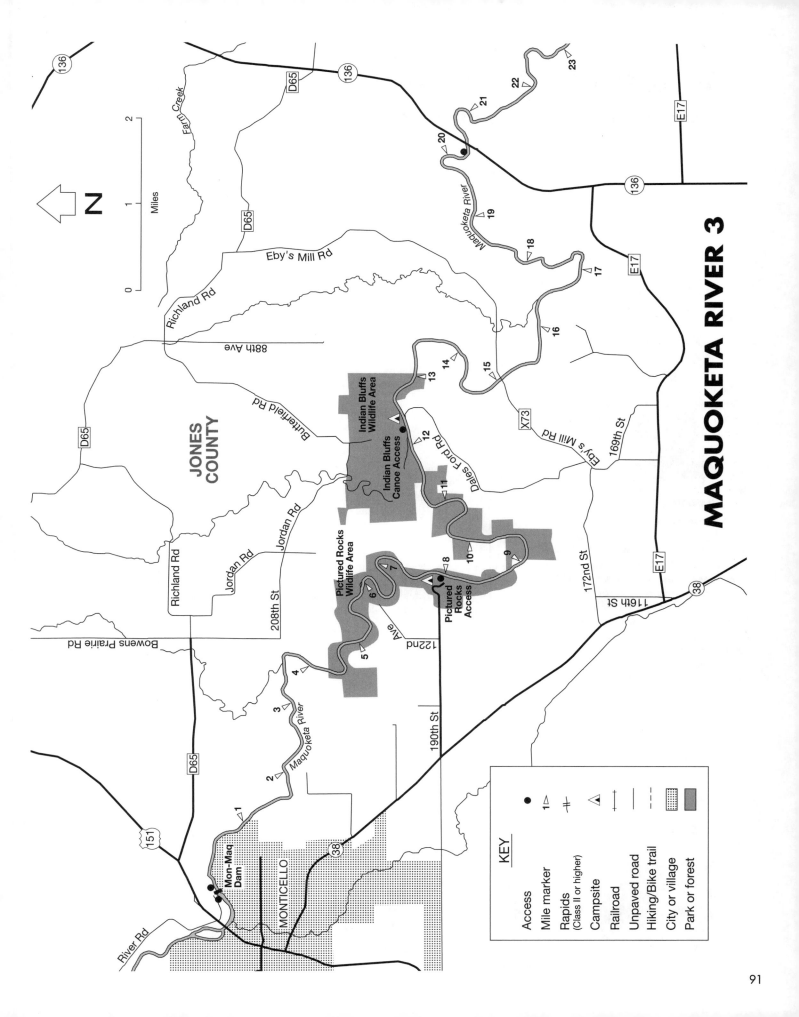

MAQUOKETA RIVER 3

KEY

- ● Access
- △ 1 Mile marker
- ⚑ Rapids (Class II or higher)
- ◮ Campsite
- Railroad
- Unpaved road
- Hiking/Bike trail
- City or village
- Park or forest

N

Miles
0 1 2

JONES COUNTY

MONTICELLO

Mon-Mac Dam

Maquoketa River

Indian Bluffs Wildlife Area

Indian Bluffs Canoe Access

Pictured Rocks Wildlife Area

Pictured Rocks Access

MAQUOKETA RIVER 4
Supples Bridge to Royertown Access (14.4 Miles)

For both dramatic scenery and wildness, this stretch of the Maquoketa is hard to beat. Averaging 120 feet wide, the river passes along high cliffs and through deeply wooded areas, and the agricultural stretches aren't as long as those in Maquoketa River 3. Fishing in the deeper holes remains good for smallmouth bass, walleye, and catfish.

Buzzard Ridge has primitive sites for river **camping**. Maquoketa Caves State Park has a campground with full amenities and great hiking trails. Joinerville Park (see "Other trips") also has a primitive campground.

Canoe rentals and shuttles are available from Bickford Canoe Rental (563-652-5855) in Canton.

The **shuttle route** (10.7 miles) from the put-in at Supples Bridge runs south on Temple Hill Road, east on County E17, and south on County Y34 to the Royertown Access.

Water levels can be approximated by checking the Maquoketa River near Maquoketa gauge (station 05418500) on the USGS Web site listed in the introduction and subtracting the reading for North Fork Maquoketa Near Fulton (station 05418400). A net reading of 300 cfs usually makes for pleasant paddling.

The **gradient** is 2.5 feet per mile.

At the **put-in**, downstream-right from Supples Bridge, you can see wooded bluffs ahead in the distance. The river flows past farmland, approaching a heavily wooded bluff, where you divert northeast past more cropland. Reaching another ridge on the north side of the valley, you bend right, and higher ridges ahead converge on the river.

Boulders and limestone outcroppings appear on the left bank. After an old bridge abutment, you pass a pasture on the left as a steep wooded bluff rises on the right. Ahead, Farm Creek enters via a scenic, wooded hollow. Vertical outcrops of limestone begin appearing, often obscured by trees in the heavily wooded, hemmed-in valley. Bending right, to the south, you head toward a much higher, dramatic 140-foot-high cliff with a cave high above the water.

As you bend back north, smaller cliffs continue, and then the bluffs slope to the river as you head east.

Pastures appear occasionally, and you pass a small settlement. Ahead on a high, wooded ridge, a log home overlooks the valley.

After you take a right bend and cross under County E17, you reach the Canton Access, privately owned (by the owners of the Longbranch Tavern just up the hill) but usually open for use. Past a stone bridge abutment on the left, you pass the Canton Church, a quaint chapel built of limestone in 1877. Curving southwest, the river begins running along a limestone wall and cuts east, away from 15th Avenue, running along blocks of limestone up to 30 feet high. A wooded ridge joins the right bank, and the river bends slightly left toward a high bluff, cedar-topped with sheer rock exposures. You bend right at its base, and straight ahead is another high bluff crowned with limestone cliffs pockmarked with caves. You bend right again and head toward the base of a high, wooded bluff to the southwest, and the river diverts 120 degrees left at its base. On the inside of this bend on the left, you'll notice a sign for the Buzzard Ridge Wildlife Area, where just up the bank is a flat area good for camping.

Heading east toward another high bluff with limestone cliffs, you bend right into a horseshoe bend to the south with beautiful rock outcroppings set back in the woods all along. The river curves along a bluff back north, and one rock outcropping resembles the remains of a stone citadel. You bend back to the right, and tall sycamore trees begin appearing among other hardwoods in the thick woods.

As you head straight south for a long stretch, you can see cliffs set back from the bank past tree trunks for half a mile. The river bends left, and Mineral Creek enters from the right. Ahead, you paddle toward 50-foot cliffs across from a pasture and bend right toward the Millertown Bridge, with access upstream on the river-right. Past it, a rocky slope on the right becomes heavily wooded again, and you curve north. As the river bends right, a cedar-topped cliff rises straight from the water at the Pine Valley Nature Area, and you head southeast past continued rock outcroppings. Remaining deeply wooded, with wooded bluffs and smaller rock outcroppings along outside bends, the river bends through a horseshoe to the north. At a left bend, the **takeout** is on the sandbar at the river-left, upstream from the Royertown Bridge.

Other trips. For a multiday trip linking Maquoketa River 3 with this one, the 2.9 miles between them passes along a couple of wooded ridges but mostly agricultural plains. The 7-mile trip from the Royertown Access to a boat ramp at Joinerville Park (east of Baldwin on Highway 64 and north on 123rd Avenue) is also pleasant, still passing along frequent rock outcroppings, although you'll see more development and pastures. Below Joinerville, the river slows behind a tall dam at Maquoketa. From there it passes perhaps the most scenic mile on the entire river, with incredibly rugged cliffs. When you reach a members-only camping area, paddle back up to Joinerville—the rest isn't worth a difficult portage at the dam (on the river-left).

Frontier Justice

The cave-strewn Maquoketa Valley wasn't just good for bears. A group of horse thieves, counterfeiters, and murderers called the Brown Gang used the numerous caves as hideouts. Jackson County was known as a lawless place where anything could happen. In 1840, law-abiding citizens had enough. They formed a posse and went after the outlaws. Shootouts ensued, and several people were killed. Law and order won the day, and 13 captured survivors were flogged and sent down the Mississippi, warned never to return.

Bluffs high above the Maquoketa upstream of Canton makes for quite a view.

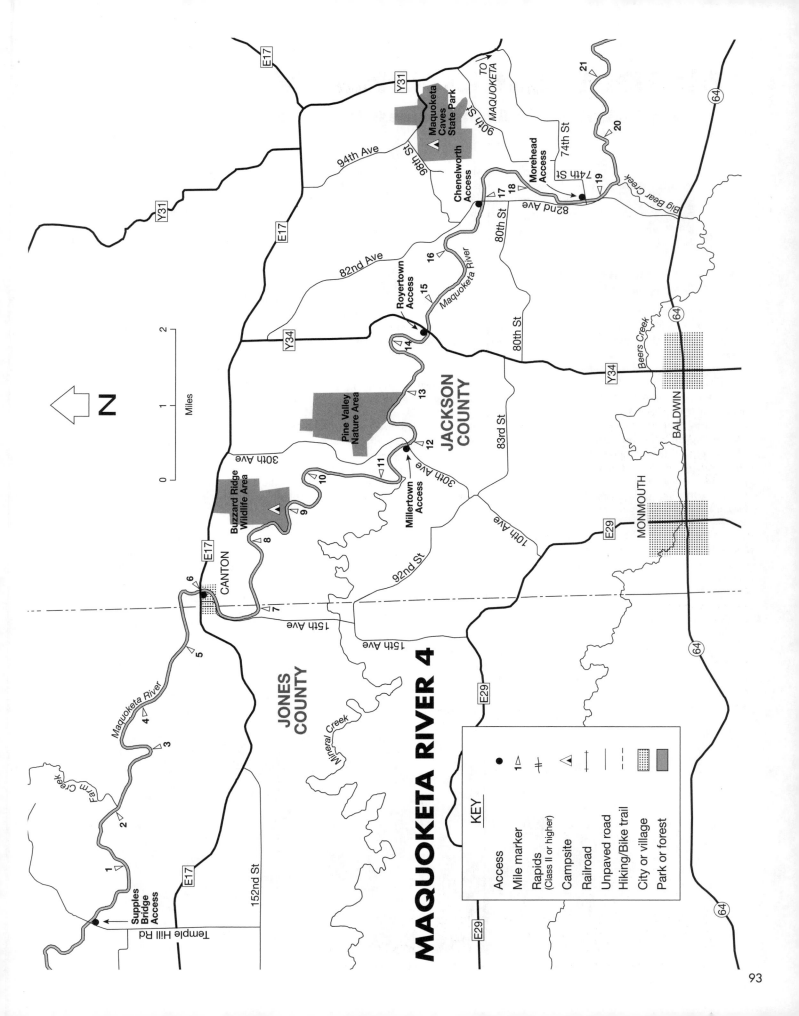

MAQUOKETA RIVER 4

N

Miles

MIDDLE RACCOON RIVER 1
Coon Rapids to Fig Avenue Access (5.8 Miles)

Is That *Glastnost* or "*Garst-nost*"?

Roswell Garst was a fascinating man who attended three colleges without getting a single degree but became wealthy by building a seed company from scratch. Despite that decidedly capitalist success, Soviet Union premier Nikita Khrushchev actually accepted an invitation from Garst to visit his farm. Khrushchev arrived in 1959. The *Des Moines Register* estimated 600 members of the press from around the world showed up with him. The visit was a prominent event in a series that led to "trade butter, not guns" diplomacy between the cold war superpowers.

A short run on a small stream averaging 50 feet wide, this section encompasses a gamut of scenery: pretty woodland hills through the town of Coon Rapids, a couple miles along deep-cut banks through agricultural territory, and finally, two sublime miles through the narrow and forested Whiterock Valley with enchanting sandstone cliffs and outcroppings.

It's hard to speak of this section without mentioning the Garst family and its colorful history that began well before it built a hybrid seed empire that helped fuel the Midwest's agricultural productivity. The grandchildren of the seed company's founder own 4,500 acres south of Coon Rapids surrounding the river, and the Garsts have begun to lovingly care for their lands where agriculture has taken its toll, restoring wetlands in plains near the river and prairie in the uplands. They've embraced ecotourism, opening homes as bed and breakfasts and allowing guests to roam their grounds on mountain bike, horseback, or foot (for a fee). The takeout, open to the public, is on their land.

Fishing is primarily for smallmouth bass.

Riverside **campgrounds** are at both the beginning and end of this trip at Riverside Park and at Garst Farm Resorts (phone number below), which also rents out a primitive, remote cabin accessible only by hike-in, all-terrain vehicle, or canoe.

Canoe and kayak rentals and shuttles are available from Garst Farm Resorts (712-684-2964).

The **shuttle route** (5.2 miles) from the put-in at Riverside Park runs southwest on Riverside Drive, west on State Street, south on 5th Avenue, southeast on State Highway 141, and south on Fig Avenue to the takeout at the Garst Farm Resorts campground.

For **water level**, check the Middle Raccoon near Bayard gauge (station 05483450) on the USGS Web site listed in the introduction. The river can be run without much scraping down to 125 cfs.

The **gradient** is 3.4 feet per mile.

Put in below the pedestrian bridge and small rapids in Riverside Park on a sandbar across from a polished-looking sandstone wall. Tree limbs hang out over the river as you approach a concrete bridge and run through a riffle. Past the next bridge, the river constricts to just 30 feet wide and falls through a riffle with a few midstream boulders.

Unfortunately, at one spot, discarded building materials and other junk cascades down a hill on the right, but then the river winds through mostly serene areas before bending right under a railroad bridge. Then the river takes a small drop. The line of trees thins along cut banks topped with grass. Riprap lines the banks to Highway 141, and the next several bends wind through cut banks and fewer riffles through an agricultural area.

After you pass under a rusting, abandoned trestle bridge, a pastured hill rises with a large home visible atop the ridge. Gradually, hills become closer on both sides to the riverbanks, and rounding a left bend you see a craggy sandstone cliff rising right from the river, where the river's character thoroughly alters. Woodlands of hardwoods interspersed with cedars cover the valley slopes, and at a left bend smaller cliffs join the bank. Just downstream, a line of prominent, low sandstone cliffs rises along the left, and the river curves to the right along them. On the right, you'll notice a mailbox on the river, where the Garsts' rental cabin is just up the bank.

The cliff ends, but the pretty valley continues with denser woods. You can see a barn and home ahead on the left, and a 200-yard-long riffle follows. Past the Fig Avenue bridge, the river bends left at a 180-foot bluff with a cliff that is the Midwest's tallest outcropping of Cretaceous Dakoka sandstone, which formed when dinosaurs roamed. The **takeout** is right across from it on the river-left.

The Cretaceous Dakota sandstone cliffs along the Middle Raccoon after a recent dusting of snow.

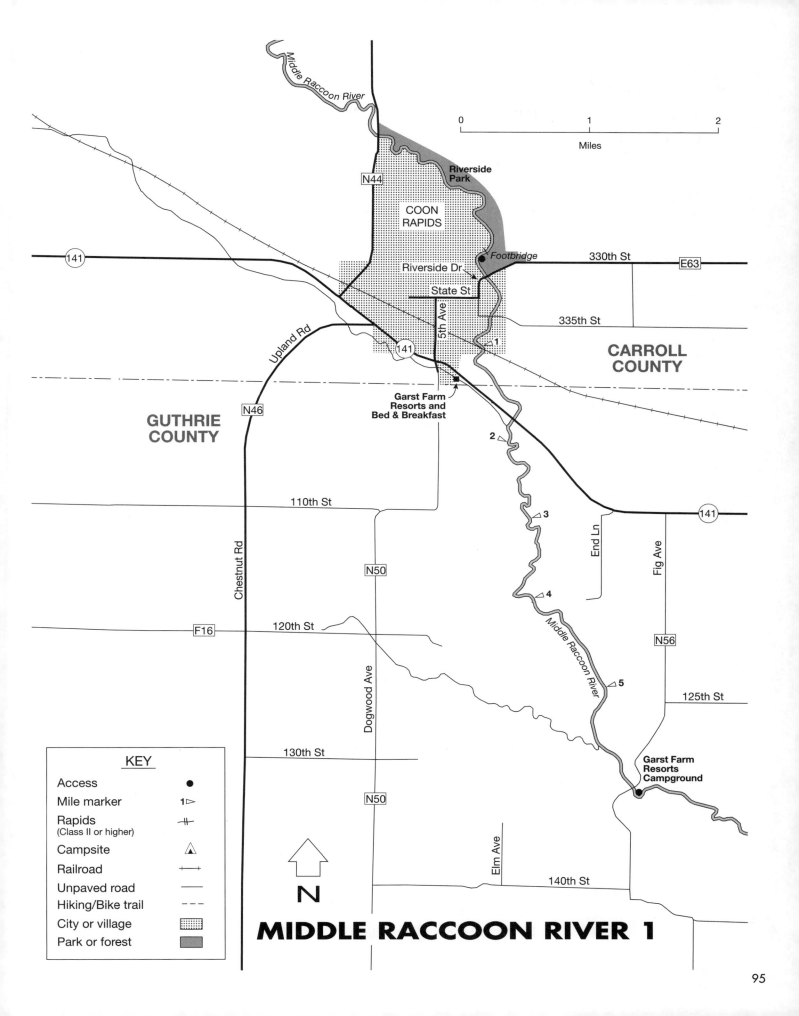

MIDDLE RACCOON RIVER 1

KEY

Access	●
Mile marker	1▷
Rapids (Class II or higher)	╫
Campsite	▲
Railroad	┼┼
Unpaved road	——
Hiking/Bike trail	- - -
City or village	▦
Park or forest	▓

N

MIDDLE RACCOON RIVER 2 AND 3

Panora to Cowles Access (7.8 Miles)
Cowles Access to Redfield (7.4 Miles)

Improbable and unrelated factors went into making one of central Iowa's most superb paddling stretches. First, the Wisconsin Glacier's Des Moines Lobe extended to its southernmost point here, depositing at its terminus "glacial-erratic" rocks and boulders more characteristic of Canada than the Corn Belt. After 10,000 years passed, some relative newcomers—state and county officials—had the foresight to establish public lands throughout much of the Middle Raccoon Valley, and they eventually granted it the ceremonial "Protected Water Area" designation. Also, in the 1970s, a tall dam was constructed for a lakeside real estate development just northwest of Panora. Lake Panorama now acts as a silt filter, with sediment falling to the lake bottom.

The result is a lengthy clear-water stream that courses around hundreds of sheep-sized boulders and rocky isles, over gurgling riffles, and through remote-feeling woods rich with wildlife. Hooting owls, screeching hawks, and chattering woodpeckers provide familiar background noises.

Without all that, the Middle Raccoon River would still be an entertaining stream. Long riffles and small rapids thrust boats from pool to pool. Some of these can be challenging at high-water levels. The Racccoon River Valley Nature Trail is good for running bike shuttles. Fishing is best for smallmouth bass.

One riverside **campground** is available at Lennon Mill Park, across the river from the access.

Canoe and kayak rentals and shuttles are available from Raccoon River Retreats (515-833-2636) in Redfield.

The **shuttle route** (8.3 miles) from the put-in for the first segment in Panora runs east on South Street, north on 3rd Street, east on State Highway 44, and south toward Linden on County P30, a blacktop road that changes to gravel and its name to Amarillo Avenue south of town on the way to the takeout.

For the second section, head west on 268th Street, south on County P28, and east on County F59 to the takeout across the Middle Raccoon River (8.5 miles).

For **water level**, check the Middle Raccoon River at Panora gauge (station 5483600) on the USGS Web site listed in the introduction. About 400 cfs is a pleasant level.

The **gradient** for both sections is 3.9 feet per mile.

Put in well downstream of Panora's dangerous Lenon Mill Dam. Around the first bend where the river turns east, anglers are often seen casting for smallmouth bass. The bass fishery is catch-and-release. Running through the first of dozens of riffles, the river bends right.

The river takes a southward path past midstream boulders. Sandbars and lightly wooded hills line the earthen banks and are followed by a savanna hill on the left. At a sharp left bend, the river is swift and may require turns around snags.

Beyond the P28 bridge, the river slows past oak, ash, and maple slopes with cedar-topped ridges. A sharp bend left followed by a hard right culminates in back-to-back riffles and a small rapids. Then the river widens and winds more lazily, with shoals that can impede progress at lower levels.

Just upstream of the next bridge is the Middle Raccoon River Access at a riffle on the left. The first real bluffs appear in the next stretch, with thin soil and scrubby vegetation lightly veiling sandstone protrusions. The bluffs give way to dense woods at the Marlowe Ray Wildlife Area on the right, and there are few riffles until the channel narrows and the current quickens through steady chop that lasts about a quarter mile, edging along a sandbar to the right.

Passing an old bridge abutment, the river flows by a log home. Further along, river-left, is another home with an open shelter and stairs leading down to a small dock. It may appear that either channel around the island downstream is passable, but in low water, keep tight against the earthen bank river-left for the faster, deeper water. The **takeout** at the Cowles boat ramp is just upstream-right from the bridge at 268th Street.

The next section begins with one of the prettiest areas on the entire river. The valley widens briefly into a meadow, as the river courses through a feisty riffle with choppy waves. Then it rushes straight toward a 40-foot limestone bluff. The current veers sharply right at the bluff's base into a narrow channel through a short rapids, and then it slows down somewhat entering a narrow, wooded valley.

After a few more wooded bends, you pass beneath the bridge at Amarillo Avenue, entering a short horseshoe bend with a scenic wooded bluff where, after a rain, you may see small waterfalls. To the south on the right is the concrete boat ramp at the Middle Raccoon Protected Water Area.

As the river heads southeast along a ridge, the valley widens and the river flows by banks topped with willows and grasses and through several riffles. Then a wooded bluff joins the left bank, routing the river south into entertaining bendlets swift with riffles. After a left bend, the channel makes a riffly split around a sandbar, and then a grassy hill becomes visible ahead and to the right. Soon the river arrives at the base of a sandy hill on the left and then bends right, to a forested hill; the water becomes swift again going through a series of riffles and passing one huge boulder. After slowing briefly, the pace quickens again as the river passes a shale outcropping on the left back.

Mosquito Creek enters from the left, and the river heads generally south, slowing behind the Redfield Dam. **Take out** 50 yards upstream of the dam on the river-left.

(See South Raccoon River 2 for a segment of the Middle Raccoon that begins at Redfield and continues into the South Raccoon.)

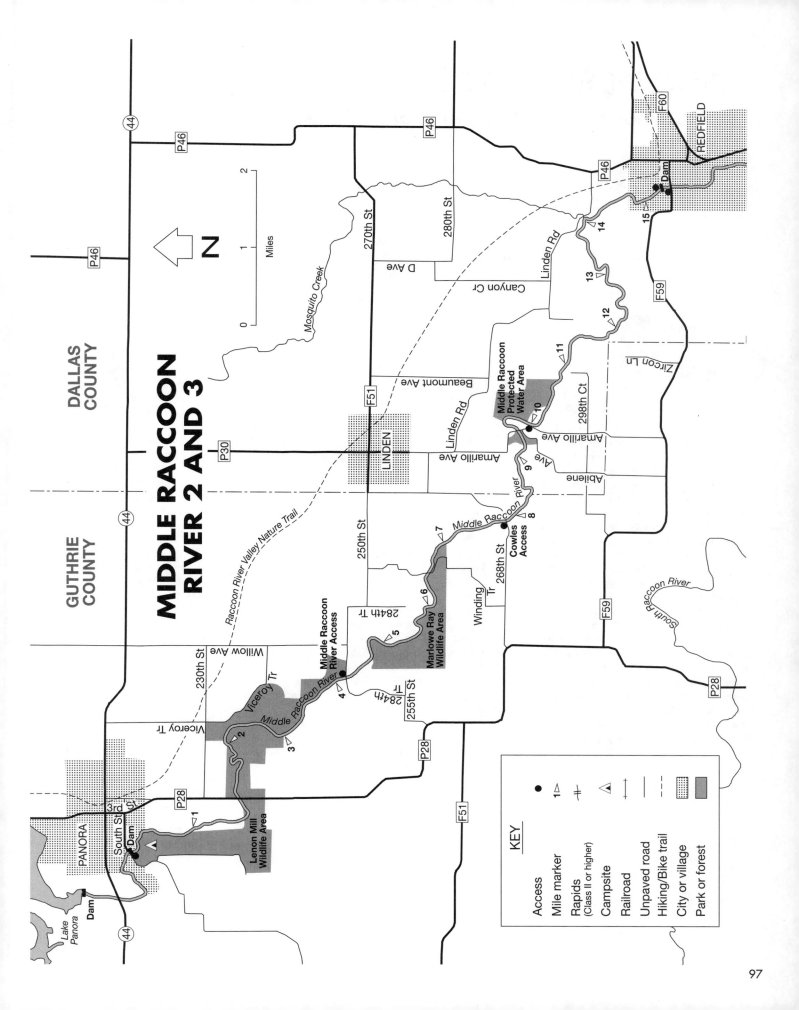

MIDDLE RACCOON RIVER 2 AND 3

GUTHRIE COUNTY

DALLAS COUNTY

N

Miles

0 1 2

Lake Panora

PANORA

Dam

South St

3rd St

Lenon Mill Wildlife Area

Viceroy Tr

Viceroy Tr

Middle Raccoon River

Willow Ave

230th St

Middle Raccoon River Access

284th Tr

255th St

284th Tr

Marlowe Ray Wildlife Area

Winding Tr

268th St

Cowles Access

Middle Raccoon River

250th St

270th St

Mosquito Creek

Raccoon River Valley Nature Trail

LINDEN

Beaumont Ave

Linden Rd

Amarillo Ave

Amarillo Ave

Abilene Ave

298th Ct

Middle Raccoon Protected Water Area

Zircon Ln

Canyon Cr

Linden Rd

D Ave

280th St

REDFIELD

Dam

South Raccoon River

44

P46

P46

P28

P30

F51

P28

F51

F59

P28

F59

P46

P46

F60

44

1
2
3
4
5
6
7
8
9
10
11
12
13
14
15

KEY

● Access

1△ Mile marker

✛ Rapids (Class II or higher)

◢ Campsite

┼┼ Railroad

| Unpaved road

- - - Hiking/Bike trail

▒ City or village

▓ Park or forest

MIDDLE RIVER
Roseman Covered Bridge to Pammel State Park (8.6 Miles)

Beginning at one of the celebrated "Bridges of Madison County" and ending at one of central Iowa's most scenic little parks, this section twists and turns through myriad natural attractions, from scenic bluffs and lowland woods to brief sections of croplands or pastures.

As the gradient suggests, you should expect moderately challenging paddling that's more so at high or low water levels. Rocks are sharp, and water levels are usually enjoyable only in the spring and early summer.

Averaging 50 feet wide, at paddleable levels the river usually runs muddy. At the put-in, don't be surprised if tourists snap your picture. North of the Roseman Covered Bridge is a small store with covered bridge souvenirs. The wooden bridges' latest round of fame, of course, was sparked by Robert James Waller's book *The Bridges of Madison County* and by the Clint Eastwood/Meryl Streep movie version that was filmed here.

Campgrounds at both Pammel State Park and Winterset City Park (about 5 miles northeast of the state park) have full amenities and scenic hiking.

Canoe and kayak rentals are available from Raccoon River Retreats (515-833-2636) in Redfield and Canoesport Outfitters (515-961-6117) in Indianola.

The **shuttle route** (9.3 miles) from the put-in runs northeast on Roseman Bridge Road to Highway 92, east to County P68, and south to Pammel State Park. Drive through the tunnel, turn right, and park near the ford.

You'll catch good **water levels** only after sustained rainy spells in Guthrie, Adair, and Madison Counties. Use the Middle River near Indianola gauge (station 05486490) on the USGS Web site listed in the introduction as a vague reference, or call Madison County Conservation at (515) 462-3536. More than 8 inches over the ford at the takeout is a good sign. As water nears or submerges the tops of the blocks at its pourover, riffles and snags become quite treacherous.

The **gradient** is 5.6 feet per mile.

Put in just upstream-right from the Roseman Covered Bridge at a small limestone jetty. The river heads east to a modern bridge at Fawn Avenue. Past a little island, at a left bend, small limestone ledges line the wooded banks.

The channel splits into shallow riffles around a sandy island. Past a high sandbar on the river-left, the banks are low and grassy. The river moves into a long, slower stretch lined with limestone boulders on a woodland slope, and then it courses over a seam of rocks, best run through the center chute. Bending north into a long horseshoe, the river widens past low limestone outcroppings. Then it constricts at a shallow riffle, passing a clearing with cut banks near Roseman Bridge Road on the left.

As the river curves southward, woods line the banks, and you may need to dodge snags through swift water. Turning right at the base of a grassy hill, the river then heads east with a farmhouse visible on a meadow ridge. The river bends right through a small chute to the left of another small island, and a shattered-looking limestone wall lines the right bank at the next left bend. The Fox Trail trestle bridge is just ahead.

Past the bridge, a limestone wall continues along the bank, leading to a small ledge drop. The river widens and slows, becoming shallow and rocky with boulders jutting from the river. A wooded ridge rises on the left, forcing the river south along it. The river becomes swift and exceedingly beautiful, with oak and elm limbs reaching high overhead as you pick your way between boulders.

Bending left, you pass boulders at the base of a wooded slope. The channel tightens into a swift S-turn and runs over a small ledge, best run through the center. Ahead, woods give way to pasture (watch for fences). You see the Harmon Avenue bridge and behind it a 140-foot bluff with a limestone cliff. A long riffle leads through the pasture to the base of the cliff, where the river bends right into dense woodlands through a fast course with several riffles.

After bending left at a 20-foot limestone wall, the river bends right along another high, wooded ridge, where stairs come down from a home. Then the river curves left along a wooded slope, slowing behind the ford at Pammel State Park. The **takeout** is ahead on the river-right, upstream from the ford.

Other trips. The 7-mile section from the Schildberg access on Highway 92 to Roseman Covered Bridge doesn't have the high bluffs of the section already described, but it does pass along scenic little limestone walls and drops down a few chutes and ledges. Expect more agricultural views.

The Pammel Loop

Hike up the bluff through noble stands of walnut and oak at Pammel State Park, and you'll observe something weird: the Middle River below flows both toward and away from you in four directions. It's no optical illusion. It's because the Middle River makes a long loop caused by an impressive rib of limestone called the "Backbone." Near the park's ford, the 100-foot bluff divides two stretches of the Middle River by only 125 yards. Harmon Tunnel, originally cut by William Harmon and his sons in 1858, diverted flows through the base of the bluff to power a sawmill. The tunnel was later abandoned, but in 1925 it was widened to accommodate vehicles. For paddlers, this creates a unique 1.9-mile paddling loop. Put in below the ford and wind past meadows and woods and over rocky riffles. Past the first bridge, take out by the culvert on the right, and hike through the tunnel to your vehicle.

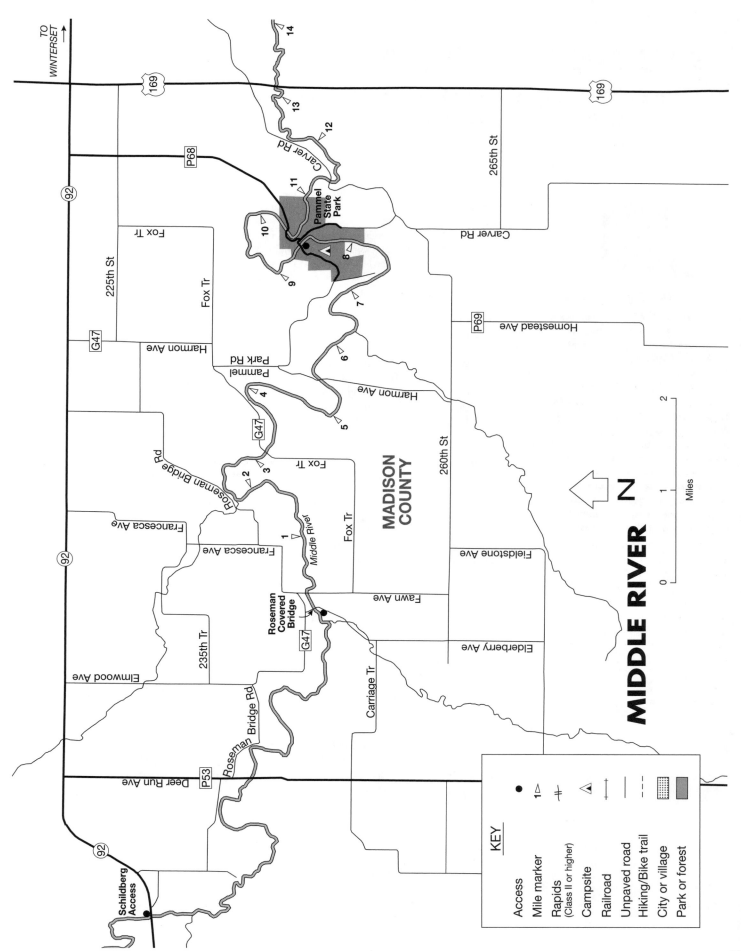

MIDDLE RIVER

KEY

Access — ●

Mile marker — ▽1

Rapids (Class II or higher) — ‡

Campsite — ◁

Railroad — ┼┼┼

Unpaved road — ┆┆┆

Hiking/Bike trail — ⣿

City or village — ▨

Park or forest — ▨

N

0   1   2
Miles

Pammel State Park

MADISON COUNTY

Roseman Covered Bridge

Schildberg Access

TO WINTERSET →

MISSISSIPPI RIVER

Upper Mississippi River National Wildlife Refuge, Lansing Area (Distance Varies)

The section described here offers a very scenic taste of the Upper Mississippi River National Wildlife Refuge. Running 261 miles from Wabasha, Minnesota, down to the Quad Cities of Iowa and Illinois, it is the longest refuge outside of Alaska, encompassing 233,000 acres of sloughs, backwaters, islands, and marshes.

Paddling the Father of Waters can seem intimidating, or at least complicated, what with all the locks and dams and barges. And in fact, the Mississippi is a large body of water requiring respect. But being so big, it also has vast, scenic areas that are simple for any canoeists or kayaker to approach. Two such areas in the Lansing area are shown on the map. More than a hundred heavily forested islands surround backwaters, creating protection from waves. By early summer, some areas fill with extensive and beautiful water lily beds. As paddlers round bends through mazelike channels (people do get lost, at least for a while), occasional views between islands unfold to massive, distant limestone bluffs that enclose the valley. Up to 400 feet high, the bluffs in this region are at the highest elevations above the river anywhere between the river's source in Lake Itasca and the mouth near New Orleans.

Except in high water, there is usually a foot or two of visibility, a far cry from the muddy river many expect to find. Spring and fall waterfowl migrations can be awe-inspiring. (Duck hunters arrive in droves in the fall.) The backwaters also make excellent fish habitat, and catches of walleye, largemouth bass, panfish, catfish, and perch are common.

Primitive **camping** along sandy islands is an excellent way to enjoy the refuge (see the introduction for information). Mosquitoes are the scourge of evening, though. Many campers prefer spots on the navigation channel or facing larger lakes, where breezes can keep insects at bay. U.S. Fish and Wildlife Service (563-873-3423) regulations apply.

Canoe and kayak rentals are available from the Upper Iowa Resort (563-568-3263) on Highway 76 north of Waukon, about 16 miles to the southwest.

You can roughly estimate **water levels** by checking the outflow of Lock and Dam 8 at Genoa online at www.mvp-wc.usace.army.mil/projects/Lock8.shtml. Typical summer flows range from 20,000 to 40,000 cfs.

The **gradient** is negligible.

Putting in at Big Slough Landing, south of State Highway 82, is a good place to begin exploring. At normal water levels, it's almost as easy to paddle upstream as downstream through the slow-moving sloughs. It is recommended that paddlers not wishing to cross the swifter navigation channel make their own loop-trail trips, setting out from one landing, exploring sloughs and backwaters, and returning to the same point. Moving toward the center of the islands, away from the navigation channel and Highway 82, is an excellent way to get a feel for the wildness that the Mississippi has to offer. Dense woods muffle the noise of highways, trains, and a power plant just a mile or two away. **Take out** where you started. You can make a similar trip based from Winneshiek Landing. DeSoto Landing accesses the navigation channel, which is much more difficult to paddle back upstream on.

For a different trip, **put-in** is at Lansing Marina, from which you can paddle north through an archipelago toward islands between Zoll Lake and Launsom Lakes. Be more wary of powerboats here, especially near Lansing Big Lake, which is about a mile wide and two miles long. Conway Lake is a perched wetlands set slightly above the river level with crystal-clear waters. From the river, when vegetation hasn't choked it off, it can be reached by paddling up its slender outlet slough, at some points not much wider than a canoe. (It can also be reached from a turnoff on State Highway 26.) Again, **take out** at Lansing Marina where you began.

Other trips. Paddlers approach the Upper Mississippi in many ways. A lifetime could be spent in thorough exploration. If you'd like to run a multiday trip on the Mississippi, plan your route thoroughly before you go. The Upper Mississippi River National Wildlife Refuge (563-873-3423) has excellent free maps of each pool from Rock Island, Illinois, to Wabasha, Minnesota. Keep the following things in mind:

• The dams' long spillways, some of which can easily be portaged at normal levels, become dangerous low-head dams at high water.

• "Pools" behind dams are huge lakes (bigger than interior impoundments such as Lake Red Rock), sometimes several miles wide. Strong winds generate high waves.

• Large, open areas of water attract drivers of personal watercraft and recreational powerboats. They probably aren't expecting paddlers.

• Canoes and kayaks are allowed to use locks, but first priority is given to commercial traffic.

• As water rises in the main channel, "pressure gradients" can develop at certain "cuts" between islands (such as No. 6 Cut, north of mile 669—no spots on this map exhibit this phenomenon) and turn into whitewater runs with standing waves up to 2 feet or whirlpool-like eddies.

• Wakes generated by massive barge flotillas or large cabin cruisers can flip your boat if you're too close.

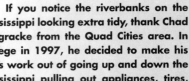

Keeping It Clean

If you notice the riverbanks on the Mississippi looking extra tidy, thank Chad Pregracke from the Quad Cities area. In college in 1997, he decided to make his life's work out of going up and down the Mississippi pulling out appliances, tires, vehicles, and questionable items from the river's banks and water. Receiving grants from large corporations like Alcoa and Budweiser, he formed Living Lands and Waters. Since then, he's gotten thousands of people together on barges during the warmer seasons to help beautify the waterway. So far, more than 800 tons of junk has been removed from the Mississippi, Ohio, and Illinois Rivers.

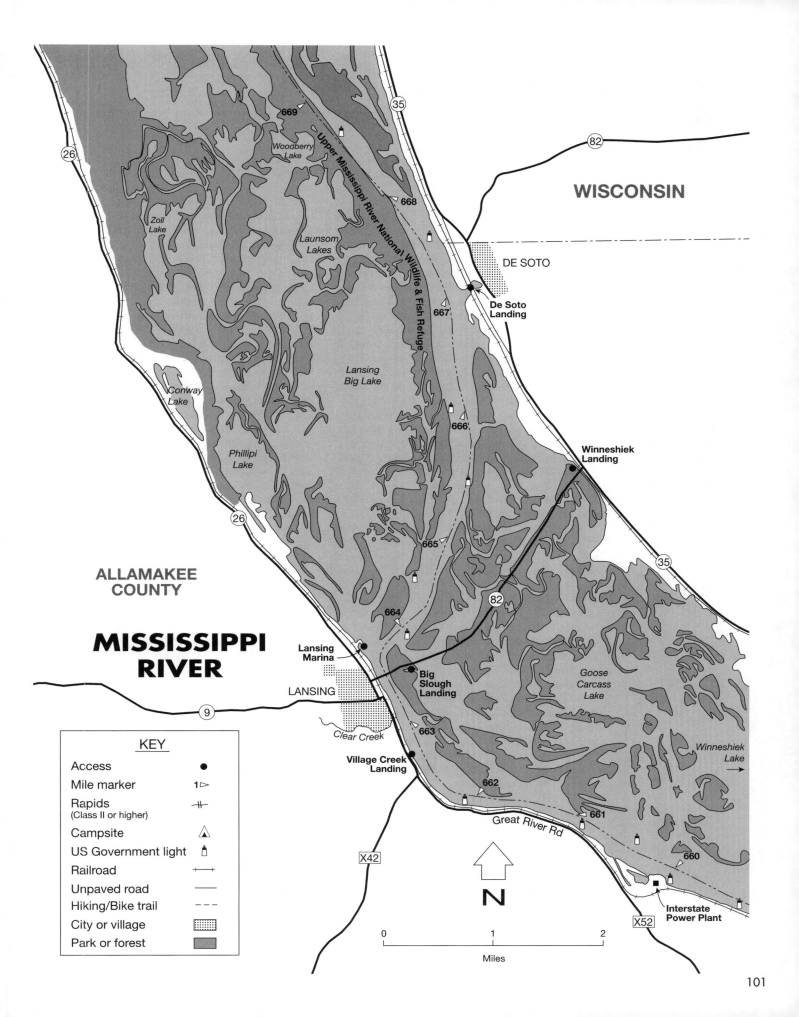

MISSISSIPPI RIVER

ALLAMAKEE COUNTY

WISCONSIN

DE SOTO

De Soto Landing

Winneshiek Landing

Lansing Marina

LANSING

Big Slough Landing

Village Creek Landing

Clear Creek

Great River Rd

Goose Carcass Lake

Winneshiek Lake

Interstate Power Plant

Woodberry Lake

Zoll Lake

Launsom Lakes

Conway Lake

Lansing Big Lake

Phillipi Lake

Upper Mississippi River National Wildlife & Fish Refuge

669
668
667
666
665
664
663
662
661
660

26
35
82
9
X42
X52

KEY

Access	●
Mile marker	1▷
Rapids (Class II or higher)	⊬
Campsite	▲
US Government light	⬚
Railroad	┼┼┼
Unpaved road	——
Hiking/Bike trail	- - -
City or village	▒
Park or forest	▓

N

0   1   2

Miles

NORTH FORK OF THE MAQUOKETA RIVER 1
Cascade to Ozark Bridge (18.3 Miles)

Flowing through a narrow gorge and along miles of wooded bluffs and cliffs, this section is certainly one of Iowa's primo paddling journeys. And it is a journey—after putting in at Cascade, there is no place to take out for 17.4 miles in Iowa's remotest valley. Paddlers come here looking for wildness and inaccessibility. After a highly scenic gorge section, the river passes two dull miles of farmland, after which wooded bluffs constantly line the river. You'll see no bridges, no homes, no people, no nothin' (OK, you might notice one building set back in the woods), for 11 blissfully forested miles.

Averaging 70 feet wide, this is a shallow, sandy stream, clear at moderate water levels, with occasional deep, aqua pools near boulders. The paddling is easygoing, with few riffles until the final 5 miles. Although it can be paddled at relatively low water levels, because of the distance commitment, its wise to go only when water is plentiful. Alternative put-ins are on Whitewater Creek. Fishing tends to be slow, but some smallmouth bass are present.

The only public land available for primitive river **camping** on this trip is at Searryl's Cave State Preserve (unmarked—see trip description to find it). See Maquoketa River 3 and 4 for more camping options.

Canoe rentals are available from Bickford Canoe Rental (563-652-5855) in Canton.

The **shuttle route** (20.4 miles) from the put-in at the Cascade City Park runs northeast on 1st Avenue and east on 2nd Avenue, which becomes County D61 out of town. Head east, south, and east on County D61, south on CountyY31, west on 254th Street, and south on 21st Avenue to Ozark Bridge.

Estimate **water levels** by checking the North Fork Maquoketa River near Fulton gauge (station 05418400) on the USGS Web site listed in the introduction. A reading of 400 cfs usually yields pleasant paddling.

The **gradient** is 4.1 feet per mile.

The **put-in** is down stairs behind the Cascade City Park shelter house, below the dam. A tiny stream just 40 feet wide here, the river is bound between concrete and rock walls through downtown. Heading out of town past homes and a radio tower, the river curves northeast into a long, lightly tree-lined stretch. A 50-foot bluff with cedars, hardwoods, and limestone exposures rises where the river bends sharply right.

Bending left, the river follows along a rock wall heading north. Hooking back to the south with a limestone bluff on the left and boulders midstream, you head straight toward a 100-foot bluff and bend 90 degrees to the east at its base. Past mossy boulders, you head straight toward a massive limestone escarpment, topped by a stone house, and then bend southwest into a long horseshoe. Steeply wooded bluffs line both banks through a gorge heading south with rock chimney formations jutting from woods on either side.

Reaching a bluff to the south, the river curves briefly east and then north past boulders the size of cattle and elephants. As the river heads northeast, bluffs draw back from the banks. Clearings become frequent, and past a farmer's ford, the next two miles pass croplands with low banks.

The river becomes more wooded past limestone bridge abutments, and Whitewater Creek enters from the left. The river bends right along a rocky, wooded ridge. You pass through the southeast curve to a sharp right bend southward, and ridges grow higher with limestone outcroppings. The valley walls converge, and on the left a precipitous bluff with limestone cliffs rises. For miles from here onward, the river is spellbinding, passing between a mature mix of hardwoods and from one bluff to another at each bend. Rock outcroppings are occasionally visible, more often covered in woods.

Past a large boulder the river drops over a seam of rocks. At a southwest bend, the river passes along moss-and-lichen-covered rock outcroppings. As the river heads generally east, a verdant carpet of ferns, yew, and other woodland plants line wooded slopes. Then the river hooks sharply south and back to the west. The river bends left, and where large boulders are spaced apart is Searryl's Cave State Preserve. Up the bluff, Searryl's Cave twists 565 feet into the bluff, with Iowa's most numerous hibernating bat colonies in the winter.

Heading east, the river drops through a spirited riffle. Ahead, a dramatic bluff rises with a high rock face flanked by cedars, and the river drops through a short riffle around a tiny island. As you continue east along a bluff on the right, another scenic bluff with limestone exposures appears on the left. Heading through a longer, gentle riffle, the river reaches an area with clay banks and then turns south along a wooded bluff.

As the bluff tapers away, a pasture joins the left bank, and at a left bend, Ozark Bridge slants across the river ahead. **Take out** on the river-right beneath it, carrying up a trail.

Other trips. The 3.7-mile trip passing through 200-foot-deep Whitewater Canyon on pretty little Whitewater Creek is quite astounding. Entirely in private land, it's accessible only to paddlers. Averaging 50 feet wide and falling at 5.1 feet per mile, the creek is by no means a whitewater run, but it courses swiftly over a rocky streambed. Put in at the Whitewater Drive bridge next to a farm (respect the landowners' property). Round a right bend, and you see that rock outcroppings begin to line the banks. Soon you're winding through a heavily forested gorge, with scenic rock faces and clefts high above the stream, passing boulders the size of recreational vehicles. Wait for rains to paddle it (more than 600 cfs on the North Fork Maquoketa is a good sign), but beware of flooding, which becomes dangerously torrential in the constricted gorge. Take out downstream of the County D64 bridge on the right.

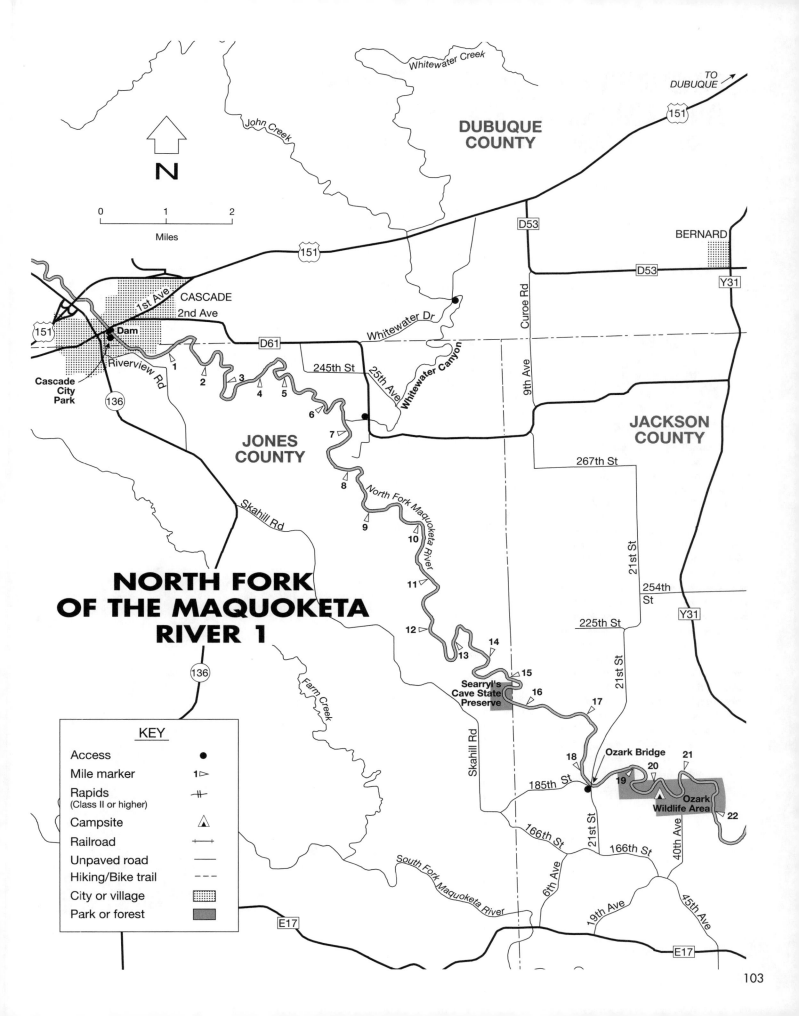

NORTH FORK OF THE MAQUOKETA RIVER 1

NORTH FORK OF THE MAQUOKETA RIVER 2
Ozark Bridge to Crab Town Bridge (7.5 Miles)

A much shorter trip with more places to access the river than North Fork of the Maquoketa River 1 (but involving steep carries), this is still an attractive stretch of river. The first half to Caven Bridge is quite isolated, too, passing along the only significant stretch of public land lining the entire river.

Similar to the main Maquoketa River, this stretch features rugged rock outcroppings frequently hidden by woods. Like the Pictured Rocks and Indian Bluffs wildlife areas, Ozark Wildlife Area attracts rock climbers who scale the hard, craggy limestone cliffs under a wooded canopy. About 70 feet wide, the river tends to run just deep enough to pass with a canoe over a generally sandy bottom. Fishing is not especially productive, but smallmouth bass and walleye can be caught.

Primitive **camping** is allowed at the Ozark Wildlife Area (boundary signs are posted). See Maquoketa River 3 and 4.

Canoe rentals are available from Bickford Canoe Rental (563-652-5855) in Canton.

The **shuttle route** (9.9 miles) from the put-in at Ozark Bridge runs south on 21st Avenue, east on 166th Street, southeast on 45th Street, southeast on County E17, and north and west on County Y31 to the Crab Town Bridge.

Estimate **water levels** by checking the North Fork Maquoketa River near Fulton gauge (station 05418400) on the USGS Web site listed in the introduction. A reading of 200 cfs usually yields pleasant paddling.

The **gradient** is 2.7 feet per mile.

The **put-in** is down a trail on the south side of Ozark Bridge. Paddling through a riffle, you see a low, rocky bluff lining the right bank, with a narrow strip of cornfield on the left. Curving south and then west, the river gains an unspoiled character in the Ozark Wildlife Area. Curving through a horseshoe bend to the northeast, you see a prairie-capped bluff looming ahead. As the river bends right, back to the southeast in a second horseshoe bend, the bluffs become thickly overgrown with vines and trees, and impressive limestone cliffs chiseled into vertical shafts appear ahead. The feeling is almost junglelike. You curve north along a lush, rocky slope to a high bluff where a boulder the size of a small home is propped on a slope by a tree. As you bend eastward, rock outcroppings are visible through trees between steep banks.

Bending right, the river curves into a long stretch with wooded slopes to Caven Bridge, upstream of which is an access with a parking lot on the river-left. Across the river is a red house. Going beneath the bridge, you pass along boulders and curve left to head northeast past bank-level rock outcroppings. Grassy clearings and cut banks become more common along the sandy-bottomed stream. Heading east, you'll less frequently pass along lower bluffs with occasional rock outcroppings. At a right bend, two steel buildings are visible atop a grassy hill on the left. The area becomes more wooded and rocky as you bend left, and Crab Town Bridge is just ahead. **Take out** on the river-right beneath the bridge, with a carry up the trail.

Other trips. Through the rest of Jackson County to the North Fork's mouth near the city of Maquoketa, each bridge is marked with a sign giving a time estimate to the next bridge. Just because there is a bridge crossing doesn't make for easy access, however. Past the bridge at 109th Avenue (locally called the Edwards Bridge), the valley bottom widens significantly, becoming increasingly agricultural, and the river passes fewer rock outcroppings. Also see Appendix 2.

Cascade

The brick and stone buildings of Cascade, at the put-in for the North Fork of the Maquoketa River 1 segment, make the town look older than the average Iowa town, and it is. Founded in 1833, the now sleepy village once boasted a large brewery, shipping 2,500 barrels per year. A nearly 19,000-cubic-foot underground vault—cut into solid limestone bedrock—was the storage tank for the beer. On the river, several mills came and went over the years, utilizing it's high gradient in this rocky area. The town was named for a 9-foot, double-tiered waterfall that flowed in the middle of town near the dam's present location. The scenery was quite picturesque in pre-1925 postcards of the falls in front of a charming stone bridge, but that year a major flood went "ripping and roaring" through Cascade, pulling homes from foundations and causing $150,000 in damage. Flood-control measures led to creating a new channel, dam, and bridge.

Wooded bluffs and rock outcroppings are common on the North Fork in western Jackson County.

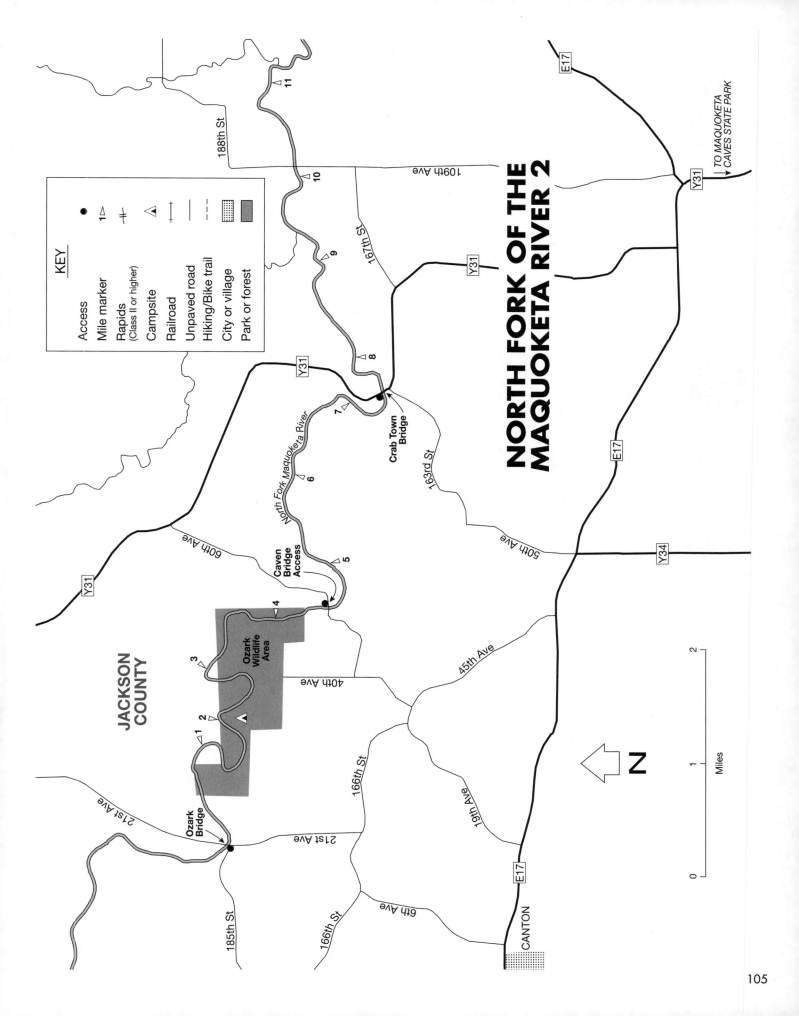

NORTH FORK OF THE MAQUOKETA RIVER 2

KEY

●	Access
1△	Mile marker
⊬	Rapids (Class II or higher)
△	Campsite
┼	Railroad
—	Unpaved road
- - -	Hiking/Bike trail
▦	City or village
▨	Park or forest

JACKSON COUNTY

North Fork Maquoketa River

Ozark Wildlife Area

Ozark Bridge

Caven Bridge Access

Crab Town Bridge

TO MAQUOKETA CAVES STATE PARK

CANTON

185th St

166th St

21st Ave

21st Ave

6th Ave

166th St

19th Ave

45th Ave

40th Ave

60th Ave

50th Ave

109th Ave

163rd St

167th St

188th St

Y31

Y31

Y31

Y31

E17

E17

E17

Y34

N

0   1   2
Miles

NORTH RACCOON RIVER 1 AND 2

Merritt Access to Horseshoe Bend Wildlife Area (9.2 Miles)
Horseshoe Bend Wildlife Area to Brown Bridge Access (9 Miles)

Many of the 150 miles of the North Raccoon from northern Sac County on down offer reasonably good paddling on a meandering prairie stream. Usually sand-, gravel-, or mud-bottomed, its watershed is roughly twice the size of the south and middle branches of the Raccoon combined, with more consistent flows.

These two sections offer some of the best paddling on the upper part of the river, with excellent scenery. You'll pass mostly wooded banks, and sporadic risings of impressive clay cliffs are a delight. In the Carroll County portion of section 1, the river also falls over two runnable rock dams (the one at the put-in is easily avoided) that form short class II drops.

Magnificent clay bluffs and surprisingly wild territory line the North Raccoon in Carroll and Jefferson County.

Although this section is not officially a canoe trail, because Carroll and Jefferson Counties both offer frequent accesses with numerous places to camp, there is a de facto one here. Muddy during high water in the spring and typically running with a foot or two of visibility the rest of the paddling season, the Raccoon averages 130 feet wide here. Fishing is excellent for catfish, and walleye are common in the fishing riffles.

There are **campgrounds** near the river at the Merritt Access, Richey Access, and Hyde Park. Primitive river camping is allowed at all public areas. Dickson Timber also has a campground, and a campground with full amenities is at Swan Lake State Park south of Carroll.

Canoe rentals are available at Butrick Bluff Wildlife Area (712-792-4614).

The **shuttle route** (8.1 miles) for section 1 from the put-in runs south on Velvet Avenue, east on 170th Street, north on Vale Avenue, east on 162nd Street, south on Zephyr Avenue, east on 165th Street, south on County N58, east on 170th Street, north on B Avenue, east on 165th Street, and north on Brentwood Avenue to the takeout at Horseshoe Bend.

For section 2 (9 miles), head north from Horseshoe Bend on Brentwood, east on 150th Street, south on County N65, east on 195th Street, and north on County E33. Turn right onto 200th Street to the takeout at Brown Bridge Access.

For **water levels**, check the North Raccoon near Jefferson gauge (station 05482500) on the USGS Web site listed in the introduction. About 500 cfs is a good level.

The overall **gradient** for both sections is 2.1 feet per mile.

Put in at the boat ramp at the Merritt Access, about 10 miles east of Carroll. Or, if you care to run the rock dam (class II), there's also a canoe launch 150 yards upstream. Scout first and run right of center.

To the 162nd Street bridge the river has low, tree-lined banks. Logjams accumulate at the bridge, and you

may need to **portage** on the river-left. As you head south, the banks are increasingly wooded. A pretty ridge with clay exposures topped by oak savanna appears ahead, diverting the river left into the Buttrick Bluff Wildlife Area (with no river access). A 100-foot wooded bluff with clay slopes briefly joins the right bank, and then Purgatory Creek enters from the left.

Bending left near a shooting range at the Bennett Access, you head northeast and then circle back southeast, where you'll see a distant grassy hill topped with trees. After a left bend and a right curve, you hear the next rock dam (class II), best run through the splashy waves in the center of the wider left chute. You can **portage** on the river right down the access road, or scout.

After it bends right into a lowland pasture, the river heads southeast in a wide valley, continuing along sparsely wooded banks to the Richey Access at the N58 bridge. The river heads northeast past expansive sandbars and then bends right; a beautiful line of cedar-and-oak-topped clay cliffs up to 35 feet tall line the river for a few hundred yards. Past a smaller wooded bluff, you head north into a huge horseshoe bend, where elms, cottonwoods, maples, and oaks line the banks past the 175th Street bridge. At a left bend around a sandbar, three piles of riprap appear on the left bank. Horseshoe Bend Access, the **takeout** for section 1, is just upstream of the first pile.

For the second section, as you head farther north, a hill appears and you bend generally east, following along sparsely wooded banks. At a southwest curve beyond Cedar Creek's mouth, you bend sharply left, and ahead is a spectacular 60-foot cliff of clay and shale. Bending right at it and passing along more woods, you reach the Hyde Park boat ramp. The river drops over a riffle. Curving southeast toward a clearing, the river then heads east into lowland woods. Heading south, you reach a striking clay bluff and bend left toward the County N65 bridge.

Past the bridge, the river turns right toward another striking set of clay cliffs topped with oaks, cedars, and walnuts. A small channel—usually logjammed—continues straight along the bluff, but most of the current makes a small horseshoe bend north toward hilly meadows. The channels rejoin at the base of the wooded bluff where an elephant-sized boulder juts from the streambed. Bending east, the river curves right, circling along a pretty ridge wooded with locusts, oaks, and cedars.

From here to the Brown Bridge, wooded ridges are constantly set back from the river with wood-lined and some pastured banks. The **takeout** is on the river-left, downstream of the bridge.

Other trips. In Sac County, the 7 miles of the Raccoon River (from the McDonald Access north of Sac City, through town, with a takeout at Hagge Park south of town) make a nice float past lowland woods and timbered ridges over a gravelly bottom. The Sac City Conservation Board (712-662-4530) rents canoes. Also see Appendix 2.

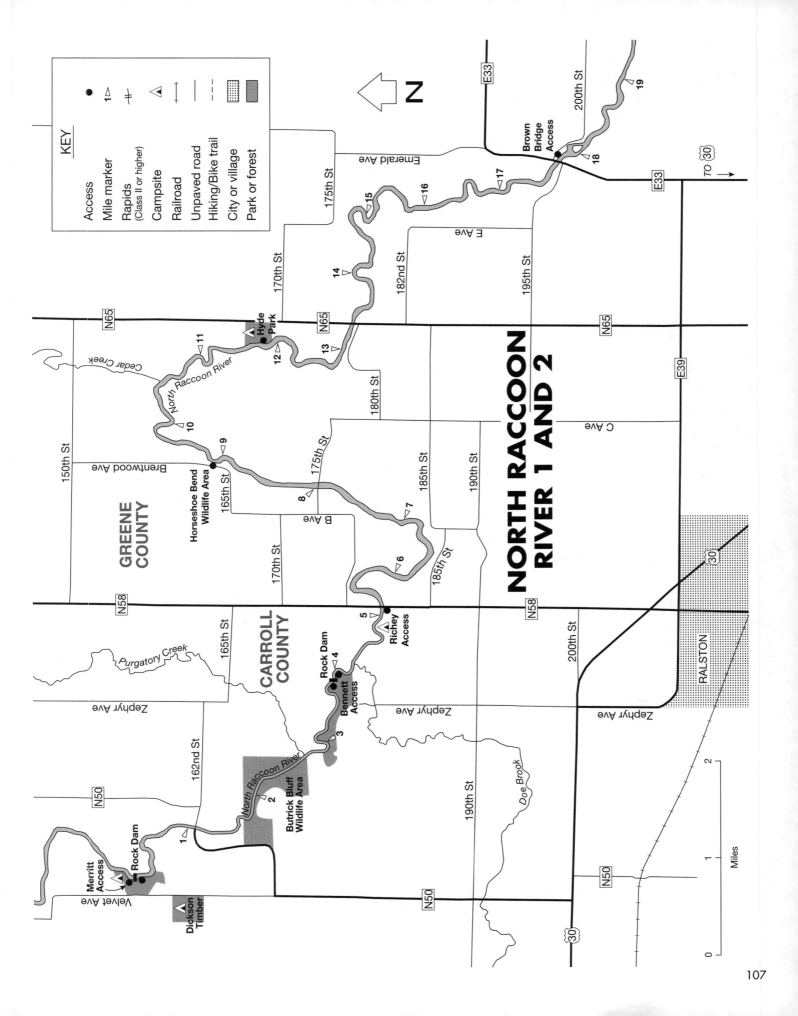

NORTH RACCOON
RIVER 1 AND 2

KEY

- Access
- Mile marker
- Rapids (Class II or higher)
- Campsite
- Railroad
- Unpaved road
- Hiking/Bike trail
- City or village
- Park or forest

N

GREENE COUNTY

CARROLL COUNTY

Cedar Creek

North Raccoon River

Hyde Park

Horseshoe Bend Wildlife Area

Brentwood Ave

150th St

162nd St

165th St

170th St

175th St

180th St

185th St

190th St

Purgatory Creek

Zephyr Ave

Rock Dam

Merritt Access

Velvet Ave

Dickson Timber

Butrick Bluff Wildlife Area

North Raccoon River

Bennett Access

Rock Dam

Richey Access

Doe Brook

RALSTON

Zephyr Ave

Emerald Ave

Brown Bridge Access

200th St

175th St

170th St

182nd St

E Ave

C Ave

195th St

200th St

N50

N58

N65

E39

E33

30

TO 30

Miles

0   1   2

NORTH RACCOON RIVER 3 AND 4

Adel to Puckerbrush Access (7.5 Miles)
Puckerbrush Access to Booneville (8.2 Miles)

Not quite so popular to paddle as the nearby Middle and South Raccoon Rivers, this part of the North Raccoon also has worthwhile scenery, along with long sandbars that make great spots to stretch your legs.

In a valley bottom up to a mile wide, the river meanders through woods or fields to reach occasional ridges at its edges. Reaching the forks of the south and north branches of the river, the Raccoon River becomes a watershed draining 3,400 square miles. Water becomes much more consistent at this point, too, so it's rare not to be able to paddle it throughout the season. With adequate water levels, these sections can easily be combined into a long day-trip. The primary game fish species is catfish, and some walleye are caught.

There is a **campground** at the put-in at Adel Island Park, and primitive river camping is allowed at Two Rivers Wildlife Area. Camping is forbidden at the Booneville Access.

Canoe and kayak rentals are available from Raccoon River Retreats (515-833-2636) in Redfield and Canoesport Outfitters (515-961-6117) in Indianola. Des Moines Rental (515-277-4401) also rents canoes.

The **shuttle route** (7.4 miles) for section 1 runs west on the park access road, south on U.S. Highway 169, east on Highway 6, and south on County R16 to the Puckerbrush Access. The route for the second trip (6.5 miles) runs south on County R16 and east on County F90 to the Booneville Access on the right.

To approximate **water levels**, check the USGS Web site listed in the introduction and subtract the South Raccoon near Redfield gauge (station 05484000) reading from the Raccoon River at Van Meter gauge (station 5484500) reading. A difference of about 500 cfs is usually a pleasant level.

Adel Island

Driving north of Adel on U.S. Highway 169, it seems as if you cross the North Raccoon River twice in about a mile. And actually, you do. At the north bridge, you cross the "main" channel, where the sign is marked "Raccoon River." Where there seems to be more water, at the south bridge, there is no sign. This part of the river is the "slough." The two channels surround Adel Island, a fairly large landmass with roads, fields, and fairgrounds, where it's easy to miss the notion that you are on an island. Due to the way the dams were constructed, more water comes through the slough than through the main channel. In early settlement days, most water took the 5-mile meandering course rather than the 2.6-mile slough that cuts a straighter path to the spot where they rejoin.

The **gradient** for both sections is 2.8 feet per mile.

Put in at Island Park in Adel, well below (about 100 yards) the dangerous dam. The river runs through rousing riffles, and after a right bend the North Raccoon River joins from the left. At the second Highway 6 bridge, watch out for the remains of rusty bridge pylons that may be just below the surface and can damage a boat.

After the river passes a few homes, the setting becomes rural heading east, and at a right bend to the south you paddle along a pretty oak-covered ridge with rock outcroppings near the water. You pass along light woods, and a small bluff rises on the right bank. At a higher point where a home tops the bluff, you bend left toward the northeast, passing a loess cliff and a less obtrusive home, and head toward the base of a rocky and wooded bluff. Bending right along prominent sandstone outcroppings, the river circles in a southwest direction, braiding through sandbars.

Toward the wooded bluff ahead on the right, you bend left at more outcroppings and run briefly east and then south near a lightly wooded ridge. The channel splits swiftly around a sandy island. Rejoined, the river bends eastward and then curves right along a planting of birch trees, approaching a ridge to the south where sheep-sized rocks are at the base of a wooded ridge. Along it, the river bends left, back to the north where fields and a home are visible on a hill, and then sharply to the southeast along riprap. In a small horseshoe bend to the north, the river doubles back past a log home and a sandy island, heading through light woods to the section 1 **takeout** at Puckerbrush Access on the left.

A nicely wooded ridge is visible ahead on the left, set back from the banks. The next two miles are lightly tree-lined. You'll pass a gravel quarry, and the noise of Interstate 80 is progressively more noticeable. Past the freeway bridge, the South Raccoon River merges from the right along a wooded ridgeline, creating the Raccoon River. The river passes wooded banks along the north edge of Van Meter, with a long, animated riffle along a riprapped bank beyond the County R16 bridge.

The banks become increasingly wooded and wild, and the river bends south toward a high, wooded ridge. You bend left at it, and limestone slabs line the bank. As you head east, the bluff tapers away and woods line the banks. You enter a horseshoe bend, and to the south you see a smaller ridge ahead at County F90, and you divert to the east and north through more woods. As you bend east, a 150-foot ridge appears ahead, with an imposing home atop it. Bending southward along the ridge, you pass beneath the railroad and County F90 bridges, with the **takeout** on the river-right.

Occasional rock outcroppings and small bluffs are found on the North Raccoon near Adel.

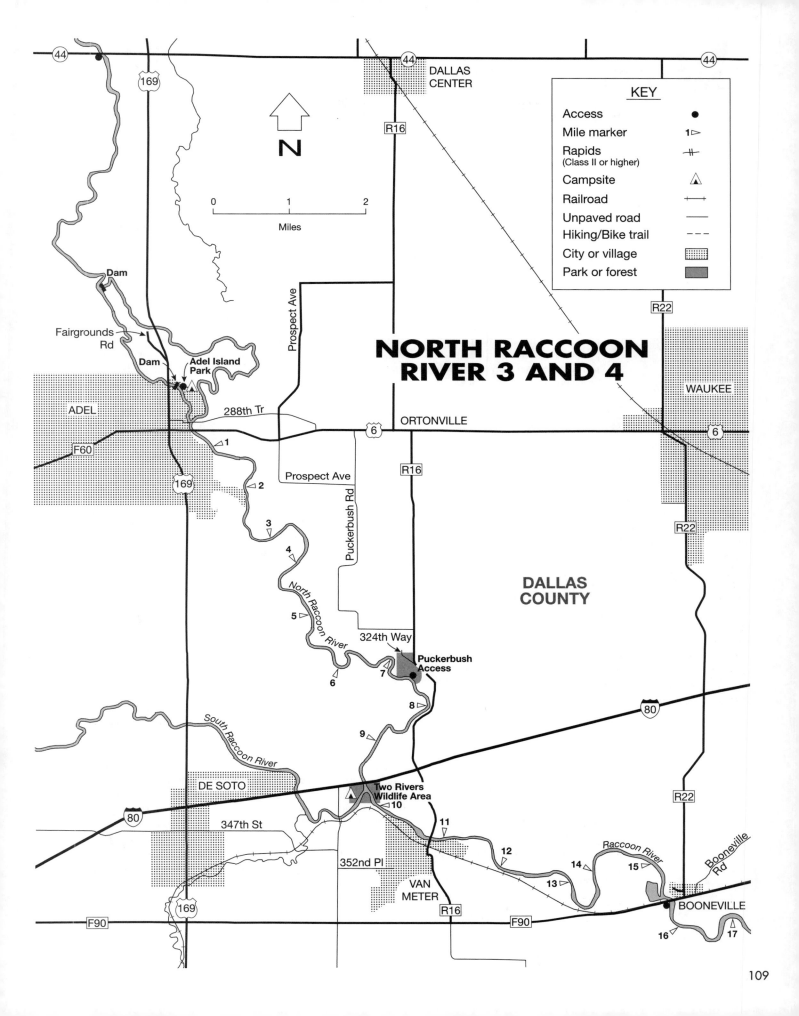

NORTH RACCOON RIVER 3 AND 4

NORTH RIVER
Elmwood Avenue to Hogback Covered Bridge (12 Miles)

Averaging just 40 feet wide in northwest Madison County, the North River is a fast, tight, tortuous, and challenging little stream. Vigilance for riverwide fences and snags is mandatory here because one or the other can appear while you swing around a swift-flowing bend. As a result, you often hear rushing water downstream and, unable to discern a riffle from a strainer, need to get out of the boat or take an eddy to check. You'll want to wait for sustained rains to paddle this one, but it's included here because of its exceptionally wild, scenic qualities.

The payoff for your constant attention is paddling where few others go, through dense, wooded areas and along beautiful rock outcroppings and occasional bucolic pastures. Just into the trip is an unusual cliff, which for several days after rainy periods showers thousands of droplets of water from a horizontal ledge midway up.

For **camping**, see Middle River.

Canoe and kayak rentals are available from Raccoon River Retreats (515-833-2636) in Redfield and Canoesport Outfitters (515-961-6117) in Indianola.

The **shuttle route** (8.4 miles) from the put-in runs north on Elwood Avenue, east on 165th Street, south on Fieldstone Avenue, east on 170th Street, north on Harmon Avenue, east and south on 166th Street, east on 168th Street, north and east on Ironwood Trail, and south on Hogback Bridge Road to the takeout.

For **water levels**, look for sustained rainy spells in Guthrie, Adair, and Madison Counties. Use the North River at Norwalk gauge (station 05486000) on the USGS Web site listed in the introduction as a general guideline, bearing in mind that levels are a full day behind this section and that tributaries skew readings. That said, you won't likely rub bottom much if the water level has remained above 250 cfs for several days. At readings above 1,000 cfs, the stream becomes treacherous.

The **gradient** is 10.3 feet per mile.

Put in downstream of the bridge on Elmwood Avenue at a carry-down on the river-right. Not far downstream is a striking cliff of limestone and coal with a swift, easy rapids running along it. Another riffle follows with a chute that can accumulate sweepers—approach with caution. After several more riffles, the river passes a pasture hillside with a farm on the left, followed by a bluff and dense woods.

The stream constricts and flows through a fun riffle and passes a 100-foot-high wooded bluff with rock outcroppings near the waterline. Curving right along it, the river bends left to a smaller wooded ride on the right with more limestone outcroppings. Watch for a fence that may be ahead. The river winds through nicely forested bends with occasional riffles. When the woods thin on the left side, you'll likely negotiate a fence and

pass along a pasture to the left, with the right slope still heavily wooded. A pretty little stream tumbles in from the right as you bend left past more rock outcroppings. Heading north, you enter a riffle perhaps 500 yards long through a pasture studded with rock outcroppings. Shortly after it is another long riffle through the undulating pasture.

As the river bends left, an electric wire may cross the stream, and the banks grow wooded again as a bluff with bedrock exposures rises on the right. After winding through pasturelands, you come to the County P57 bridge.

Between here and the next bridge, the gradient ratchets up to 13.8 feet per mile, resulting in numerous swift riffles and a few small rapids. The river bends south, and a riffle runs along little rock outcroppings; then the river diverts left into a swift riffle at a wooded ridge with more prominent rock exposures. The river bends right at another bluff, winding in small bends southward to a 120-foot bluff with a line of limestone cliffs at its top in the woods. After a sharp left at the bluff's base, the river bends slightly left away from it and descends a brief class I rapids—watch out for snags.

The river bends back to the bluff, and a short limestone wall picks up along the bluff's base. Past another small rapids (again, watch for snags!), scenic limestone walls form the left bank. A pasture joins the left bank with a farm visible, but the right bank remains wooded with hardwoods and cedars up a bluff and little limestone walls edging the river. The stream abruptly leaves the bluff, entering the pasture heading north. After several jogs to the right, the stream heads east and then doubles back south along a 25-foot undercut shale and limestone cliff.

The next mile has a tortuous series of swift, tight bends through dense forests. It can be demanding, especially at high water. Check each corner for frequent strainers or sweepers. After a left bend, you head toward a 30-foot earthen cliff, and the river curves right through a 50-yard-long rapids along the cliff's base that you'll want to scout for snags before running.

After a left bend, the twisting river straightens out along a pretty wooded ridge, leading to a short class I rapids, which you can actually see well from upstream as you approach. The current remains swift with riffles into a lightly wooded area mixed with pasture, and at a left bend are orangish rock outcroppings. Passing along a small wooded ridge, you reach the bridge at Ironwood Trail. The final segment to Hogback Covered Bridge becomes somewhat less challenging, passing through woods until joining a ridge on the left that has brightly tinted orange sandstone outcroppings protruding from a small dirt cliff. You'll see the covered bridge ahead. **Take out** on the left downstream of it, and upstream of the concrete bridge.

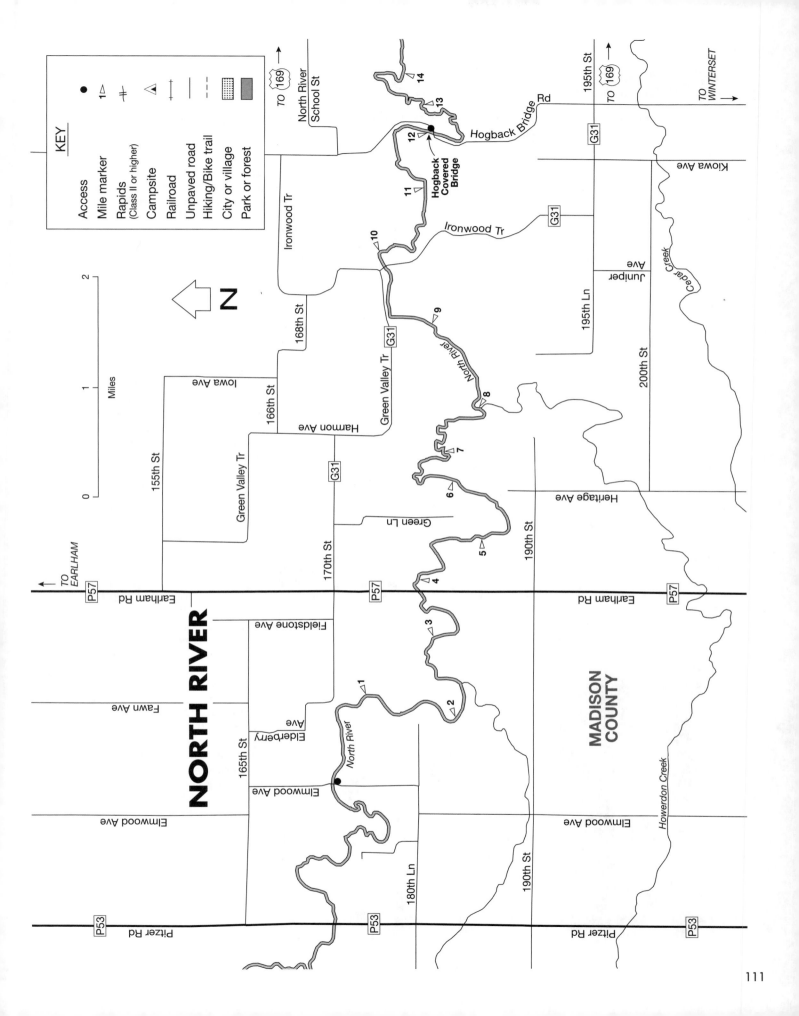

NORTH RIVER

KEY

- Access ●
- Mile marker △1
- Rapids (Class II or higher) ⫤
- Campsite △
- Railroad ⟊
- Unpaved road
- Hiking/Bike trail
- City or village
- Park or forest

N

Miles
0 1 2

MADISON COUNTY

Hogback Covered Bridge

TO 169
TO WINTERSET
TO EARLHAM

RACCOON RIVER
Boonerville Access to West Des Moines (11.9 Miles)

A good section of river for escaping the city, the Raccoon River for the most part here has its characteristic personality—quite easygoing, with numerous good sandbars and a sandy bottom. At two points, though, it courses over bedrock that creates riffles. One of these spots, right at the end of the trip, involves a pair of ledges that develop class I–II waves.

Generally, the river flows through a plain up to 1.5 miles wide, meandering on the south edge of its valley, joining, leaving, and rejoining a scenic, heavily wooded ridgeline. As you near suburban West Des Moines, it may come as no surprise that signs of development are encroaching upon the river, including riverfront homes and landscaping companies. With no access in between the put-in and takeout, plan for a full day of paddling. Fishing is primarily for catfish, and some walleye.

Walnut Woods State Park has a **campground**. At the Polk County line, the river bottom is "meandered," meaning you can camp on high sandbars (see introduction), although areas near the freeway and homes are not ideal.

Canoe and kayak rentals are available from Raccoon River Retreats (515-833-2636) in Redfield and Canoesport Outfitters (515-961-6117) in Indianola. Des Moines Rental (515-277-4401) also rents canoes.

The **shuttle route** (11.9 miles) runs east on County F90, south on Interstate 35, and briefly east on State Highway 5. Get in the right lane, and take the first exit at the sign for Walnut Woods State Park. Turn left, heading north to Old Highway 5. Then head west to Southwest 105th Street, following the curve east to the park entrance.

For **water levels** check the Raccoon River at Van Meter gauge (station 05484500) on the USGS Web site listed in the introduction. About 700 cfs is a friendly level.

The **gradient** is 3.2 feet per mile.

Paddling south from the **put-in**, just downstream from the County F90 bridge, you pass along light woods approaching a forested ridge to the southeast. As you bend northeast, a ridge with large homes is visible across the valley, and the river curves southeast again toward another wooded ridge. At the left curve away from the ridge, the channel parts around a large, sandy island, the tail end of which is secluded enough and high enough for river camping at moderate water levels.

Heading north, you can hear traffic along County F90 on the left before the river bends to the right away from the road and then runs in a long eastward stretch along high sandbars and wooded banks, at one point along the base of a wooded ridge. As the river turns left into a horseshoe bend, the trees thin out, and you pass along a cornfield topping cut banks at the north part of the bend. Curving back southward into the woods, the river bends left at a 70-foot-high wooded bluff and heads east along scenic ribbons of sandstone and limestone bedrock.

Continuing along the bluff, the river drops through a 50-yard riffle. A second riffle culminates dropping over a small ledge near large rocks, and homes are perched on the banks to the right. Heading northeast, the river approaches County F90 again, curving back to the southeast past riprap on the banks.

After the river takes a bit of a bend to the left, the banks are more wooded, and at a right bend the river flows straight south into the first of a series of horseshoe bends. Passing several pumping stations for Des Moines' water supply, including an old brick one, the river bends north, coming very close to county F90, where the river bends south along riprapped banks.

After the final horseshoe bend, the river heads east under the twin I-35 bridges, and then its pace quickens a bit around a sandy island. After a jog to the north through pleasant woods, you begin seeing homes of the former town of Commerce (since absorbed by West Des Moines) on the left bank at a right bend. A boulder midstream announces that two main bedrock ledges (class I–II) are just ahead. Easily scoutable from your boat, they range from quite easygoing below 700 cfs to developing waves high enough to swamp a canoe at higher levels. Usually the adequate water depth is on the left. At higher levels, there are no easy portage spots except along the riprap on the left, but if you paddle along the river-right bank, the waves are not intense.

The river becomes sandy-bottomed again, and just ahead on the river-right, **take out** at the Walnut Woods State Park boat ramp.

Other trips. For information about the section downstream of here and more on the ledges in this section, see Appendix 1 and Appendix 2.

Just outside West Des Moines, the serene Raccoon may surprise you at a couple of rockier swift spots.

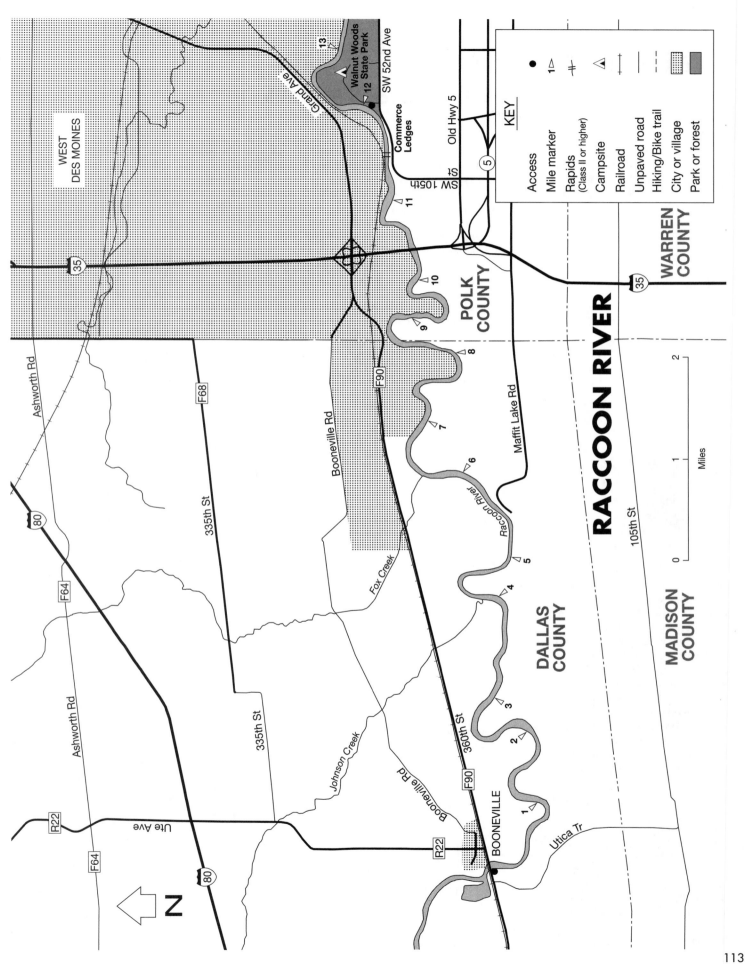

RACCOON RIVER

WEST DES MOINES

Walnut Woods
12 State Park

Commerce
Ledges

POLK COUNTY

WARREN COUNTY

DALLAS COUNTY

MADISON COUNTY

BOONEVILLE

Grand Ave

SW 52nd Ave

SW 105th St

Old Hwy 5

Booneville Rd

Maffit Lake Rd

Raccoon River

Fox Creek

Johnson Creek

Booneville Rd

105th St

Ashworth Rd

Ashworth Rd

Ute Ave

335th St

335th St

360th St

Utica Tr

N

KEY

●	Access
1△	Mile marker
⌿	Rapids (Class II or higher)
△	Campsite
╫	Railroad
	Unpaved road
┆	Hiking/Bike trail
▦	City or village
▨	Park or forest

0   1   2
Miles

ROCK RIVER
340th Street to Rock Sioux Access (8.9 Miles)

Often overlooked, the Rock River is a local favorite in Sioux County, in far western Iowa. Despite the river's name, and although you will see occasional piles of glacial-erratic rocks along the banks, the Rock is mostly a sandy stream. It flows through more croplands than perhaps any other trip in this book. Occasionally, the scenery is quite impressive, including a high bluff with earthen cliffs and some heavily wooded sections.

Averaging 100 feet wide and running shallow, the river is smaller and more intimate than the nearby Big Sioux, with plenty of sandbars to stop at along the way. When it's high, it runs as chocolaty as the Big Sioux, but at moderate levels it is somewhat clearer. Fishing is best for channel catfish.

Oak Grove and Big Sioux Parks share a **campground** with full amenities up the ridge from the river.

Canoe rentals are available from the Rent All Center (712-722-3928) in Sioux Center.

The **shuttle route** (9.8 miles) runs east on 340th Street, south on Dipper Avenue, west on County B30, south on County K22, west on County B40, and south a short distance on County K18.

To estimate **water levels**, see the information in Big Sioux River 2.

The **gradient** is less than 2 feet per mile.

The **put-in** is a carry-down beneath the 340th Street bridge on the river-left. The river curves left beyond the bridge, and the banks are heavily wooded with silver maples. Rocks line the right bank and then the left bank, where at a boulder you bend into a long, fairly straight section heading southwest.

The line of trees along the banks alternates between sparse and dense, with cornfields visible atop cut banks in spots. At a left bend the river begins bending regularly, and extensive sand and gravel bars line the water. A small, wooded hill with oaks and walnuts joins the left bank, and at a right bend sharply right away from the hill, the river widens, becoming shallow. At the next left bend, a long sandbar leads to the County B30 bridge.

The banks are low and scrubby as the river heads generally west through gentle bends. Passing a horse corral, you bend left, heading southwest where trees begin to line the river. As you head generally south, the banks become more heavily wooded with mature trees. Past a line of glacier-deposited rocks on the right, occasional clearings

make cornfields visible. Ahead, a gracefully sculpted grassy ridge dotted with boulders appears in the distance on the left. A small creek enters from the left through a deep-cut bank as the river curves right. After a left bend, the channel splits around a long, wooded island. In the narrow, deeper left channel, a cathedral of tree limbs hangs over the swift water.

Once the channels have rejoined, you round a small right bend, and then a bend left, to the south, heading straight toward loess cliffs on a 100-foot bluff, wooded with oaks. You bend southwest at the bluff's base, and woods continue along the banks as the bluff recedes. At a left bend to the south, corn tops a cut bank on the river-right. Views of mixed wooded and grassy rolling ridges continue on the left. Heading northwest and then hooking straight south along sparsely tree-lined banks, you continue southward through a mix of croplands and groves to the Cherry Avenue bridge.

In a rightward curve through sparsely wooded banks, you reach a left bend, where the **takeout** is on the high sandbar on the river-left, 300 yards upstream from the confluence with the Big Sioux River.

Other trips. You can easily extend this trip by 1.6 miles, continuing into the Big Sioux to the canoe landing at Oak Grove Park. It's a much larger river, about 180 feet wide, passing along lowland woods and croplands, until reaching the parks where an impressive 120-foot wooded ridge joins the bank. Another pleasant trip on the Rock River begins just west of Doon at the County A52 bridge, just upstream of the fork with the Little Rock River. After floating 8.1 miles past pastures and some croplands, along with some very heavily wooded sections, take out at the boat ramp north of Rock Valley on County K42. Above the confluence with the Little Rock River, both streams tend to be of canoeable depth only sporadically, and they pass mostly through heavily agricultural areas.

Rocks and Stones

The Rock River is named for the Sioux quartzite bedrock outcroppings that appear along the river farther north at places like Rock Rapids and Blue Mound State Park near Luverne, Minnesota, all extensions of the *Couteau des Prairie* (see Big Sioux River 1). One of the southernmost Sioux quartzite outcroppings is in the southwest corner of Oak Grove Park. Quartzite is an extremely hard rock, more like granite than softer limestones, shales, and sandstones typically found in Iowa. Many buildings in Sioux City, Iowa, and Sioux Falls, South Dakota, were constructed of it, colloquially called "redrock." Iowa's oldest exposed rocks, they formed about 1.7 billion years ago. The Rock River's headwaters are near Pipestone National Monument near Pipestone, Minnesota, where various tribes quarried a much softer kind of red stone geologists call "catlinite," named after artist George Catlin, who recorded Native American ways of life in paintings. The Indians used it to fashion peace pipes. On at least one early map, the Rock River was labeled the Red Pipe Stone River.

The Rock is a smaller alternative to the nearby Big Sioux, with simular scenery.

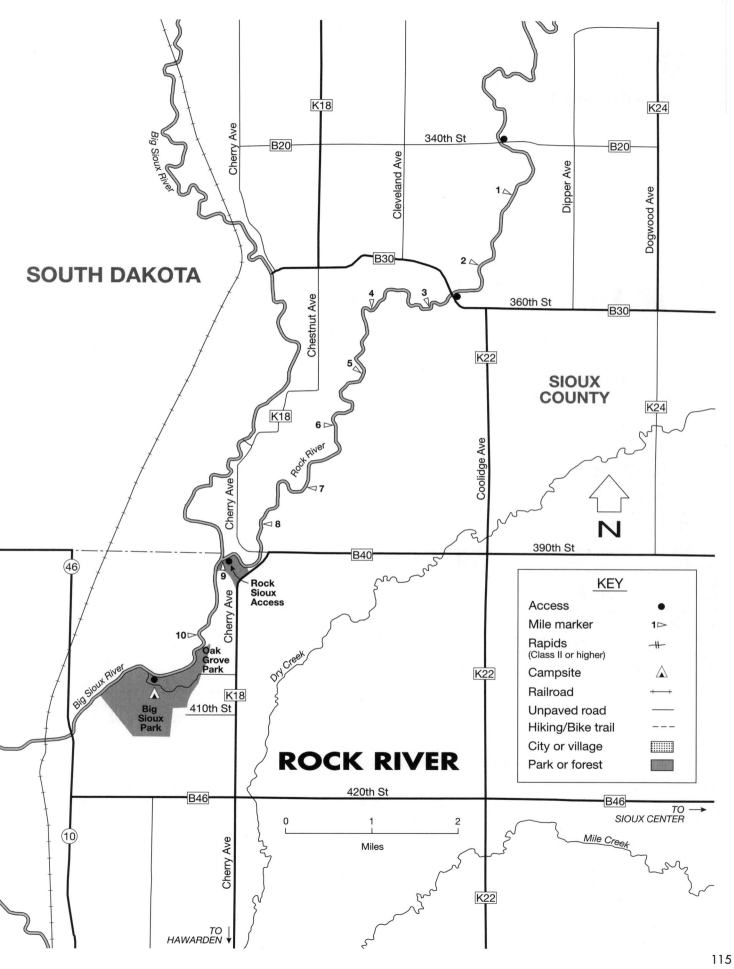

SHELL ROCK RIVER 1
Northwood to Plymouth (16.6 Miles)

In Worth County, Cerro Gordo County, and a portion of Floyd County, the Shell Rock River free-flowingly passes along and over quite a lot of "shell rock," better known as limestone. Not the most vaunted trip on the Shell Rock (see Shell Rock River 2), the landscape here—where meadow, field, pasture, and rock meet rushing water—give it an entirely different atmosphere from most Iowa paddling trips. Most often, you'll pass low, grassy banks or small limestone exposures, usually appearing like stair steps lining the banks.

Averaging 60 feet wide, this is a small, oft-rocky-bottomed stream, and your boat will thank you if you wait to run it at moderately high water. The pastures make for quite a number of fences, and you will periodically need to get out of the boat to portage where it's unsafe to go under them. Fishing for northern pike is good, and some catfish and smallmouth bass are caught. You can shorten this long trip using one of the many bridges as an access—most are not difficult.

Ochee Yahola Park, 4 miles northwest of Northwood, has a **campground** near the river. Camping is prohibited at Land of Two Waters.

The **shuttle route** (15.8 miles) from the put-in in Northwood runs east across the Shell Rock River bridge on 2nd Avenue, south on U.S. Highway 65, east on State Highway 9, south on County S56, and east on 340th Street across the bridge to the Strand Park access.

For **water levels**, see Shell Rock River 2; look for slightly higher levels.

The **gradient** is 4.6 feet per mile.

Below the low-head dam at Swensrud Park is a bridge too low to paddle under. **Put in** downstream-right of the bridge, and paddle down the swift and rocky stream meandering in a wooded corridor through town. After the trees thin out, ahead you see a sign reading "low-head dam," but the dam has been reduced to rubble. If water is adequate, you can run either through a left or a center chute without trouble.

Following grassy banks with occasional thickets of willow shrubs, the river makes only subtle bends heading south to the 450th Street Bridge, where a farm is near a cornfield. The water is shallow and sandy heading south along crops and grassy banks; at a left bend, the banks become wooded. You pass under Highway 65, where the river deepens and narrows to a railroad bridge and then to a swift section past grain bins over a rocky substrate.

As the river slows again, rocks line the banks, and lines of trees line one bank or the other. Sporadically, little limestone ledges begin to jut from the banks. Passing through cornfields and pasture, you come to the 430th Street bridge, past which you might encounter a streamwide fence. Limestone boulders begin lining the banks. Past a home and more pasture, an abrupt right turn past a gnarled cottonwood brings you into a series of swift, S-shaped bends, still through pasture, with growing limestone walls and boulders along the banks. You pass under a farmer's wooden bridge, and the setting is idyllic and unique.

Past a fence, you enter nicely wooded Land of Two Waters, a public area. Elk Creek tumbles in from the right, and limestone ledges switch from one bank to another as you pass between mature cottonwood, willow, and ash trees. The river bends east, and a little creek joins from the left as you leave Land of Two Waters, where woods give way to grassy meadow.

Through a swift riffle, the river widens to 100 feet, quite shallow around a grassy island. Past the County A38 bridge, you briefly run between cornfields. Bending left into a riffle, you pass a mix of trees and grassy meadows. Turning right, the river constricts and drops over a small ledge. Limestone walls appear intermittently. Past the 400th Street bridge, the river widens into another shallow riffle near old bridge abutments. Narrowing along grassy banks, the river widens again around a large, sandy island with a lone cottonwood, and you reach the County A39 bridge.

You pass through a long flatwater section along meadow banks just as the next bridge becomes visible, and little limestone walls rise along the banks again. The river drops over a small bedrock ledge, entering a riffle leading to the 380th Street Bridge. Sporadic limestone outcroppings continue as you head south into a pasture with low banks.

The river twists and turns through grassy banks resplendent in wildflowers, and it flows fast through riffles and past a nearby barn. After a right bend, you go over a riffle that leads to the Highway 9 bridge. Past it, another riffle leads toward a home, passing along stairlike limestone formations. As you continue along occasional rock exposures in a deeper channel, the Plymouth grain elevator becomes visible in the distance. Nearing town, the river bends sharply right along a crumbly limestone wall and past a home. At the next left bend, **take out** at Plymouth's Strand Park, just downstream-left of the 340th Street trestle bridge.

Shell Rock Revival

Native Americans knew the Shell Rock as the Neshonagaton, or Otter River, and river otters swim here again today. For years leading up to the 1970s, though, Albert Lea, Minnesota, didn't consider its natural lake—the Shell Rock's source—or the river it feeds, to be such special places. Pumping unfiltered sewage into the lake, at times the city fed the upper Shell Rock with such nutrient intensity that the river flowed green with algae blooms. People living near the river didn't open windows due to its reek, and the stream was devoid of game fish. Under pressure from Iowa, the town finally built a wastewater treatment plant, allowing both the lake and river to regenerate. An incredible success story, the Shell Rock now runs cleaner, and fish have returned.

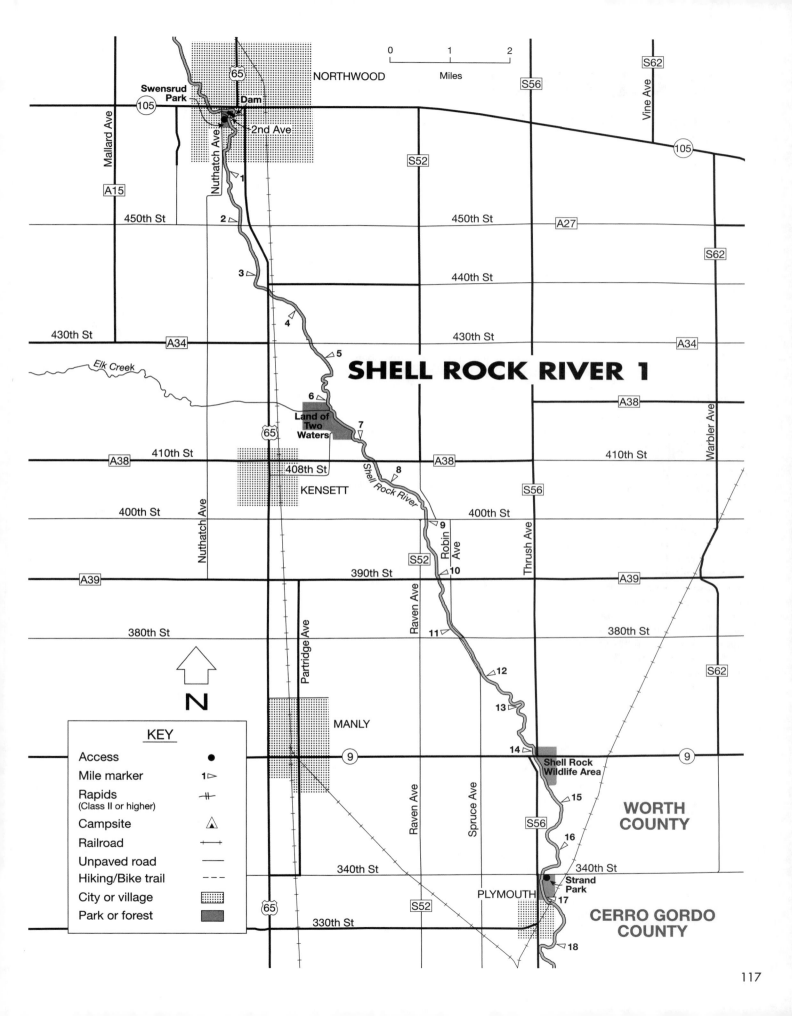

SHELL ROCK RIVER 1

SHELL ROCK RIVER 2
Plymouth to Nora Springs (11.9 Miles)

With fast water and frequent small cliffs, this section of the Shell Rock is immensely fun when the water is up. The first segment from Plymouth to Rock Falls runs through both speedy riffles and exhilarating ledge rapids, mostly class I. At higher water levels, three of these ledges become (very short) class II drops with waves that attract whitewater play boaters. It's not overly dangerous; still, novice boaters may swim. The second portion from Rock Falls to Nora Springs sustains the same gradient but drops in longer, still quite spirited riffles where the scenery is heavily wooded with dramatic bluffs. Fishing is primarily for smallmouth bass and catfish.

Camp of the Woods (641-696-3413) is a privately run riverside **campground** on Falls Park Drive just northwest of Rock Falls. Wilkinson Pioneer Park has a campground with full amenities up the hill from the river. Shell Rock River Preserve has a primitive campground accessible from the river (see trip description).

The **shuttle route** (15.8 miles) from the put-in at Plymouth runs west on 340th Street, south on County S56, east on State Highway 122, and north on Hooker Avenue to Mill Dam Park in Nora Springs.

Determining **water levels** is tricky, as the Shell Rock's only gauge is more than 60 miles downriver. Check the Shell Rock at Shell Rock gauge (station 5462000) on the USGS Web site listed in the introduction, subtracting the flow of the Winnebago River at Mason City gauge (station 05459500). Look for a minimum difference of 400 cfs, along with rainfalls around Albert Lea, Minnesota. Whitewater play boaters will enjoy higher levels.

The **gradient** is 5.9 feet per mile.

Put in downriver-left from the 340th Street bridge in Plymouth's Strand Park. The river heads swiftly past the backyards of Plymouth homes, dropping over a small ledge at an island tufted with grasses and wildflowers. Past a railroad ridge, you drop through a riffle, bend right, and head toward a rusty trestle bridge.

Through a rock-strewn, riffly course, the river heads west, curving south near County S56 on the right and dropping over another ledge with the larger waves on the right side of the river. Ahead, past two homes, a cracked limestone wall with cedars joins the left bank. Heading southeast, the stream drops over another small ledge, and you briefly see a cornfield. The river is tree-lined again, and a rock wall joins the left bank. The next ledge (class I–II) can be a little tricky, dropping about 2 feet. The rocky center is not runnable at moderate levels; approach the left chute head-on. Running the right chute requires a left turn in swift current, culminating in a splashy wave.

Heading swiftly east, you reach Camp of the Woods campground. You bend right, and picturesque Rock Falls Creek drops over several tiers of dams, and the Shell Rock falls over a wavy ledge best run through the center. Southward through several riffles, the river slows along tree-lined banks, bending left. You hear the roar of another drop, Shell Rock Falls, this one dropping 3 feet. It's easiest to run on the far river-right chute.

Passing under the scenic arched bridge at the village of Rock Falls, you'll see limestone walls joining the banks, followed by the rock-and-prairie banks of Wilkinson Pioneer Park on the right. Past stairlike limestone formations is a red covered bridge on the right.

Past an abandoned trestle bridge and its concrete replacement at 295th Street is a flat slab of rock. You follow a cedar-lined limestone wall eastward through a savanna (watch for fences) in the Shell Rock River Greenbelt, and the river is glassy until it reaches a 30-foot-wide, fast chute. Then it slows, curving along small, cedar-topped cliffs to the 290th Street bridge.

Dividing around a small island, the river enters a swift, highly scenic section in the Shell Rock River Preserve. At a left bend, past a small limestone wall, the river runs southeast. The river is forced into a right bend at an impressive 30-foot overhanging cliff, and half a tunnel of rock forms over the swift channel. As you head south, you see a similar higher cliff. Making a sharp right, the river follows along a small limestone wall on the left. Directly across the river from a bluff-top home on the right, you can hike up a trail to the preserve's primitive campground.

With more fast water heading south, the river slows as the bluff on the right recedes. Past the next bridge, at a left bend, the velocity increases past heavy woods and rocky banks. Beyond an island, the river flows over riffles and easy rapids. At a left bend into a rightward curve, the channel tightens into a 40-foot-wide, swift chute into a longer leftward curve. The current slows to a crawl, and wooded banks give way to grasslands. Turning southeast, the river becomes lakelike heading into the Mill Pond approaching Nora Springs. **Take out** near the shelter house at Mill Dam Park on the right shore.

Other trips. The paddling is nice below the dam at Nora Springs (put in on the river-left, below the dam)—especially in Nora Springs itself—as far south as the 180th Street bridge. You may prefer to avoid going any farther south toward Rockford if winds are from the south; otherwise, you'll likely experience hog-confinement stench.

Shell Rock Falls

The tidy town of Rock Falls was originally called Shell Rock Falls after the 4-foot falls on the river that enticed Euro-Americans to pick this spot for settlement. The falls still exist, in a somewhat altered form. The first settler, Elijah Wiltfong, arrived in 1856 and built a mill with a 20-foot dam at the falls. Some of its rock rubble remains today.

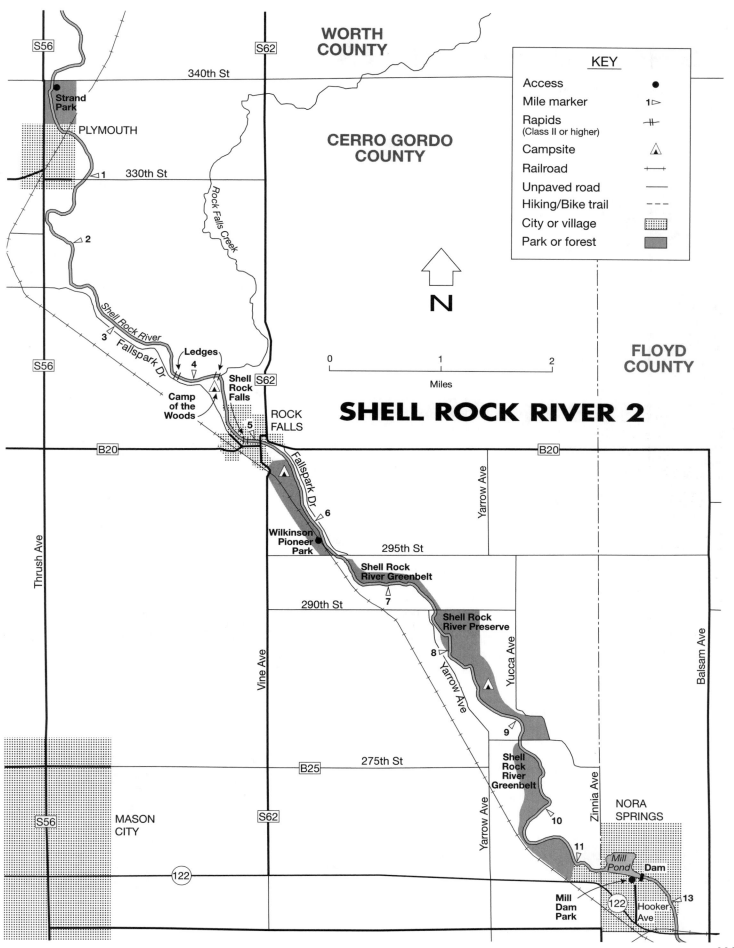

SHELL ROCK RIVER 2

KEY

Access	●
Mile marker	1▷
Rapids (Class II or higher)	╫
Campsite	▲
Railroad	┼
Unpaved road	——
Hiking/Bike trail	- - -
City or village	▦
Park or forest	▧

WORTH COUNTY

CERRO GORDO COUNTY

FLOYD COUNTY

N

0   1   2
Miles

S56

340th St

Strand Park

PLYMOUTH

330th St

1

2

Rock Falls Creek

S62

Shell Rock River

3

Fallspark Dr

Ledges

4

Camp of the Woods

Shell Rock Falls

S62

5

ROCK FALLS

B20

Fallspark Dr

6

Wilkinson Pioneer Park

295th St

Shell Rock River Greenbelt

7

290th St

Shell Rock River Preserve

8

Yarrow Ave

9

Yucca Ave

B20

Yarrow Ave

B25

275th St

Shell Rock River Greenbelt

10

11

Thrush Ave

Vine Ave

S56

MASON CITY

S62

Yarrow Ave

Zinnia Ave

Balsam Ave

NORA SPRINGS

Mill Pond

Dam

122

Mill Dam Park

122

Hooker Ave

13

SHELL ROCK RIVER 3
Clarksville to Shell Rock (8.6 Miles)

Wizardry and Water

Before author Robert James Waller became famous outside Iowa for penning *The Bridges of Madison County*, he wrote a lyrical series of essays for the *Des Moines Register* about canoeing from the Shell Rock's source to its mouth. It was later compiled into a long essay called "Going Soft upon the Land and Down Along the Rivers" for his collection *Just Beyond the Firelight*. The book is prominent in the canon of Iowa paddling literature. Having grown up in Rockford, Waller writes that upon his death his ashes will be spread at a spot most magical to him—the confluence of the Winnebago and Shell Rock Rivers, "where the wizard lives."

A lot has happened to the Shell Rock since its waters left the swift segment in Shell Rock River 2. It's gone past several towns and through several impoundments, including a lake section above Greene where noisy powerboats careen up and down the river. Not at all a high-octane stream here, the Shell Rock has become a lazy river good for a lackadaisical, very pretty float along lowland woods, wildflowers, and extensive sandbars. Passing along no bluffs and through only a few riffles, it's an attractive river anyway, with good camping at the beginning and end.

The Butler County Nature Trail is also excellent for running a shuttle from Heery Woods State Park in Clarksville to the mill access at Shell Rock. Fishing is productive for catfish. The Department of Natural Resources stocks this section with walleye, and some northern pike are also caught.

Heery Woods has a scenic riverside **campground** right at the put-in. Shell Rock Park also has riverside campsites, plus a campground with full amenities.

Canoe rentals are available from the River Ranch Campground (641-435-2108) near Nashua, about 20 miles north of Clarksville.

The **shuttle route** (5.5 miles) from the put-in runs south on State Highway 188 and east and southeast on State Highway 3 to Shell Rock Park.

For **water levels** check the Shell Rock at Shell Rock gauge (station 5462000) on the USGS Web site listed in the introduction. About 500 cfs is pleasant.

The **gradient** is less than 2 feet per mile.

Put in beyond the rocks on the river-left, well below the dangerous dam at Heery Woods State Park in Clarksville. The Highway 188 bridge is just ahead, followed shortly by a railroad bridge, then banks covered in lowland woods.

As the river curves north into a horseshoe bend, sandbars lined with willow shrubs become common, and the river becomes narrower and deeper. The woods continue as the river doubles back, heading southeast, east, and then south through a very deeply wooded floodplain and then briefly past a cornfield. As the river heads east past another field, the banks become increasingly wooded again. Then the river widens to 350 feet where it joins a large backwater, a good spot to spy aquatic birds such as herons and egrets.

Heading south into a second horseshoe bend, the river nears 205th Street on the right, where there is a privately owned access near a line of riprap. Bending left at a log home on a small ridge, the river runs past mobile homes and passes into another woodland area heading northeast. As you curve southeast, the stream's character begins changing. Limestone rocks line the left bank with an attractive forest of mixed hardwoods with seasonal wildflowers in the understory.

Bending northeast, the river passes a small, wooded ridge on the right. As the river curves back into a long, straight stretch southeast, the banks are still rocky and the river courses through several little riffles. Then you begin seeing homes with retaining walls and decks just before a brief jog into a sharp bend right. Bending left to the southeast again, the river heads through more lowland woods and widens into a left bend where the channel braids around several sandy islands covered in woods and grasses. Reaching a prominent log home with giant weeping willow trees, you bend right along riprap, curving to the right toward the Highway 3 bridge. Just beyond that, the **takeout** is at the boat ramp, downstream on the river-right.

Other trips. Well upstream of here, the 10.2-mile trip from Rockford to Marble Rock also offers reasonably good paddling, and the first part of it is riffly along rocky, wooded ridges before it slows behind a high dam at Marble Rock. Also see Appendix 2. If you enjoy lazy float trips on a sandy river, try the shallow Little Cedar River near Nashua, about 20 miles northeast of Clarksville. Put in at Chickasaw Park on County B47, below the rapids, and float to either the River Ranch Campground (which runs shuttles on the Little Cedar and Cedar Rivers near Nashua; 641-435-2108) or the dead-end road just south of the Highway 346 bridge on the east side of the river.

Woods and wildflowers are common along this stretch of the Shell Rock.

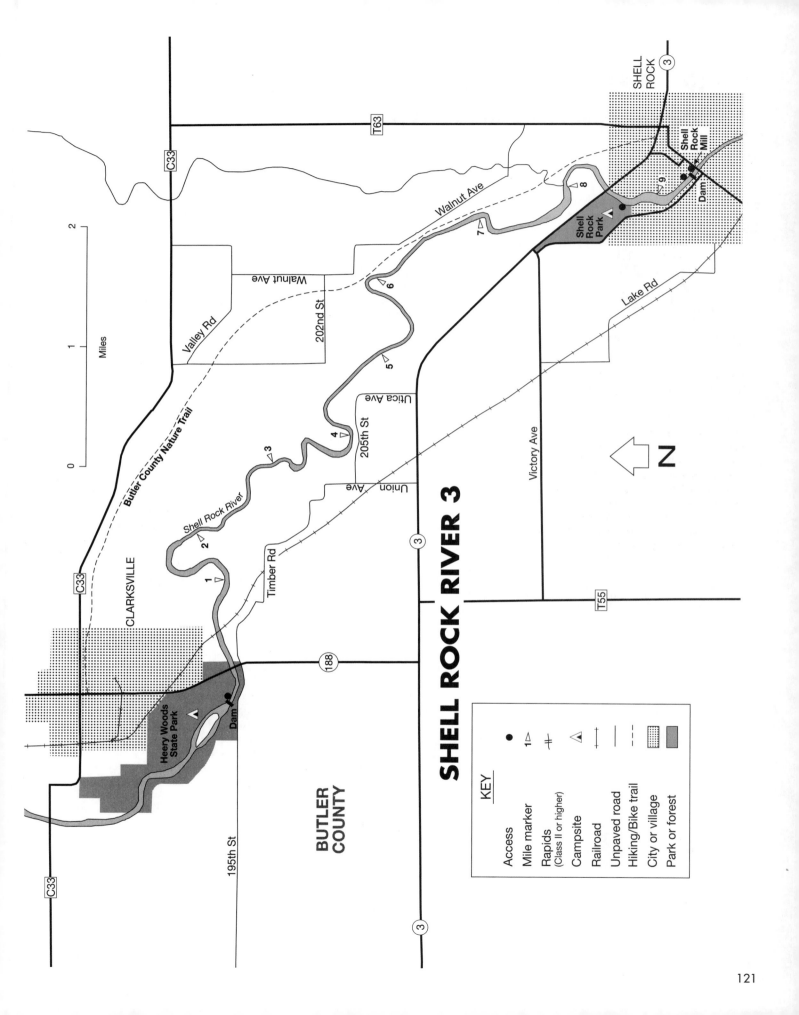

SHELL ROCK RIVER 3

KEY

Access	●
Mile marker	1△
Rapids (Class II or higher)	✝
Campsite	◁
Railroad	┼┼┼
Unpaved road	───
Hiking/Bike trail	- - -
City or village	░░░
Park or forest	▓▓▓

SHELL ROCK

Shell Rock Mill

Shell Rock Park

Heery Woods State Park

CLARKSVILLE

BUTLER COUNTY

Butler County Nature Trail

Shell Rock River

Walnut Ave

Valley Rd

202nd St

205th St

Union Ave

Utica Ave

Victory Ave

Lake Rd

Timber Rd

195th St

Dam

N

Miles

SKUNK RIVER
Oakland Mills Park to Lowell (15.7 Miles)

As it runs through southeast Iowa, the Skunk is a big river, with an average width of 180 feet. But it's not nearly as large as the neighboring Des Moines and Iowa Rivers. Here, it flows along scenic bluffs carpeted in hardwoods and ridges up to 150 feet high, as well as lowland woods in a mostly tree-lined corridor.

During the summer, it usually runs with lots of silt, appearing chocolaty. Something to keep in mind about this stretch is that traveling to it can help extend the paddling season. Fall colors are at their brightest in mid-October, a full week later than in northern Iowa. By that time of the year, like most rivers in Iowa, the Skunk is running crystal clear, and it usually behaves like a somewhat smaller stream.

Catfishing is excellent.

Oakland Mills Park has two **campgrounds**, one riverside and one up the bluff. Stephenson Park at the takeout also has a riverside campground. Scenic Geode State Park, southeast of Lowell, has full amenities but no canoe access.

Canoe and kayak rentals and shuttles are available from River Basin (800-748-3712) near Burlington.

The **shuttle route** (15.9 miles) from the put-in runs south on County W55, east on County J20, and north on County X23. The takeout is just across the Skunk River bridge on the left.

For **water levels** check the Skunk River at Augusta gauge (station 05474000) on the USGS Web site listed in the introduction. About 700 cfs makes for pleasant paddling.

The **gradient** is less than 2 feet per mile.

The scenic **put-in** is on the river-left, at the stairs below the dam in Oakland Mills Park. There's a small rapids to run through just ahead; at lower water levels, it's best run either through the center or through the spirited chute along the limestone wall at the base of the wooded bluff on the river-right.

The bluff tapers off, and past a few cabins, a timbered ridge rises on the left. The river bends left along the rock outcroppings at the ridge's base. Soon, you arrive at the Faulkner boat ramp on the river-left, an alternative put-in. The banks are rock-lined slopes as you continue, and they are followed by a section of dirt banks and a thinner line of trees until you begin to pass tall, noble sycamores.

At a sharp left turn at a small, wooded ridge, the river runs through a riffle, and a tree-covered bluff rises on the right. As you head east along the bluff, you see a line of mobile homes and cabins along the left bank to the Highway 218 bridge. After the Skunk heads southeast through wooded banks with occasional cabins and past limestone shelves, a long riffle leads along a rock bar, and you near a wooded ridge on the right.

Bending right at a high cut bank with a clearing and more cabins, the river runs straight south into a more wooded area, and Fish Creek enters from the right. At the bridge at Lexington Avenue, there is a private boat ramp on the downstream-right side. Just past here, the river runs into a wavy 200-yard riffle that curves around a rock bar and then heads northeast. At a bend to the southeast along a 20-foot clay bank with a clearing, the river drops through a brief riffle and turns left at another rock bar. Both sides of the river slope down with heavily vegetated banks, and Big Creek joins from the left.

With light woods on both sides of the river, you bend east along high, tree-topped cut banks toward a heavily timbered bluff to the east. Near a cabin in the woods, the river curves rightward along the base of the scenic 150-foot wooded bluff with interesting limestone formations at the river level. Heading southwest away from the bluff, you turn abruptly left along small rock outcroppings on the right. Heading south through the narrow, wooded valley, the river joins a wooded ridge on the right and curves along it past the homes of Lowell to the northeast. The **takeout** is at the boat ramp upstream of the County X23 bridge on the river-left.

Other trips. The 9.9-mile trip from Stephenson Park to the boat ramp a mile northwest of Augusta offers scenery similar to that in the described section, along wooded banks with occasional scenic ridges and intermittent limestone outcroppings, with some crop fields. There are campgrounds at Indian Path Park and Welter Park in Augusta, and both camping and cabin rentals (but not ideal access) at Gray's Landing. Well upstream, in Washington County, the river periodically passes along smaller wooded bluffs, as do both the smaller North Skunk and the South Skunk to their union in Keokuk County. From Ames to Keokuk County, the South Skunk has been channelized and doesn't offer much of interest for paddlers.

Nice River, Rank Name

Being somewhat unknown to paddlers, the Skunk River has something of an image problem. That its name conjures up images of fetid, striped creatures does not make the situation better. Perhaps a little etymology can help. Our name for the river derives from an Algonquin word, *Checauqua*, the same root for the city of Chicago. The name roughly translates as "smelly." Hmmm. Some suppose that the name for the Skunk River derived from the skunk cabbage that sometimes grows on its banks. That doesn't make perceptions all that much better, either, as the plant—in order to attract flies and gnats that pollinate its cabbagelike flowers—generates high heat and emits a foul odor. For the record, the Skunk River isn't foul smelling.

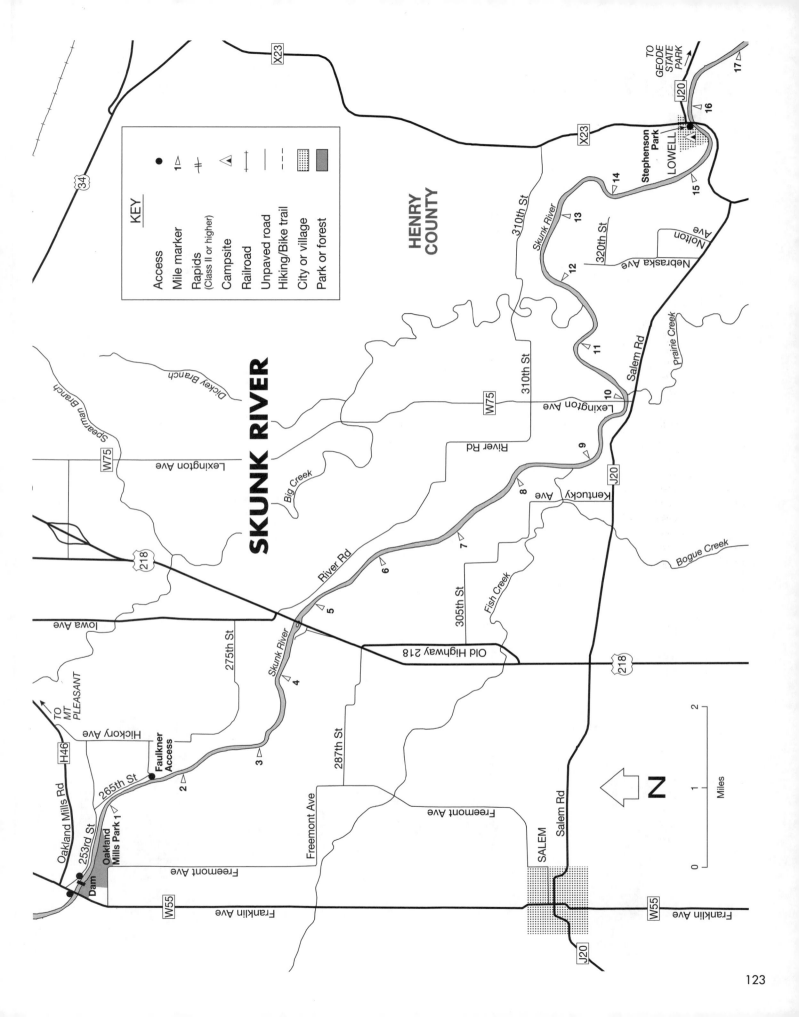

SKUNK RIVER

KEY

Access
Mile marker
Rapids (Class II or higher)
Campsite
Railroad
Unpaved road
Hiking/Bike trail
City or village
Park or forest

HENRY COUNTY

TO GEODE STATE PARK

Stephenson Park

LOWELL

Skunk River

Nebraska Ave

Notion Ave

320th St

310th St

Salem Rd

Prairie Creek

Lexington Ave

River Rd

W75

Big Creek

Dickey Branch

Spearman Branch

Lexington Ave

Kentucky Ave

Bogue Creek

Fish Creek

305th St

Old Highway 218

River Rd

Skunk River

275th St

287th St

Freemont Ave

Freemont Ave

Salem Rd

SALEM

Franklin Ave

W55

Iowa Ave

TO MT PLEASANT

Hickory Ave

Faulkner Access

265th St

253rd St

Oakland Mills Park 1

Oakland Mills Rd

H46

Dam

Franklin Ave

N

Miles

SOUTH RACCOON RIVER 1
Nation's Bridge to McCammond Access (11.7 Miles)

In close proximity to the larger Middle Raccoon River before they join at Redfield, this segment of the South Raccoon has more in common with Madison County's Middle River than the river it will soon join. Averaging approximately 60 feet wide, the South Raccoon usually rises and falls fairly quickly. Its geology, being just beyond the end moraine of the most recent glacial advances, exhibits age-worn bedrock outcroppings and some sandstone cliffs.

This river doesn't pass along nearly as much public land, so expect to see some agricultural activity near the river. But there are also some pristine areas that may surprise a paddler who's never tried this float. Fishing is for catfish and occasional smallmouth bass.

Nation's Bridge Park has a riverside **campground** with full amenities.

Canoe and kayak rentals are available from Raccoon River Retreats (515-833-2636) in Redfield.

The **shuttle route** (8.3 miles) from the put-in runs north on County P28, east on County F59, south on County P48, and briefly west on County F61 to the McCammond Access.

Water levels are somewhat sporadic, and there is no gauge on this river, so you must check visually. Look for sustained periods of rainfalls in Guthrie, Carroll, and Audubon Counties. If you arrive to find too much or too little water, you can also check the Middle Raccoon River 2 and 3 segments or Madison County's North or Middle Rivers.

The **gradient** is 4.1 feet per mile.

After the **put-in** at the ramp at Nation's Bridge Park, the river runs through a riffle. Past the P28 bridge, you curve left along a wooded ridge heading generally north. You briefly pass through a sparsely wooded lowland, and the river reaches a ridge to the north and bends right at its base along small, dark outcroppings of sandstone.

At another wooded ridge on the right, the river bends northeast along more sandstone outcroppings. You curve back to the south in a horseshoe bend, and more prominent low outcroppings line the left bank as you head toward the Walnut Trail bridge. Past the bridge you reach a wooded bluff with mature trees, an earthen slope, and a pretty sandstone wall at its base. Running east past wooded banks, you bend right along a wooded ridge, continuing to curve with it for nearly a mile. Bending left, the river drops through a zesty riffle, and the trees become sparse as you head south, seeing a few cornfields.

As you continue southeast, a colorful cliff with strata of stone, clay, earth, and shale in thin ribbons appears. Dropping through a short riffle, you bend straight east at a wooded bluff. The river circles to the northwest and then hooks back to the right at a junked car, makes a quick left toward concrete riprap, and braids swiftly through sandbars on the way to the 310th Street bridge.

The setting becomes quite wooded again as you curve north toward a pretty ridge with rock outcroppings and cedars along the river as you bend right. Heading east past a clearing on the left, the river bends southeast, passing lowland woods for several very gentle bends. After the river takes a sharper bend to the north, the banks grow more heavily wooded as it bends right, and then left. Reaching a point at the north, the river bends right and curves along a long and very scenic line of sandstone cliffs up to 30 feet tall.

You see riprap as you head straight south toward County F61. Bending left along more riprap and heading east, the river drops over a short, splashy rapids (class I). Heading south past the County F61 bridge, you paddle straight to the base of an impressive, 160-foot wooded bluff with a slanting clay and sandstone exposure. Bending left at the bluff, the river heads northeast along wooded banks. After a right bend, the **takeout** is at the sandbar on the river-left, 200 yards upstream of the County P48 bridge.

Pretty riffles and small bluffs attract paddlers to this intimate little stream.

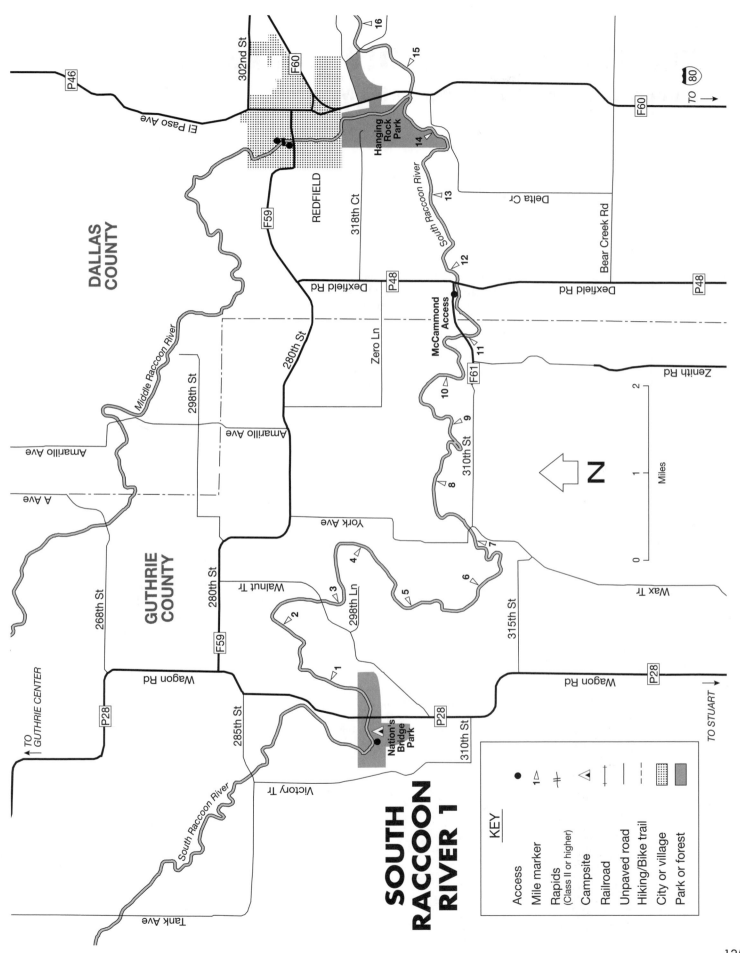

SOUTH RACCOON RIVER 1

KEY

- Access ●
- Mile marker △1
- Rapids (Class II or higher)
- Campsite △
- Railroad
- Unpaved road
- Hiking/Bike trail
- City or village
- Park or forest

N

0 1 2 Miles

DALLAS COUNTY

GUTHRIE COUNTY

Middle Raccoon River

South Raccoon River

Hanging Rock Park

REDFIELD

Nation's Bridge Park

McCammond Access

TO GUTHRIE CENTER

TO STUART

TO → 80

P46
El Paso Ave
302nd St
F60
F59
318th Ct
Delta Cr
Bear Creek Rd
F60
P48
Dexfield Rd
P48
Dexfield Rd
Zenith Rd
F61
310th St
Zero Ln
280th St
Amarillo Ave
298th St
A Ave
Amarillo Ave
268th St
Tank Ave
Victory Tr
285th St
Wagon Rd
P28
F59
280th St
Walnut Tr
298th Ln
York Ave
315th St
Wax Tr
P28
Wagon Rd
310th St
P28

SOUTH RACCOON RIVER 2
Redfield to Earlham Bridge (11.7 Miles)

This beautiful run on the South Raccoon actually begins on the Middle Raccoon River. The atmosphere below the Redfield Dam, where the put-in for this segment is located, is different from that of Middle Raccoon River 2, however. Rather than passing mostly glacial-erratic boulders—and there still are some here—the river flows along numerous sandstone boulders and bedrock outcroppings, including spectacular Hanging Rock, a large undercut cliff, right at the beginning of this trip.

The second half of the trip has fewer rock outcroppings, and the river doesn't run as swift, but the 160-foot deep valley has a pristine, deep-woods feel. In this mid-sized river averaging 80 feet wide, fishing is good for smallmouth bass in the rockier first half, and it's better for catfish in the sandy second half.

The Des Moines West KOA (515-834-2729), a mile south of the takeout on County P58, has a **campground** with full amenities. The Kuehn Conservation Area has hike-in campsites (not accessible from the river). Camping is prohibited on the other side of the river at the Pleasant Valley Access.

Canoe and kayak rentals are available from Raccoon River Retreats (515-833-2636) in Redfield.

The **shuttle route** (10 miles) from the put-in runs east on Thomas Street, south on 1st Street, east on Omaha Street, and then east on County F60 and south on County P58 to the Earlham Bridge Access just across the river bridge on the right side of the road.

For **water levels**, check the South Raccoon at Redfield gauge (station 5484000) on the USGS Web site listed in the introduction. A pleasant level is 600 cfs.

The **gradient** is approximately 3.2 feet per mile.

Put in downstream of the Redfield Dam on the river-right. Through a riffle, you head straight south under the Thomas Street bridge past wooded banks to Hanging Rock, a high sandstone cliff rising straight up from the river and "hanging" out over the channel because the river has undercut its base. The river turns left and runs around the remains of a dam, heading to another sandstone bluff ahead. The river widens heading south, and the landscape becomes cut banks with trees becoming sparse.

As you bend left, the smaller South Raccoon River merges from the right, and the new segment created by the conjoined rivers has been given that name. Past the Highway 6 bridge, the river curves left at a long, unfortunate line of riprap. The banks become more natural and grow wooded as the stream falls through a small riffle. Bending left and passing beneath the G Trail bridge, the river makes a right bend along the woods and drops through a spirited riffle.

Curving left, you reach a small cabin, and then the river curves gently right along small sandstone cliffs. Head south toward a 160-foot, deeply wooded bluff ahead, and you reach its base, where sandstone boulders the size of cattle are strewn about the bank in the river. Small sandstone cliffs appear as the bluff guides the river north.

Bending right along a small, wooded ridge to the H Avenue Bridge, the channel splits around a sandy island. Where a bluff rises on the left, the river bends south and then passes several large boulders and runs through a short riffle. The character of the landscape begins changing as the bluff tapers off heading south. Dirt cut banks and sandbars become more common, and the woods briefly thin allowing meadows to become visible. The river bends sharply left and then right where it reaches a wooded hill.

The river curves into a long, fairly straight section to the east along heavily wooded hills, bending right slightly through the Kuehn Conservation Area. At a sandbar to the right, the channel tightens and speeds up a bit, and the next sandbar on the left is the Pleasant Valley Access, where a dirt trail leads up the embankment to the parking area.

Bending left into a long, rightward arc along a wooded ridge, the river widens to 90 feet, and near a gravel bar you have an unobstructed view of the heavily timbered valley's hills. Reaching a wooded hill on the right, the river bends left, and the channel tightens briefly before widening to more than 300 feet and splitting into two channels around a huge sandy island. Past the island, a home tops the high ridge ahead, breaking the aura of wildness.

Bending left, the river begins passing numerous glacier-deposited rocks and speeds up a bit. Shale ledges begin jutting from the right bank. One unique formation is rather bulbous. In a long rightward curve, you pass a home on the right, and then the mouth of Panther Creek. **Take out** upstream of Earlham Bridge on the river-right.

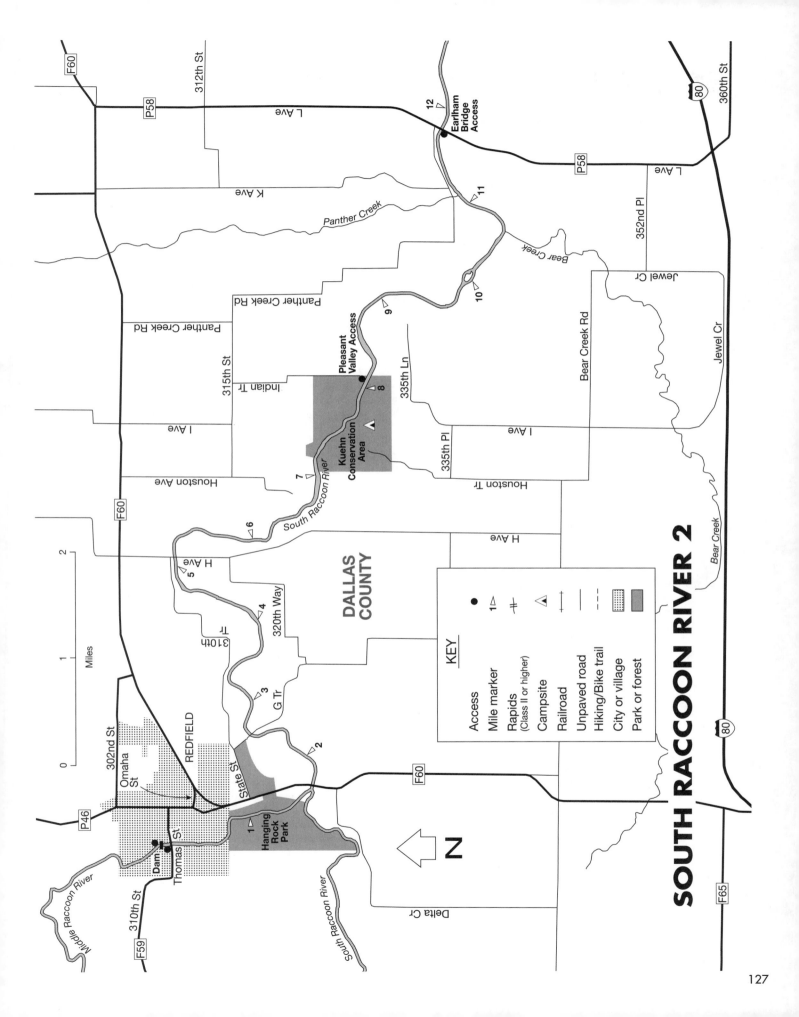

SOUTH RACCOON RIVER 2

KEY

●	Access
1△	Mile marker
⚓	Rapids (Class II or higher)
△	Campsite
┼	Railroad
——	Unpaved road
- - -	Hiking/Bike trail
▦	City or village
▨	Park or forest

SOUTH SKUNK RIVER
Story City to Ames (17.2 Miles)

Many miles of both the North Skunk and South Skunk have been channelized and hold little interest for paddlers, but this segment is a remarkable exception. The U.S. Army Corps of Engineers purchased land along this unaltered stretch in the 1970s with an eye on submerging Story County's only large, uncultivated valley. A general outcry stopped the scheme, leaving swaths of public land and the civic will to create the Skunk River Green Belt, prohibiting development along the river.

Winding through the valley are 19 miles of bike and foot trails, and popular parks attract Ames' outdoors enthusiasts. The river is only 30 to 50 feet wide, and streamwide snags would be a problem but for local paddling and conservation clubs, which clean up trash and informally maintain the channel. In 2002 this segment became the Skunk River Water Trail.

The river bottom alternates between sand, gravel, rock, and sometimes mud. At lower levels, the water clarity is fairly good, although agricultural runoff is present, as it is in many Iowa rivers. Smallmouth bass fishing can be good in the riffles, and channel catfish are common near snags. Usually, this section is divided into two trips. The run from Story City to the Anderson Canoe Access is a quick-running stretch passing over several riffles with glacially deposited rocks along the banks and pleasant lowland woods. The second half of the journey seems somewhat slower for long periods, but occasionally tall, wooded banks rise up, and below the mouth of Bear Creek, long pools become broken up by energetic riffles.

Primitive riverside **camping** is allowed at the mouth of Bear Creek, half a mile upstream from the Soper Mill Access. Three primitive riverside campsites are also available at McFarland Park; they can be difficult to find but are on the left bank, just downstream from where Keigley Branch enters on the right. If you are planning to use them, notify the Story County Conservation Board (515-232-2516).

Canoe and kayak rentals are available in Ames at Ames Outdoor Gear (515-292-2276).

The **shuttle route** (15 miles) from the put-in runs east on Broad Street to Interstate 35 and south to Ames' 13th Street exit. Head west on 13th Street until crossing the Skunk River. Take a right into River Valley Park. The takeout is about 60 yards upstream from the dam.

The **gradient** is 4.4 feet per mile.

For **water levels**, check the South Skunk River near Ames gauge (station 05470000) on the USGS Web site listed in the introduction. About 300 cfs is ideal.

Put in on the river's west side, about 200 yards south from the parking lot at Story City's South Park. The river here is attractive, crossed by a footbridge with stone archways and a dangerous dam. Put in directly below the small rapids.

The trip begins swiftly, snaking through a wooded tunnel of overhanging maple and elm branches. Snags can be tricky. Downstream, the wastewater treatment plant appears, and the river widens and slows. After heading generally eastward, it flows past a housing development while bending south. Grain silos are visible to the west above the trees, and the river quickens pace and tightens into a long bend back east.

Small hills rise, and the channel widens above a ford, best run through the waves right of center, although a quick **portage** is necessary at low levels. A 30-foot-high earth cliff rises on the right and leads to a wide riffle where a logjam accumulates. After shallow riffles, at a bend Long Dick Creek tumbles in from the left. The E18 Access is just ahead, downstream from the bridge on the river-right.

Below County E18, the river bends left and then right, passing sandbars and a tall, sandy bank. The course widens, passes concrete riprap, and heads toward a hilltop home at a leftward bend. The whir of traffic on I-35 can be heard through much of this stretch. At a bend left, junked cars protrude into the river from the right bank. After some island sandbars and a right bend, the Anderson Canoe Access is on the left, just upstream from the 150th Street bridge.

The route is heavily wooded for several miles, and snags are likely, but low, sandy banks make quick portages easy. Bear Creek joins from the left, followed by a riffle. The river enters a valley with steep, wooded banks lined by footpaths. A spirited riffle passes beneath the 170th Street trestle bridge. Downstream one-half mile is the Sopers Mill Access Area on the right. Run the short rapids at the access straight through the center. There are put-ins and takeouts below it and above it that you can use to **portage**. Just downstream, a submerged pipe is a potential hazard in low water, and the river may be **portaged** on the left. Keigley's Branch joins from the right, and the river braids through sandy chutes above the 180th Street bridge. A mile downriver is an access at Peterson Park, across the river from where it connects to a sandpit on the left.

Limestone riprap causes a short riffle. The river passes through two more riffles and by a large home. It slows behind a dam, where limestone outcroppings poke out on the left. **Portage** on the concrete to the right. The Sleepy Hollow Access is downstream-right from the Riverside Road Bridge. Concrete riprap becomes common, and the scenery is briefly dismal with steel buildings and homes before oak-and-hickory-covered ridges rise up and the river regains its woodsy character. After a gentle riffle, the stream passes beneath a steel footbridge at River Valley Park. The **takeout** is just around the next bend to the right, upstream from the big dam.

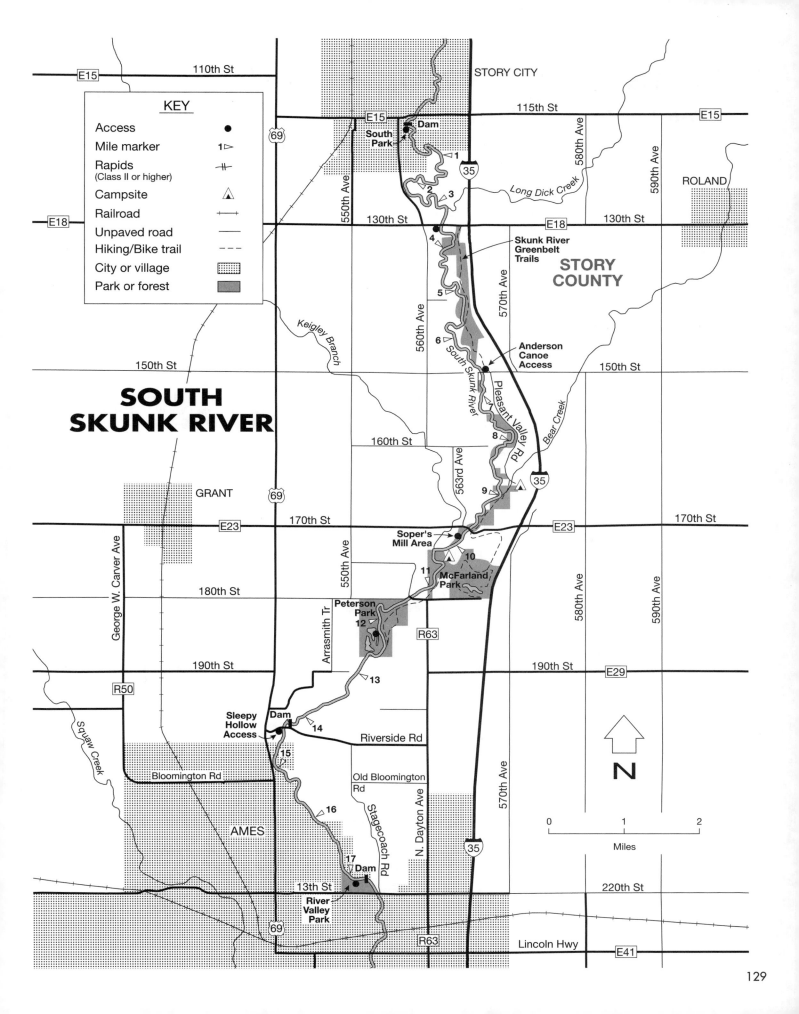

SOUTH SKUNK RIVER

TRUMPETER TRAIL 1 AND 2

Trumbull Lake to County N18 (3.1 Miles)
Lost Island Lake through Barringer Slough (2.8 Miles)

The Trumpeter Trail travels a set of interconnected marshlands, lakes, and sloughs that were once a part of a larger lake known as Pelican Lake, approximately 10 miles northeast of Spencer. In places, scenery is unspoiled as you paddle through seas of enveloping cattails.

At other times, you'll see reminders—small dams and levees—of how drastically settlers changed all of north-central Iowa in their quest to convert wetlands into fertile farmlands. The trail often cannot be paddled from beginning to end, nor is that recommended. Lost Island Marsh can be dry; if it is, you'll face a mile-long portage around it rather than the regular 300-yard portage to the access on Lost Island Lake. Except for the east shore, Lost Island Lake itself does not offer pristine scenery—lakefront homes line its north, west, and south shores. For this reason, two separate trips are recommended here, focusing on the best-quality segments.

That said, approaching the Trumpeter Trail in pieces is a great diversion, and in the two sloughs the abundance of birds—from trilling red-winged blackbirds to honking geese—can be humbling. There are well over 3,500 acres of adjacent wetlands here. Incidentally, the area is brimming with waterfowl hunters during the fall hunting season. Remote lakes and ponds offer excellent fishing for northern pike, bass, walleye, crappy, bluegill, and perch.

Given adequate water conditions, if you do want to paddle the whole trail, the entire route is nearly 12 miles, not all of it easy. Many paddlers may prefer a two-day trip, with a night spent at Lost Island–Huston Park.

Lost Island–Huston Park has a **campground** with full amenities.

The Expedition Co. (712-332-9001) in Arnold's Park on Lake Okoboji **rents kayaks**. **Canoe rentals** are available from Linn Grove Landing (712-296-3635) in Linn Grove.

The **shuttle route** for the first segment (7.4 miles) runs from the put-in south of 310th Street on Trumbull Lake, west on 310th, north on County N14, east on County B17, and south on County N18 to the bridge over Smith's Slough at Mud Lake, where there is parking on the east side of the road.

For the second segment (5.3 miles) from Lost Island Lake, drive northwest on the access road, west on 330th Street, south on 325th Avenue, west on 340th Street, south on 315th Avenue, and east on 350th Street to the access.

For **water levels**, check visually—especially at Lost Island Marsh, North Trumbull Creek, and Barringer Slough—before you go. These areas often cannot be paddled. Don't be surprised if low water conditions turn you back.

The **gradient** is negligible.

For the first part of this trip, Trumbull Lake to County N18, **put in** on the access on the west-central side of Trumbull Lake, south of 310th Street. The lake is mostly undeveloped. Paddle three-quarters of a mile straight east across the lake toward a wooded shore. High waves can develop on windy days; use good judgment.

Approach a point that juts into the water and paddle south around it. To the left, you'll see a marker for the Trumpeter Trail with an arrow pointing into the inlet. Ahead, you'll approach a low-head dam from downstream. Take out on the left by the willows and **portage** 30 yards to the upstream access. Paddle against inconsequential current into charming and serene Smith's Slough, a shallow, sandy-bottomed channel only 10 to 15 feet wide with cattails and reeds lining the banks. Beaver dams can span the slough, requiring a portage or two. Occasionally the channel opens into wide, deep "potholes," or ponds. Trail markers clearly delineate the route.

The **takeout** is at the County N18 bridge. A grate prevents you from paddling straight into Mud Lake, but you can portage across the road and paddle that lightly developed lake, where pelicans often congregate. On the official trail route, you'll reach a dock with a short portage to Lost Island Marsh. If the marsh has water, it can be interesting to paddle. If not, return to the N18 bridge.

For the second part of this trip, Barringer Slough has two main lakes and several ponds connected by shallow marshes that make for challenging paddling. **Put in** at the access on the southwest arm of Lost Island Lake and paddle past a peninsula to a spot 20 yards right of the outlet dam. Carry over the levee and put in at the pond below. You'll pass through a concrete structure to enter a 10-foot-wide creek leading to the north lake. You may need to push through vegetation to enter.

Paddle across to the south side of the lake, where a channel leading out is apparent. Again, you may need to push through mats of vegetation to enter, but then the channel opens into a pond. Beyond here, the trail proceeds into a smaller channel, which splits. If water is low, take the right channel to an island and **portage** through tall grass across it, and then paddle through the marshy area to a southbound channel that opens into the lake. Otherwise, proceed through the cattails and reeds through the increasingly indistinct and marshy left channel before you enter a pond. Through a narrow channel to the south, the water opens into the south lake. Hug the right shore, and the access is past a point through a narrow swath of open water between reeds leading to the 325th Avenue boat ramp, one possible takeout.

The larger channel to the left leads to a network of marshy islands, an area that can be confusing. Generally, navigate just to the right of a stand of cottonwoods ahead. After the channel opens into a larger pond, the **takeout** is on the south shore near the dam.

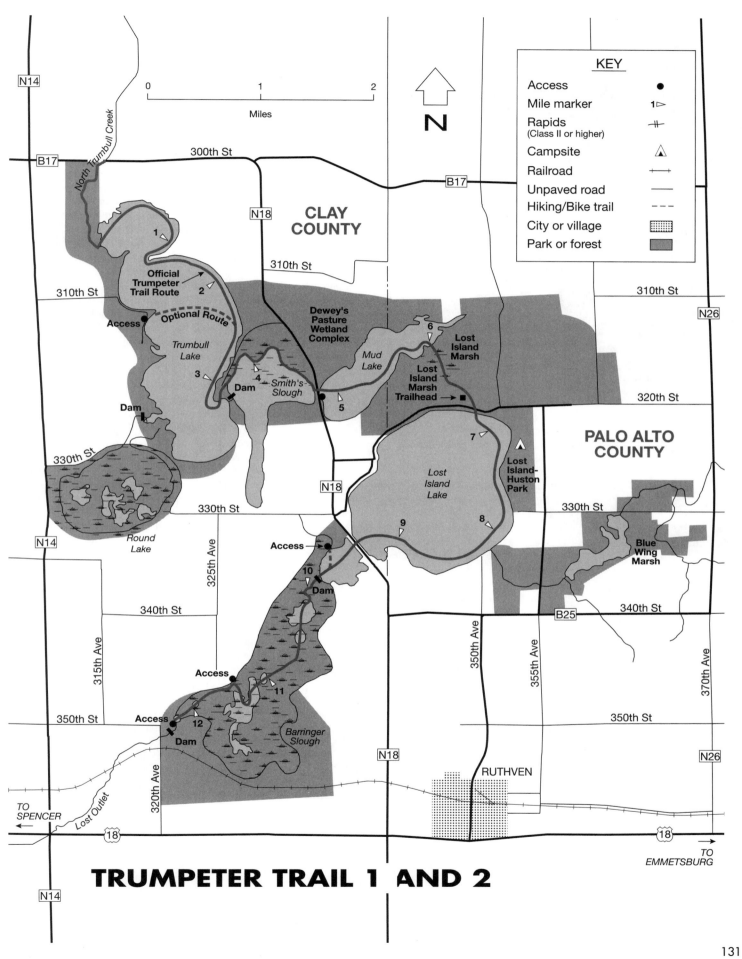

TRUMPETER TRAIL 1 AND 2

TURKEY RIVER 1 AND 2

Eldorado to County W42 (6.1 Miles)
County W42 to Clermont Park (15.6 Miles)

The Turkey is a scenic river sometimes overshadowed by its even showier neighbors, the Upper Iowa, the Yellow, and the Volga. And sure, winding through a heavily agricultural valley, you will notice more cut banks and fields along much of the Turkey than you do on other rivers. But there are also outstanding, serene stretches that make it worthwhile. Plus, while other waters dwindle by late summer, you can often look to the larger Turkey for more consistent flows.

The Turkey is swift and fun, passing woods and some native pines below Eldorado.

These two stretches have especially scenic areas, with several stands of pines and paper birch and small limestone formations. Don't expect complete seclusion; County B40, also known as Great River Road, crosses the river no fewer than five times. Water clarity on the Turkey is usually fair. Fishing is good, primarily for smallmouth bass and catfish.

Privately run Skip-A-Way Resort has a riverside **campground** with full amenities in Clermont on Highway 18, with cabin rental also available. Dutton's Cave County Park, 2 miles south of the river on Ironwood Road, also has a campground.

Canoe rentals are available from Turkey River Canoe Rentals (563-245-1559) in Elkader.

The **shuttle route** (5.4 miles) for section 1 begins on the only street going out of tiny Eldorado and heads north on Highway 150, east and southeast on County B40, and north on County W42 to the put-in.

For section 2 (10.8 miles), head south on County W42 to B40, then generally southeast on B40, and northeast on Highway 18 into Clermont. Turn into Clermont Park on the left just before the river bridge.

For **water levels**, check the Turkey River near Eldorado gauge (station 05411850) on the USGS Web site listed in the introduction. Look for more than 200 cfs to avoid scraping in riffles.

The total **gradient** for both sections is 3.9 feet per mile.

Put in upstream of Eldorado's scenic, but closed, bridge on the river-right. The current is slow. As you bend in a sharp hook to the right, a pretty limestone cliff topped with pines rises on the left. As you bend left, you pass a modern sawmill followed by a home with a deck built into the trunks of two impressive pines growing from a hunk of limestone.

Past two long islands, a riffle leads to a ridge covered in hardwoods with some pines. You bend eastward, past a brief view of crops and a silo, and the ridge continues along with paper birch, other hardwoods, and other pines atop small limestone outcroppings. The river drops through a very spirited riffle and runs northeast past occasional limestone walls up to 20 feet high.

Beyond the County B40 bridge, be cautious where snags accumulate at a small island. The river slows, and you pass along an abused stretch with corn-topped cut banks that have exposed a buried car. As you bend right, everything changes, and you run through a swift riffle toward a wooded ridge. You bend southeast at an impressive clay cliff topped with cedars, and past a riffle are more treeless cut banks ahead. At a sharp left bend at a wooded ridge, you'll see the County W42 bridge ahead, where the **takeout** is on the gravel bar downstream-right of the bridge.

On section 2, the river runs through several riffles around lightly tree-lined double horseshoe bends. As it hooks to the right, a beautiful wooded bluff with limestone step formations at the water line forms the left bank. You head south, the bluff tapers off, and you pass cornfields to the County B40 bridge. Past it, the banks become more wooded with low limestone outcroppings. As you bend west, a ridge with a pretty grove of pines joins the left bank for three-fourths of a mile. The river continues straight west and then curves left at a 100-foot wooded bluff.

Through light lowland woods, the river winds past a home and small gravelly islands. Heading due east, you reach the Ironwood Road bridge. Continuing along light woods with grassy banks, you pass a farm and then bend right into a wilder area where the river braids through small gravel islands. At a riprap-lined bank, the stream falls through a riffle toward a wooded ridge covered in stands of cedars, and sculpted ridgelines undulate in the distance.

Heading south, you approach a wooded bluff with striated limestone exposures near the water. Bending northeast, you pass under County B40 again and pass an old barn. The river enters a series of bends through lowland woods past a farmyard and a rocky island. At a hook to the right, the river joins a 140-foot bluff, heading south through several riffles along limestone walls and passing under County B40 yet again.

The river arcs left along a heavily timbered bluff. As a low limestone wall forms the right bank, you cross under County B40 for the final time. Past a private encampment, the river bends right at a wooded bluff, and soon small limestone cliffs join the left bank. Through several riffles heading southeast, the setting becomes quiet and unspoiled. The water slows, and turning left at an undercut cliff with a house atop it, you enter Clermont, where you'll see warning signs for the dam. **Take out** on the river-right.

Other trips. Locals love the easily accessed 4-mile float from Clermont (access is where State Street ends) to the Elgin Canoe Access, usually on inner tubes. Passing along some limestone outcroppings and more often light lines of trees, the river is quite placid with a few riffles and trash receptacles on sandbars all the way along. There's one access at the midway point on County W51.

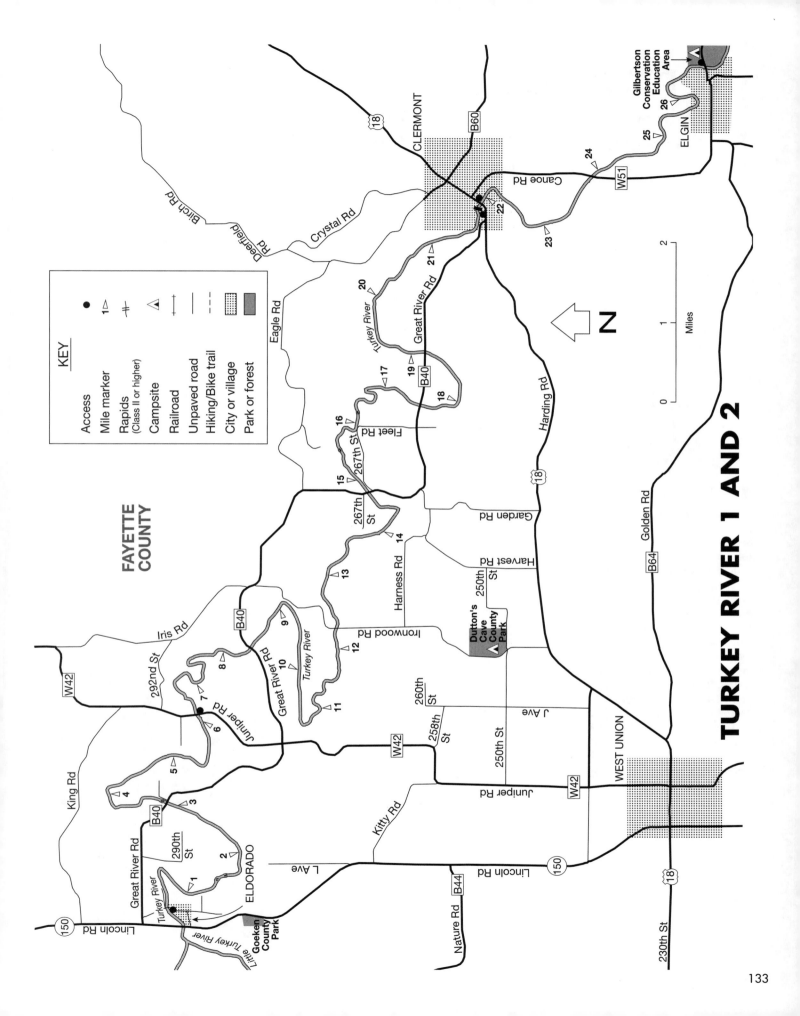

TURKEY RIVER 1 AND 2

TURKEY RIVER 3 AND 4
Elgin Access to Big Spring Fish Hatchery (10.8 Miles)
Big Spring Fish Hatchery to Elkader (7.3 Miles)

The Turkey River's valley is wide here, and these sections continue with the Turkey's odd dichotomy of uninspiring cornfield paddling along with some interesting sights. In this case, the springs, both little and big, add interest, as does low-key scenery of wooded bluffs.

Fishing is best for smallmouth bass and catfish. Where cold water pours into the river at the trout hatchery, trout can be caught near the bank.

There is a riverside **campground** with full amenities at Gilbertson Conservation Education Area at the put-in. There is another riverside campground at Frieden Park (not a good canoe access), and primitive camping is allowed at the canoe access for Big Spring Fish Hatchery. The Turkey in this section is a "meandered stream," so sandbar camping, using appropriate caution (see introduction), is acceptable. Also see Turkey River 5 and 6.

Canoe rentals and shuttles are available from Turkey River Canoe Rentals (563-245-1559) in Elkader.

The **shuttle route** (13.7 miles) from the put-in for section 3 of the Turkey runs east and northeast on County B64, southeast on County B60, south on Depot Road, west on Country Road, and south on Big Spring Road. Take a left onto the hatchery road, and turn right to the access before reaching a large pond or the hatchery itself.

For section 4 (9.5 miles), head north and east on Big Spring Road, east on 210th Street, and south on County X16. In Elkader, turn right onto High Street, follow the left curve, turn right onto Bridge Street, cross the bridge, turn right onto Main Street, and proceed to the access behind the baseball diamond.

For **water levels**, check the Turkey River above French Creek Hollow at Elkader gauge (station 05412020) on the USGS Web site listed in the introduction. Look for more than 250 cfs to avoid scraping in riffles.

The total **gradient** for both sections is 3.9 feet per mile.

Put in on the river-left, near the campground at the Gilbertson Conservation Education Area. Float beneath the County B64 bridge, bending left and passing along a small limestone wall. The river constricts and quickens heading to the base of a small wooded bluff to the southeast. It then heads into a long clearing with cornfields visible, through riffles, and past occasional light lines of willows and a farmhouse. Flowing southeast, the river heads to a 100-foot wooded bluff and bends right, following the bluff straight to the south.

The bluff tapers off, and you come to a road; you bend left and have a view of grain silos ahead. It's one mile to the bridge at Cable Avenue. Past several riffles, you approach a cedar-covered bluff, making a right bend at its base. The river passes through a lowland timbered area and bends left, a high bluff rises on the right, and a moss-encircled spring bubbles into the river below a road.

The bluff recedes, and the river rejoins the right bank as you bend slightly left. Upstream of a right bend into a riffle, the **takeout** for this segment is on the left at the Big Spring Fish Hatchery (see sidebar). You go through the riffle and see water pouring from culverts; you'll often see trout anglers fishing from the bank near these, as well as a stair-stepping artificial waterfall.

At the start of the second segment, a wooded bluff joins the left bank, and you curve to the right along it. A road is seen running up a wooded hill where the river bends left. Past a wooded bluff on the left, the channel splits around a wooded island, and a grain silo with crops appears on the right. Turning left at a wooded bluff, you can see the road again briefly, and a short limestone wall picks up on the right bank. Ahead is a higher wooded bluff at a bend to the right. You pass a stand of tall cottonwoods. Then you head along a bluff on the right, and near a weeping willow a spring gurgles out near the river.

You see Elkader's water tower along with a limestone cliff ahead. You paddle along the backyards of homes, and as you turn right, a pretty bluff with cedars and blocky limestone formations is on the left. You can see the clock tower of Elkader's charming Italianate courthouse ahead. At the sign reading "STOP!" **take out** on the river-right, well above the dam, behind the baseball diamond.

Downtown Elkader is a great place to relax, where you can stroll to the 346-foot-long limestone Keystone Bridge over the Turkey or have a bite at a local restaurant or bakery. However, the **portage**, if you care to continue on from here, requires a four-block carry directly down sometimes bustling Main Street to get around *two* dams. You can put in down the steps at Riverview City Park on Main.

Approaching Elkader, the banks of the Turkey become heavily wooded.

That's One *Big* Spring

Living up to its name, Iowa's largest spring is a real gusher, releasing between 15,000 and 25,000 gallons of cold, clear water every minute. In 1938, Otto and Mary Bankes fulfilled a dream by opening a trout ranch, where anglers could come and pay a fee to fish for trout. They raised the spring's level with a concrete structure and diverted its cold water to ponds before it spilled into the Turkey. But floods kept sweeping away their fish and silting in the ponds and spring. They managed to stay in business until 1961, when the State Conservation Commission bought the hatchery and constructed the present 24 raceways that teem with trout. Trout are hatched near Manchester, trucked here, and reared to catchable size.

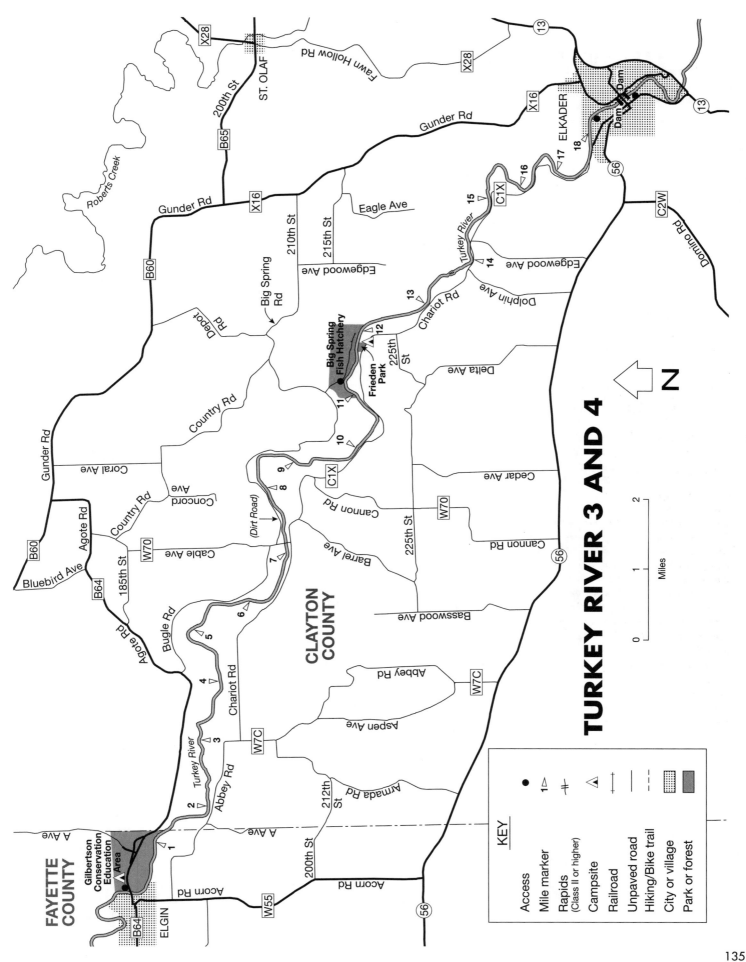

TURKEY RIVER 3 AND 4

KEY

●	Access
1▷	Mile marker
ⱶ	Rapids (Class II or higher)
▷	Campsite
ⱶ	Railroad
│	Unpaved road
╎	Hiking/Bike trail
▨	City or village
▨	Park or forest

N

0   1   2
Miles

TURKEY RIVER 5 AND 6

Turkey River Park to Motor Mill (5.8 Miles)
Motor Mill to Garber (12.3 Miles)

These stretches of the Turkey are a radical departure from sections 1 through 4. In a much narrower valley, the river runs between heavily timbered valley walls in a deeply unspoiled setting. The river averages 120 feet wide, and there are few swift riffles in this primarily lazy float.

An interesting site just before the takeout for section 5 is the mill at the tiny village of Motor, which was constructed of native limestone from the bluff top. To get the limestone down from the bluff, builders used two sets of rail tracks and cars cabled in a long pulley system. The weight of rocks going down pulled empty cars back up. Despite being a state-of-the-art facility in the 1850s, the mill was difficult to reach because of the valley's rugged topography. Before a rail line could be built to Motor, a chinch bug blight destroyed widespread cultivation of wheat in Iowa. The mill closed in the 1880s.

Anglers concentrate primarily on smallmouth bass and catfish. Some walleye are caught, too.

There are riverside **campgrounds** at the put-ins for both trips, one at Turkey River Park and the other across the road from the Motor Mill Access. Abdel Kader City Park (named after the Algerian freedom fighter the town is named for) on Highway 13 in Elkader has all amenities. Privately run D&D Campground in Garber has full amenties. There's also Deer Run Campground in Elkader (563-245-3337), which has a rental cabin. The Turkey in this section is a "meandered stream," so sandbar camping, using appropriate caution (see introduction), is acceptable.

Canoe rentals and shuttles are available from Turkey River Canoe Rentals (563-245-1559) in Elkader.

The **shuttle route** (7.8 miles) from the put-in for section 5 runs north on Highway 13, east on Grape Road, and south on Galaxy Road to the Motor Mill Access (around a curve in the road past the mill itself).

For section 6 (21.5 miles), retrace the same route back to Highway 13 and then head south to County X3C, southeast to County C7X at Elkport, and northeast across the Turkey River to Garber. Turn right on Front Street and right again on County X41 to the access on the left before the bridge.

For **water levels**, check the Turkey River above French Creek Hollow at Elkader gauge (station 05412020) on the USGS Web site listed in the introduction. Look for more

than 250 cfs to avoid scraping in riffles, which become increasingly rare throughout.

The total **gradient** for both sections is 3.4 feet per mile.

After the **put-in** on river-right, at Turkey River Park, float beneath the Highway 13 bridge toward a wooded hillside ahead. Bending right at another wooded ridge, the river is wide until the channel constricts through an easy 40-foot-wide chute. Ahead is a high, wooded bluff with a rocky promontory flanked by tall cedars, where you bend left.

Past several small sandy and grassy islands, you bend right along a densely forested bluff on the left. As you head south, wooded ridges line both sides, creating a serene atmosphere through the enclosed valley. Beyond a brief cornfield segment, the river jogs right toward the remains of a bridge and six-story Motor Mill, one of Iowa's most iconic river sights, set between scenic limestone cliffs on both sides of the river. Past the bridge, the river falls over three little drops. Around the leftward bend is the canoe access, the **takeout** for the first segment.

For section 6, the Turkey continues from the Motor Mill access northeast past a farm and small limestone formations. Past homes, the river runs through a riffle and bends right along a wooded bluff with a limestone boulder, leaving signs of civilization behind.

Heading south, the river passes nice vistas. You run along a 20-foot limestone cliff, and a tall, scraggly pine grows straight from the rock. Formations on another small cliff are topped with pines, birch, and hardwoods. Bending northwest into a tight horseshoe bend, the river quickens pace heading back south. A 200-foot-high wooded bluff with a mix of conifers, birch, and hardwoods rises as you bend left.

Beyond an acute right bend at another high bluff, the river flows south through a continued wild, isolated, narrow valley, following along a bluff carpeted in deciduous trees for nearly two miles. Small limestone outcroppings are occasionally seen. Past an island with an animated chute on the left channel, the river becomes placid, near a meadow clearing.

Heading east, the river begins a series of 90-degree bends. Wooded bluffs keep alternating sides. Past a crop field are more wooded bluffs. At a final 90-degree bend to the right along a bluff with van-sized boulders at its base, you begin regularly seeing signs of humanity again: cornfields, power lines across the river, a road running along the river, and deeply cut banks. The Volga (see Volga River 2) joins from the right, and you pass beneath the Elkport-Garber bridge. You bend left along a wooded ridge, and the **takeout** is just past the next bridge on the river-left.

Dvorak on the Turkey

Czech composer Antonín Dvořák, working in New York City, was tired of city life and missed his homeland. But his four-month summer vacation in 1893 wasn't time enough to reach Bohemia by ship, so he did the next best thing: he hopped a train to the Iowa village of Spillville on the banks of the upper Turkey. The bawdy musician mixed with local Czech immigrants. He also enjoyed strolls along the Turkey and was often seen wandering into the woods with a violin in one hand, a bucket of beer in the other. Dvořák was a bird-listener more than a bird-watcher. Musical trills echoing Iowa avian species sometimes surfaced in his compositions, such as String Quartet in F, op. 96, thought to be inspired by the scarlet tanager.

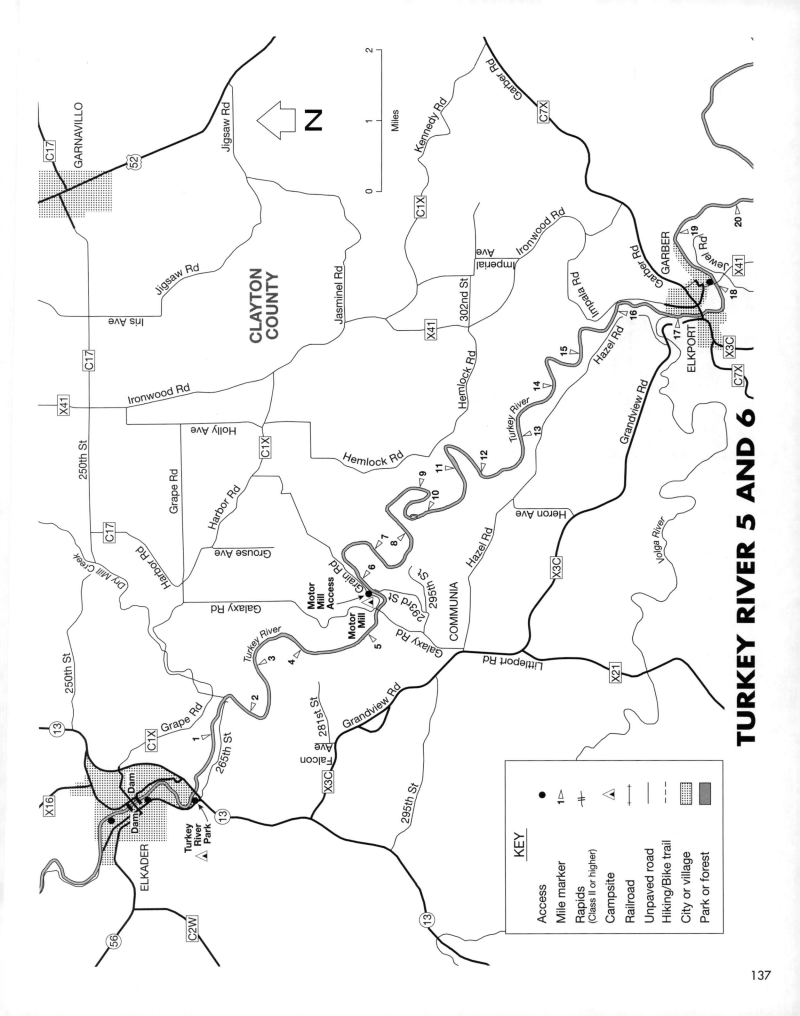

TURKEY RIVER 5 AND 6

CLAYTON COUNTY

GARNAVILLO

ELKADER

ELKPORT

GARBER

COMMUNIA

KEY

●	Access
1 △	Mile marker
╫	Rapids (Class II or higher)
△	Campsite
╪	Railroad
│	Unpaved road
┊	Hiking/Bike trail
▦	City or village
▨	Park or forest

N

Miles
0   1   2

Motor Mill Access
Motor Mill

Turkey River Park
Dam
Dam

Dry Mill Creek

Turkey River

Volga River

UPPER IOWA RIVER 1
Plumber's Park to Kendallville (11.8 Miles)

Many paddlers can't believe they're still in Iowa when they first take to the Upper Iowa. In fact, at the put-in to this trip, you're actually in Minnesota—momentarily. The river is heavily spring-fed, and the water clarity is excellent. The river is swift with enjoyable riffles and runs, and pines with occasional stands of balsam fir trees top breathtaking limestone cliffs of great beauty. It's also just the right size stream for paddling.

This stretch of the Upper Iowa has more than its share of showy riverside cliffs.

The result is that hundreds of paddlers flock here from around the Midwest on summer weekends. Some revelers float with coolers full of beverages, most often to float on the ultra-scenic Upper Iowa River 2 and 3 segments, but a weekend party scene hasn't overtaken the river as it has on, say, Missouri's Current River. If avoiding droves of weekend paddlers on an exceptionally scenic tract of the Upper Iowa is your goal, this stretch is a pretty good bet, but you'd encounter even fewer fellow paddlers below Decorah.

Dairy farming is an important part of the local economy, and that shows up repeatedly in this stretch. While you paddle along cliffs of picturesque grandeur on one bank, cows graze green pastures on the opposite side. Perhaps that makes this section feel less secluded than others, but the gentle bovines really don't ruin the view. The primary game fish species is smallmouth bass—where the river's in Minnesota, you need a Minnesota fishing license.

Campgrounds with full amenities are found at Kendallville Park (riverside) and at privately run Harvest Farms on 318th Avenue.

Canoe and kayak rentals and shuttles are available from Hruska's Canoe Livery (563-547-4566) in Kendallville and Harvest Farms (563-883-8562) near Kendallville.

The shuttle route (9.6 miles) from the Plumber's Park put-in on Minnesota County Road 30, east of Granger, runs southwest to Florenceville, Iowa, south on County V58, east on County A23 (50th Street), south on 345th Avenue, east County A23, and northeast on State Highway 139 to Kendallville Park.

Water levels can be checked on the Upper Iowa at Bluffton gauge (station 5387440) on the USGS Web site listed in the introduction. Look for more than 180 cfs to avoid scraping on riffles, although many paddlers will run this scenic stretch to lower levels.

The **gradient** is 5.1 feet per mile.

After the **put-in** at Plumber's Park (there are no signs or facilities at the park—just parking and an access where the road splits away from the river), the river bends left at the base of a ridge where it curves right. Pretty limestone cliffs begin lining the left bank with lots of hardwoods and birch trees. Heading southwest into a pasture, you enter Iowa, where a nice bluff topped with pines and some balsam fir trees line the right bank and the pasture continues all along the left. The pine-topped cliffs continue along the long horseshoe bend as you head north, crossing back into Minnesota, where the cliffs taper off and pastures surround the river.

Several riffles lead to another line of pine- and cedar-covered cliffs where you curve right. Just ahead on the left, you'll notice a small spring branch fed by three springs right out of the bluff. The middle spring is set back in a cave. Continuing along the same bluff, the river bends back into its namesake state, staying in Iowa to its mouth. As you bend right, there is an amusing small rapids with rocks and boulders to dodge next to scenic rock walls. You pass a farm and through a riffle, and another pasture begins as the river diverts left along sheer and very scenic cliffs on the right with overhanging promontories capped with firs and pines.

Following the cliffs for about a mile to the east, the river bends right along similarly scenic bluff. Past the 20th Street bridge, the river heads through prairie areas through several riffles. Past the next bridge, woods with occasional limestone outcroppings line the bank. A ridge begins to rise on the right, and then the river slowly bends left away from it through a sparsely wooded area. Bending slightly right, the river becomes swifter, and a pretty bluff wooded with pines and birch rises on the right.

The river heads south, and after a right bend, strikingly rugged cliffs topped with conifers rise on the left bank. At a cut through the bluff, Harvest Farms has an access. Leaving the bluffs, you'll soon arrive at the 360th Street trestle bridge, which is followed by a sandy island. The right channel is quite swift. Curving left along a pine-topped ridge, the river makes a 45-degree bend to the right at some scenic 30-foot bluffs with more pines.

Passing through several riffles heading southwest, the river begins curving along the final wooded bluff with hardwoods, pines, and a line of limestone cliffs. The **takeout** is ahead on the right.

Other trips. The stretch of river from Lidke Park below the dam in Lime Springs to either County V58 (13.6 miles) or the Plumber's Park Access (15.3 miles), both near Florenceville, also offers excellent paddling. Passing through long stretches of pasture, the river also flows through isolated wooded valleys and past some limestone cliffs and outcroppings, none rivaling bluffs downstream. The river often flows slowly through long pools and only the briefest of riffles in the first part of this trip. On the second half, the river runs through a long, swift, and winding stretch along cedar thickets and scrubby banks that is like no other part of this river. Look for higher levels (somewhere near 200 cfs on the Bluffton gauge) to avoid getting stuck in many shallow riffles. (See inset map on opposite page.)

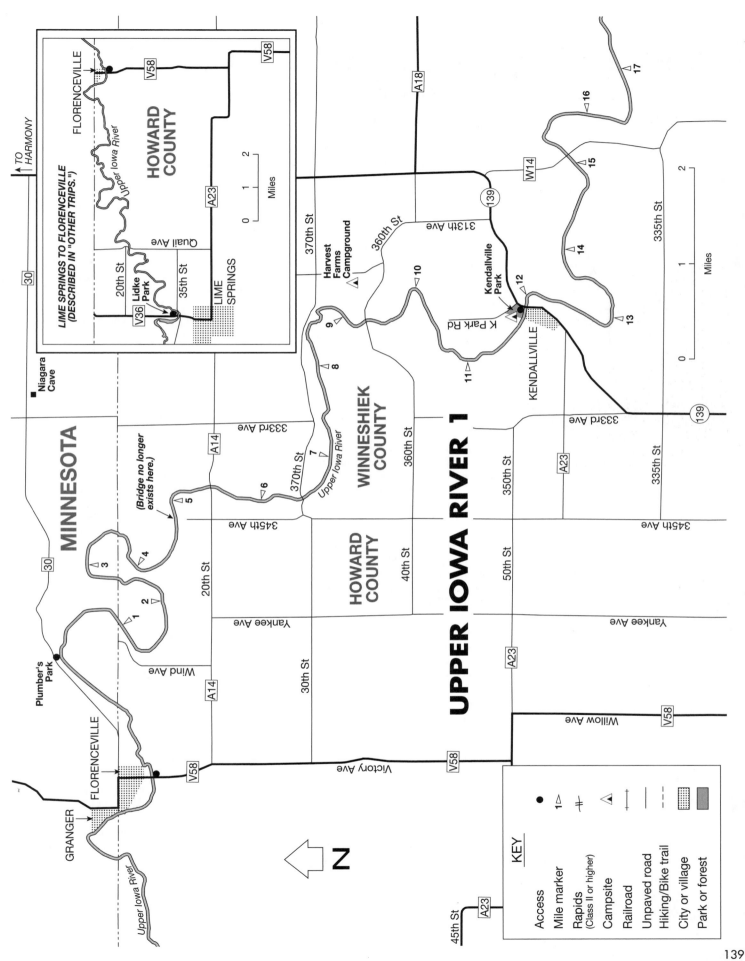

UPPER IOWA RIVER 1

UPPER IOWA RIVER 2 AND 3

Kendallville to Chimney Rock Park (12.6 Miles)
Chimney Rock to Bluffton (5 Miles)

Considered by many to be Iowa's premier paddling experience, there's good reason the river on these two sections becomes crowded on summer weekends. Massive rock formations and stands of conifers are at their showiest here, and paddle-in-paddle-out campgrounds are excellent places to base a trip. The river is of an intimate size, about 60 feet wide, with clear waters. It's just challenging enough that you'll almost certainly see someone dump a canoe somewhere along the way.

Don't let the many paddlers lull you into a false sense that this river is a theme park ride. Local canoe liveries do a reasonable job of clearing paths through snags, but you should be wary of sweepers and strainers in swift sections. Fishing is a dicey proposition on the weekends because of the canoe traffic, but during the weekdays and off-season weekends, smallmouth bass are caught in good numbers. Trout can be caught near the mouths of spring branches, such as Coldwater Creek.

Riverside **campgrounds** with full amenities are found at Kendallville Park and at the privately run Randy's Bluffton Store. Harvest Farms near Kendallville (see Upper Iowa 1 map) also has full amenities up the bluff from the river. Chimney Rock Park has attractive primitive sites set in the woods along the river, and the privately run Chimney Rock Campground and Hruska's Campground are also riverside. Primitive river camping is also allowed at the Upper Iowa Access Area and Coldwater Creek Wildlife Area.

Canoe and kayak rentals and shuttles are available from Hruska's Canoe Livery at Kendallville (563-547-4566), Harvest Farms near Kendallville (563-883-8562), Chimney Rock Canoe Rental south of Chimney Rock Park (563-735-5786), and Bluffton Store Canoe Rental (563-735-5738).

The **shuttle route** (10.5 miles) for the first trip, from the put-in at Kendallville Park, runs northeast on Highway 139, east on County A18, south on County W20, and west on Chimney Rock Road to the access just across the river bridge.

For the second segment (2.6 miles), head east on Chimney Rock Road, southeast on County W20, and briefly west on Village Road to the Bluffton canoe access.

Water levels can be checked on the Upper Iowa at Bluffton gauge (station 5387440) on the USGS Web site listed in the introduction. Look for more than 150 cfs to avoid scraping on riffles, although many paddlers will run this scenic stretch at much lower levels.

The total **gradient** for both sections is 4 feet per mile.

Past the first bridge from the **put-in** at Kendallville Park, the river bends 90 degrees right at the first of many scenic limestone outcroppings. Small homes are set back in the woods, and then the river bends left at scalloped-looking cliffs covered in ferns and mosses. As you head east through meadows and lowland woods, a bluff rises on the left, and the river curves south before joining more cliffs on the right. Past back-to-back riffles, the County W14 bridge is just ahead.

After a right turn, tall wooded bluffs rise straight ahead. The river constricts, and snags tend to accumulate in fast water here, so use caution. After you pass through a fun chute and past a cornfield, a set of cliffs rises on the left. One dramatic formation called Plymouth Rock looks like a medieval fortress with turrets and ramparts. A sawmill that cut pine logs and sent boards to Decorah stood here for 50 years, beginning in 1853.

Past the Coldwater Creek Road bridge, the river bends left 90 degrees along a bluff with angular rock outcroppings. At an island, the left channel has deeper water—watch for overhanging branches that can capsize paddlers. As you go through a swift, constricted channel, again, watch for potentially dangerous snags.

The river flows by more prairie, woodlands, and bluffs, bending south and then east. At a sharp bend right, a small island splits a shallow riffle. As you head southeast, a limestone wall on the right gradually recedes, and a pasture lines the left bank. You'll likely have to negotiate a fence before the next bridge.

As the river curves left, an impressive limestone cliff looms on the right bank, with a cave and a worn-looking tower formation visible. Cliff swallows flit here and there, and cedars and pines cling to the rock. The bluff briefly drops back from the river, and where it rejoins, beautiful little Blue Spring pours into the river from the base of the cliff.

Pine woodlands with young firs line the right slope. Past an island, the river drops 2 feet through an entertaining chute. After a long gravel bar and prairie grasses with wildflowers, you bend left at another high bluff thickly topped in mature pines. You head into a long horseshoe bend, and as the river doubles back south, dramatic limestone cliffs rise straight from the river, including noble Chimney Rock. The **takeout** for the first segment is ahead on the right, just upstream from Chimney Rock Bridge.

For the second segment, begin by passing under the bridge. After the river curves left along bluffs through another horseshoe, at a right bend pine boughs hang over a 15-foot sheer rock wall. Past the bridge at Bluffton and a riffle, an incredible line of undulating cliffs, the Bluffton Palisades, joins the right. Pines and Iowa's best stands of balsam firs grow from crevices in the sheer cliffs and atop the bluff. The bluffs continue for a mile to the **takeout** on the left.

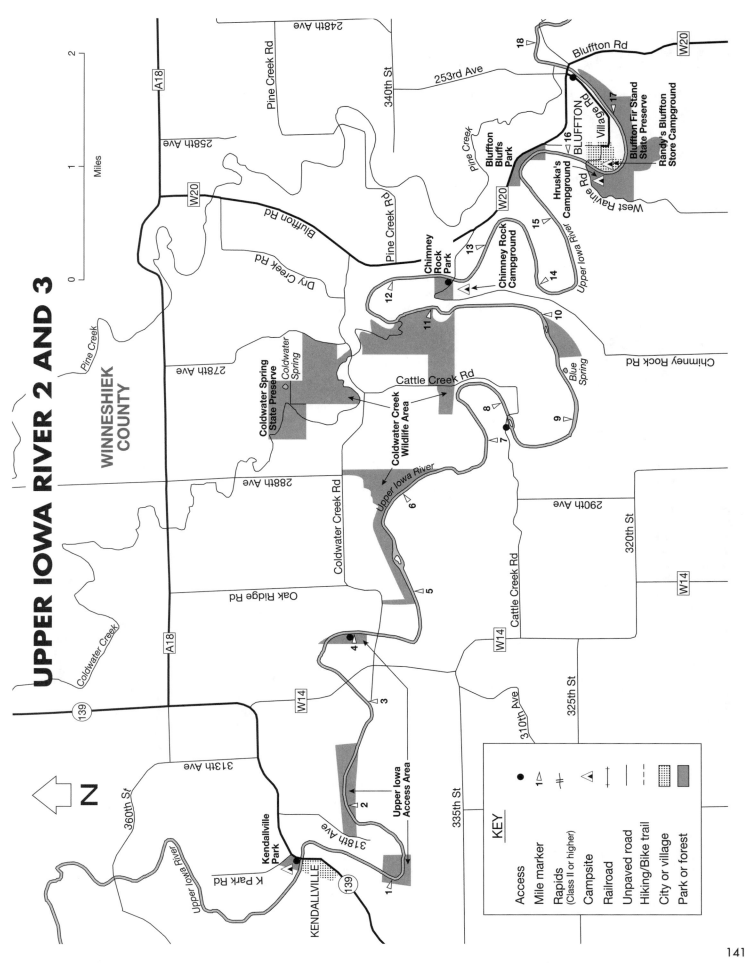

UPPER IOWA RIVER 2 AND 3

WINNESHIEK COUNTY

N

Miles

KEY

●	Access
1△	Mile marker
⊬	Rapids (Class II or higher)
◁	Campsite
┼	Railroad
---	Unpaved road
┆	Hiking/Bike trail
▦	City or village
▨	Park or forest

Kendallville Park

KENDALLVILLE

K Park Rd

Upper Iowa River

360th St

313th Ave

318th Ave

Upper Iowa Access Area

335th St

310th Ave

325th St

320th St

Oak Ridge Rd

288th Ave

278th Ave

Coldwater Creek Rd

Cattle Creek Rd

Coldwater Spring State Preserve

Coldwater Spring

Coldwater Creek Wildlife Area

Upper Iowa River

Blue Spring

Chimney Rock Rd

290th Ave

Cattle Creek Rd

Chimney Rock Park

Chimney Rock Campground

Dry Creek Rd

Pine Creek Rd

Bluffton Rd

258th Ave

340th St

253rd Ave

248th Ave

Pine Creek Rd

Pine Creek

Bluffton Bluffs Park

BLUFFTON

Hruska's Campground

Village Rd

West Ravine Rd

Bluffton Fir Stand State Preserve

Randy's Bluffton Store Campground

Bluffton Rd

Upper Iowa River

Coldwater Creek

A18

W20

W14

139

141

UPPER IOWA RIVER 4
Bluffton to Malanaphy Springs State Preserve (8.7 Miles)

If you like swifter waters, you'll enjoy this stretch of the Upper Iowa. The bluffs aren't quite so showy as those upstream of here or below Lower Dam, but the trip culminates with one of the most magnificent sites on the entire length of the river at Malanaphy Springs (see description).

Smallmouth bass are the dominant game fish, with some trout in pools near spring creeks.

For **campgrounds** see Upper Iowa River 2 and 3. Also, Decorah City Campground has riverside camping with full amenities; and primitive riverside camping is allowed at the Chattahoochie Access and Malanaphy Springs State Preserve.

Canoe and kayak rentals and shuttles are available from Upper Iowa Canoe Rental (563-382-2332) in Decorah. Also see Upper Iowa River 2 and 3.

The **shuttle route** (5.9 miles) from the put-in on Village Road runs east and south on County W20 to the Malanaphy Springs State Preserve.

Water levels can be checked on the Upper Iowa at Bluffton gauge (station 5387440) on the USGS Web site listed in the introduction. Look for more than 150 cfs to avoid scraping on riffles.

The **gradient** is 6.9 feet per mile.

Put in on the river-left, across from the downstream side of the Bluffton Palisades. Float beneath the County W20 bridge, and after a riffle and a right bend you see a rusty trestle bridge with a limestone bluff rising behind it. After another riffle, you enter a meadow with some cropland visible.

Pass through several riffles and chutes, the last of which can get quite shallow at low water. Curving around a bluff on the right, you see a farm, at which the river constricts and drops over a ledge. At a small island just ahead, take the left channel and you'll drop through a small rapids.

The river runs through more riffles, leaving the bluff. The river becomes snaggy and sandy, and then it rejoins the wooded bluff on the right and returns to its rocky character. The river speeds up as it curves along the bluff, and heading east you fall through a half-mile-long riffle past mostly deciduous trees with a few pines on the ridge.

Slowing for another half mile, the river begins bending right along another wooded bluff, narrows to 20 feet, and drops through a fast chute. Beautiful little Christopher Spring pours in from the bluff on the left, which is wooded with cedars, pines, and hardwoods. For a long stretch, the river heads south through a savanna setting with distant bluffs visible. The river passes through riffles until reaching the Scenic River Road bridge, where pretty bluffs with limestone exposures are set back from the stream. A steep carry-down access can be used on the river-left here.

Bending left, the river heads straight east through light woods and open pasture. Turning right at a wooded bluff with small limestone outcroppings, you'll see and hear Malanaphy Springs ahead. First visible is the gushing cascade that falls more than 10 feet straight into the river. Look up, and you'll see a network of cascades up the bluff. You can scramble up the verdant slope to where the spring issues from a cliff 80 vertical feet above the river.

Past an island that splits an energetic riffle, the river bends right at a midstream boulder. The **takeout** is upstream of the bridge on the river-left, with a 100-yard carry to the parking lot. A hiking trail leads back to the spring from here.

Other trips. The two miles from the Malanaphy access to the one near Pole Line Road isn't particularly interesting except for a very long riffle in the last mile, but the following 4.8 miles from Pole Line Road into Decorah are pleasant enough. They pass through an unusual wood-lined set of bends where the river seems to come to a T at a bluff, with a backwater to the left and the main channel continuing to the right. Riffles, a long segment through a pasture, and a high, wooded bluff follow. Entering town past Highway 52, the river drops through riffles and a small rapids on the way to the takeout at Will Baker Park.

Malanaphy Springs is a cold spot to drench yourself on a hot summer's day.

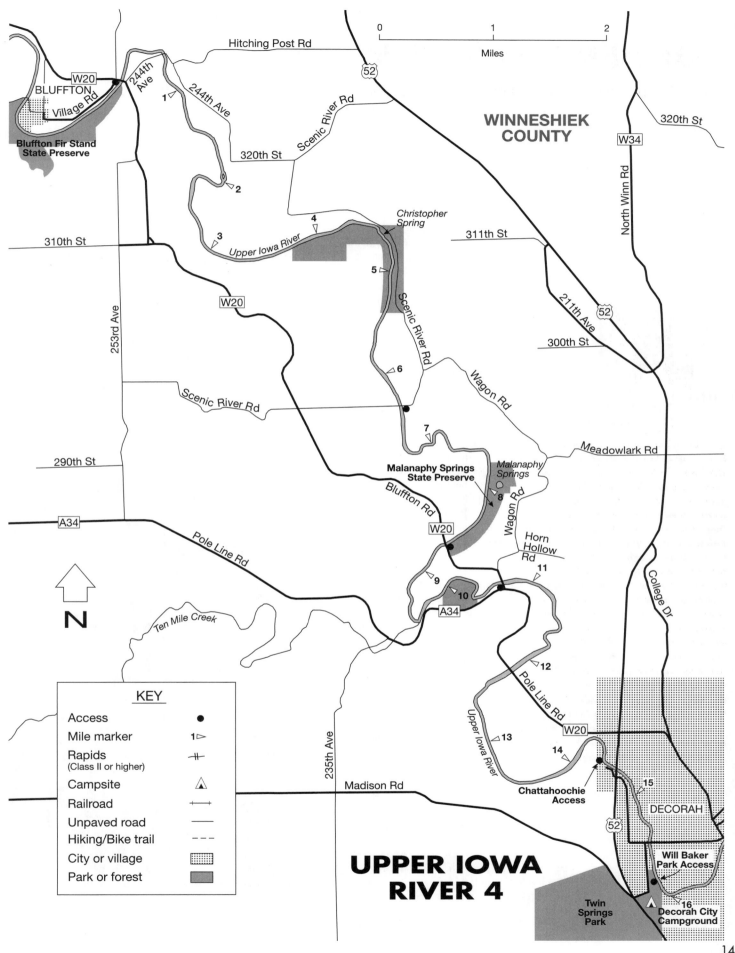

UPPER IOWA RIVER 4

KEY

Access ●

Mile marker 1▷

Rapids ‖
(Class II or higher)

Campsite △

Railroad ┼

Unpaved road ─

Hiking/Bike trail ┄

City or village ▦

Park or forest ▨

UPPER IOWA RIVER 5
Trout Run to Upper Dam (8.5 Miles)

The Upper Iowa heading out of Decorah has a little of everything, from the backside of a Wal-Mart that was court ordered not to open because it was constructed partly in the river's flood zone, to tall, wooded bluffs and long segments of public land. In between are fun riffles, a few homes, and some farmland, along with wilder stands of pine trees along small ridges.

For those who like to mix paddling with other pleasures, it's worth mentioning that Decorah is a scenic base for a multisport weekend. Dunning's Spring Park (where there's a 40-foot waterfall), Van Peenan Park, Phelps Park, and Palisades Park all have good hiking, cycling, and mountain-biking trails. Plus, Decorah is a bike-friendly town, so pedaling between the parks is easy. Cross-country skiing options abound in the winter. The town has numerous bed and breakfasts and a historic hotel, none directly on the water.

This entire section of the Upper Iowa is a catch-and-release smallmouth bass fishery, so the fish run larger than average, but you must return them to the water immediately, unharmed.

Decorah City **Campground**, with full amenities, is riverside. Primitive camping is allowed at Lower Dam (see Upper Iowa River 6).

Upper Iowa Canoe Rental (563-382-2332) in Decorah **rents canoes** and runs shuttles.

The **shuttle route** (5.4 miles) from the put-in at Trout Run Park on the southeast edge of Decorah runs east a short distance on Highway 9, northeast on County A52, and northeast on River Road to Upper Dam.

Often when **water levels** are inadequate in the upper stretches, paddling any stretch below Decorah works just fine. Check on the Upper Iowa at Decorah gauge (station 5387440) on the USGS Web site listed in the introduction. Look for a reading above 150 cfs to avoid scraping.

The **gradient** is 4.5 feet per mile.

From the **put-in**, on river-right at Trout Run, the Upper Iowa runs through a series of tight bends and along some riprap. Turning right at a small island, the river falls through chutes—take the narrower left chute at low water.

Past a cornfield and Decorah's wastewater treatment plant, the scenery gets better as the river bends left toward a low, wooded bluff. Bending right, the river splits into riffles around a small island. Passing a bridge,

you bend northwest toward one last wooded bluff and leave ridges behind as you run into a lightly tree-lined area with some small limestone outcroppings.

The next several bends take you through shallow riffles with lightly wooded low banks, past a farm and some homes. Approaching another bluff, you bend right toward a bridge. Past this the river becomes extremely scenic within the Upper Iowa Access Area, flowing along a limestone wall topped with pines. Pretty rock outcroppings continue as the bluff tapers off at another bridge and red cedars become more common than pines.

Ahead, a 300-foot-high wooded bluff forces the river to bend southeast toward a pine-lined ridge ahead. As you round a left bend, a limestone wall forms the left bank and the river slows behind Upper Dam. After bending right along more pines, cedars, and oaks, **take out** on the right, 100 yards above the dam.

Other trips. The trip through Decorah itself from the access at Will Baker Park to the Trout Run access passes along a levee that protects the town from flooding but is also quite enjoyable, moving swiftly and always with a view of beautiful bluffs that surround the town. (See accompanying map.)

The Decorah Ice Cave

In the beautiful bluffs above the river in Decorah, one cave is particularly interesting. Most caves have air temperatures averaging about 47 degrees. The Ice Cave in the summer months is below freezing, and depending on the year, by June ice can coat the walls up to 10 inches thick. The freezing is due to the limestone cave's unique shape that, unlike most caves, allows frigid winter air to circulate through the cave in the winter. That makes the rock frigid, too. In the summer, when water atop the bluff is no longer frozen and percolates down, the insulated limestone acts like a gigantic freezer mug. In 1897, 18-year-old Aldis Kovarik from nearby Spillville made scientific observations that helped to explain the phenomenon of ice caves to the world. This "glaciere" is thought to be the largest in North America east of the Black Hills. The cave is open for exploration, but it is not lit. You usually need to enter more than 10 feet past the mouth to encounter ice, so bring a flashlight.

Pine-topped bluffs are a treat on this portion of the Upper Iowa.

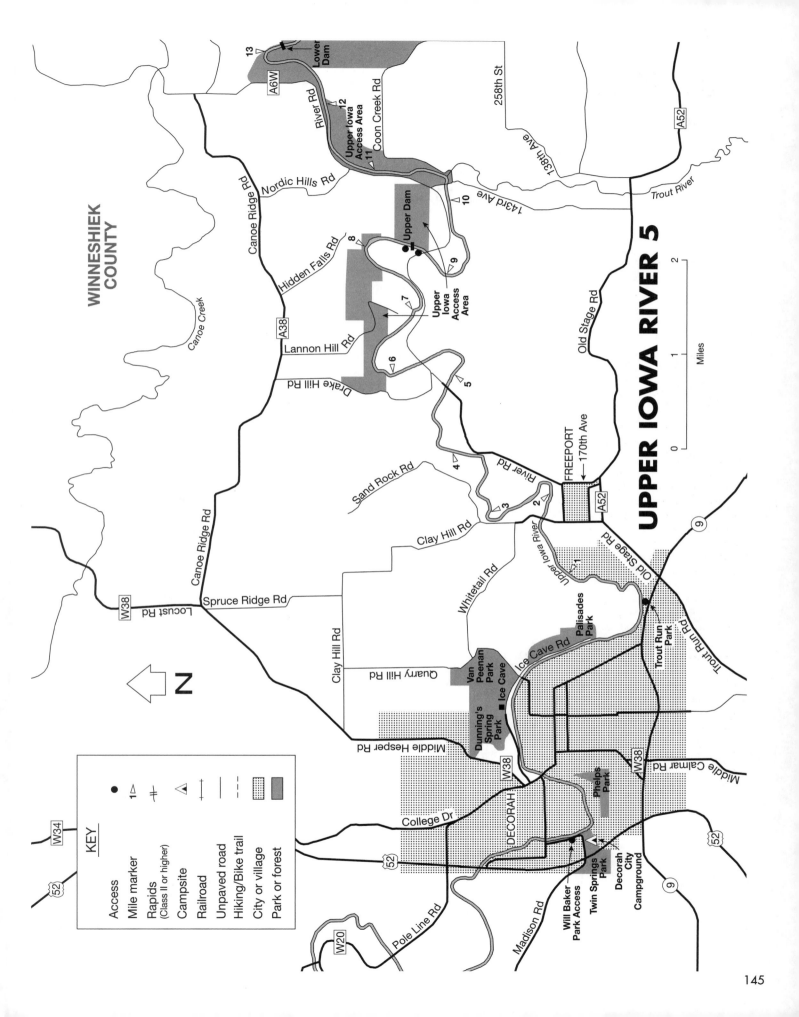

UPPER IOWA RIVER 5

WINNESHIEK COUNTY

N

UPPER IOWA RIVER 6
Lower Dam to Iverson Bridge (15.8 Miles)

It's just fine by locals that most outside paddlers congregate at the Kendallville-Bluffton section. That way, paddling along the highest bluffs remains blissfully uncrowded on this section and on Upper Iowa River 7, both exceedingly scenic stretches.

The feel of the river alters considerably, making a quick transition from a 90-foot-wide stream in a tight valley to 150-foot-wide river through big-sky scenery, arcing along towering and arid prairie slopes crowned by woods and majestic limestone outcroppings. It's not just pretty—the scenery is grand, and completely unique in the Midwest.

If there's a scenic drawback, it's that a few parts of the valley bottom are flat and fertile. Row crops are sometimes planted right up to the river's edge with no riparian buffer strips, contributing to the lower river's occasional turbidity after rains. Allamakee County has little public land along the river. Usually, though, the river runs as clear as it does upstream.

It's easy to shorten this long day-trip by putting in at Lundy Bridge, where the access is less demanding than at Lower Dam. At Canoe Creek, you can put in on the creek at Ferris Mill Road and float or drag approximately 100 yards to the river. The smallmouth bass and walleye fishing are excellent.

Primitive **campsites** are among the bluff-top pines at Lower Dam. Also see Upper Iowa River 7.

Canoe and kayak rentals and shuttles are available from Upper Iowa Resort (563-568-3263).

The **shuttle route** (11.7 miles) from the put-in runs northwest on Lower Dam Road, north on River Road, east on County A26 where the road turns to gravel in Allamakee County, very briefly north on Balsam Road to Iverson Bridge Road, and southeast to the bridge.

Water levels can be checked on the Upper Iowa at Dorchester gauge (station 05388250) on the USGS Web site listed in the introduction. More than 200 cfs allows you to avoid most scraping.

The **gradient** is 4.6 feet per mile.

The Lower Dam area is a beautiful **put-in**, but it requires a 200-yard carry down a steep trail *below* the dam. The access above it is the takeout for the trip from Upper Dam. The bluffs are heavily covered in pines, and the dam causes the river to spill about 15 feet over a limestone outcropping, creating a roaring waterfall. Directly below the dam, the river channel splits, with a small amount of water flowing south into a horseshoe bend. Most of the river's flow heads straight east, falling through a fun class I rapids.

Bending left where the channels rejoin, the river is intimate, swift, and rocky with heavily wooded banks. Pines protrude above oaks and other hardwoods on the 150-foot bluff on the left. The remote atmosphere continues to Lundy Bridge, where a limestone promontory overlooks the river and the access is downstream-right of the bridge.

Bending right along a cedar-cloaked bluff, the river widens and slows. Past light woods with sporadic views of fields, the river approaches a small, timbered ridge and turns left into a lengthy riffle. Past a trailer house and cornfields, you pass under Ferris Mill Bridge. Bending left at a 250-foot ridge, you see the first of several prairie-covered slopes on this trip. Native plants live here in an arid ecosystem called a glade, in which thin soils hold little water on sun-baked, south-facing slopes.

The valley is narrow. A wooded ridge rises ahead. Beyond a sandy island, at a right bend, Canoe Creek enters from the left. The Upper Iowa continues along a bluff in a riffly run, which is followed by a section of cut banks topped with cornfields and then a cedar-covered bluff.

Ahead, a scenic set of bends begins. A high, partially wooded ridge with a large cedar-fringed glade rises. Beyond a long riffle, a wooded bluff crested with prominent limestone escarpments appears ahead. As you bend right, more undulating bluffs with multiple glade-sloped ridgelines and rock cliffs high above the valley floor stretch into distant views ahead. Past a short riffle, the river turns right along the base of a bluff. Straight ahead is another spectacular gladed bluff, and after bending left at its base you approach Ellingson Bridge, where a farmer has barricaded access to the river. (Friendly note: air has been drained from paddlers' tires here.)

Past a cornfield, the river splits around an island for the next third of a mile. The right channel has a small rapids and passes near a bluff rather than cornfields. The bluff continues past the island, guiding the river on a long arc to the left. As you head west along the bluff, its slopes become dominated by cedars with stands of cottonwoods and birch. The river is wide, flat-bottomed, and often just deep enough for a canoe to pass. As the river curves right along the base of another bluff, limestone outcroppings protrude from the banks. Past a farm, the current flows slowly east and then north, where a striking 300-foot bluff looms ahead, crowned with rugged limestone cliffs above gladed slopes studded with cedars and a few stands of birch and cottonwoods.

Bending west at the bluff's base through several riffles, the river then bends right along another wooded bluff. **Take out** on the river-left, upstream of Iverson Bridge.

Other trips. For one mile, the stretch downstream of the put-in below Upper Dam is quite scenic. A hanging pedestrian bridge spans the river from a 4-H camp to a bluff thickly wooded with pines. Just beyond the mouth of little Trout River, the Upper Iowa slows behind Lower Dam. Sandy sediment flattens the stream bottom for the rest of the way, creating shallow shoals not ideal for paddling. The takeout is on the river-left above the dam, requiring a steep uphill haul to the parking area.

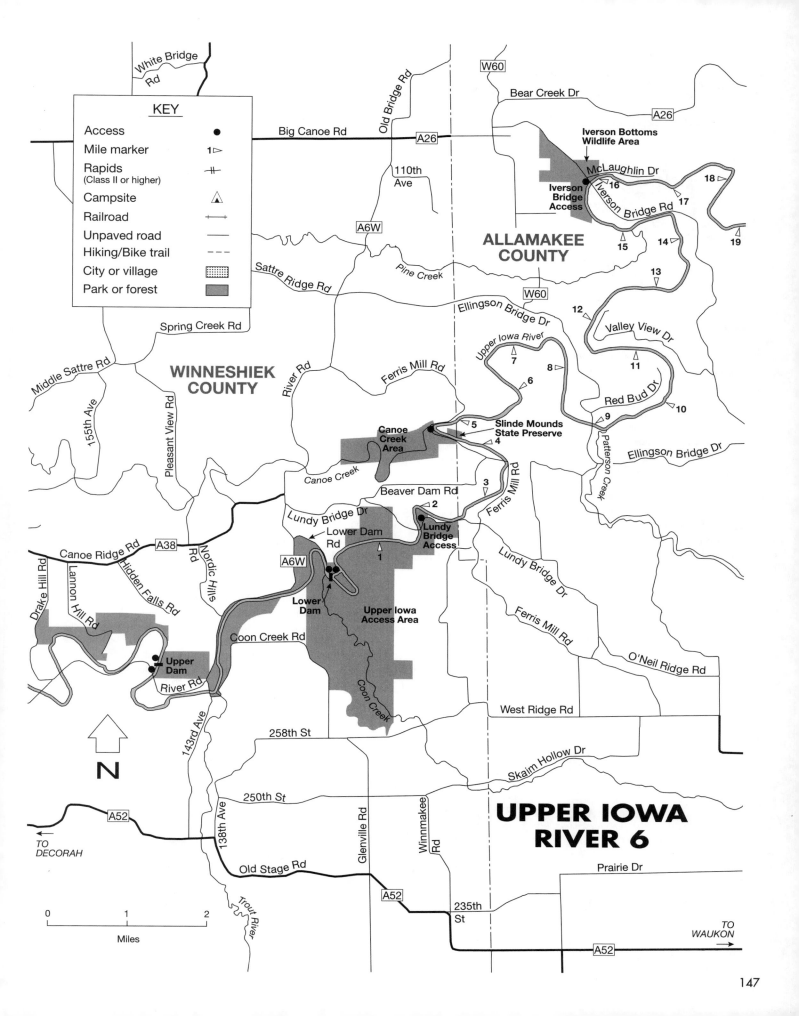

UPPER IOWA RIVER 7

Iverson Bridge to Upper Iowa Access (9.4 Miles)

Upper Iowa, or Oneota?

In the late nineteenth century, state geologist Samuel Calvin began a movement to rename the Upper Iowa River the Oneota River. Actually, the stream had long been called Oneota by the Winnebago tribe, which inhabited the valley until 1849, when Euro-Americans displaced them. Calvin's idea was part homage to the original name, but he also argued it would avoid confusion between this and an entirely unconnected river, the Iowa. Although his effort never caught on, the name Oneota was selected to describe a pre-Winnebago culture that built villages along the Upper Iowa's banks beginning around 1200 A.D. Archaeological evidence now suggests that some of the "Oneota" natives, displaced when the Winnebago moved in, probably moved further into the Iowa interior. Oddly enough, there they became known as the Iowa.

This section begins at one very scenic bluff and ends near another, with dramatic ridgelines continuing along most of the river to Highway 76, past which are interesting riffles and smaller bluffs. The river feels somewhat more enclosed and wooded in this section than in Upper Iowa 6, but the vistas are similar in scale.

Fishing continues to be good for smallmouth bass and walleye. Brown trout are sometimes caught near the mouth of Bear Creek.

A **campground** with full amenities and cabins is available at Upper Iowa Resort on Highway 76.

Canoe and kayak rentals and shuttles are available from Upper Iowa Resort (563-568-3263).

The **shuttle route** (10.7 miles) from the put-in runs northwest on Iverson Bridge Road, north on Balsam Road, east on Bear Creek Drive, south on Highway 76, and east on County A26 to the Upper Iowa Access.

Water levels can be checked on the Upper Iowa at Dorchester gauge (station 05388250) on the USGS Web site listed in the introduction. Look for 200 cfs or higher on the Dorchester gauge to avoid most scraping.

The **gradient** is approximately 3.9 feet per mile.

Downstream of the Iverson Bridge from the **put-in**, the trip begins splendidly, heading through a boulder-strewn riffle toward a spectacular wooded bluff with limestone cliffs high above the river. As you pass between woodlands, a high bluff appears on the right. After you descend a riffle, cornfields are visible through lightly tree-lined banks.

Beyond an island with a long riffle through the right channel, a high bluff with gladed slopes and mural-like limestone escarpments appears ahead. Bending sharply right at the bluff's base, the river becomes shallow with riffles and sand shoals. Curving right at a wooded bluff, the river constricts to 70 feet wide and deepens somewhat.

To the northeast, the valley becomes quite narrow and wooded. A gladed slope of a ridge is seen ahead, and you bend right where the river becomes sandy-bottomed with fewer riffles, running along a wooded bluff on the right with occasional glimpses of cornfields on the left. As you bend left past an eroded pasture and a junky area near a farm, a few pines poke above hardwoods on the right. Bending right at a wooded bluff to the north, you pass a few mobile homes and the Upper Iowa Resort's boat access (not public, although it can be used for a fee) on the way to the Highway 76 bridge.

Turning left beyond the bridge, the river runs through several riffles along a bluff. At a deep pool, Bear Creek enters from the left and the Upper Iowa curves right through sparse woods with cornfields visible. The river passes through more deep pools from here on, where walleye fishing can be excellent. At a left bend ahead you'll see a distant bluff called "the Elephant," which does look vaguely like a pachyderm. As you continue toward it, power lines cross the river. Look on the river-left for stairs leading down to the river at the **takeout**.

Other trips. Paddling and fishing continue to be reasonably good for 3.2 miles downstream of the Upper Iowa Access to Hartley's Bridge, where County X6A crosses. You'll pass a few more wooded bluffs, with mostly a light line of trees with glimpses of cornfields along the way. Take out upstream and right of that bridge. The 8.9-mile trip from Hartley's Bridge to the river's final access at Blackhawk Point on Highway 26 is not highly recommended; due to channel straightening, the river becomes extremely shallow and difficult to paddle during normal water conditions.

High bluffs tower above the riffled river just below Iverson Bridge.

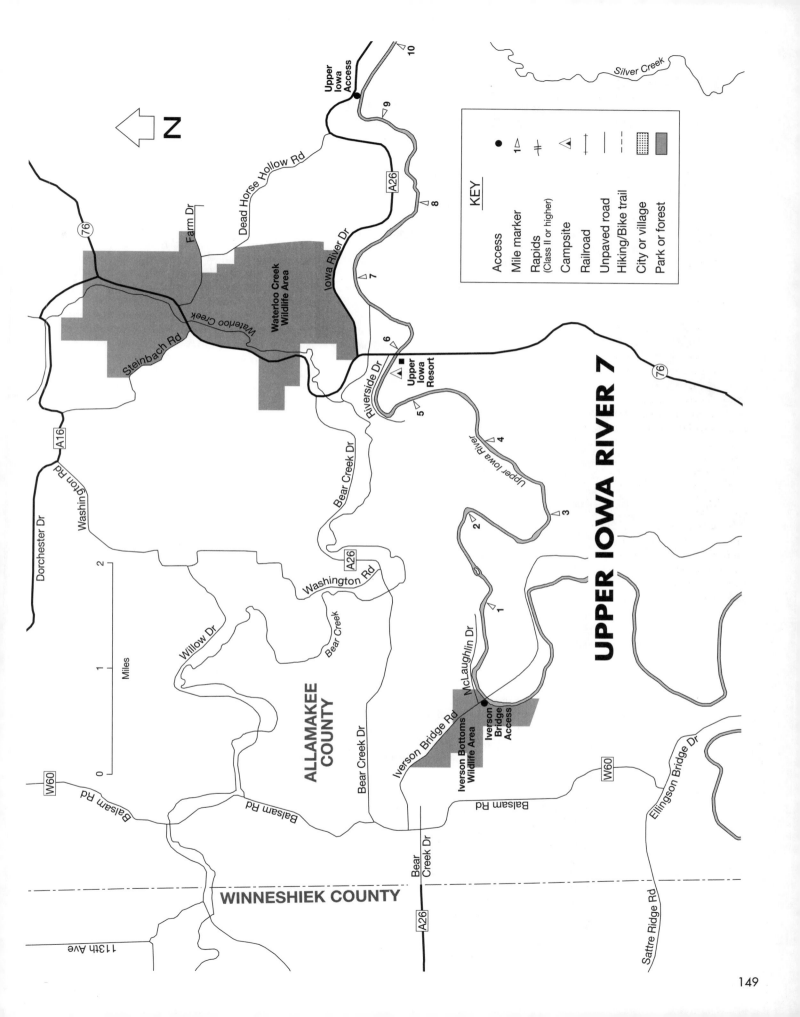

UPPER IOWA RIVER 7

KEY

Access
Mile marker
Rapids (Class II or higher)
Campsite
Railroad
Unpaved road
Hiking/Bike trail
City or village
Park or forest

N

Silver Creek

Upper Iowa Access

Dead Horse Hollow Rd

Farm Dr

Iowa River Dr

Waterloo Creek Wildlife Area

Waterloo Creek

Steinbach Rd

Washington Rd

Dorchester Dr

Riverside Dr

Upper Iowa Resort

Bear Creek Dr

Bear Creek

Washington Rd

Willow Dr

Upper Iowa River

McLaughlin Dr

Iverson Bridge Rd

Iverson Bottoms Wildlife Area

Iverson Bridge Access

ALLAMAKEE COUNTY

Bear Creek Dr

Balsam Rd

Balsam Rd

Balsam Rd

Bear Creek Dr

WINNESHIEK COUNTY

113th Ave

Sattre Ridge Rd

Ellingson Bridge Dr

Miles
0   1   2

VOLGA RIVER 1

M Avenue to Volga River State Recreation Area (12.1 Miles)

Iowa has a handful of small streams that, given good water levels, compel paddlers to call in sick to work or school, drop all responsibilities, and take to the water. The upper Volga is such a stretch of river. It's sublimely scenic, with cliffs both delicately and ruggedly sculpted, deeply secluded portions, and springs bubbling from bluffs. The fast waters continue running clear after all but the heaviest of rains.

Averaging 40 feet wide and dropping fairly swiftly, this isn't exactly a novice river tour. It has a few tricky turns and a couple of short rapids. The Volga River State Recreation Area is a 5,500-acre state park, second only to Brushy Creek State Recreation Area in size. Where the river is surrounded by parkland, the setting is amazingly pristine and remote. You can also divide this trip into two shorter stretches focusing on the prime scenery, the first from M Avenue to Klock's Island Park, the second from Langeman's Ford to the state recreation area.

Fishing is best for smallmouth bass and rock bass.

Volga River State Recreation Area has a riverside **campground**. Farther upriver, Twin Bridges Park also has riverside camping at the forks of the Volga and the Little Volga Rivers, 2.5 miles north of Maynard on County W25.

Canoe rentals are available from Turkey River Canoe Rentals (563-245-1559) in Elkader.

The **shuttle route** (9.4 miles) from the put-in runs north on M Avenue, east on Highway 93, north on Highway 150, and east on Ivy Road. Turn right onto the park road, following signs to the campgrounds, and continue past the campgrounds to the canoe access.

To approximate **water levels**, check the Volga River at Littleport gauge (station 5412400) on the USGS Web site listed on the introduction. The gauge is well downstream from this section, but with more than 250 cfs, this section will probably be runnable. This river flash floods in constricted sections: check rain forecasts.

This section sustains a steady **gradient** of 8.8 feet per mile.

Put in upstream from the M Avenue bridge. Beyond it, a wooded bluff with small limestone outcroppings joins the right bank, followed by another as you hook right. Heading south, the bluff forms ragged cliffs rising from the streambed. Along a breathtaking set of cliffs, the river has cut off an old meander through a bluff and runs through a fun rapids (class I), dropping through several pitches.

Passing swiftly through lowland woods, the river bends right toward a line of wooded bluffs. Through frequent riffles, the river bends left at a wooded ridge

The Milwaukee-Turkey Line

Every now and then as you paddle down the Volga, you'll notice flat spots in the woods. Most of these are old railroad grades from the Milwaukee-Turkey Line that stretched from Garber to West Union. Completed in 1882, the line closed in 1938, and the tracks were pulled out that same year.

toward Klock's Island Park, where there's an access 300 yards upstream of Highway 93.

Just past the bridge, the river bends sharply right at a limestone bluff, running through riffles to the Highway 150 bridge. After a left bend, you'll see the Main Street bridge at Fayette. Through town, the stream falls through several spirited riffles and briefly follows along a small limestone wall. Beyond homes, the river is forced left at a limestone wall covered in mosses and ferns. Through a long pool, the river passes a golf course, bending left at diminutive undercut limestone formations.

After the river takes two right bends, 20-foot limestone cliffs line the left bank on a straight, slow stretch as the river flows southeast toward Langeman's Ford. At the ford (the access is on the right), the river drops through brief rapids. As you bend left, a high bluff covered with deciduous trees, red cedars, and yew lines your right side. Springwater tumbles from its base into the river. Continuing the left curve, you'll pass a junky area as the river moves away from the bluff.

Rejoining the bluff, the river becomes rockier with boxy limestone formations and then 30-foot cliffs with overhanging rocks. Volga River State Recreation Area now surrounds the river, which becomes swifter. As you bend right, a ridge looms ahead. A long, swift riffle leads to its base, where the river makes a tricky right turn at a midstream boulder. Turn right into the eddy to avoid a collision. The river follows along the bluff, which is wooded with birch and hardwoods for 1.5 miles, arching right. Toward the end of the bluff are tortured-looking cliffs, abruptly ending where the river flows through wild meadows.

Bending right at a wooded ridge, the river widens and then constricts into a swift run curving left along rock outcroppings verdant with moss, wild ginger, ferns, and spindly yew. After a right bend, the river heads straight for a high, wooded bluff topped with paper birch ahead. Again, an instream boulder lurks—this time stay left through the fast left turn. As you paddle along boulders the size of vans and cabins, the river curves left and another pretty spring gushes down a steep slope. Past more limestone cliffs and woods curving left, the bluff tapers off.

Reaching a smaller wooded bluff ahead, the river curves right. Dropping over a ledge, the river approaches a trestle bridge. The **takeout** is 100 yards downstream at the gravel bar on the river-left.

Other trips. The paddling remains riffled and wild—but doesn't pass along scenic cliffs—to the access at Heron Road. The section from Heron Road to the Grannis Creek Wildlife Area passes mostly through lowland areas with glimpses of farmland all along. Beyond Grannis Creek, the river runs through a pretty, hemmed-in, wooded valley, with a couple of challenging snag-ridden sections on the way to Wadena.

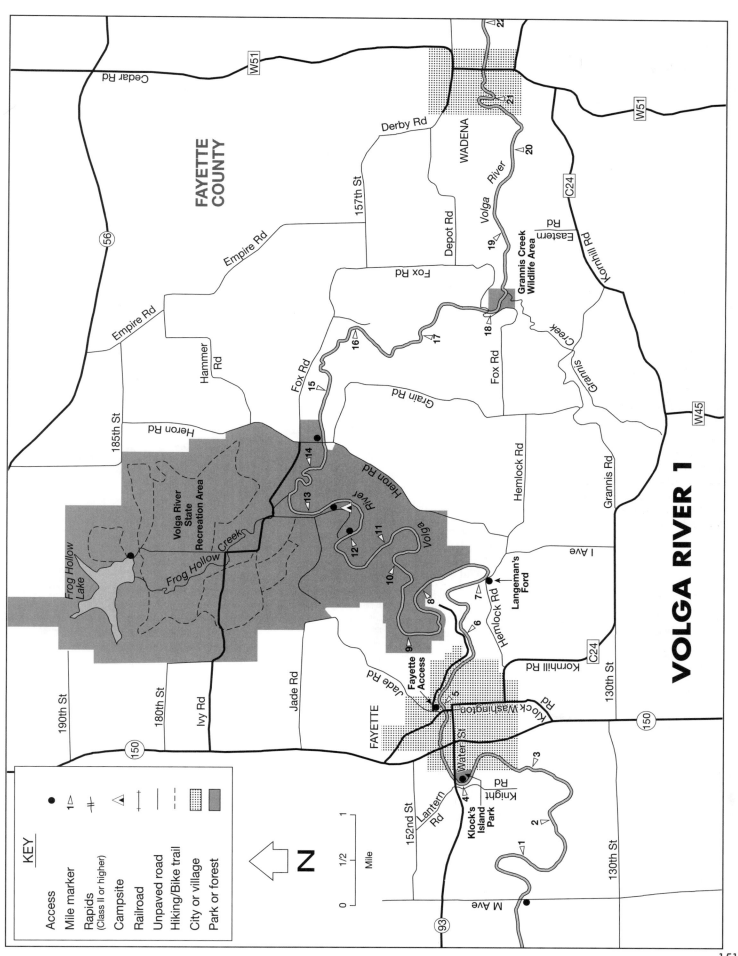

VOLGA RIVER 1

KEY

- Access
- Mile marker
- Rapids (Class II or higher)
- Campsite
- Railroad
- Unpaved road
- Hiking/Bike trail
- City or village
- Park or forest

FAYETTE COUNTY

Volga River State Recreation Area

Frog Hollow Lake

Frog Hollow Creek

Grannis Creek Wildlife Area

WADENA

Volga River

Grannis Creek

Langeman's Ford

Fayette Access

FAYETTE

Klock's Island Park

N

VOLGA RIVER 2
Osborne Park to Garber (19.3 Miles)

Another fantastic trip, this long tour to the Volga's mouth flows by its most impressive large-scale rock formations, along with extensive stretches of secluded valley. In places, stands of tall, upright red cedars (a contrast to their typical gnarled appearance), cast the impression of coniferous woods.

This section can be enjoyed more often than Volga River 1, due to its increasingly riverlike character. Although its drainage basin spans more than 400 square miles when it reaches the Turkey, the Volga is still a small river. Spring-fed and usually running clear, it will remain silt-laden for a day or so after a good rain. The trip easily can be shortened using the Mederville Access. Access over riprap at Littleport is not ideal, but it is possible. Smallmouth bass are present throughout the Volga, and catfishing gradually improves near the mouth.

Osborne Park has a riverside **campground**, as well as an education center that cares for injured or abandoned wild animals, from raptors to cougars. Privately run Littleport Campground in Littleport (563-245-2536) is also riverside.

Canoe rentals are available from Turkey River Canoe Rentals (563-245-1559) in Elkader.

The **shuttle route** (11.9 miles) from the put-in runs northeast on Highway 13, southeast on County X3C to Elkport, and northeast on County C7X across the Turkey River to Garber. Turn right on Front Street and right again on County X41 to the access on the left before the bridge.

For **water levels**, check the Volga River at Littleport gauge (station 5412400) on the USGS Web site listed on the introduction. Look for 125 cfs for reasonable passage through riffles. This river flash floods in constricted sections: check rain forecasts.

The **gradient** for this section is 5 feet per mile.

Put in on a sandbar at the Osborne Park campground, accessed on a park road. As the river runs south, wooded ridges rise and fall along either bank. After a left bend, you come to a pretty little bluff with tall cedars and then bend sharply right. At the next left, rock outcroppings appear as riffles lead from one emerald pool to the next.

You'll notice public hunting signs along the left at the Leonard Wildlife Area. Spring Creek enters from the right, and through back-to-back riffles you head south toward a wooded bluff. Bending left, the river winds through a scenic wooded stretch around two islands. Through lowland areas, you bend toward a scenic bluff near its base and turn right, where low cliffs and rock outcroppings line the river.

Ahead are the bluff-top homes of Mederville, and past a left bend an arched bridge spans a gorge with sheer limestone walls about 30 feet high. A more utilitarian concrete bridge is ahead, and limestone remains of a mill built sometime after 1838 by Henry Meder can still be seen. Beyond the little gorge and the canoe access on the

right is a spirited riffle bending left. As the river curves right, a longer riffle courses along the base of a boulder-strewn bluff. Through more riffles, you bend left at the base of a wooded ridge. Past bluffs covered in a pleasant mix of hardwoods, the river curves north, where unusually tall red cedars begin appearing on a ridge. At a right bend, the towering cedars line an eastward curve along a high ridge.

A riffle splits around a high, sandy island that's a fine place to stop. The stream constricts to just 20 feet wide, running fast past small limestone outcroppings. Beyond a smaller ridge, the Volga bends east past a limestone wall up to 15 feet high with a pasture across the stream. The river bends right, and an incredible 100-foot-high cliff looms ahead. Sadly, someone has plopped a home atop it. Past the first cliff are fantastical rock formations rivaling the Upper Iowa's, including chimney-like spires, a balanced rock, and a castlelike formation. The woods obscure these somewhat. Ahead on the right are smaller, still impressive, rock monoliths.

Curving left into a long, straight stretch, you reach Littleport. Past the tiny town and the County X21 bridge, the Volga is more riverlike, ranging from 50 to 80 feet wide, flowing through longer pools between riffles. Beyond a sharp hook right, it flows at the base of scenic cliffs and heads southwest until turning left. As the river heads generally east, the valley becomes narrow and forested again, bound by ridges. Rocky hollows periodically incise the valley.

You bend south and then back north through a double horseshoe bend, and at the north point you reach a wooded bluff with limestone cliffs. The bluff continues as you head south through the tight valley. Then the valley bottom begins widening into the river's last phase. Clearings become more common, and heading east, north, and then generally northeast, the stream runs back and forth through a one-fifth-mile-wide plain between 140-foot bluffs. Occasional dramatic cliffs appear high above the river, sometimes obscured by dense woods. Past the County XC3 bridge high above the river, you enter the much wider Turkey (see Turkey River 5 and 6). After the bridge connecting Elkport and Garber, you bend left along a last wooded ridge. The **takeout** is just past the next bridge on the river-left.

Other trips. The 6.8-mile trip from the old bridge in Volga City to Osborne (shown on the map) is also worth paddling. Mostly passing along lowland woods and some pasture, the stream itself is quite delicate and beautiful. In the last two miles, scenic bluffs rise along the river. If you're willing to carry down riprap, the 2.5 miles from Birch Road down to Volga City pass along a nice pine stand and scenic long cliffs before dropping over the easily run remains of an old dam at Volga City.

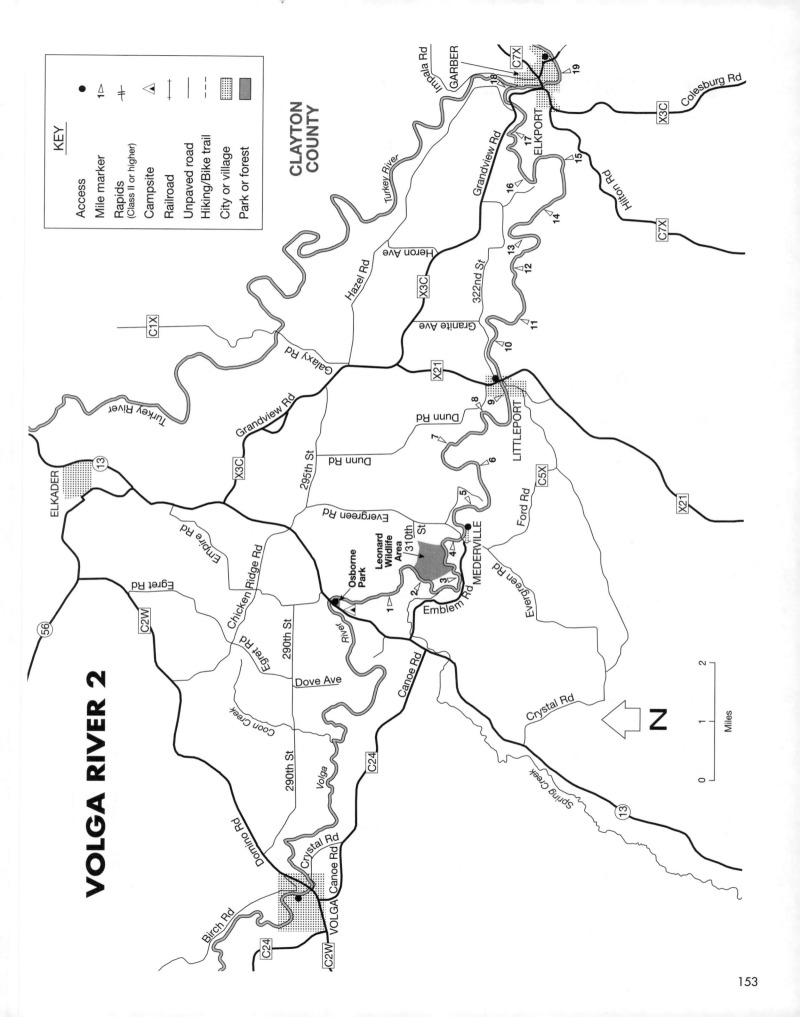

VOLGA RIVER 2

KEY

- Access
△ Mile marker
⌇ Rapids (Class II or higher)
▽ Campsite
╪ Railroad
│ Unpaved road
┆ Hiking/Bike trail
▦ City or village
�▦ Park or forest

CLAYTON COUNTY

N

Miles
0   1   2

WAPSIPINICON RIVER 1 AND 2

Iron Bridge to Quasqueton (4.9 Miles)
Quasqueton to Troy Mills Wildlife Area (8.3 Miles)

Wapsie and Pinnekon

Here's a melodramatic legend of lust, canoeing, and retribution: a Sauk band teamed up with the Mesquakie to attack the Sioux to avenge a fallen warrior. During preparations, handsome Pinnekon, son of the Sauk chief, and Wapsie, the Mesquakie chief's lovely daughter, fell for each other in a river village near what's now Quasqueton. Everyone was cheerful about the upcoming regal wedding, save for Long Fleet Foot, a Mesquakie warrior who'd struck out trying to woo Wapsie. As Wapsie and Pinnekon went for a lovers' paddling excursion on the river, Long Fleet Foot couldn't contain his rage and let loose an arrow straight into Pinnekon's heart. Wapsie leaped to help her beloved, flipping the canoe, and the lovers drowned in swift water. Their names were given to the river, though, unifying them for eternity.

It's a fine story with a good moral (don't jump in canoes!) but was likely crafted by Victorian-era settlers. See Wapsipinicon River 3 for a more mundane explanation of how the Wapsi got its name.

The Wapsipinicon River begins trickling near Taopi, Minnesota, fewer than five miles from the birthplace of the Upper Iowa River. The "Wapsi," as it called, forms the southern run of northeast Iowa's small bluff country rivers. In Bremer and Blackhawk Counties, the Wapsi flows through a long, swampy greenbelt of lowland river birch and silver maple woods, with backwaters extending all over the flat-bottomed valley. That segment is an Iowa Protected Waterway and, taken in small bites, can make for a unique paddling experience. But the river's narrowness and dense woods make for frequent riverwide snags and portages. Joined at Littleton by the second of two rivers with the name "Little Wapsipinicon," the river emerges from impoundment at Independence to make a pleasant paddling river on much of its remaining length.

In the first section described here, the Wapsi flows past wooded bluffs, and in the second, it more often flows through lowland woods. Cedar Rock, a home designed by Frank Lloyd Wright to suit the small bluff it's perched atop, is a distinctive sight. The river is almost never swift. It is sandy-bottomed except at rare riffles and averages 140 feet wide here. Fishing is best for catfish, with some northern pike and walleye also caught.

Quasqueton Park has a riverside **campground**, and camping is also allowed near the access at the Troy Mills Wildlife Area. Up the bluff and overlooking the river, the Boies Bend Access Area also offers camping.

The **shuttle route** for the first trip (4 miles) runs from the put-in at Iron Bridge south on Nolan Avenue and east on 278th Street to Quasqueton Park.

For the second trip (8.1 miles), head across the bridge from the park, east on Linn Street, which becomes County D47, south on County W45, west on 310th, and south on Stewart Avenue to the access on the northeast side of Troy Mills Wildlife Area.

Water levels can be checked on the Wapsipinicon at Independence gauge (station 05421000) on the USGS Web site listed in the introduction. The river here is generally sandy-bottomed, and you'll begin dragging at levels below 150 cfs.

The **gradient** is less than 2 feet per mile.

Put in just downstream of the Iron Bridge boat ramp between the old iron bridge and the new concrete one. You paddle southeast toward the base of a rocky,

wooded ridge, and the river bends left toward a higher wooded bluff ahead and then turns right along scenic limestone outcroppings. Beyond some homes at another right bend, you see an impressive brick boathouse exhibiting the Prairie School design sensibilities of Frank Lloyd Wright. Up the hill, built into a limestone outcropping, is his matching contextual masterpiece, Cedar Rock. Feel free to get out and explore the grounds, now managed by the Iowa Department of Natural Resources.

As you round the horseshoe bend to the south, you see a stairway that leads up the pretty wooded bluff to the Boies Bend Access Area (not a canoe access). Heading northeast, the river becomes lakelike behind the dam at Quasqueton. The **takeout** for the first trip is 50 yards above the low-head dam on the river-right.

If you want to link to the second trip, the **portage** is an easy 150-yard carry to an access below the dangerous low-head dam. You can **put in** either upstream or downstream of a rock dam—a short, class-I rapids runs straight through on the river-right chute—between the low-head dam and the W35 bridge.

Below the bridge, banks are low and lightly wooded. You bend right to a pasture, and a home tops a small ridge with a rocky base. Ahead are smaller limestone outcroppings, followed by a curve to the east toward a small ridge with a 15-foot clay cliff. Through lowland woods heading generally south, the river bends left along a rocky, wooded ridge in a tighter, deeper channel. Heading southeast, you'll pass a riverside home followed by lowland woods of the Sand Creek Wildlife Area. In the next several bends, at high water, the river can connect with numerous backwaters.

The river occasionally passes homes, all through dense lowland woods of silver maples with some willows and cottonwoods. Past some limestone outcroppings and more woods, the river passes some row crops, and after a sharp right bend, the **takeout** is at the boat ramp on the river-left.

Cedar Rock makes an interesting stop on the Wapsipinicon.

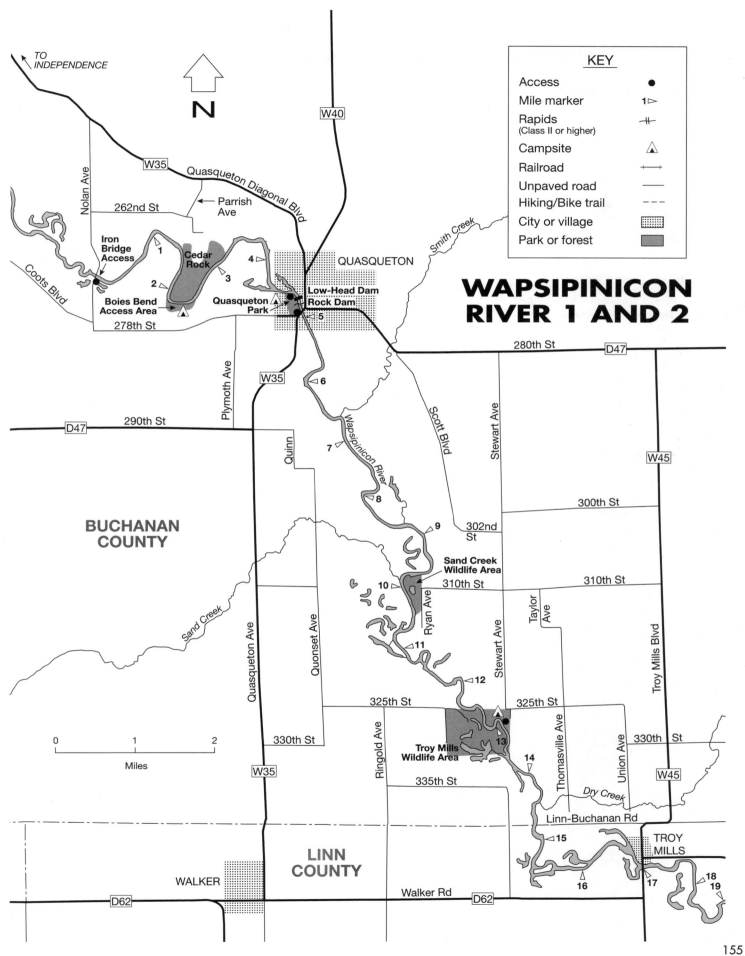

WAPSIPINICON RIVER 3
Troy Mills to Central City (12.2 Miles)

River of Swans and Potatoes

The Wapsie-Pinnekon legend described in the previous section is sometimes still passed off to local children as a true story. But more likely, the name "Wapsipinicon" derives from the arrowhead plant, an edible white tuber that thrived in the river and still grows there. Native Americans collected them by wading barefoot and dislodging the starchy vegetables—about the size of a new potato—with their toes. Because they float, the tubers rose to the surface where they were gathered to eat. Originally, the river's name was likely Waubessa pinneac, called by French traders and soldiers the *Pomme de Cigne*, or roughly, Swan Potato River. "Swan" signified the whiteness of the tubers. The modern-day spelling "Wapsipinicon" is no more a corruption than Wapizipinka, one of many ways this river's name has been mangled in historical texts over the year.

This popular stretch of the Wapsipinicon certainly has its appealing points. It's easy to access from Cedar Rapids (20 miles to the south) and the Waterloo-Cedar Falls area (about 35 miles to the northwest). It has pretty bluffs and pleasant woods all the way along. If you don't own a boat, rentals are available.

By no stretch of the imagination is this a remote section of stream, however. It is heavily wooded, but you'll also see dozens of riverside homes and corresponding lines of concrete riprap piled along the river, protecting home owners' investments.

Note that this trip begins at the village of Troy Mills, not at the Troy Mills Wildlife Area (the takeout for Wapsipinicon River 2), which people can find confusing. Beginning here cuts out paddling past numerous river shacks and saves you a portage around the dam. Anglers will find catfish, walleye, northern pike, and smallmouth bass throughout this run.

Pinicon Ridge Park has an excellent riverside **campground** with full amenities.

Canoe rentals and shuttles (for this section only) are available at Pinicon Ridge Park (319-892-6450).

The **shuttle route** (15 miles) from the put-in at Troy Mills runs south on County W45, east on County E16, north on Highway 13, west on Maple Street in Central City, and north into Pinicon Ridge Park to the river access.

Water levels can be checked on the Wapsipinicon at Independence gauge (station 05421000) on the USGS Web site listed in the introduction. This section is generally sandy-bottomed, and you'll begin dragging at levels below 150 cfs.

The **gradient** is less than 2 feet per mile.

In the village of Troy Mills, **put in** downstream of the W45 bridge and dam, on a rocky beach, on the river-right. Run the rocky riffle, and you pass small homes on the way out of town. Bending to the south, the river passes a battered-looking limestone outcropping with cedars clinging to it. Then the river begins bending through lowland woods with numerous sandbars as it curves back to the northeast, where there's another home on a small ridge with riprap lining the stream.

Beyond a wooded ridge sloping to the river, you bend right along some riprap with more evidence of homes. Curving left, you head east toward a low ridge with a rocky bank and then float past cabins toward a higher wooded bluff with limestone outcroppings. Turning left at the bluff's base, you see a line of homes across from the bluff that capitalize on the nice view near the end of Dix Road, an alternative put-in.

Ahead, an even higher bluff rises with beautiful rock outcroppings at its base, turned green with a generous covering of moss and lichens. Passing more homes, one of them set on the wooded bluff to the east, you turn right at the bluff's base and pass more homes across the river. Shelflike limestone formations protrude from the left bank. Ahead, you reach another low bluff, this one with scenic rock cliffs up to 30 feet high. Past more cabins, some wooded grazing land, and more cabins with a long line of riprap, you hook to the northeast through lowland woods dominated by silver maples. Reaching a small bluff, you see cabins ahead with a high, wooded ridge in the background.

More riprap-lined wooded banks ensue, and then the setting becomes more serene, with a high, wooded ridge ahead. Bending left, you'll soon reach the Sutton Road bridge.

Past the bridge, a car, appliances, and other junk line the river near two homes, and the river enters a snag-strewn area of lowland woods that leads to the next bridge at Paris Road. Either side of the river makes a decent canoe access. A rocky ridge rises ahead, and you bend left as the river widens and slows behind Central City's dam. You bend southeast toward a bluff to the east, with both pretty rock outcroppings and a road running along it, and then the river turns right at the bluff's base. The area ahead is nicely wooded as you enter Pinicon Ridge Park. A wooded ridge rises on the south bank of the river, and beyond a wooded island, the easily accessible campground is seen on the river-left. The **takeout** at the park's boat ramp is a few hundred yards downstream on the river-right.

The "Wapsi" is most often a glassy stream lined with rocks and woods.

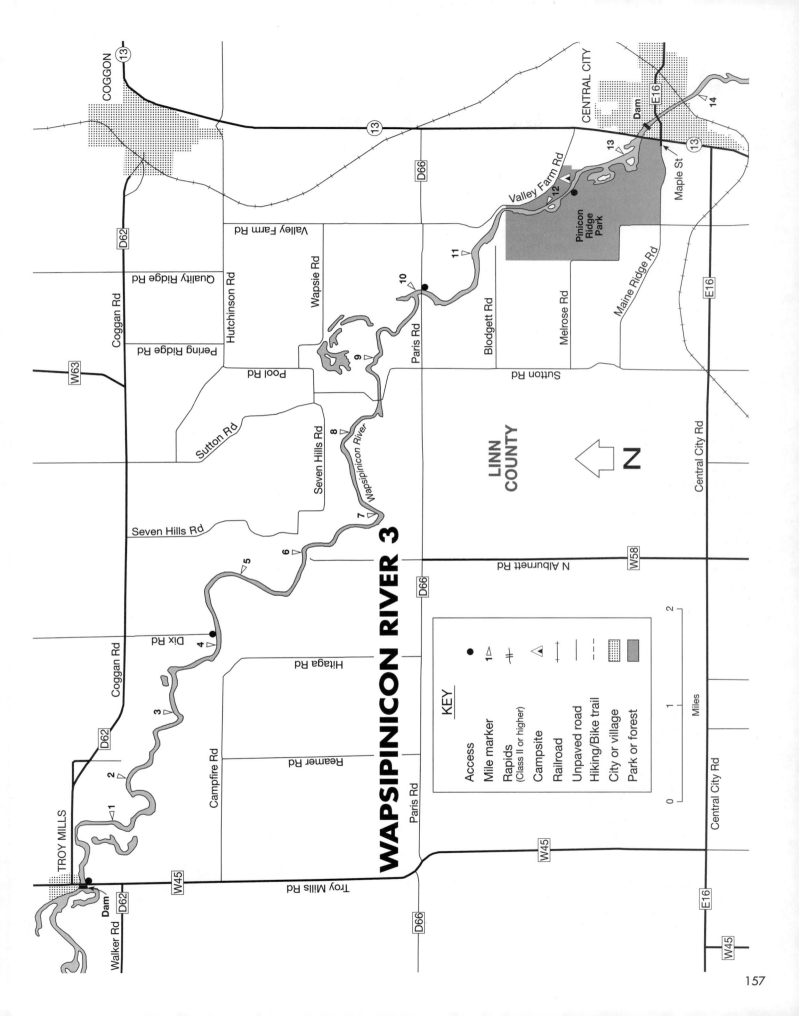

WAPSIPINICON RIVER 3

KEY

●	Access
1△	Mile marker
⊬	Rapids (Class II or higher)
◢	Campsite
┼	Railroad
		Unpaved road
– – –	Hiking/Bike trail
▦	City or village
▨	Park or forest

Miles
0   1   2

N

LINN COUNTY

Pinicon Ridge Park

CENTRAL CITY

TROY MILLS

COGGON

WAPSIPINICON RIVER 4 AND 5

Central City to Waubeek (6.6 Miles)
Waubeek to Stone City (10.7 Miles)

Taken together, these two sections make up the quintessential Wapsipinicon River trip. For two miles upstream of Waubeek, the river cambers through a narrow valley along very scenic bluffs. Section 4 is uncharacteristic for this river, with numerous riffles that aren't a wild ride but do add interest. Downstream from Waubeek, the river regains its languid personality, entering a widely braided, heavily wooded section that would be frustrating were paddlers not regularly sawing paths through the snags. Ending where Grant Wood ran an artists' colony in the tiny village of Stone City, the trip covers the breadth of what the Wapsipinicon has to offer paddlers.

Angling is best for catfish, smallmouth bass, walleye, and northern pike.

Riverside **camping** is allowed at the Wakpicada Natural Area. Matsell Bridge Natural Area has camping up the ridge from the river, as well as rental cabins (319-892-6450). At Central City, the Wapsipinicon becomes one of the state's smaller "meandered streams," meaning that sandbar camping—using appropriate caution (see introduction)—is acceptable.

The **shuttle route** (6 miles) for the first segment runs west out of Wakpicada Natural Area past the fairgrounds, north on Highway 13 to Central City's Maple Street, east to Main Street, and over the river bridge in Central City. Continuing east out of town on Main Street, the road becomes County E16. Turn south on Duck Point Road and then southeast on Boy Scouts Road, which leads to the access across from the bridge in the village of Waubeek.

The shuttle route (9.5 miles) for the second trip heads north of the Waubeek access on Boy Scouts Road, west on Wapsi Banks Road to County E28, southeast to County X28, and south to the put-in at Stone City.

Water levels can be checked on the Wapsipinicon at Independence gauge (station 05421000) on the USGS Web site listed in the introduction. This section is generally sandy-bottomed, and you'll begin dragging at levels below 150 cfs.

The **gradient** is less than 2 feet per mile.

Put in at the Wakpicada Access, just south of Central City, and paddle generally south in little bends through lowland woods. A sharp left turn leads into a small riffle along cut banks. Bending left, you see a cabin, and a long riffle follows. Pass a small rocky ridge, and the Jordans Grove Road bridge is ahead, with an access downstream on the river-right.

The river drops 8 inches over a seam of rocks, followed by a shallow riffle. Bending north, you approach another small, wooded ridge, and after a left bend you hook back south past a log home. Heading south, you bend left at a rocky bank, passing two more homes.

You join a pretty ridge with a rocky bank, and limestone rock outcroppings begin appearing on a ridge slope. The valley narrows considerably. Further along, blocky cliffs appear, and you bend along them to the right. As you head southeast, higher bluffs rise, and cliffs up to 35 feet high are festooned with yew and ferns. You bend straight to the south, and a long line of prominent cliffs stretches out ahead. The river curves a bit left, the bluffs drop back from the river, and you see the Waubeek bridge ahead. On the downstream side of the bridge is another rock seam; the middle chute affords easiest passage. The **takeout** for this segment is at the boat ramp just downstream of the bridge, where an 80-foot walk up the hill leads to a pub in a stone house.

For the second segment, which begins at the same boat ramp south of town, the river curves east and then north along a pretty bluff with limestone formations. Past a couple of cabins on a ridge to the left, you bend left along another bluff with Wapsi Banks Road running along its base. Past here, the valley suddenly opens wide, and you're paddling along a cornfield. Bending right, the river runs next to dozens of small cabins around a long bend. At a sharp right turn by a sandbar, you leave cabins behind and enter a wilderness bottomland of maples and river birch. There are several possible routes. Navigation here changes yearly; your route depends on where a clear path is available. You may need to **portage** several times over fallen tree trunks or drag through shallow, sandy-bottomed areas. Keep your wits about you: there are many potential strainers here.

All the channels do join back together eventually, and you come to a gradual left bend along a rocky bank by a wooded ridge. Just after a right bend, the Matsell Bridge Natural Area boat ramp is on the left. Just up the hill are restrooms and drinking water. Beyond Matsell Bridge, you pass through a small riffle and come to a scenic 30-foot limestone cliff with boulders the size of cows and hippos at its base. Mosses, tiny ferns, and yew grow up the jagged rock exposures. As another high bluff rises on the left, you see homes set back in the woods on the right. The river curves right along more cliffs with red cedars clinging to crevices.

There's no doubt you're near Stone City. Among the homes on wooded lots to the right, one toolshed displays a facsimile of Grant Wood's *American Gothic* (see sidebar in Wapsipinicon River 6 for more on Wood). You may hear pounding in a quarry. Just ahead is the town's pretty double-trestle bridge. Past a stone building on the left, you curve along a splintered rock wall covered in shiny green liverworts. The **takeout** is at the boat ramp on the river-left.

Upstream of Waubeek, the "Wapsi's" subtle beauty is at its peak.

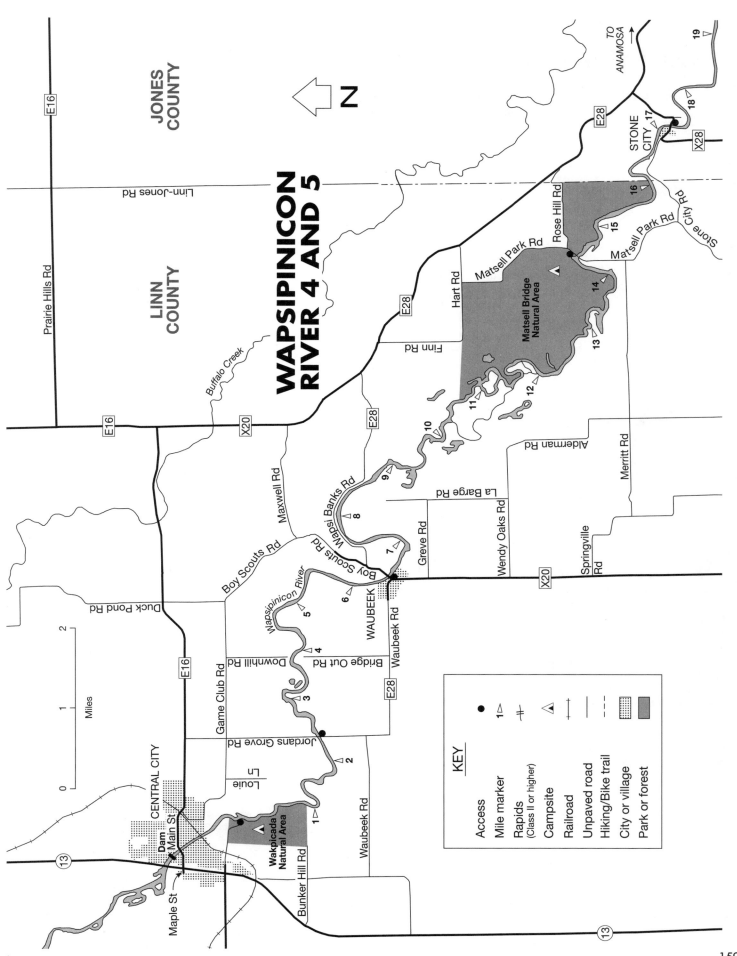

WAPSIPINICON RIVER 4 AND 5

JONES COUNTY

LINN COUNTY

N

TO ANAMOSA

KEY

●	Access
1△	Mile marker
⊹	Rapids (Class II or higher)
△	Campsite
⊢	Railroad
—	Unpaved road
- - -	Hiking/Bike trail
▦	City or village
▨	Park or forest

Matsell Bridge Natural Area

Wakpicada Natural Area

CENTRAL CITY

WAUBEEK

STONE CITY

Miles

0   1   2

WAPSIPINICON RIVER 6
Anamosa to Newport Mills Access (8.6 Miles)

Why this stretch is paddled less frequently than others upriver is puzzling. It begins in the river's attractive namesake state park, ends at a good access, and in between passes some of the most rugged little cliffs and limestone formations on the entire river. The stretch is much less developed with riverside cabins, the paddling is excellent, and a sense of seclusion sets in.

When a lot of water is released from the hydropower dam at Anamosa, the water in this section does appear muddier than in the sections upriver. Catfish and smallmouth bass are the primary game fish, and some walleye and northern pike are caught.

A **campground** with full amenities is up the ridge at Wapsipinicon State Park. The Wapsipinicon in this section is classified a "meandered stream," meaning that sandbar camping—using appropriate caution (see introduction)—is acceptable.

The **shuttle route** (10 miles) from the put-in runs southwest from the Wapsipinicon State Park entrance on E34, southeast on Forest Chapel Road, northeast on U.S. Highway 151, south on County X40, and east and northeast on Newport Road.

Water levels correspond to power generation at Anamosa and can be sporadic. Check the Wapsipinicon near Anamosa gauge (station 05421740) on the USGS Web site listed in the introduction. Look for a minimum reading of 5 feet to avoid scraping on numerous sharp rocks.

The **gradient** is 2.4 feet per mile.

Put in at the boat ramp at Wapsipinicon State Park. Just downstream, pretty limestone cliffs line the water in a bit of limestone gorge, with rock outcroppings visible on both sides. Past the park's picnic shelters and through light riffles, a creek enters from the left. The bluffs taper off, and the river bends right into a riffle through lowland woods.

Approaching a wooded and rocky slope to the south, you bend left, passing beneath the two Highway 151 bridges and then immediately beneath a bridge for a rural road. Bending slightly right, you see a quarry, where boulders are stacked in the river-right side of the channel, constricting the left side into a spirited riffle. The river bends right, southward away from Lead Mine Road, where the twisted remains of what look like railroad tracks are on the bank at the beginning of a wooded ridge.

Heading straight south, you see a dramatic bluff rise on the right, with cliffs up to 50 feet high and angular formations topped with woods. Boulders protrude from the riverbed on the right side of the channel as well as on the left further along, running through a riffle.

The woods grow sparse, and you see a cornfield ahead. You bend right, and past the Lands Road bridge are

deep-cut banks with strange concrete islands in the river. But then, as you bend left, a small rocky ridge forms the left bank, with limestone walls topped by a thin line of trees. Heading west, the river reaches a wooded ridge and bends along small exposures of limestone. Gradually, the setting becomes increasingly wooded, and the rock outcroppings are more prominent.

Past a cabin, the river bends right into a very scenic part of the river. On the right, a knobby-looking piece of limestone appears, the first of several remarkable limestone formations. Just downstream, cliffs pockmarked with crevices and caves hang over the river where it has worn undercuts in the base of the cliffs.

Bending left into a long southeastward stretch along more dramatic bluffs, you may occasionally hear and see cattle grazing the woodlands on the left. Past a small riffle, a bluff rises on the left. An eye-catching monolith of limestone appears ahead on the right. After a right bend, you'll see another conspicuous outcropping, rugged and cedar-topped, with a cave near its waterline. Just downstream of it, Hog's Den Hollow appears as a depression in the woods. Ahead is one last glorious set of jagged white limestone cliffs tinted with reddish and yellowish tones.

The bluffs drop back from the river, and you pass a cabin. Past power lines across the stream, stay to the river-right of an island, where the **takeout** is at the Newport Mills boat ramp.

Other trips. Downstream of the Newport Mills Access, the Wapsi Valley widens considerably into a sometimes agricultural lowland not of great interest to paddlers. But after the river passes the town of Olin on Highway 38, the 6.6-mile stretch of river between the Olin and the Jungletown boat ramp is well worth a trip, winding through heavily wooded areas and past scenic bluffs. To reach the Jungletown Access, head south of the "town" of Hale on 100th Avenue, cross the river bridge, and head east a half mile down Jungletown Road to the takeout.

Stone City

In 1930, regionalist artist Grant Wood painted *Stone City*, his first major landscape painting, to showcase his newfound style—highly idealistic, almost cartoonlike renderings. They also were meant to represent an idea. The painting depicted a curvy Wapsipinicon Valley from a field high above, with the river and double-trestle bridge at the center. Although it's been said he was trying to depict the decline of the limestone quarries, you'll notice the rattle of jackhammers as you paddle through town, where the bluffs are still being gradually reduced to rubble. Wood ran an artists' colony in Stone City during the summers of 1932 and 1933. *Stone City* now hangs at the Joslyn Art Museum in Omaha, Nebraska.

The Wapsipinicon runs along numerous scenic lines of cliffs nearing Newport Mills.

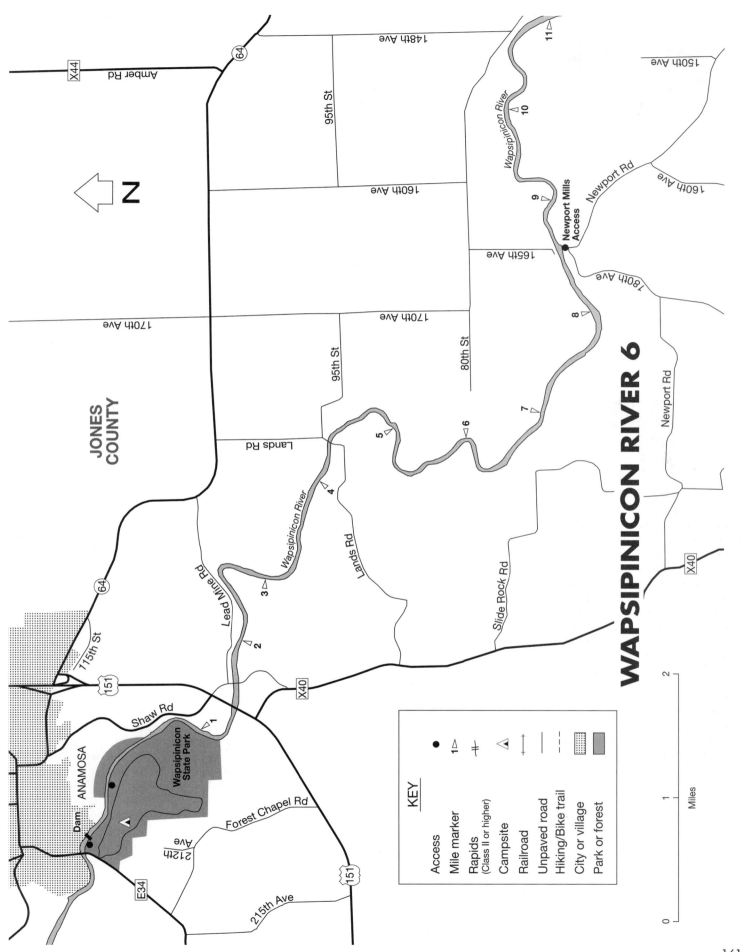

WAPSIPINICON RIVER 6

WEST FORK OF THE DES MOINES RIVER
Humboldt to Gotch Park Access (4.7 Miles)

The West Fork of the Des Moines River rises in Lake Shetek near Curie, Minnesota, and dozens of other southwest Minnesota lakes and marshes feed the stream before it enters Iowa near Estherville. At normal flows, it's paddleable from the state line to Frank A. Gotch Park, where it joins the East Fork to become the Des Moines River.

This short section is fun and scenic. One of nicest views is near the put-in, right in the town of Humboldt. Small limestone outcroppings are visible throughout much of the trip, and the river descends near-constant riffles along low, wooded bluffs for the first several miles, with rocks and boulders midstream. There are dams—each dangerous—at both ends of this trip, but the put-in is well below the dam in Humboldt, and the takeout is half a mile upstream from the Cornbelt REC Dam. *Do not paddle over the Cornbelt REC dam*, which has killed several canoeists. There is one rock dam in Humboldt that you'll want to scout. Smallmouth bass, northern, and catfish are commonly sought here.

Excellent **campgrounds** are found near both the put-in and takeout for this trip. Joe Sheldon Park overlooking Lake Nokomis (the backed-up river) on the west edge of Humboldt has showers and electricity, as does Gotch Park, where campsites overlook the confluence of the Des Moines River's two main forks.

The **shuttle route** (6.8 miles) begins by heading a block east on 3rd Avenue to U.S. Highway 169. Take a right and head south 4.5 miles to County C49. Go east one mile and north one more mile on Gotch Park Road, and enter the park after crossing the bridge over the Des Moines. The takeout is a fourth of a mile into the park on the right side of the road.

For **water levels**, see the Humboldt gauge (station 05476750) on the USGS Web site listed in the introduction. At 300 cfs or below, you will scrape sharp rocks often and have a frustrating time.

The **gradient** for this section is 6 feet per mile.

The **put-in**, river-left and downstream from the Humboldt dam, is just across the Cottonwood Trail at the west end of 3rd Avenue. The river is glassy, running along 8- to 15-foot limestone cliffs next to the stream. With normal water conditions, a small creek cascades through a crevice in the rock. Pass beneath Highway 169, and shortly ahead you'll hear the roar of the first rock dam. Scout this on the right before deciding whether you should run it. The rock dam rapids (solid class II) course through a pushy 15-foot-wide chute in the center. At higher levels a large hole develops on the right side of this chute that should be avoided. The left side of the chute has a fun wave train. **Portage** on the river-right if you're not comfortable with this one.

You can also begin your trip at the park at the bridge on Sumner Avenue, avoiding the first rock dam altogether. Just downstream from the bridge on the left, a worn-looking brick Coca-Cola bottling plant stands on a limestone outcropping. Decades ago, discarded bottles were tossed from the windows into the river, and some collectors still enjoy scouring the downstream gravel bars for them.

The river enters a long riffly section, coursing past homes and buildings on the right. Gradually the banks become more wooded with fewer homes. After a home on the left with a large deck, the river widens as you come to a second rock dam. You can run the left or middle chutes, although at low levels you may need to **portage**.

A riffle nearly a mile long curves to the east and continues where the river bends right along a small wooded ridge that rises on the left side. At lower levels you may have to dodge rocks. The river slows a bit, with rocks and boulders still jutting up from the river. Both banks are wooded. Curving left at the beginning of a 70-foot wooded bluff with a few houses atop it, the river heads southeast past small limestone outcroppings and an island. Indian Creek enters from the right. Just upstream from the Gotch Park Road bridge, there are some rocks to avoid. **Take out** at the concrete boat ramp after a left bend past the bridge.

Other trips. The West Fork has other stretches of interest. The 4.6-mile trip from Rutland to Joe Sheldon Park in Humboldt has scenic bluffs and limestone outcroppings, although the flow soon becomes sluggish behind the Humboldt Dam. The 16-mile section from the Peterson Access east of Wallingford to the Basswood Access northwest of Emmetsburg on Highway 18 runs through light woods and pastured ridges with occasional riffles over glacial till, channelized in the last 3 miles. In approximately 33 miles from the Basswood Access to the boat ramp at County P19 southwest of Bradgate, with several accesses in between, the channelization continues, but the river also passes constantly between woods that sometimes form a canopy over the river. Long tracts of public land offer excellent wildlife viewing. From Bradgate to the old milldam in Rutland (10 miles) is a slow, tree-lined river briefly flanked by dramatic loess bluffs. Much of the East Fork of the Des Moines River is heavily wooded and beautiful, but profuse snags make the going difficult near its headwaters. The 11-mile stretch from County C26 to Dakota City, or to Gotch Park (14.6 miles; paddle upstream to the takeout on the West Fork) passes through deeply wooded hills without much snag trouble.

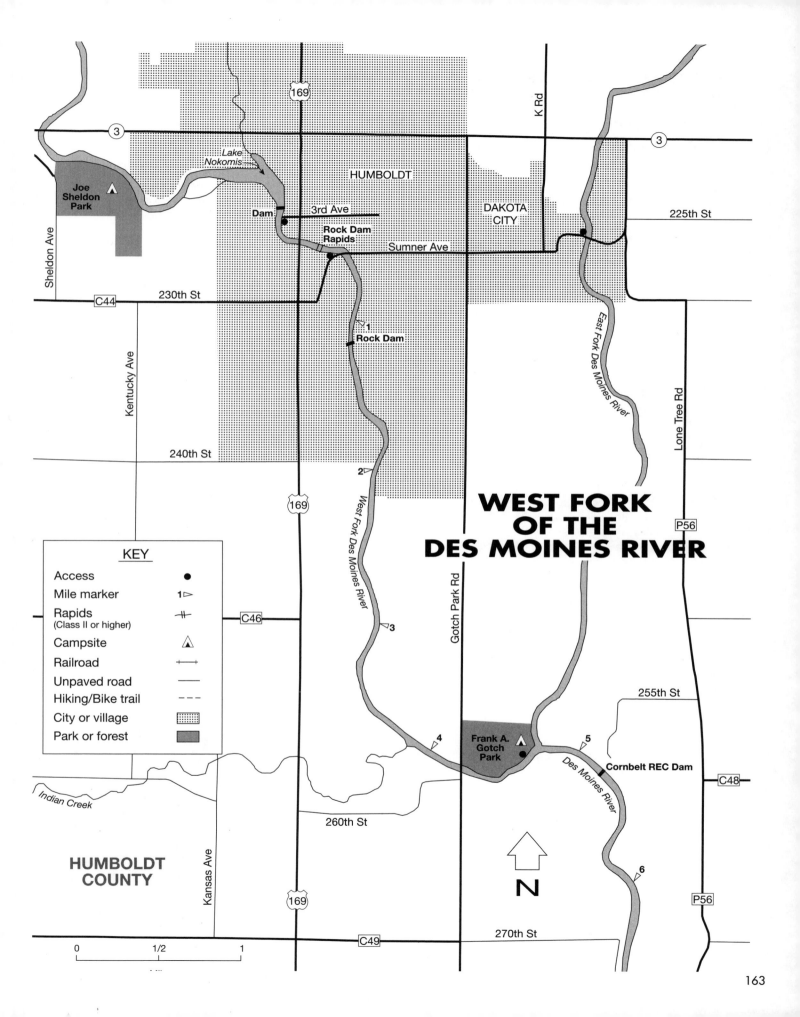

WEST FORK OF THE DES MOINES RIVER

KEY

Access	●
Mile marker	1▷
Rapids (Class II or higher)	╫
Campsite	▲
Railroad	┼─┼
Unpaved road	───
Hiking/Bike trail	─ ─ ─
City or village	▦
Park or forest	▨

HUMBOLDT COUNTY

Joe Sheldon Park

Lake Nokomis

HUMBOLDT

DAKOTA CITY

Dam

3rd Ave

Rock Dam Rapids

Sumner Ave

1 Rock Dam

West Fork Des Moines River

East Fork Des Moines River

Frank A. Gotch Park

Cornbelt REC Dam

Des Moines River

Indian Creek

Sheldon Ave

Kentucky Ave

Kansas Ave

Gotch Park Rd

Lone Tree Rd

K Rd

169

3

3

C44

230th St

240th St

225th St

255th St

260th St

270th St

C46

C48

C49

P56

P56

169

N

0   1/2   1

WEST NISHNABOTNA RIVER
Hancock to Macedonia (16.5 Miles)

Early described as a "silvery stream," the West Nishnabotna River suffered greatly at the hands of Euro-American settlement. Due to the erosive nature of soils in the wide valley, pioneer sodbusters quickly found fragile loess washing away into the river. Heavy sediment raised the level of the riverbed, in turn causing flooding in riverside towns several times a year. The first answer was to dig new, deeper, straight channels for the rivers, but that didn't stop the floodwaters. Eventually, agricultural practices were modified, and steadily the rivers have cut into banks, regaining meanders ever since.

The stretch that best illustrates how far the river has made a comeback is the easily accessed portion of river between Hancock and Old Town Park near Macedonia, a trip that can be shortened with the access at the town of Oakland. Some locals still remember looking from the bridge where Hancock's Botna Bend Park now is and seeing straight upriver for a mile or more. Now the river winds through two small horseshoe bends there. Expect no dramatic bluffs or fast water on the West Nishnabotna—it is a very lazily meandering, tree-lined prairie stream, typically brown as cocoa for much of the season, with a sandy and occasionally muddy bottom. That said, it's a relaxing getaway with dense concentrations of wildlife such as deer, turkeys, herons, and waterfowl, and it has nice sandbars for stopping to splash around.

At Botna Bend Park, there is a riverside **campground** with full amenities (plus buffalo, elk, and deer for your viewing pleasure), and Old Town Park also has camping near the river.

Canoe and kayak rentals are available from Botna Bend Park (712-741-5465) and Canoesport Outfitters (402-296-0522) in Plattsmouth, Nebraska, south of Omaha.

The **shuttle route** (11.9 miles) from the Hancock put-in runs briefly east on County G30, south on U.S. Highway 59, west on County G66, and south on 385th Street to Old Town Park, near Macedonia.

Water levels can be checked at the West Nishnatbotna at Hancock gauge (station 06807410) on the USGS Web site listed in the introduction. Look for more than 125 cfs to avoid constantly hitting sand shoals. Above 400 cfs, only the highest sandbars still appear.

The **gradient** is less than 2 feet per mile.

Put in at the boat ramp just upstream of the County G30 bridge in Hancock's Botna Bend Park. Past the bridge, the river heads southeast through banks lined by maples, ash, cottonwoods, and elms. Bending left, you pass beneath a railroad bridge and along cut banks with an occasional view of crops topping the outsides of the channel in the next two bends; sandbars are on the insides of the bends.

As you head southwest, dense woods with tall cottonwood trees line the pleasantly uneroded banks. The views for the next several miles alternate between long stretches of woods and short segments where fields covering rolling hills are visible. After passing some decidedly un-scenic junk and concrete riprap piled on a cut bank, you bend left and can see the town of Oakland ahead. After another long stretch of woods, at a bend to the east you'll see the backs of downtown Oakland's buildings. The County G42 bridge is just around the next bend, and the access at Oakland's Chataqua Park is a quarter mile ahead on the left.

Mixed views of crops and woods with cut banks ensue, and as you make a little hook to the right, you'll see the Highway 6 bridge. Past it, young woods line the banks, followed by agricultural views and then a farmyard atop a 5-foot-high loess cut bank.

Tall cut banks begin lining the left bank. Past more views of the crop-covered valley at a bend to the west, the woods become denser, and gradually you approach Carson, where you could use the area behind the baseball diamond as an access.

Past the Highway 92 bridge, the river passes over a bit of a riffle and enters a long woods-lined section heading due south. Bending to the southeast, you can see Macedonia's water tower after views of fields. Bending right and then left for another view of the town above corn or bean fields, the river heads southwest into a pretty and wild-feeling area of light woods and marshlands. The **takeout** is at a boat ramp in Old Town Park about 70 yards downstream of the County G66 bridge on the right.

Nishnabotna Means Canoeing

The singsong word *Nishnabotna* derives from a Native American utterance that scholars agree has something to do with canoeing. The word may have been Sioux, or it may have been Otoe. One linguist said it meant "crossed in a canoe," referring to the river's depth at the time, but it also may have meant something more like "river where canoes are built." One Mormon record said it meant "good canoeing river." In any case, early explorers had a difficult time spelling it, scribbling anything from "Nishnay Baton" to "Ichinpokina."

The West Nishnabotna is a pleasant prairie stream in recovery mode.

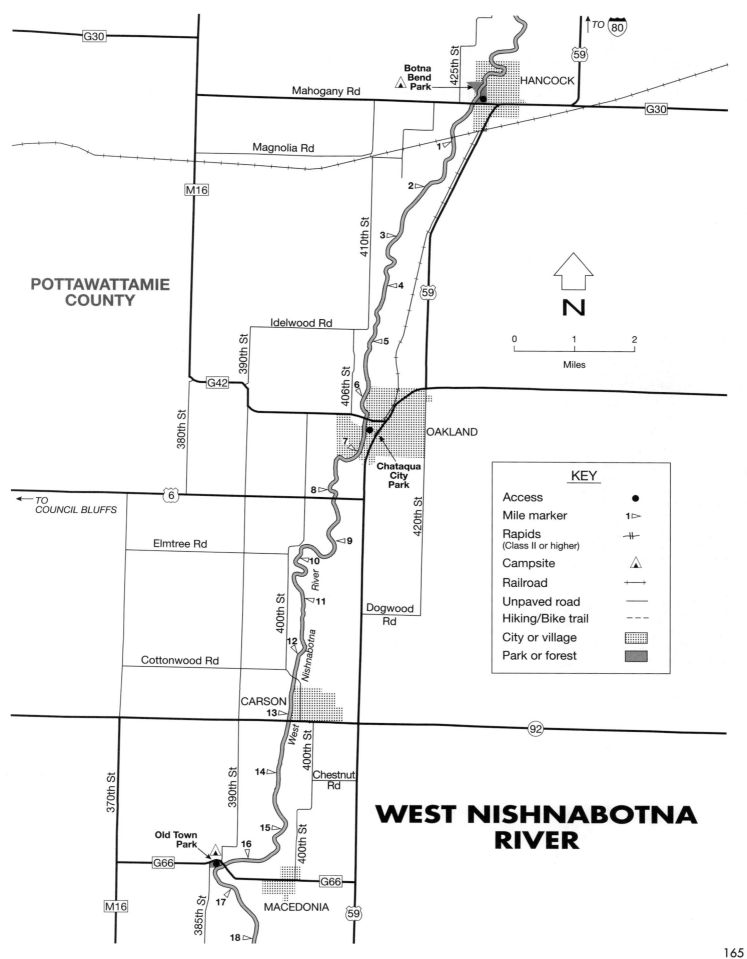

WEST NISHNABOTNA RIVER

KEY

Access	●
Mile marker	1▷
Rapids (Class II or higher)	╫
Campsite	⚠
Railroad	┼┼┼
Unpaved road	──
Hiking/Bike trail	─ ─ ─
City or village	▒
Park or forest	▓

POTTAWATTAMIE COUNTY

Botna Bend Park

HANCOCK

Mahogany Rd

Magnolia Rd

Idelwood Rd

OAKLAND

Chataqua City Park

← TO COUNCIL BLUFFS

Elmtree Rd

Dogwood Rd

Cottonwood Rd

CARSON

Chestnut Rd

Old Town Park

MACEDONIA

TO 80

N

0   1   2
Miles

WINNEBAGO RIVER
Mason City to Claybanks Forest State Preserve (10.3 Miles)

A close cousin to the nearby Shell Rock River, the Winnebago, too, drops over exciting ledges and skirts small limestone cliffs. Taken together, they make a great pair of rivers to run on the same weekend (see Shell Rock River 2).

Running muddier than the Shell Rock in the spring, some of the best parts of the Winnebago are right inside pleasantly wooded Mason City. Traffic noise isn't distracting, except under Highway 18. Surprises arise too, such as a cave you can paddle into and a place fossil hunters will love—Claybanks Forest State Preserve, with its slopes rich in fossilized sea critters from the Devonian era, back when Iowa was under a muddy sea.

Whitewater play boaters will find numerous waves and eddies to exploit on the section between Mason City's 12th Street Access and the Averydale Access, which holds the most interest at levels above 400 cfs. The wildest single rapids (still, not terribly difficult) falls between the access at Clay Banks Drive and Wren Avenue. The river averages 75 feet wide, and fishing on this stretch is best for smallmouth bass and reasonably good for catfish and walleye.

The **campground** at Clear Lake State Park on the southeast edge of Clear Lake, about 10 miles west, has full amenities. The Cupola Inn Bed and Breakfast (641-422-9272) is just across Clay Banks Drive from the access; it also provides shuttles. Also see Shell Rock River 2.

The **shuttle route** (9.5 miles) from the put-in runs east on 12th Street in Mason City to County S56, south to Clay Banks Drive, southeast to Wren Avenue, and south to just past the bridge over the Winnebago.

Water levels can be checked on the Mason City gauge (station 05459500) on the USGS Web site listed in the introduction. Between 250 cfs and 600 cfs are fun levels, while the river becomes wild and pushy at higher levels.

The **gradient** is 4.9 feet per mile.

Put in southwest of the 12th Street bridge in Mason City. Heading swiftly south over a rocky bottom, you bend 90 degrees left and head past East Park, where a trail runs along the river. You'll drop over the remains of an easily run low-head dam, and you'll then pass beneath the Kentucky Avenue bridge and a rail bridge. The river turns south into a riffle. Watch the next left turn at higher levels (approximately 1,000-plus cfs)—a chaotic pillow wave can develop on the far river-right, and right past it is a 2-foot ledge drop that develops sticky holes.

The river slows, coursing south between low, tree-lined banks. Crossing under the Highway 122 bridge and curving left past the wastewater treatment plant, the river rounds a right bend, drops through a riffle with a wave hole, and then slides over a sheet of solid limestone with a small island separating channels. At scrapingly low levels here, a **portage** is in order.

Just ahead on the river-right is the Averydale Access. Past another spirited riffle, the river continues through a light tree line. You turn right past a railroad bridge, a limestone wall rises up to 20 feet, and the river drops over a ledge. You approach a small island and bend left at a small cliff, and another rock wall rises on the left. Bending south beneath 250th Street, the stream falls through an animated riffle to a beautiful cliff with angular limestone formations.

Past homes and County S56, slightly higher cliffs line the river. Water has splendidly carved the rock, creating eddies, limestone overhangs, and caves. You can paddle into one cave large enough for several canoes. Past the two U.S. Highway 18 bridges, the lines of rock walls continue. You bend left over a class I rapids and then curve right; at an eddy on the river-left, natural limestone steps leading to Clay Banks Drive make a convenient access.

The river continues along a small cliff, where a tiny waterfall pours off a cliff after rains. Through more riffles, the river bends left, briefly joining Ulmus Avenue, a possible access. Passing agricultural views, the river widens to 150 feet, and you hear Big Gully Rapids ahead. The 60-yard-long rapids (class I–II) drops several feet in two main ledges, with a few minor ones between. Most paddlers will prefer to avoid holes forming at moderately high levels, but play boaters will enjoy them. Scout from the bank or your boat.

As the river continues past one last limestone outcropping, the banks become increasingly wooded, and the river constricts to 60 feet in places. After a wooded ridge, you see the first of the "clay banks" that are part of the state preserve that bear their name. These eroded tan soil exposures are surrounded by prairie slopes, where you can explore for small fossils. One clay bank ahead comes right down to the stream, and a nice mix of woods and cedar-studded prairie lines the banks until you swiftly bend north and then east through woods to the **takeout** at the bridge.

Trouble... Right Here in *Creek* City

Mason City claims to be the basis for River City, the fictitious Iowa town in Meredith Willson's 1957 Broadway musical, *The Music Man.* Peculiarly, when Willson was a boy in Mason City, the town officially had no river—just Lime Creek. But it *looked* like a river, and local residents also wanted to honor the Native Americans who had shared food, helping early settlers survive. In 1930, at Forest City's diamond jubilee, a contingent of Winnebago arrived from Nebraska for a rechristening ceremony. Chief Eagle Neck dipped a cup into the water. Noted conservationist Louis H. Pammel poured it back, pronouncing the waters to be of the Winnebago River, it's original name.

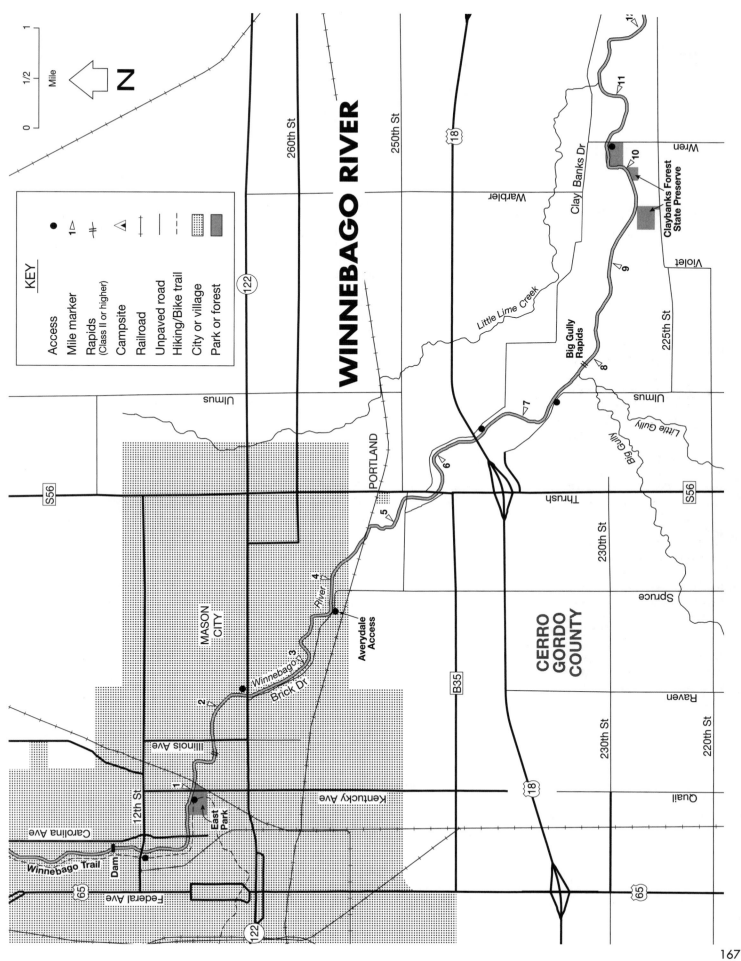

WINNEBAGO RIVER

KEY

- **Access** •
- **Mile marker** ◁1
- **Rapids** (Class II or higher) ≠
- **Campsite** ◬
- **Railroad** ┼
- **Unpaved road** │
- **Hiking/Bike trail** ┆
- **City or village** ▨
- **Park or forest** ▨

260th St

250th St

18

Clay Banks Dr

Warbler

Wren

◁11

◁10

Claybanks Forest State Preserve

Violet

◁9

Little Lime Creek

225th St

Big Gully Rapids

≠
◁8

◁7

Ulmus

Little Gully

Big Gully

Ulmus

230th St

Thrush

S56

S56

◁6

PORTLAND

◁5

122

Ulmus

MASON CITY

Illinois Ave

River ◁4

Winnebago Tr ◁3

Brick Dr

Averydale Access

◁2

Kentucky Ave

CERRO GORDO COUNTY

Spruce

Raven

Quail

220th St

230th St

B35

18

65

65

12th St

Carolina Ave

◁1

East Park

Federal Ave

Winnebago Trail

Dam

122

N

0   1/2   1
Mile

YELLOW RIVER 1
Volney to Sixteen Bridge Access (5 Miles)

There's been a recent resurgence of local pride in the tiny Yellow River—new accesses were built, a canoe livery has opened, woodsy-chic cabins near the river are available, and two watershed-protection groups have formed to help keep this beautiful little river pristine.

Part of this has to do with a recently emerged trout fishery. In a parry against global warming, the river has actually gotten colder in recent years, probably thanks to soil conservation programs that keep more water on the ground, seeping into spring aquifers rather than directly into the river. The Department of Natural Resources now manages the Yellow River from Highway 50 to Ion as a coldwater stream, stocking 75,000 trout fingerlings annually. Trout are growing to trophy size. An electroshock survey recorded brown trout up to 28 inches long.

Because this stretch is a shorter one with easy access, it is a good run for taking your time fishing or just enjoying the meadows, woods, and limestone cliffs along the way. Still swift, this section focuses on a part of the river somewhat easier to run than Yellow River 2. The river drops over some small ledges. Snags can be troublesome, as on any small stream.

Named for tinted clays long ago carried to the Gulf of Mexico, this tiny spring-fed river usually runs clear. It is only 45 feet wide, and its rocky bottom can make for stop-and-start paddling. Most canoeists and kayakers wait for medium water. Much of the valley's topography is quite rugged, due to the fact that—to an even greater extent than other northeast Iowa streams—the area was not pummeled into flatness by geologically recent glaciers.

Riverside **camping** is available at Scenic Valley Campground near the Sixteen Bridge access. The Paint Creek Unit of the Yellow River State Forest, northeast of the access, also has campgrounds. The nearest campground with full amenities, and a great view, is at Pike's Peak State Park near McGregor. Primitive river camping is allowed in the Yellow River State Forest (but not at Effigy Mounds). The Natural Gait and Ion Inn on Old Mission Drive (800-291-2143) has bluff-top cabins that overlook the Yellow River Valley and are just a short walk from the river.

Canoe and kayak rentals and shuttles are available from Big Foot Canoe Rental (563-539-4272) in Volney.

The **shuttle route** (3.6 miles) from the put-in in Volney runs northeast on Big Foot Road and southeast on Linton Drive to the Sixteen Bridge access.

There is no gauge for the Yellow River, so **water levels** must be checked visually. You can call Big Foot Canoe Rental (563-539-4272) to see if the river is too low, too high, or about right.

The **gradient** for this section is 7.4 feet per mile.

Put in at the County X26 access near tiny Volney, and paddle downstream along a wooded bluff where limestone walls form the right bank. Right off, you drop through several riffles past rock outcroppings and paper birch. Just past the mouth of Bear Creek, the Volney access is on the river-left. You curve left and pass under a bridge, and just ahead the fast stream carries you past a farmhouse with occasional rock walls lining the banks. The river slows as you pass a view of meadows and crops with tree-covered hills rising in the backdrop, and Suttle Creek joins from the right. As the river quickens pace, the scenery transitions from sparse lowland woods to a wooded bluff joining the bank where the river curves right. The river bends left at pretty limestone cliffs cloaked by walnut and maple trees, and then it heads beneath a canopy of trees into a long section with several riffles.

You may briefly see crop fields on the right, followed by more woods at a left turn with scenic limestone rock faces. Don't gawk too long—this corner is prone to collecting logjams, and you may need to **portage** along the right side of a grassy island. After a flatwater section, the riffles pick up again, and a 40-foot-high cliff rises as you bend left. After a sharp bend left, the river drops over a 2-foot ledge with protruding rocks that can be hard to see from upstream—take the left side of the channel for an easy run over waves. The river snakes through the narrow basin of the 300-foot-deep valley, through riffles and along wooded bluffs and boulders. After a left, it drops over a smaller ledge and comes to a deep pool with cliffs and a rope swing at Sixteen Bridge. **Take out** on the river-left, downstream of the bridge.

Other trips. The 12.3 river miles from County W60 to County X26 is not for everyone. With no official accesses, put-ins and takeouts at bridges tend to be steep. The river is shallow, requiring frequent portages over rocky shoals at normal water levels. However, rewards are great. Below Livingood Springs, just upstream of County W60, the stream triples in size. The brown trout fishery is at its peak quality from there to County Road X16. With private land lining the banks all along, the best way to access trout-filled pools is by canoe. It also is beautiful, with sandstone bluffs, caves, and stands of pines and balsam fir, and with segments through pasture and fields as well. Select short trips between bridges. At higher water levels, when fishing is not as good, the shoals become small rapids or energetic riffles, and the Yellow River can be paddleable as far upriver as Highway 50. With the gradient averaging 10.2 feet per mile, at high water it can be as challenging as Yellow River 2.

Short River, Long History

A river little more than 50 miles long, the Yellow River had a disproportionate influence on Iowa's history and prehistory. After 500 A.D., it must have impressed Eastern Woodland Indians, who at its mouth constructed unique effigy mounds in shapes of eagles, bison, and bears. It was a fur-trade stop for French voyageurs. Settlers capitalized on the river's high gradient by building lumber mills on it. More than 30 years before he became president of the Confederacy, Jefferson Davis, then a lieutenant in the Union Army, oversaw the construction of Iowa's first mill. Wood sawn there was used to construct Fort Crawford in Prairie du Chien, Wisconsin. Dozens more mills followed, as did villages. As steam power gained currency and freshets frequently washed towns off the map, settlements moved to high ground or dwindled. By the early 1900s, the Yellow was called "the River of Lost Mills," beginning a return to wildness. Today, you'll be hard-pressed to find evidence of the river's bustling days.

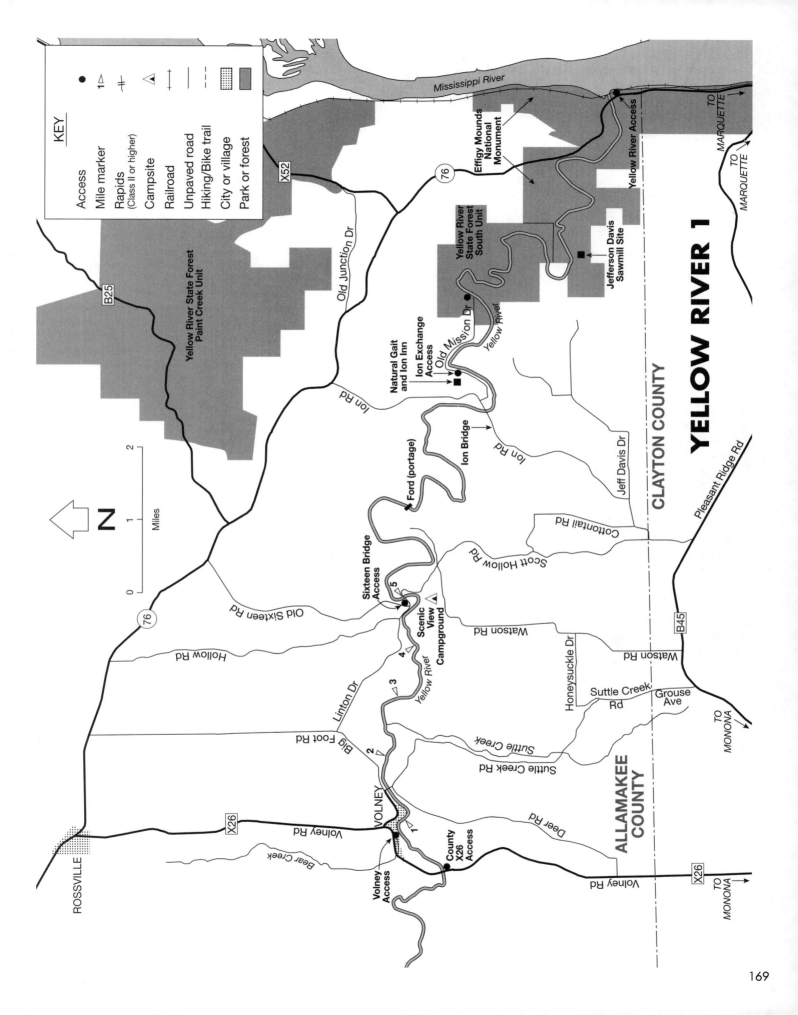

YELLOW RIVER 1

KEY

- • Access
- 1△ Mile marker
- ╫ Rapids (Class II or higher)
- △ Campsite
- ┼ Railroad
- ─ Unpaved road
- ┄ Hiking/Bike trail
- ▦ City or village
- ▨ Park or forest

Mississippi River

Effigy Mounds National Monument

Yellow River Access

TO MARQUETTE

TO MARQUETTE

TO MARQUETTE

Yellow River State Forest South Unit

Jefferson Davis Sawmill Site

Yellow River State Forest Paint Creek Unit

X52

76

B25

Old Junction Dr

Ion Rd

Natural Gait and Ion Inn

Ion Exchange Access

Old Mission Dr

Yellow River

Ion Bridge

Ion Rd

Jeff Davis Dr

CLAYTON COUNTY

Pleasant Ridge Rd

N

Miles

0 1 2

Ford (portage)

76

Old Sixteen Rd

Hollow Rd

Sixteen Bridge Access

Scenic View

Yellow River Campground

5

4

3

Cottontail Rd

Scott Hollow Rd

Watson Rd

Linton Dr

Big Foot Rd

2

Honeysuckle Dr

Suttle Creek Rd

Grouse Ave

Watson Rd

B45

TO MONONA

X26

ROSSVILLE

Bear Creek

Volney Rd

VOLNEY

1

Volney Access

County X26 Access

Deer Rd

Suttle Creek Rd

Suttle Creek

ALLAMAKEE COUNTY

Volney Rd

X26

TO MONONA

169

YELLOW RIVER 2
Sixteen Bridge Access to the Mississippi River (16.4 Miles)

This stretch of the Yellow River runs swiftly through a deep, forested valley past some remote stands of white pine and birch; at times, paddling here seems as if you've left Iowa to paddle a stream much farther north. Sightings of river otters, bald eagles, and osprey are likely, especially in the thousands of acres at Yellow River Forest and Effigy Mounds National Monument (Iowa's only national park), where public lands flank most of the river's final 7.5 miles.

This is one of the more challenging traditional canoe runs in Iowa; expect short rapids and tricky turns. Some trout can be caught as far downstream as the Yellow River State Forest, but smallmouth bass gradually become dominant as the water warms. Past the state forest, catfish, walleye, and sauger become common. Special regulations apply at Effigy Mounds National Monument. For example, the area where Jefferson Davis Sawmill once stood is an off-limits archaeological site. For more information, visit park headquarters on Highway 76.

For **camping**, see Yellow River 1.

Canoe and kayak rentals and shuttles are available from Big Foot Canoe Rental (563-539-4272) in Volney.

The **shuttle route** (10.8 miles) from the put-in at Sixteen Bridge runs north on Old Sixteen Road and southeast on Highway 76 until it crosses the Yellow River near its mouth. The take-out is on the Mississippi River, east across the railroad tracks.

For **water levels** see Yellow River 1.

The overall **gradient** from Sixteen Bridge to the Yellow River State Forest boundary is 10.3 feet per mile, after which the gradient slows to 3 feet per mile.

For the first 8 miles beyond the **put-in**, just downstream of the Sixteen Bridge, the river is at its most challenging. Past a pasture with goats, elk, and horses at the Scenic Valley Ranch, you curve right along pretty rock outcroppings. The banks become enclosed in a mix of hardwoods. The bluff tapers away as the river runs swiftly south and bends left, coursing along a bluff with an understory of coniferous yew. You head north for half a mile, and a 100-foot bluff looms ahead. The river makes a beeline for the bluff's base and makes a sharp right turn—probably the river's trickiest. Turn into the eddy on the right, or the swift current may bring your boat into a large rock, flipping you at a potential pinning hazard.

The river runs east along the bluff through pristine territory. Bending right, the river slows into a long pool. Downstream, you come to a mass of concrete at a farmer's ford—because of dangerous culvert grates, there's a mandatory **portage** on the river-left over the riprap.

Past the farm, bluffs again rise, and the river enters perhaps its most magical phase. After an abrupt right bend at a van-sized boulder, the river curves right along a 200-foot-high wooded bluff. After two sharp left bends, you're heading generally east through fast riffles and chutes, one dropping about 3 feet over 30 yards, where ragged-looking pines top a bluff.

Making a 110-degree right bend at the base of the next bluff, the river runs through an easy class I rapids with waves up to 2 feet. Passing large boulders at the end of the rapids, the river constricts into a swift chute, widens, and passes through several more riffles along scenic bluffs to Ion Bridge. You head through a very long riffle leading past small islands, and the Ion Exchange access is ahead on the left. It's on private land, but the owner has granted permission for public access.

In the next mile, the river drops more than 20 feet. Around the next right bend, you'll see why. The river drops 3 feet down a rock-strewn class I–II rapids—line up your boat before entering it; rocks can catch you sideways, and a swim would be jostling. After a couple of easier rapids (still significant drops), the river enters the Yellow River State Forest.

A high, pine-crowned limestone bluff lines the right bank, which is festooned with mosses, vines, and tiny ferns. Beneath a willow tree on the left, there is a dirt access, reachable in dry times from Old Mission Drive. The next several bends run along high, wooded bluffs with fewer rock exposures and through a narrow valley now 400 feet deep. The current slows for longer periods between riffles, but you should still be vigilant in swift sections for strainers and sweepers. Widening to 60 feet, the river becomes sluggish as it nears Highway 76. You float under a pedestrian bridge at Effigy Mounds and then under the highway and railroad bridges, and your view opens to the wide valley of the bluff-lined Mississippi. The **takeout** is 300 yards downstream on the right.

The Yellow River State Forest has some of Iowa's most pristine settings.

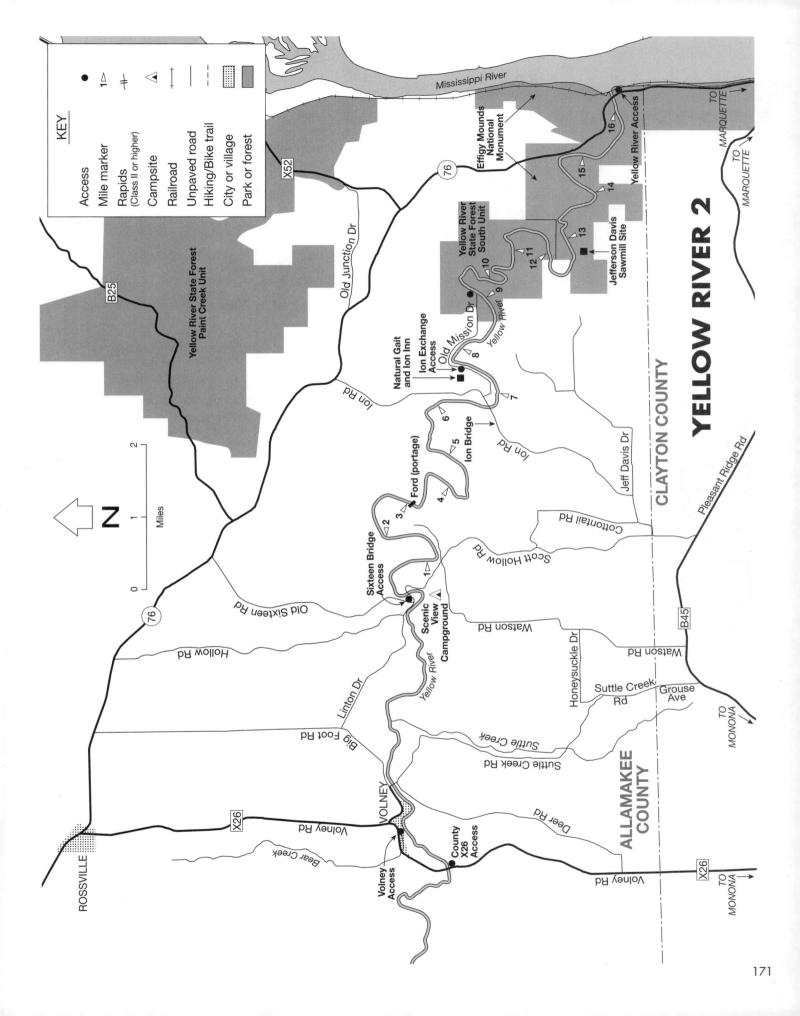

KEY

Access
Mile marker 1
Rapids (Class II or higher)
Campsite
Railroad
Unpaved road
Hiking/Bike trail
City or village
Park or forest

N

Miles
0 1 2

Mississippi River

X52

76

Yellow River State Forest
Paint Creek Unit

B25

Old Junction Dr

Effigy Mounds
National Monument

16

15

14

13

Yellow River
State Forest
South Unit

12 11

10

9

Jefferson Davis
Sawmill Site

Yellow River Access

TO MARQUETTE

TO MARQUETTE

TO MARQUETTE

Ion Rd

Natural Gait
and Ion Inn

Ion Exchange
Access

Old Mission Dr

8

7

6

Ford (portage)

5

Ion Bridge

Ion Rd

Jeff Davis Dr

CLAYTON COUNTY

4

3

2

Sixteen Bridge
Access

1

Scenic View
Campground

Cottontail Rd

Scott Hollow Rd

Pleasant Ridge Rd

B45

Old Sixteen Rd

Hollow Rd

76

Linton Dr

Yellow River

Watson Rd

Honeysuckle Dr

Suttle Creek
Rd

Grouse Ave

Watson Rd

TO
MONONA

Big Foot Rd

Suttle Creek

Suttle Creek Rd

ALLAMAKEE
COUNTY

Deer Rd

ROSSVILLE

X26

Volney Rd

Bear Creek

VOLNEY

Volney
Access

County
X26 Access

Volney Rd

X26

TO
MONONA

YELLOW RIVER 2

171

APPENDIX 1

URBAN PADDLING

It's sometimes startling to see how serene and wooded streams can be in the heart of a city, and with much more wildlife than you might expect. These urban sections tend to be noisier than others you'll find in this book, but you'll likely be pleased with some quiet portions, too. Most urban areas in Iowa have good paddling opportunities either right in town or somewhere not far off. Here is a list of cities in the state that have paddleable river segments not covered in the main section of this guide.

BURLINGTON

See "Other trips" in the Skunk River section.

CEDAR RAPIDS

Cedar River

Put-in: Sac and Fox access
Takeout: Upper Palisades access
Distance: 8.2 miles

This trip on the sandy, wide Cedar passes along nicely wooded banks with pretty islands and ridges; you pass a wastewater treatment plant and may encounter some train noise.

DAVENPORT/BETTENDORF

Duck Creek

Put-in: Brady Street bridge, Davenport
Takeout: Devil's Glen Park, Bettendorf
Distance: 6.3 miles

Duck Creek runs through the hearts of two cities, and yet, thanks to a greenbelt, its banks are splendidly wooded along nice ridges as the creek runs over rocky riffles and one fun ledge drop near the takeout. The 12-mile Duck Creek Parkway Trail winds along the length of this trip, so a bike shuttle is easy to arrange. Unfortunately, Duck creek is paddleable only after recent rains. Check the Duck Creek at DC Golf Course gauge on USGS web site listed in the introduction. More than 100 cfs will do. Being in an urban area, storm-water sewers can lead to flash flooding and dangerous paddling conditions; don't paddle during a rain.

DES MOINES

The capital city was built on the forks of the Des Moines and Raccoon Rivers, and both rivers are blessed with urban green space. Unfortunately, the historic spot where the rivers merge is dangerous due to low-head dams that have killed paddlers and others in the past. Portages are difficult there, so please avoid the downtown area. That said, try these nice stretches.

Raccoon River

Put-in: Walnut Woods State Park
Takeout: Waterworks Park
Distance: 8.4 miles

The most wild-feeling stretch through the metro area, the banks are constantly tree-lined with occasional wooded ridges and excellent sandbars for stopping.

Des Moines River Urban Section 1

Put-in: Sycamore access, NW 66th Avenue
Takeout: Birdland Marina, Pennsylvania Avenue
Distance: 7.9 miles

Paddling up the river and back down to where you started is probably as popular as running a shuttle for this trip. You'll see more homes than on the Raccoon River, but you'll also see nicely forested areas and wooded bluffs, with sightings of wildlife such as bald eagles and beavers being common.

Des Moines River Urban Section 2

Put-in: Harriet Street access, near SE 14th Street
Takeout: Yellow Banks Park
Distance: 8.2 miles

You'll begin in the city near where eagles congregate in the winter, and you'll pass a mix of wooded and industrial views and an eagle nest on the way to the Highway 65 bridges, where the scenery is more pristine. High, wooded bluffs are visible as you approach Yellow Banks Park, with its loess cliff visible from the most scenic angle.

Nicely wooded areas are often found in the middles of cities, such as the Raccoon in West Des Moines and Des Moines.

DUBUQUE

Catfish Creek/Mississippi River

Put-in: Mines of Spain State Recreation Area access

Takeout: Massey

Distance: 4.6 miles

This interesting geological tour begins as you paddle along a towering cliff on Catfish Creek. Then you enter the river, where you'll pass distinctive Horseshoe Bluff, which looks like a small mountain standing apart from the rest of the bluffs. Farther down are nice sandbars on large islands. Barges and other large motorized craft use the navigation channel—stay well out of their paths and close to shore, and avoid paddling in stiff headwinds. Also see Little Maquoketa River.

FORT DODGE

Des Moines River

Put-in: Fort Dodge (lower dam launch)

Takeout: Kalo

Distance: 6.2 miles

On this short run, you'll pass along wooded bluffs and quiet territory until passing beneath the Highway 20

bridges near the takeout. Also see Des Moines River 1 and Lizard Creek.

IOWA CITY/CORALVILLE

Iowa River

Put in: Tailwater West, Coralville Dam

Takeout: Edgewater Park (west side of river, Coralville)

Distance: 4.5 miles

Backed up behind a dam in Coralville, the water is quite slow, but the scenery is excellent; you'll pass small rock outcroppings, wooded ridges, some riverside homes, and, toward the end, a not-so-scenic quarry.

MASON CITY

See Winnebago River.

MUSCATINE

Cedar River

Put-in: Moscow

Takeout: Saulsbury Bridge Park

Distance: 9.1 miles

Wild feeling and quite scenic with long tracts of woods (and now and again a cabin), this stretch of river is less

Aleuts of old probably never imagined their seafaring skin kayaks would ever be adapted for use so far from the ocean.

Prairie ridges in O'Brien and northern Cherokee County offer glimpses of scenery that's become uncommon in a state once covered in native grasslands.

than 10 miles northwest of Muscatine. Canoe rentals and shuttles are available from the park (563-264-5922).

SIOUX CITY

Missouri River

Put-in: Mulberry Point, NE (across the bridge from Vermillion, South Dakota)

Takeout: Ponca State Park, NE

Distance: 27 miles

It's not a novice trip, but this unaltered, freely meandering piece of the Missouri National Recreational River just 20 miles from Sioux City is a refreshing alternative to the channelized river along the Iowa border. A full-day trip that can be broken up by camping on one of the ample sandbars, this trip offers views of bluffs wooded with exposures of loess and shale. The biggest dangers are snags in the fast-flowing (up to 5 miles per hour) current and high headwinds that can create large waves on the big river. You'll see occasional powerboats, but Jet Skis are banned. On this and other parts of the 98 miles of Missouri National Recreational River, two guide services approach tours very differently: Missouri River Expeditions (605-360-2646) leads three-day touring kayak trips accompanied by an ornithologist (to help your bird-watching) or astronomer (aiding your stargazing). Stone Outdoor Adventures (605-661-4169) leads day-trips in a 29-foot birch-bark canoe. Also see www.nps.gov/mnrr.

SPENCER

Put-in: Thunder Bridge

Takeout: West Leach Park

Distance: 2.5 miles

See map for Little Sioux River 1. The river meanders through nicely wooded lowlands and past some homes, dropping over one easily run rock dam.

WATERLOO/CEDAR FALLS

Put-in: Gateway Park

Takeout: Cedar Bend Park

Distance: 5.7 miles

The river runs along wooded banks past George Wyth State Park.

APPENDIX 2

WHITEWATER PLAYSPOTS AND RUNS

Some paddlers may say "Iowa whitewater" is an oxymoron. True, Iowa has no long, continuous class II–III runs like those in some neighboring states. But there are a number of rapids and waves where whitewater boaters can have plenty of fun and hone skills close to home. This appendix is organized into park-and-play spots and whitewater runs.

These directions to some of the state's wilder waters are intended for skilled whitewater paddlers. Swift-water paddling—yes, even in Iowa—can be dangerous, especially for unaccompanied novices. If you are using this appendix, it is assumed that you know how to read water, scout rapids, turn from swift water to slow eddies, use bracing strokes, and so on. If you do not have these skills, there are several ways to learn them before heading out. For a list of organizations and commercial establishments offering instruction, see Appendix 6. Water levels reference Web sites listed in the introduction.

PLAYSPOTS

Breens Rapids

See map for Des Moines River 1. At levels above about 2,500 cfs on the Des Moines River at Fort Dodge (station 05480500), what might be the state's biggest natural wave hole forms here, dropping over what at lower levels is a limestone slab jutting above the waterline. About three vertical feet from entrance to trough, an arch-shaped wave with a foam pile about 30 yards long forms across the river-left half of the channel at a 30-degree angle to the shore. Quite big and retentive, it can sometimes be a struggle to get out of. Advice from paddlers who've been stuck is to flip over and let your body and paddle catch the current to get downstream of the hole before rolling back up. At the far river-left, a second, smaller wave is better for beginners. Unless you ask a home owner for permission to cross his or her yard to put in just above the rapids on the river-left, this is not an ideal park-and-play spot. For public access, put in alongside the point where Madison Avenue leaves the river, and paddle upstream one-fifth mile to the rapids, where you can easily carry upstream of the rapids on the river-left rock outcropping.

Camp Comfort

This is a rock dam located on the Shell Rock River in Butler County at a county campground. At most levels, surfing isn't great, but there are hard eddy lines, and the river drops 3.5 feet in solid class II rapids through two separate channels, either of which requires turns to get through clean. On the USGS Shell Rock at Shell Rock gauge (station 05462000), look for more than 1,000 cfs. Directions: head five miles north of Allison on Highway 14, 3.5 miles east on County C23, and 1 mile north on Nobel Avenue.

The Chickasaw Rapids on the Little Cedar.

Chickasaw Rapids

At the remains of a milldam on the Little Cedar River at Chickasaw Park west of Ionia on County B57, several decades back the state dumped rocks and boulders over the breached dam, creating a rock-garden rapids (solid class II). It is a longer rapids (for Iowa) about 70 yards long. Stay far on the river-right at the entry because part of the dam remains on the river-left, creating a dangerous hole. Due to all the boulders, foot entrapment is another big hazard here—under no circumstances should you try to stand if you swim (and a swim is likely to be bone-jangling). The waves aren't the best surfing waves, and if caught they must be done on the fly because they are not easily reached from eddies. There are multiple routes, including around an island on the left. The stretch is runnable but bony at 200 cfs on the USGS Little Cedar near Ionia gauge (station 05488000); more than 800 cfs is better.

Surfing at Clay Hole on the Cedar.

Clay Hole

Located across the river from downtown Cedar Falls, a demolished dam creates riverwide waves (solid class II). A local paddling club has removed dangerous rebar from the former dam. The waves behave differently at different water levels, but there is something worthwhile at levels from 500 to 3,500 cfs on the USGS Cedar River at Cedar Rapids gauge (station 05464500), at which the features become washed over. Generally, from river-left to river-right, the waves increase in size. There are waves for sidesurfing and, at higher levels, anything from flat spins to cartwheels or multiple loops. On the far river-right is an extremely sticky hole (class III) that only advanced whitewater paddlers should enter. Camp nearby at Big Woods Park or George Wyth State Park. Eateries and pubs are nearby, in downtown Cedar Falls.

Commerce Ledges

See map for Raccoon River. At bedrock ledges on the Raccoon River at the former town of Commerce, with some concrete chunks from an old bridge, there are surfing waves from approximately 700 cfs to 3,000 cfs. One large midstream boulder creates an eddy good for practice turns and squirts. Park at a pull-off across Southwest 52nd Avenue from the entrance to West Des Moines Sand and Gravel Company, and carry your boat up a trail through the woods upstream of the ledges. You can take out at the mouth of a gully near your vehicle. Alternatively, you can put in at the Walnut Woods State Park boat ramp and paddle upstream to the playspot at moderate levels. There is camping at the state park.

Davis City Ledges

See map for Grand River 3. About 400 yards downstream of the Highway 69 bridge at Davis City on the Grand River, this is a natural set of two main ledges (class II). Check the USGS Thompson River at Davis City gauge (station 06898000). At 350 cfs or more, the ledges have playable water. The first ledge is not river-wide but can develop a sticky hole in the center of the channel. The second ledge, which the river turns left into, is the more significant drop. A sticky wave develops on the downstream-right portion of the rapids. Other wave holes can develop on the river-left portion at various levels. Paddle down a third mile from Davis City to play, carry back above the rapids (easiest on the river-right), and paddle back up to Davis City Park when you are done.

Humboldt Rock Dam

See map for West Fork of the Des Moines River. The upper rock dam is easily reachable as a park-and-play spot. The hole on the river-right side of the chute can be very sticky at high levels, but it does flush. There are strong eddy lines on both sides of the chute. Check the USGS Des Moines River at Humboldt gauge (station 05476750), looking for more than 300 cfs.

Lehigh Rock Dam

See map for Des Moines River 3. At a limestone rock dam created by locals just upstream of the bridge, the wide Des Moines River develops numerous waves. The larger waves, usually better for surfing, are on the river-right half of the channel. There is a boat ramp on the river-left upstream of the rapids, and a canoe access downstream of the bridge, also on the river-left. Look for levels roughly between 700 and 2,200 cfs on the USGS Des Moines River at Fort Dodge gauge (station 05480500).

North Raccoon River Rock Dams

See map for North Raccoon River 1 and 2. There are numerous rock dams, which the DNR refers to as "fishing riffles," all up the North Raccoon River in Greene, Carroll, and Sac Counties. For play boaters, a few of these create excellent waves with good eddy service. Three have significant drops, creating nice waves, mostly over glacially rounded boulders. For water levels, see the USGS North Raccoon near Jefferson gauge (station 05482500). At levels between 300 to about 1,000 cfs, the best bet is the "Jefferson" rapids, one mile south of Jefferson at Henderson Boy Scout Park (not shown on map), which has a campground. At higher levels, head to Carroll County, where two rock dams have bigger drops. The rapids at the Merritt Access have more retentive waves. Waves at the Bennett Access rapids may be too steep for play, but strong eddy lines are good for squirting. Camping is allowed at both accesses.

North Fork of the Maquoketa River

About 300 yards downstream of the Highway 61 bridge

Whitewater play on a North Raccoon rock dam near Jefferson.

north of the town of Maquoketa, the river cuts straight through a small, limestone ridge that was dynamited to create a new channel for the river during highway construction. The result is a short class II rapids in a scenic mini-gorge. There's one surfable wave at the 2-foot drop on the entry, with a little wave train following it. Downstream there's another small drop. The best parking is off the road on the northwest side of the river on the southbound lane. Look for more than 300 cfs on the USGS North Fork Maquoketa near Fulton gauge (station 05418400).

WHITEWATER RUNS

High-gradient creeks can be found in most parts of the state. With a little homework, contacts with other paddlers, and a willingness to patiently wait for rain, you can discover some surprisingly swift water right here in Iowa. For checking rainfalls, the following Web site is quite useful: www.crh.noaa.gov/cgi-bin-ncrfc/uncgi/igmapx. Most creeks are not within the scope of this book, but a few such runs are listed here. In addition to these, see the following sections in the main part of this guide, each of which has at least some small rapids or waves: Lizard Creek, Shell Rock River 2 (Plymouth to Rock Falls), Winnebago River, the "Other trips" section of Little Sioux River 5, Middle Raccoon River 2 and 3, and Boone River 1.

Ditch Number 206 (Class III)

Briggs Woods Park, South of Webster City (1/3 mile) See the map for Boone River 1 and 2. An extremely brief run dropping about 60 feet in a third of a mile, this series of solid class III sandstone ledges along beautiful rock outcroppings runs for a day or two (sometimes more) after localized heavy rains in the Webster City area. Despite its romantic name and origins, it

actually is a pretty place. Water runs from the field drain tiles of former wetlands, as well as from the spillway of the park's lake. Follow park roads back to the signs that say "Waterfalls," and carry your boat below the spillway to the put-in. If water is rushing, not trickling, over the spillway, the ledges are worthwhile. Otherwise, go play on the Boone (see Boone River 1).

There are a total of six drops, the highest being 4 feet. The first two are the most vertical and require the highest water levels to get over without scraping (rare). Stay right at the second drop to avoid penciling into rocks. The third drop is great fun, with a side-curling wave. The fourth comes immediately after it through the center of a rock seam, and then there's a slow stretch (perhaps with a beaver dam) leading to the two final drops. In the two final ledges, the creek drops a total of 6 feet. Approach these from the river-left, following the tongue of water near the rock wall on the final drop to avoid the boat-grinding sharp rocks on the river-right. When you reach the Boone River, carry back up the trail and repeat.

Rapids at a rock cut on the North Fork of the Maquoketa.

The ledges on Ditch Number 206 near the Boone.

Little Maquoketa River (Class I–II)
Twin Springs to Durango (6.1 Miles)
See map for Maquoketa River 1. Above Durango, the Little Maquoketa is essentially a creek, but one that's of interest to skilled whitewater paddlers for a couple of days after rains. Drive to the Budd Bridge and look downstream to determine whether it's runnable—if the rapids are passable, but not lapping at tree trunks, the rest will work. If they're too high, check again in a few hours. Sustaining a gradient of more than 15 feet per mile through a very picturesque run, the stream runs along limestone cliffs, a few pastures (watch for fences!), deep woods, and numerous short rock-garden rapids (class I–II, more difficult at higher levels). The biggest drops—scout them—are the rock-garden rapids just downstream of Budd Bridge and the chute on a rock dam at the base of the slopes at the Sundown Mountain ski area. Putting in near Graf adds about 3 miles to the trip—also a high-gradient stretch that demands respect. The Heritage Trail here works perfectly for running a bike shuttle, with trailheads at either Graf or Twin Springs as possible put-ins.

White Breast Creek (Class II–III)
Highway 181 to 92nd Avenue (5.3 Miles)
This largish creek runs high for whitewater boaters only now and then, but with a single rapids like no other in Iowa, it's worth watching for the right conditions. You need to check two gauges. For adequate flows, you need 7.5 to 13 feet on the USGS White Breast Creek near Dallas gauge (station 05487980). This stretch is part of Lake Red Rock's floodplain, so when the lake rises above 750 feet on the Corps of Engineers Lake Red Rock pool gauge (station PELI4) online at water.mvr.usace.army.mil, the rapids begin to become submerged.

At Stickle Rapids, 250 yards upstream from the 70th Avenue bridge, locally called Stickle Bridge, scout from shore on either side. There are two main routes, 60 to 100 yards long over hard sandstone bedrock, dropping a bit over 6 feet in several ledges. The river-right channel (class II) has two main ledges, ending in a rock-strewn, wavy chute curving leftward. The left channel (class III) drops over three main drops, the second being a slanting 3-foot chute culminating in a wave hole, followed immediately by a left turn into rapids and the next drop. At levels over 9 feet on the gauge, water courses over the rock outcropping in the center, and the entire width becomes a runnable class III rapids, with several large holes, the biggest of which is on the river-left. Large, sharp rocks can injure both boat and paddler.

About a quarter mile past Stickle Bridge is a ledge drop with good surfing waves. At the lower end of the runnable range, you can put in at Stickle Bridge, treating both rapids as park-and-play spots if you are willing to do some paddling upstream and carrying around the rapids. Marion County Park on the west edge of Knoxville has camping with all amenities.

Wapsipinicon River (Class I)
Central City Dam to Wakpicada Access (1 Mile)
See map for Wapsipinicon 4 and 5. Not a creek, this is a short stretch that runs consistently. It's not big water, either. It begins with a class I rapids splitting around a large rock in the center of the river below the dam. Put in well downstream to avoid the dam's dangerous hydraulics. Beyond the Main Street Bridge, a class I–II rapids leads to a railroad bridge. At moderate water levels on the river-left channel, a steep wave hole forms directly underneath the tracks. The fast tail of water below the bridge forms a sharp eddy line, good for practice ferries, eddy turns, and squirts with a deep recovery area. To get to the put-in, head north of the bridge across the river on Highway 13, take the first right onto Grove Street, and then take the following right. Head south to the fishing access by the dam. For the takeout, head south on Highway 13 to where E16 heads west, but turn left (east) on the road leading past the fairgrounds to the Wakpicada Access. Look for at least 250 cfs on the USGS Wapsipinicon at Independence gauge (station 05421000).

APPENDIX 3

PADDLING SECTIONS GROUPED BY SKILL LEVEL

Most sections detailed in this book don't require expert-level skills (for sections that do, see Appendix 2), but there is plenty of "in-between" water that's not ideal for novice paddlers. For a first-time paddler, it's best to first paddle a slower stream at a moderate water level just to get the feel for moving water and to cut back on distance to a few miles instead of running a whole section.

New paddlers will find streams under the "Beginner" heading to be most friendly, at least under normal circumstances—low to moderate water levels in gentle weather. Be aware that even on so-called beginner streams the unexpected arises: tricky snags or logjams that must be portaged can accumulate, road crews may install a temporary low bridge, and so on. Bodies of water listed in the "Intermediate" group are there because they include one or more of the following: swifter waters with some tricky turns, open water where high waves can develop, long distances between accesses, difficult access, numerous fence crossings, or numerous logjams or snags. Novice paddlers can handle most of these trips if accompanied by more experience paddlers. Where there's any doubt, I've placed the trip in the more difficult category.

Bodies of water in the "Experienced" category have fixed hazards or imminent potential for them that can spell trouble for novice paddlers, even those accompanied by some-one more experienced. They require a degree of skill, such as being able to take an eddy when you need to, being able to make turns in rapids, being able to navigate, and so on.

BEGINNER

Big Sioux River 1, 3
Boone River 3
Cedar River 1, 2
Des Moines River 2, 3, 4, 5, 6
DeSoto Lake
Iowa River 3 (not including dam portage)
Little Sioux River 1, 2, 3, 4, 5, 6, 7
Maquoketa River 1, 2, 3, 4
Middle Raccoon River 1
North Raccoon River 3
Rock River

Shell Rock River 3
Skunk River
Turkey River 1, 2, 3, 4, 5, 6
Upper Iowa River 5, 7
Wapsipinicon River 1, 2, 3, 4, 6
West Nishnabotna River

INTERMEDIATE

Big Cedar Creek 1, 2
Big Sioux River 2
Boone River 1, 2
Cedar River 3, 4
Des Moines River 1, 7, 8, 9, 10
East Nishnabotna River
Grand River 1, 2, 3
Iowa River 1, 2, 4, 5
Little Maquoketa River
Little Turkey River
Middle Raccoon River 2, 3
Middle River
Mississippi River
North Fork of the Maquoketa River 1, 2
North Raccoon River 1, 2, 4
Raccoon River
Shell Rock River 1
South Raccoon River 1, 2
South Skunk River
Trumpeter Trail 1 and 2
Upper Iowa River 1, 2, 3, 4, 6
Volga River 1, 2
Wapsipinicon River 5
West Fork of the Des Moines River
Yellow River 1

EXPERIENCED

Lake Red Rock
Lizard Creek
North River
Shell Rock River 2
Winnebago River
Yellow River 2

APPENDIX 4

RECOMMENDED READING

If you'd like to both widen and deepen your perspective on Iowa's rivers and streams, as well as the landscapes that surround them and the history that's unfolded along their banks, here's a short list of excellent books.

Dinsmore, James. *A Country So Full of Game: The Story of Wildlife in Iowa*. Iowa City: University of Iowa Press, 1994. To unveil the abundance of wildlife and habitat in Iowa before settlement, the author spent a decade researching early accounts of wildlife in Iowa, such as Indian agent Joseph Street's 1833 excursion through Iowa. Back in Wisconsin, Street commented, "I had never rode through a country so full of game." He wasn't the only one. Early explorers and settlers observed that elk were more common than deer, and there were mammals from wolves and bears to lynx and massive herds of bison. Some of the vignettes are tragicomic viewed from the lens of our era, such as the woman boiling a now-endangered whooping crane for two days to try to make it chewable.

Harris, Eddy L. *Mississippi Solo: A River Quest*. New York: Nick Lyons Books, 1988. A young St. Louis musician decides to paddle the Mississippi from Lake Itasca to its mouth, naively setting off without knowing the first thing about paddling, or about the mighty Mississippi. The travelogue grows along with the author's paddling skills, as well as his understanding of regional attitudes toward an African-American in a canoe. Harris writes glowingly about Iowa's bluffs, and he runs into both the best and worst of humanity along the way. (The most recent reprint is by Owl Books.)

Heusinkveld, Harriet. *Saga of the Des Moines River Greenbelt*. Pella, Iowa: Pella Print Company, 1989. This is an excellent history of the Des Moines River Valley's Native American and pioneer history, along with a chronicle of efforts to protect it. (Not in print, available at libraries.)

Knudson, G. E. *A Guide to the Upper Iowa River*. Decorah, Iowa: Luther College Press, 1971. Probably Iowa's most thorough river guide. The maps and outfitters listed are rather dated, but the book does provide excellent context for the Upper Iowa's history, archeology, and geology. Available at may outfitters' shops.

Kurtz, Carl. *Iowa's Wild Places*. Ames: Iowa State University Press and Iowa Natural Heritage Foundation, 1996. This is mainly a collection of mind-alteringly gorgeous photography, along with some text, showing Iowa's precious places.

Peterson, William J. *Iowa: Rivers of Her Valleys*. Iowa City: Iowa State Historical Society, 1941. Rivers, of course, were the most important determiner of settlement patterns. Petersen offers the most comprehensive overview available of how Iowa's rivers affected early European settlers and gives etymologies of the Indian roots of river names. He also includes interesting vignettes about streams, such as Tete de Mort (Death's Head) Creek, where French traders found skulls of Dakota warriors thrown over cliffs by rival warriors. (Not in print, available at libraries.)

Prior, Jean C. *Landforms of Iowa*. Iowa City: University of Iowa Press, 1991. This is a nicely illustrated overview of Iowa's geology that strikes a good balance between conveying solid science and being understandable to a layperson.

Waller, Robert James. *Just Beyond the Firelight*. Ames: Iowa State University Press, 1988. This is a moving collection of essays pondering life in Iowa. Two essays address the Shell Rock River, one of them chronicling a canoe expedition from its beginning to its end, weaving in the dilemmas of conservation along the way.

Riffles and wooded bluffs with hardwoods and pines are common near Steamboat Rock on the Iowa.

APPENDIX 5

INSTRUCTIONAL RESOURCES

The books and videos listed are available in most paddling shops. If you can't find an item, any bookstore will be glad to order it for you, or you can use an online book retailer.

INTRODUCTORY PADDLING

Jacobson, Cliff. *Canoeing.* Rev. 2nd ed. Old Saybrook, Conn.: Globe Pequot, 1999.

Kallner, Bill, Donna Jackson Kallner, and Kym Lutz. *Whitewater Kayaking.* 2nd ed. Old Saybrook, Conn.: Globe Pequot, 2000.

Wyatt, J. Michael. *Sea Kayaking.* 2nd ed. Old Saybrook, Conn.: Globe Pequot, 1999.

Globe Pequot also publishes several other brief and inexpensive paddling books in their Basic Essential series.

INTERMEDIATE/ADVANCED PADDLING

Heads Up! River Rescue for River Runners. Video, 29 min. American Canoe Association, 7432 Alban Station Boulevard, Suite B226, Springfield, Va. 22150, 1993.

Ray, Slim. *The Canoe Handbook: Techniques for Mastering the Sport of Canoeing.* Mechanicsburg, Pa.: Stackpole Books, 1992.

Ray, Slim. *Swiftwater Rescue.* Asheville, N.C.: CFS Press, 1997.

WHITEWATER PADDLING

Grace Under Pressure: Learning the Kayak Roll. Video. Rapid Progression, www.paddlefilms.com.

Nealy, William. *Kayak: A Manual of Technique.* Birmingham, Ala.: Menasha Ridge Press, 1986.

Play Daze. Video. Heliconia Press, P.O. Box 200, Clayton, Ontario, Canada, KOA 1PO, 1999.

Whitewater Self Defense. Video, 65 min. Performance Video and Instruction, 550 Riverbend, Durango, Colo. 81301, 1999.

Whiting, Ken. *The Playboater's Handbook 2.* Clayton, Ontario, Canada: Heliconia Press, 2002.

CAMPING

Jacobson, Cliff. *Canoeing and Camping: Beyond the Basics.* 2nd ed. Old Saybrook, Conn.: Globe Pequot, 2002.

Kuhne, Cecil. *Kayak Touring and Camping.* Mechanicsburg, Pa.: Stackpole Books, 1999.

The Middle Raccoon River almost always runs clear.

APPENDIX 6

PADDLING CLUBS, ORGANIZATIONS, AND INSTRUCTION IN IOWA

Members of paddling clubs and other organizations are good resources to help new paddlers learn the basics in a safe and fun environment. Also, many beginners and veterans alike find that trips offered by these groups are fun and educational ways of experiencing Iowa's rivers.

CLUBS

Calhoun County Canoe and Kayak Club, Manson, conducts paddling trips to nearby waterways; www.man son-nw .k12.ia.us/faculty/pettyb/kayakers.htm

Canoe and Kayak Adventure Club of Northeast Iowa offers periodic trips in northeast Iowa; P.O. Box 66, Waukon, IA, 52172, (563) 778-8575.

Central Iowa Paddlers takes local and regional paddling trips, sometimes offering informal instruction; www.paddleiowa.org

Drifters Canoe-n-Kayak, Fort Dodge, paddles rivers in the Fort Dodge area; communities.msn.com/drifters canoenkayak

Iowa State University Canoe and Kayak Club, Ames, has twice-weekly pool sessions with whitewater kayaks available for practicing rolling and strokes and takes primarily whitewater trips to various parts of the country. Informal instruction, with membership open to the public; www.scc.iastate.edu/~kayak

Prairie Rapids Paddlers, Cedar Falls, is a whitewater play-boating-oriented group often found at Clay Hole in Cedar Falls; sweliver.home.mchsi.com/kayak.html

Saukenuk Paddlers, Quad Cities, offers a regular roster of both flatwater and whitewater excursions in Iowa, Illinois, Wisconsin, and beyond; (563) 326-3921, www.rivers-end.org/saukenuk

Skunk River Paddlers, Ames; groups.yahoo.com/group/ skunkriverpaddlers

University of Iowa Kayak and Canoe Club, Iowa City, offers weekly pool sessions with whitewater kayaks available for practicing rolling and strokes and takes whitewater trips to various parts of the country. Informal instruction, with membership open to the public; www.uiowa.edu/~boating

OTHER ORGANIZATIONS

Iowa Canoe Association supports paddlesports, disseminates paddling information, and assists canoe and dragonboat racing festivals and whitewater activities; 1630 19th Street NW, Cedar Rapids, IA 52405; dhillma@rockwellcollins.com.

Iowa Water Trails Association advocates access and amenities for paddlers, as well as dam safing and removal; www.desmoinesriver.org

Iowa Whitewater Coalition advocates development of whitewater courses and safe paddling in Iowa; groups. yahoo.com/group/IowaWhitewater

INSTRUCTION

Canoe and Kayak Institute, Duluth, Minnesota, offers an important swift-water-rescue course not available in Iowa, in addition to numerous other paddling courses; www.um doutdoorprogram.org/paddlingm.htm

Canoesport Outfitters, Indianola, offers instruction for all types of paddling in both canoes and kayaks, including basics, moving water, sea kayaking, and whitewater; (515) 961-6117, www.canoesportoutfitters.com

River Basin, Burlington, provides canoe and kayak instruction, including basics, moving water, and sea kayaking; (319) 752-1857, www.canoeskayaks.com

APPENDIX 7

USEFUL WEB SITES

Flood Forecasts
www.crh.noaa.gov/ncrfc

Iowa Paddling Destinations
skunkriverpaddlers.tripod.com
www.desmoinesriver.org
www.iowadnr.com

Magazines
www.canoekayak.com
www.paddlermagazine.com

Maps
State Parks (PDF): www.exploreiowaparks.com
Topographic: terraserver-usa.com

National Organizations
American Canoe Association: www.acanet.org

American Rivers: www.amrivers.org
American Whitewater: www.americanwhitewater.org

Online Paddling Community Information
boatertalk.com
www.paddling.net

Rainfalls
iwin.nws.noaa.gov/iwin/ia/climate.html
www.crh.noaa.gov/cgi-bin-ncrfc/uncgi/igmapx

Water Levels (Current and Archival)
waterdata.usgs.gov/ia/nwis/current/?type=flow
flowwater.mvr.usace.army.mil

Weather
www.nws.noaa.gov
www.weather.com

The cliffs and crags of Lake Red Rock are great fun to explore.

More Great Titles
FROM TRAILS BOOKS & PRAIRIE OAK PRESS

ACTIVITY GUIDES
- Great Cross-Country Ski Trails: Wisconsin, Minnesota, Michigan & Ontario, Wm. Chad McGrath
- Great Minnesota Walks: 49 Strolls, Rambles, Hikes, and Treks, Wm. Chad McGrath
- Great Wisconsin Walks: 45 Strolls, Rambles, Hikes, and Treks, Wm. Chad McGrath
- Paddling Illinois: 64 Great Trips by Canoe and Kayak, Mike Svob
- Paddling Southern Wisconsin: 82 Great Trips by Canoe and Kayak, Mike Svob
- Paddling Northern Wisconsin: 82 Great Trips by Canoe and Kayak, Mike Svob
- Wisconsin Underground: A Guide to Caves, Mines, and Tunnels in and around the Badger State, Doris Green
- Minnesota Underground & the Best of the Black Hills: A Guide to Mines, Sinks, Caves, and Disappearing Streams, Doris Green

TRAVEL GUIDES
- Great Little Museums of the Midwest, Christine des Garennes
- Great Minnesota Weekend Adventures, Beth Gauper
- The Great Wisconsin Touring Book: 30 Spectacular Auto Tours, Gary Knowles
- Tastes of Minnesota: A Food Lover's Tour, Donna Tabbert Long
- Wisconsin Lighthouses: A Photographic and Historical Guide, Ken and Barb Wardius
- Wisconsin Waterfalls, Patrick Lisi
- Wisconsin Family Weekends: 20 Fun Trips for You and the Kids, Susan Lampert Smith
- County Parks of Wisconsin, Revised Edition, Jeannette and Chet Bell
- Up North Wisconsin: A Region for All Seasons, Sharyn Alden
- Great Wisconsin Taverns: 101 Distinctive Badger Bars, Dennis Boyer
- Great Weekend Adventures, the Editors of Wisconsin Trails
- Eating Well in Wisconsin, Jerry Minnich
- Acorn Guide to Northwest Wisconsin, Tim Bewer

NATURE ESSAYS
- Wild Wisconsin Notebook, James Buchholz
- Trout Friends, Bill Stokes
- Northern Passages: Reflections from Lake Superior Country, Michael Van Stappen
- River Stories: Growing Up on the Wisconsin, Delores Chamberlain

HOME & GARDEN
- Wisconsin Country Gourmet, Marge Snyder & Suzanne Breckenridge
- Wisconsin Herb Cookbook, Marge Snyder & Suzanne Breckenridge
- Creating a Perennial Garden in the Midwest, Joan Severa
- Wisconsin Garden Guide, Jerry Minnich
- Bountiful Wisconsin: 110 Favorite Recipes, Terese Allen
- Wisconsin's Hometown Flavors, Terese Allen

HISTORICAL BOOKS
- Prairie Whistles: Tales of Midwest Railroading, Dennis Boyer
- Barns of Wisconsin, Jerry Apps
- Portrait of the Past: A Photographic Journey Through Wisconsin 1865-1920, Howard Mead, Jill Dean, and Susan Smith
- Wisconsin: The Story of the Badger State, Norman K. Risjord
- Wisconsin At War: 20th Century Conflicts Through the Eyes of Veterans, Dr. James F. McIntosh

GIFT BOOKS
- The Spirit of Door County: A Photographic Essay, Darryl R. Beers
- Milwaukee, Photography by Todd Dacquisto
- Duck Hunting on the Fox: Hunting and Decoy-Carving Traditions, Stephen M. Miller
- Spirit of the North: A Photographic Journey Through Northern Wisconsin, Richard Hamilton Smith

GHOST STORIES
- Haunted Wisconsin, Michael Norman and Beth Scott
- W-Files: True Reports of Wisconsin's Unexplained Phenomena, Jay Rath
- The Beast of Bray Road: Tailing Wisconsin's Werewolf, Linda S. Godfrey
- Giants in the Land: Folktales and Legends of Wisconsin, Dennis Boyer

For a free catalog, phone, write, or e-mail us.

Trails Books
P.O. Box 317, Black Earth, WI 53515
(800) 236-8088 • e-mail: books@wistrails.com
www.trailsbooks.com